NEGLECTED PERSPECTIVES ON SCIENCE AND RELIGION

Neglected Perspectives on Science and Religion explores historical and contemporary relations between science and religion, providing new perspectives on familiar topics such as evolution and the Galileo affair. The book also explores common differences in science and religion with respect to their various treatments of doubt, curiosity, and the methods by which truth claims are assessed. The book includes discussions of religious and scientific treatments of the origins of males and females, evolving views of sex and gender, and contemporary tensions about topics such as same-sex marriage. Viney and Woody also include a chapter exploring the effects of social science research on religious topics such as prayer, prejudice, and violence. The rise of social sciences such as psychology, sociology, and anthropology has resulted in discoveries that contribute to new ways of thinking about the relations of science and religion. This book is ideal for graduate and upper-level undergraduate students, as well as anyone interested in science and religion.

Wayne Viney is Professor Emeritus of Psychology and Emeritus University Distinguished Teaching Scholar at Colorado State University, USA. He has served as President of the Society for the History of Psychology.

William Douglas Woody is Professor of Psychological Sciences at the University of Northern Colorado, USA. He has received Early Career Achievement Awards from the Society for the History of Psychology and the Society for the Teaching of Psychology.

NEGLECTED PERSPECTIVES ON SCIENCE AND RELIGION

Historical and Contemporary Relations

Wayne Viney and William Douglas Woody

NEW YORK AND LONDON

First published 2017
by Routledge
711 Third Avenue, New York, NY 10017

and by Routledge
2 Park Square, Milton Park, Abingdon, Oxon OX14 4RN

Routledge is an imprint of the Taylor & Francis Group, an informa business

© 2017 Taylor & Francis

The right of Wayne Viney and William Douglas Woody to be identified as authors of this work has been asserted by them in accordance with sections 77 and 78 of the Copyright, Designs and Patents Act 1988.

All rights reserved. No part of this book may be reprinted or reproduced or utilised in any form or by any electronic, mechanical, or other means, now known or hereafter invented, including photocopying and recording, or in any information storage or retrieval system, without permission in writing from the publishers.

Trademark notice: Product or corporate names may be trademarks or registered trademarks, and are used only for identification and explanation without intent to infringe.

British Library Cataloguing in Publication Data
A catalogue record for this book is available from the British Library

Library of Congress Cataloging in Publication Data
Names: Viney, Wayne, author.
Title: Neglected perspectives on science and religion : historical and contemporary relations / Wayne Viney, William Douglas Woody.
Description: 1 [edition]. | New York : Routledge, 2017. | Includes bibliographical references and index.
Identifiers: LCCN 2016043171 | ISBN 9781138284753 (hardback : alk. paper) | ISBN 9781138284760 (pbk. : alk. paper) | ISBN 9781315213750 (ebook)
Subjects: LCSH: Religion and science.
Classification: LCC BL240.3 .V563 2017 | DDC 201/.65--dc23
LC record available at https://lccn.loc.gov/2016043171

ISBN: 978-1-138-28475-3 (hbk)
ISBN: 978-1-138-28476-0 (pbk)
ISBN: 978-1-315-21375-0 (ebk)

Typeset in Bembo
by Taylor & Francis Books

To the memory of American psychologist and
philosopher, William James.

And to Lisa Woody for her patience and encouragement.

And finally, in loving memory of Wynona Rose Viney.

CONTENTS

Preface   *viii*
About the authors   *xii*
Acknowledgements   *xiv*

1. Intellectual Warfare: Arguments Pro and Con   1
2. The Problem of Knowledge   23
3. The Problem of Causality   44
4. Causality Continued: Angels and Demons   63
5. Soul and Body   80
6. Evolution   95
7. Galileo and the Church   112
8. Advances in Understanding of the Origins of Sex   131
9. Women and Men: Scientific and Religious Perspectives   151
10. Sexual Orientation: From Harmony to Discord to Diaspora   173
11. Religion and Social Metrics   197
12. Absolutism: The Disease of Philosophical Thought   217

Bibliography   *233*
Index   *256*

PREFACE

This book explores historical and contemporary relations between science and religion, providing new perspectives on familiar topics such as evolution and the Galileo affair. There is also a strong focus on religious and scientific treatments of knowledge, curiosity, and doubt. In addition to these traditional topics we include materials that have often been overlooked or neglected in standard histories. For example, we argue that the microscope no less than the telescope resulted in deeply troublesome problems for both scientists and religious leaders. Specifically, microscopic discoveries of sperm cells in the late 16th century resulted in heated debates about a host of questions with deep scientific, religious, and philosophical implications. What was the possible role of such lowly creatures in the generation of life? Were they gendered? Why were there so many of them? The untold multitude of sperm was troublesome because of long-standing moral concerns about the enormous waste associated with any form of sex, particularly sex without an explicit goal of reproduction.

Questions multiplied. With definitive evidence that sperm were necessary for fertilization there were debates about the relative contributions of the egg and the sperm. So-called "ovists" argued for the primacy of the egg, while "spermists" argued for the primacy of the sperm. Such arguments raised questions about older theories of preformation, a belief, in at least some of its iterations, that creation was an all-at-once affair completed in advance of conception such that we were all preformed in extreme miniature in the ovary of Eve. Each person was thus known to the creator from the very foundations of the earth. Tensions thus surfaced between preformation theory and epigenesis, a competing theory that individuals emerge from the interaction of many parts originally indifferent to each other but including, at a minimum, male and female gametes coming together in a complex environment that also contributes in multiple ways to final outcomes. The religious and scientific implications of these questions are relevant to a comprehensive understanding of the history of the relations between science and religion, relations that include both conflict and accommodation.

This book also investigates the evolving history of religious and scientific views of males and females and their abilities and social roles. Little-known early scientific studies of the intellectual abilities of males and females are especially relevant to this discussion. We investigate long-standing religious and early scientific assumptions that sex and gender occur in binary categories. We then focus on scientific research that has challenged binary classification. We explore the complexities of sexual and gender identities as well as early 21st century debates on issues such as birth control and abortion. Finally, we turn to a discussion of changing religious and scientific approaches to sexual orientation and same-sex marriage.

Discoveries in the social sciences are also relevant but often neglected in discussions of scientific and religious worldviews. Social science research aided by the development of new statistical techniques extended the power of measurement into previously inaccessible areas. Controversial studies were conducted on such topics as the relations between religious belief and prejudice, the efficacy of prayer, and religion and violence. To be sure, there were methodological and interpretive difficulties associated with such studies, but optimism was sufficient to promote the development of a science of religious belief with organizational support including the development of scholarly journals. New metrics were applied to a great variety of topical areas. For example, the time of death had been attributed to the specific action of deity, but statistical studies of death yielded data sufficiently reliable to support the life insurance industry. Time of death could now be viewed in probabilistic terms. With such studies, science had invaded an arena previously dominated by religious concepts. Relations between the empirical sciences and religion had played out in the fields of astronomy, geology, and biology, but social science research must also be included in any survey of the relations between science and religion. The present book includes samples of work in this previously neglected history.

We also explore religious and scientific approaches to the problems of causality and epistemology. Two chapters on causality are included partly because of the historical and contemporary problem of demonology. Indeed, an entire chapter is devoted to that topic because of its continuing prevalence and its devastating effects in the 15th and 16th centuries and because so many major religious organizations and sacred literatures continue to include demonic forces in their assessment of causality. Under epistemology, or the problem of knowledge, we explore differences and similarities in religion and science with respect to their treatments of doubt, curiosity, and the roles played by authority, observation, and reason in knowledge claims.

We agree with scholars who argue that there is no single satisfactory definition that captures all of the meanings of religion. In both religion and science we encounter convictions or persuasions about the nature of reality, what it is that constitutes truth, and the means by which truths are discovered and supported. Throughout the book, we will see that various religions and sciences sometimes agree and sometimes disagree on the nature of reality, truth, and the means by which truths are uncovered. A multi-patterned tapestry will emerge rather than any kind of single linear thread. We hope the pattern will trigger new appreciations as well as more informed and balanced critical judgments. In the chapters that follow we will find that religion and science are partly defined by what they do in their various expressions. There are some generic characteristics associated with the two entities along with many variations with respect to major intellectual categories such as cosmology, epistemology, ontology, and axiology. As with a majority of books on science and religion, the focus in this book is on science primarily in relation to the three Abrahamic religions: Judaism, Christianity, and Islam.

Historiographic problems are visited and revisited throughout this work. How can historians bracket or control their personal and contemporary biases as they write history? Such a question is especially relevant when the subject is science and religion. Is there any sense in which the historian can be objective? Can we truly recapture a sense of earlier mental pictures of the world? Most historians agree on the importance of understanding the context in which historical events take place, but context is multidimensional. It has economic, political, scientific, religious, artistic, geographic, philosophical, sociological, cultural, and technological components and these are dynamic and changing in almost any era. How can any historian claim to recapture a robust sense of context?

There is one historiographic problem we have pursued in considerable detail, especially in our first chapter. Early major works set forth the thesis that science and religion have been locked in continuing intellectual warfare. Numerous recent historical treatments however have challenged the warfare thesis or have taken the additional step of arguing that there never has been anything approaching intellectual warfare between science and religion. Are we to believe historians who make the claim that there has been no real warfare between science and religion or are we to believe those who argue that there have been and continue to be instances of intellectual warfare between the two?

Unfortunately, scholars who have argued pro and con about the warfare metaphor have often failed to define their terms. What is intellectual warfare and are there parallels between intellectual and physical warfare? There are serious disagreements between scientists and many religious leaders on a variety of topics, but when do such disagreements spill over into intellectual warfare? Early in Chapter 1 we set forth some meanings of intellectual warfare.

Our approach to the relations between science and religion is decidedly developmental and pluralistic. The relations are not, and never have been, frozen and thus cannot be reduced to a single all-pervasive, timeless, descriptive category. We argue that science, religion, and their various relations are best understood as works in transition. Evolution, adjustment, adaptations, and accommodations constantly occur. There have been cooperative efforts and isolated instances of historical and contemporary intellectual conflict by criteria we set forth in Chapter 1. There has also been a proliferation of methodologies in both science and religion. For example, faith traditions, once based exclusively on authority, revelation, and tradition, have been challenged and often supplanted by a growing emphasis on experience, reason, critical philosophy, and hermeneutics. Process theology and philosophy have also challenged literalism and the more static epistemologies and ontologies of the past. Similarly, numerous scholars in the history and philosophy of science have challenged the concept of a single fixed scientific method. Scientific methodologies have evolved with discoveries of new instruments and methods, new statistical techniques and expansion into new areas of inquiry. Though some ideas or approaches may be counted as canonical, the methods of field biologists, astronomers, and historical scientists such as paleontologists and geologists, are nevertheless quite different from the methods of wet lab chemists, mathematicians, or theoretical physicists.

The book consists of 12 chapters with documentation in the form of endnotes following each chapter. A bibliography and index are also included. Chapter 1 provides a brief overview of the conflicting claims regarding the relationship between science and religion. Chapter 1 also explores treatments of science and religion in the popular press where one regularly encounters the language of warfare. Subsequent chapters explore how these conflicting claims play out in specific topical areas such as human sexuality, evolution, and causality.

Scholars in the physical sciences as well as academicians from other disciplines such as sociology, philosophy, theology, and history have explored the relationships between science and religion. Though psychologists have established organizations for the study of psychology and religion and have contributed to scholarly journals in the psychology of religion, there have been few major works by psychologists on the larger problems associated with science and religion. We hope this work forges a small beginning in a new direction, particularly because psychological insights are highly relevant to problems associated with the relations of science and religion. Works in science and religion are often written by scholars for scholars. Many such works are highly linear detailed treatments of very specific topics while others, like the present work, are more wide ranging. We have attempted to write on a range of topics for a general audience and hope that the work will also be useful to specialists.

ABOUT THE AUTHORS

Wayne Viney is Emeritus Professor and Emeritus University Distinguished Teaching Scholar from Colorado State University where he taught undergraduate and graduate courses in the development of scientific thought, the history of psychology, and the psychology of religion. Viney has published extensively in the history of psychology with a special focus on historiography, the psychology and philosophy of William James, and the contributions of women in the history of psychology. He is co-author with William Douglas Woody of a major textbook, *A History of Psychology: The Emergence of Science and Applications*. In addition to his professorial work, Viney worked for a number of years as Head of the Department of Psychology and later as Associate Dean of Natural Sciences and as Director of the University Core Curriculum in Biology. Throughout his career, Viney always placed strong emphasis on the importance of classroom teaching. He is the recipient of over 20 major teaching awards in his career at Colorado State University including a life-time achievement award from the Society for the History of Psychology of the American Psychological Association. He has also been recognized by the Colorado State University Alumni Association with the Distinguished Faculty award for 2012. Earlier in his career, he served as President of the Society for the History of Psychology and as President of the Rocky Mountain Psychological Association.

William Douglas Woody is Professor of Psychological Sciences at the University of Northern Colorado where he teaches undergraduate and graduate courses in the history of psychology, the psychology of religion, university teaching, and psychology and the law, among others. Woody has published in the history of psychology, the psychology of religion, and teaching of psychology, among other areas, and, as noted previously, he is a co-author of the major textbook *A History of Psychology: The Emergence of Science and Applications*. Woody shares Viney's deep commitment to university teaching. He has published many peer-reviewed and invited works about the teaching of psychology, and he has received numerous college, university, and national teaching awards, including being named Best Professor by the students at two of the three universities at which he has taught. Additionally, he has received national Early Career Awards from both the Society for the History of Psychology and the Society for the Teaching of Psychology. Recently, he served as President of the Rocky Mountain Psychological Association.

ACKNOWLEDGEMENTS

We express appreciation to literally dozens of graduate and undergraduate students enrolled in our courses in the Psychology of Religion and in courses in The Development of Scientific Thought offered at Colorado State University and the University of Northern Colorado. Some of the ideas set forth in this book were presented in our classes, and the enthusiasm and appreciative and critical feedback from students have been of great value in the evolution of our manuscript. We owe a special debt of gratitude to philosopher Donald A. Crosby who team taught courses with Viney on the Psychology and Philosophy of William James and who has engaged in helpful dialogue with us on many of the topics covered in this book. Donald Wayne Viney, son of Wayne Viney, has shared his expertise on a great range of topics we have covered including: the problem of freedom and foreknowledge, process philosophy, evolution, and William James. Friends of the senior author from the fields of physics (Sanford Kern), biology (Robert Zimdahl), and neurology (Howard Nornis) who have met regularly for years have patiently endured extensive commentary about the project and have made numerous supportive comments. Also, many thanks to Michael Viney, son of Wayne Viney, for his thoughtful comments especially on the topics of evolution, geology, and philosophy of science. The senior author's interactions with Professors Holmes Rolston III and Bryan Dik have also been very valuable. Specifically, Rolston's book *Three Big Bangs: Matter-Energy, Life, and Mind* served as a basis for rich, formal, and sometimes heated but friendly exchanges on numerous topics we have covered.

We have had the pleasure of working with publication and production teams at Taylor & Francis. We remain particularly grateful to Editor Christina Chronister, Editorial Assistant Julie Toich, and the strong production team who helped complete the work. The entire Taylor & Francis team has been extremely professional, personable, and helpful throughout the publication process.

We dedicate this work to the memory of William James, whose pioneering work in psychology, philosophy, religion, and history continues to inspire us in our teaching and scholarship as well as in our daily lives. We also express appreciation to Eric Schmidt for his encouraging comments on an earlier version of this work and to Diana Lee for sharing her extensive knowledge of fundamentalism and extreme religious groups.

We remain exceedingly grateful to our families for their support, encouragement, and patience throughout this project. We thank Thomas, Marcus, and Seth Viney for their assistance on technical and philosophical issues and Lisa Woody for her wisdom and good humor; and Nate and Ian Woody, who remained patient with their father as he worked long hours. Finally, in loving memory of Wynona Rose Viney (1934–2009).

Wayne Viney and William Douglas Woody

1

INTELLECTUAL WARFARE
Arguments Pro and Con[1]

> There has always been a conflict between religion and science.[2]
>
> There was never anything approaching intellectual warfare between theologians and scientists.[3]

Historical treatments of the relationship between science and religion are riddled with bewildering contradictions. One extreme position, the "warfare thesis" was set forth by John William Draper in a book titled *History of the Conflict Between Religion and Science*.[4] Another example is found in Andrew Dickson White's book *A History of the Warfare of Science with Theology in Christendom*.[5] The warfare thesis is also encountered in Bertrand Russell's *Religion and Science*; a book that revisits and amplifies the claims of Draper and White.[6] Michael Ruse, in an introduction to Russell's book, notes that Russell was an "ardent proponent of the conflict thesis" believing that "religion and science have long been at war, claiming to themselves the same territory."[7] Jerry Coyne, in his book *Faith vs. Fact: Why Science and Religion are Incompatible* argues that there are inherent epistemological and substantive differences between science and religion.[8] Keith Thompson, in a book that explores why the religion and science debate continues, points out that "science and religion are two very different entities with different ways of arriving at 'truth'."[9] But do these differences rise to the level of intellectual warfare between religion and science or between theologians and science?

Historian David Lindberg challenged the idea that there has been intellectual warfare between theologians and scientists. Indeed, Lindberg made the claim, as noted in the second epigraph for this chapter that "there was never anything approaching intellectual warfare between theologians and scientists." Rodney Stark, in his book, *For the Glory of God* argues "there is no inherent conflict between religion and science" and makes the further claim that science has been dependent on religion, and more specifically that *"Christian theology was essential for the rise of science"*[10] Jonathan Sacks points to "A Great Partnership" between science and religion.[11] Lawrence Principe, in a course entitled "Science and Religion," produced by The Teaching Company, makes the claim that "No serious historians of science or of the science religion issue today maintain the warfare thesis."[12] If this is indeed true of historians of science, it is by no means true of many scientists and philosophers who still believe strongly that the idea of intellectual warfare between science and religion is applicable both historically and on the contemporary scene.[13] Scientists however, have been and continue to be highly variable with respect to their positions on religious faith and the relations between science and faith. The variability is amply illustrated by Nancy K. Frankenberry, in her book *The Faith of Scientists*.[14]

Conflicting Historical Narratives: Importance of the Problem

Conflicting accounts of the history of the relations between science and religion are interesting in their own right, but also important because they touch on values, political movements, and general public interests. Conflicting historical narratives also present perplexing challenges for instructors who cover topics in courses such as the history of science, religious history, evolution, the history of ideas, the history of mental disorders, or the history of philosophy, sociology, anthropology, or psychology. Those who teach history must now adjudicate among deeply conflicting claims and tensions encountered in historical and scientific literature. Is the warfare thesis credible or is it manufactured by the popular press or by those in the scientific and academic communities who are hostile to religion or by some of the members of the faith community who are uncomfortable with scientific discoveries that conflict with religious doctrines? How believable are the claims of historians who now question the warfare thesis? Have these historians been unduly influenced by their religious biases or are they merely conveying truths of history overlooked or distorted by warfare theorists? Samuel Butler, in lines applicable to those who embrace the warfare thesis as well as to those who deny it, noted that "God cannot alter the past; [but] historians can; it is perhaps because [historians] can be useful to [God] in this respect that [God] tolerates their existence."[15]

The persistence and importance of the warfare debate is set forth graphically in the book *War of the Worldviews: Science vs. Spirituality* by Deepak Chopra and Leonard Mlodinow.[16] Chopra, arguing for spiritual and religious viewpoints, and Mlodinow, arguing for traditional scientific views, cover such topics as evolution, mind and brain, the problem of design, and free will and determinism. The title of the book and its contents supports popular beliefs in deep divisions between the two worldviews and their implications for values and morality. To be sure, there are differences between science and religion or science and some varieties of spirituality. Such differences are clearly visible in contemporary and historical events. But, once again, we can ask whether there is reasonable justification for claims of warfare between the worldviews as suggested by the title of Chopra and Mlodinow's book. Kenan B. Osborne and Ki Wook Min, in their book *Science and Religion: Fifty Years after Vatican II*, remind their readers that relations between science and religion are not static but evolving and they point to reconciliations that have occurred since Vatican II.[17] A book of essays from the International Society for Science and Religion (ISSR) edited by Fraser Watts and Kevin Dutton titled *Why the Science and Religion Dialogue Matters* provides helpful information on variations in the relations of science and religion across major faith traditions including Christianity, Islam, Judaism, Hinduism, and Buddhism.[18] Clearly, there is no one kind of relationship between the two entities and there are differences in orientations toward science within as well as between various faith traditions.

One of the major problems associated with the warfare thesis is that most of those who have written pro and con have neglected to define exactly what they mean by warfare. Intelligent discussion of a concept hinges upon clear definitions. What do we mean by intellectual warfare? Does intellectual warfare share some things in common with physical warfare? We will explore the concept of intellectual warfare and then turn to a consideration of arguments by those who believe the concept is not applicable to the history of the relations between science and religion. Counterarguments will also be set forth.

Defining Warfare

Physical warfare and intellectual warfare are multidimensional so any definition must tease out some of the most salient components of these concepts. Historian Edward J. Larson has noted that we are not "talking about an actual war between science and religion as if mental constructs can fight like countries do, marshalling armies and taking territory."[19] Still, in what follows, we will discover some interesting parallels between physical and intellectual warfare. At a minimum, intellectual and physical warfare include the following:

1. Warfare inevitably includes interest groups engaged in organizational activities, including plans and strategies for challenging, engaging, and defeating an enemy.
2. Warfare involves legislative and legal activities as manifested in litigation along with attempts to elect lawmakers who are favorable to a given position. There will also be lobbying efforts to influence the direction and construction of legal structures and the appointments of judges.
3. Warfare has demonstrable effects on educational activities. In a time of heightened tensions, it is particularly important for the youth to be thoroughly immersed in "proper interpretations" of the conflict. There may be lists of "forbidden books" or careful screening of educational materials and teachers.

Private schools may be established to assure that perspectives are focused on those things deemed "appropriate and orthodox." Battlegrounds can be for intellectual or physical territory.
4. The character and intensity of language employed by adversaries is one mark of warfare. There may or may not be a formal declaration of war, but the language of warfare including terms such as *battle, skirmish, combatant, clash, victory, duel,* and *defeat* will be evident in scholarly and popular literature. Warfare influences language in another way. The enemy is often portrayed in strident, vociferous, demeaning, and denigrating terms. We war with words, but also with actions.
5. Warfare includes attempts to influence the flow of information through propaganda, outright distortions and lies, demonstrations, surveys, petitions, control of the media, pickets, protest rallies, and censorship.
6. The tools of physical as well as intellectual warfare may also include: censure, excommunication, the threat of torture, withholding promotions, restrictions on the right to travel or publish, isolation of combatants, death threats, and capital punishment.
7. Most of the foregoing activities cost money, so economic considerations including fundraising, taxation, and sacrifice play prominently in the equation.
8. Warfare provokes intense emotional loyalties often resulting in "blind certitude" and in ideologies seemingly immune to contradictory evidence.
9. Warfare produces martyrs, heretics, heroes, and heroines.
10. Physical and intellectual warfare also play out in historiography or how history is written. Historical narratives inevitably produce divergent interpretations of the causes, conditions, villains (including historians themselves), heroes, successes, failures, and final outcomes.

Larson suggests that warfare where science and religion are concerned "is just a metaphor," but nevertheless a metaphor that is "seductive and tenacious [such that] people respond to it and feel it has validity."[20] It can also be argued that some of the current and historical tensions between science and religion rise to a level that justifies the application of a substantive concept of intellectual warfare. People have been tried, confined, denied the right to publish, excommunicated, threatened with torture, and have received death threats because of their beliefs about science and religion.

The Warfare Thesis: Brief Overview of Arguments and Counterarguments

In what follows, we examine four standard arguments employed by those who reject the warfare thesis or the idea that science and religion are natural enemies. We also explore counterarguments by those who believe there are irreconcilable differences between science and religion and that such differences often result in conflict that rises to the level of intellectual warfare.

Argument Based on Variability of Religious Traditions and Practices

Those who argue against the warfare thesis point out, appropriately, that religions are highly variable and there is no one perspective that can speak for all religious beliefs. Karen Armstrong has argued that for the past 50 years "it has been clear in the academy that there is no universal way to define religion."[21] Variations in religious communities with respect to attitudes toward science are illustrated by faith communities that have supported new scientific thought along with faith communities that have strongly resisted important scientific discoveries and explanations. Ronald Numbers, in his carefully researched book *The Creationists: The Evolution of Scientific Creationism*, calls attention to deep divisions in faith communities over evolution and creationism.[22] Clearly, it is a mistake to lump all religions together and to declare there has been warfare between religion (as if this term referred to one thing) and science. Variation within religious communities may sometimes be as great as variation between scientific and religious communities.

In fact, however, some of the warfare theorists agree with this argument. For example, Andrew Dickson White has been accused of treating religion in an undifferentiated manner, but this accusation is unfounded. Throughout his classic work, White repeatedly acknowledged enlightened religious leaders who supported or even initiated major scientific discoveries.[23] White's work is directed primarily at conservative theologians who take scriptures and church doctrine literally and who often convey the idea that they are speaking for the one true religious viewpoint. In such cases, White was adamant that there had indeed been continual skirmishes and intense battles. Such skirmishes or battles can serve as case histories or illustrations of most of the components of the definition of warfare offered above.

Others argue that the extreme variability encountered in religious groups does not mask irreconcilable differences between religion and science even when both terms are taken generically. In her book *Defending Science within Reason*, philosopher Susan Haack notes that "Religion, unlike science, is not primarily a kind of inquiry, but a body of belief – 'creed' is the word that comes to mind."[24] She calls attention to major differences in treatments of disbelief in religion and in science. Disbelief, doubt, and skepticism are regarded as necessary and central virtues in science, but rarely enjoy the same status in the overwhelming majority of faith communities.[25] Further, when old beliefs are challenged by new data, there are differences in science and religion with respect to rate of change. Religion is inherently more conservative with respect to rate of change than science.

There are also differences in the role and use of emotion in religious and scientific belief systems. Some degree of affect may attend all cognitive functions, but the way affect is nurtured stands out as a consequential difference in scientific and religious communities. Francis Bacon believed that rhetoric or the "grand style" should be avoided in scientific presentations.[26] He believed scientific presentations should focus on substance rather than style with its attempts to secure persuasion through the skillful selection of inflated phrases and images that distort data. Emotion, if anything, should be held in abeyance even at the risk of dry and sometimes tedious presentations. By contrast, powerful emotional attachments are cultivated with great care in religious traditions. Special holidays are set aside that call for sacrifice, devotion, remembrance, and celebration. Music, art, and architecture are powerful tools for the production of praise, gratitude, thanksgiving, affirmation, worship, and allegiance. Religious authorities are present in our most vulnerable times (births, marriages, funerals) to authenticate, comfort, validate, or even threaten. Religious authorities are often known for audacious promises that play on our deepest longings and our strongest needs for justice, pleasure, spiritual superiority, and personal permanence. Shrines, monuments, statues, cathedrals, and pilgrimages to special holy places also evoke enduring emotional attachments. William James warned that emotion in religion is "apt to be tyrannical."[27] By contrast, science seeks to temper or even harness the role of emotions in favor of nurturing and establishing cognitive truths.

As an aside, physicist Richard P. Feynman lamented the exclusively cognitive emphasis in science resulting in the failure of science to produce the rich emotional experiences often observed in unscientific people. He speaks of the adventures and joys of deep penetration into the mysteries of the world. Yet, according to Feynman,

> Our poets do not write about it; our artists do not try to portray this remarkable thing. I don't know why. Is nobody inspired by our present picture of the universe? The value of science remains unsung by singers, so you are reduced to hearing – not a song or a poem, but an evening lecture about it.[28]

Feynman is underscoring here a major generic difference between religion and science where the advantage clearly lies with religion. We are feeling and thinking creatures and to the possible disadvantage of science, feeling may often appeal as the deeper source of truth.[29]

Another difference between religion and science, where the two are taken generically, is encountered in the role of ritual and distinctive compulsive features of their practitioners. In their practice, scientists are as dedicated, compulsive, rule-ridden, and as obsessive as anybody in any disciplinary area. The forms of compulsion however are idiosyncratic and seldom promulgated systematically by authority or tradition. It is said that Isaac Newton could be so obsessed with a problem that he would forget to eat.[30] Charles Darwin at times appeared to be in a trance as he pondered a problem.[31] B. F. Skinner sometimes kept track of the actual number of words he produced in fixed temporal intervals as he worked on his manuscripts.[32] Religious compulsions can also be highly idiosyncratic, but in addition there are many more stereotyped, blindly followed and orchestrated compulsions promoted and sustained by institutions and modeled by authority figures. Thus, one may learn that one needs to pray a fixed number of times and at precise hours each day. Further, it may be that one cannot pray authentically without assuming a given posture, a repetitive movement, a specified spatial orientation, or the meticulous recitation of an exact word sequence. Varieties of repetitive gestures and bodily movements may signify sincerity, celebration, obeisance, submission, or repentance. "Responsive readings," obligatory valorized memory work, and prescribed recitations are also promoted and viewed as marks of proper dedication or even as penitential requirements.

Those who argue against the warfare metaphor are correct in calling attention to the high variability in religious beliefs and organizations. At the same time, there are characteristics broadly associated with religion that are commonly recognized and that are clearly modal in religious beliefs and practices. The role and use of affect is evident in religion and is clearly different from its role and use in science. Variability in religious beliefs and practices should be recognized, but should not be used to mask conflicts with science when they have occurred. Masking is sometimes evident when recurring conflicts are dismissed as exceptions.

Argument Based on the Religious Face of Selected Scientific Works

A second argument by those who dispute the warfare thesis is that many scientific discoveries have come from scholars who have been strongly committed to various faith traditions. An entire issue of the magazine *Christian History* was devoted to "The Christian Face of the Scientific Revolution."[33] Articles on the works of luminaries such as Galileo, Copernicus, Newton, and Boyle were written to demonstrate how scientific discoveries have come from the work of Christians. Muslims also take pride in showing how scientific breakthroughs came from the work of scholars such as Rhazes, Alhazen, or Avicenna. The goal was to demonstrate compatibilities between faith and science and to show how faith has sometimes motivated scientific activity. In other words, faith and science are not necessarily natural enemies because both religious and scientific interests are encountered within the same individual. The assertion of a connection between one's identity with a faith tradition and one's scientific interests is demonstrably true in many instances, but such an assertion should be balanced with the fact that many of these same individuals have also experienced painful and sometimes debilitating tensions between the demands of their faith and the demands of their science. Examples abound.

Descartes, a devout Catholic, could not bring himself to publish his book *The World*, because many of its conclusions ran counter to Catholic doctrine. In fact, Descartes' work supported many of the conclusions published by Galileo who had been condemned by church authorities. Descartes believed very strongly that his arguments in support of the movement of the earth were based on sound reasoning and solid proofs, but he was distraught by the tensions between his religious beliefs and his scientific findings. In a letter to his friend Marin Mersenne, Descartes said "I would not wish, for anything in the world, to maintain them [i.e., his arguments and proofs for the movement of the earth] against the authority of the church." In that same passage, Descartes noted that he liked to live by the Motto "*to live well, you must live unseen.*"[34] Descartes' religious beliefs or more likely his fear of retaliation from the church prevailed. Though he had written *The World* in the four-year period from 1629 to 1633, he suppressed its publication during his lifetime. It would be over a decade after the death of Descartes before the book was finally published. There is no way to assess the number of incidents in which scholars have been punished or have suppressed their works out of fear of retaliation from religious authorities. Neither is there a way to assess the extent of inner turmoil and pain resulting from such self-denial. Descartes however, observed that he was "more happy to be delivered from the fear of my work's making unwanted acquaintances than I am unhappy at having lost the time and trouble which I spent on its composition."[35]

Galileo is the prime example of a Christian whose scientific discoveries are widely recognized, but whose scientific work and philosophy brought him into conflict with his church. Ultimately, in his Inquisition trial, Galileo was forced to swear he would abandon his false belief that "the Sun is the center of the world and does not move from east to west and that the Earth moves and is not the center of the world."[36] In his abjuration he was also forced to acknowledge that he had been warned that the doctrine of a Sun centered universe was contrary to the teachings of Holy Scripture. The conflict between Galileo and the church clearly illustrates Galileo's internal conflicts between his faith and his science. His internal conflicts and his bitterness are nowhere better expressed than in a letter to a friend in which he said "You have certainly understood which was the true and real motive that caused, under the lying mask of religion, this war against me that continually restrains and undercuts me in all directions"[37] Galileo experienced wrenching personal conflicts between his faith tradition and his science. It is arguable as to whether he could have whole-heartedly approved of an expression such as "the Christian face of the scientific revolution."

A more recent example of internal turmoil between the demands of faith and science is encountered in the work of the paleontologist and Jesuit priest Pierre Teilhard de Chardin who lived from 1881 to 1955. Teilhard published over 175 technical scientific papers in paleontology and related fields, but his chief interest was in a synthesis of evolution and the Catholic faith. The technical scientific papers presented no problems to church authorities, but, as noted by Donald Viney, Teilhard's deep commitment to evolution created a "'crisis of obedience' that reached its peak in July 1925, coincidently the same time as the Scopes Trial in Tennessee."[38] Viney goes on to note that, as a Jesuit priest, Teilhard had taken the vow of obedience which, among other things, gave the church authority over such matters as where and what Teilhard could teach, travel rights including conferences he could attend, and what he could publish. Church authorities repeatedly denied permission to Teilhard to publish works that explored evolutionary thought and its implications for theology. Further, Teilhard was not permitted to attend some of the scientific and philosophical conferences that might have been receptive to his ideas. For his part, Teilhard remained officially loyal to the church, but experienced understandable anguish when the church repeatedly used its authority to isolate him from the intellectual community. In private letters Teilhard expressed faith that he would experience divine influence independent of official church directives.[39] He hoped he could die without bitterness.

Prior to his death, Teilhard transferred his major works to his secretary Jean Mortier who would see to it that "the Church censors would not have the last word."[40] Following his death, major works such as *The Phenomenon of Man*, *Man's Place in Nature*, *The Divine Milieu*, and *Hymn of the Universe* were published and widely distributed. Teilhard societies have been formed and Teilhard is celebrated in many quarters as an important proponent of evolutionary thought. Apologists for the church might argue that it was Teilhard's philosophy, not his science that threatened Catholic doctrine. Teilhard, however, did not see it that way though he recognized the tensions between his approach to evolution and classic church doctrine based largely on the teachings of Thomas Aquinas. For his part, Teilhard insisted that his major work, *The Phenomenon of Man* "to be properly understood, must be read 'exclusively as a scientific study.'"[41] In Teilhard's view, it was his science *and* its philosophical implications that fell victim to censorship.

Following the Teilhard fiasco, the Catholic Church has ostensibly made peace with much of evolutionary thought.[42] John Caiazza has pointed out however, that the Catholic Church has enjoyed two distinct advantages in dealing with the evolution–creation issue. The first is a fallout benefit from the earlier Galileo affair when the church rushed too quickly "to condemn empirical discoveries on the basis of apparent contradiction of Biblical texts."[43] The second is that the church has always been free to move from literal to more spiritual or metaphorical approaches to scripture. A third, but problematic advantage centers on the authority of the Pope to speak definitively on all matters that influence theology.

We return now to the basic argument as to whether Western science has a Christian face because so many scientists were Christians. It is true that a great many scientists in the Western tradition were Christians, but does this observation justify the conclusion that science thus has a Christian face? Was it something in scriptures or in church teachings that motivated scholars such as Descartes and Galileo or was it their empirical observations in the "book of the world" that inspired their scientific work?

Argument Claiming that Western Science is a Result of Christian Doctrine

Still another argument against the warfare hypothesis is encountered in the claim of Rodney Stark in his book *For the Glory of God* that "Christianity depicted God as a rational, responsive, dependable, and omnipotent being and the universe as [God's] personal creation, thus having a rational, lawful, stable structure, awaiting human comprehension."[44] There is little question that some early scientists and philosophers envisioned new possibilities for human knowledge based on their growing belief in the regularities and lawfulness of nature. One may ask whether such beliefs were indeed intrinsic to original Christian teachings or were they the product of the influence of the late Middle Age and early Renaissance Christian hermeneutics that had been influenced by Greek thought? Stark quotes Alfred North Whitehead who "grasped that Christian theology was essential for the rise of science in the West, just as surely as non-Christian theologies had stifled the scientific quest everywhere else."[45] Whitehead, however, as we pointed out in the epigraph at the beginning of this chapter, never denied "there has always been a conflict between religion and science." Whitehead understood the important distinction between early Biblical Christian doctrine and later doctrine surfacing in the late Middle Ages and early Renaissance under the influence of Greek thought. If science grew out of an exclusively Christian belief in the rational nature of God resulting in a lawful world, then why didn't Western science enjoy a much earlier beginning? Western science developed and was nourished in a complicated context including: the rediscovery of the Greek classics and their influence on Christian thought, the printing press, a larger reading public, new geographic studies with the accompanying need for improved measurement techniques, the diffusion of authority, the growth of secular perspectives, and the influence of the earlier discoveries of such Islamic luminaries such as Rhazes, Avicenna, Alhazen, and Averroës who incidentally, like many early Christian philosophers and scientists, often suffered debilitating tensions with conservative religious authorities.

Stark's claim that science grew out of Christian doctrine deserves further examination. As noted, some early philosophers and scientists embraced the notion of God as a kind of beneficent mechanic or clock maker whose laws and works were well fitted to human comprehension. Our question is whether this God is truly the God of the Bible or of early Christianity? The God of the Bible may indeed share some of the attributes ascribed by Stark, but the Biblical God is also capable of human-like emotions such as regret, anger, jealousy, and grief. The Biblical God is also portrayed as in Job, chapters 38 through 41, as an inscrutable God whose ways are unpredictable and far beyond human comprehension. The Biblical God is also a God who shows favoritism without a clear underlying rational explanation as in the story of Cain and Abel. In the scriptural account, it is not clear why God preferred Abel's offering to Cain's offering. One may also question whether the God of the New Testament is a God who inspires the kind of epistemic structures necessary to the development of science. In the New Testament, the virtues of blind faith are often celebrated while doubt and rational inquiry are denigrated. The idea that "Christian theology was necessary for the rise of science in the West" is not without serious problems.

Argument from Whig History

Finally, it is often argued that the warfare thesis is an example of the outdated historical methodology criticized by Herbert Butterfield in his *Whig Interpretation of History*.[46] The claim of Butterfield was that whig history, among other problems, promotes narratives that vindicate or even glorify the present and that celebrate the heroic efforts of luminaries fighting against and overcoming the ignorance and dark forces of the past. Whig historians present history in a teleological framework as a progressive march out of the wilderness to the present state of enlightenment. In the context of the history of the relations of science and religion, it is argued that whig histories have portrayed religion as adversarial and as an impediment to major scientific advances. Such histories provide a celebratory story of the steady advance of science against the dark forces of superstition and ignorance.

William Cronon, past President of the American Historical Association, while recognizing whiggish distortions of history, nevertheless calls attention to the danger of the "capacious usage of the word 'whig' ... applied indiscriminately ... to anyone writing histories in which something becomes better over time and is so judged A Good Thing."[47] Cronon calls attention to Butterfield's concern with oversimplified or abridged histories, but acknowledged that all history is abridged history. Technical histories, properly attuned to the fine detail, complexities, and contexts of historical events presumably serve as correctives for overly simplified and celebratory whiggish history. But, as noted by David Wilson, the "pursuit of complexity could produce ever narrower studies that are void of generalizations."[48] Further, a narrow focus or obsession with fine detail can result in histories of things that are not true. Later in the chapter, we will explore some examples.

The Press and the Warfare Hypothesis

It can be argued that it is the popular press always eager for sensationalism that is guilty of the perpetuation of the warfare hypothesis. However, it is not just the popular press that uses the language of warfare. In fact, many scholarly works also employ the language of warfare. Our earlier definition of warfare included the idea that scholarly and popular literature will magnify tensions by employing the language of warfare. Indeed, the case in favor of the warfare thesis would appear to be settled if one were to judge it in terms of the language encountered in popular and scholarly usage. It is clear that the language of warfare is pervasive in ongoing debates over topics such as stem cell research, human sexuality, and evolution. For example, an article published in *The New York Times* by Amy Harmon explores the tensions a science teacher encounters in his attempts to teach evolution. The title of the article is "A Teacher on the Front Line as Faith and Science Clash."[49] The article refers to the clash between religion and science as a "culture war." A scholarly article by Kenneth Miller refers to the famous Dover Pennsylvania trial on evolution as a victory for science, but then notes that "the greater war goes on."[50] Miller is referring to efforts of creation theorists to challenge evolution through attempts to influence lawmakers, textbook selection, and school boards. The use of the word *war* is undoubtedly no accident. The cover of the March 2015 issue of National Geographic is emblazoned with the caption "The War on Science" referring to an article on battles over climate change, evolution, the moon landing, vaccinations, and genetically modified food.[51] In another scholarly work, Barbara Forest calls attention to the idea that "the United States is the world's only industrialized country in which people are still fighting over evolution."[52] Again, the word *fighting* betrays the intensity of the intellectual conflict and the nature of the methods employed by the adversaries. Regardless of the position one takes on whether there has, in fact, been warfare between science and religion, the foregoing materials illustrate that both scholars and popular writers employ the language of warfare.

A Deeper Look at the Warfare Thesis

Arguably, the most visible advocate of the warfare thesis was Andrew Dickson White who was a historian, the first president of the American Historical Association, and, co-founder and first president of Cornell University. As president of Cornell, White hoped to establish a strong scientific secular university free of the theological constraints typically encountered in most American universities in the 19th century. As a result, White was subjected to sustained angry criticism from religious conservatives worried that the rapidly expanding scope of science in the university was encroaching into territories long regarded as the exclusive, sacred, and inviolable domain of religion. Religious conservatives understood that White's agenda would forever change the nature of the university so students were advised from pulpits to stay away from Cornell University. Cornell was one of the early visible manifestations of the land grant tradition initiated by the Morrill Acts of 1862 and 1890. Science, now more closely aligned with technology, was no longer an esoteric and abstract curiosity, but an increasingly visible and tangible force demonstrably relevant to the problems of agriculture, transportation, health, economics, communication, and our ways of understanding ourselves and our world. The relentless reach and march of science was an inevitable and understandable threat to older ways of thinking.

White, for his part, was not one who could ignore what he regarded as unfair and misguided criticism. Still, the battle was painful as White admitted he had been very active in church and that some of his greatest sources of joy were in religious music, poetry, and ecclesiastical architecture. His misgivings were exacerbated by his belief that an open conflict between science and theology was bad for both. He always expressed belief in a "pure and undefiled" faith that, in theory, could be perfectly compatible with science. Nevertheless, he fought back against religious conservatives in fiery speeches, magazine articles, and finally in his massive two-volume influential but controversial classic titled *A History of the Warfare of Science with Theology in Christendom*. White called attention to the transition in 19th century Europe and America from control of universities by theologians to more secular control. One manifestation of the transitions is that there were diminishing religious tests for students and for professors.

White's book was developed over an extremely difficult and demanding 20 year period complicated by his work as president of Cornell, along with U.S. government assignments as commissioner to Santa Domingo in 1870, minister to Russia in 1879, and minister to Germany in 1892. The positive side of extensive travels was that they afforded access to many libraries in the old world and the new. White understood there would be bitter attacks against his work and that it would include inevitable errors of omission and commission. It was a massive work covering a great range of topics in 20 chapters. There are numerous errors, but White's hope was that the overall direction of the work would accurately capture important historical conflicts as well as the tensions he and others faced from religious conservatives in the late 19th century. His book was translated into many languages and has remained in print in English language sources.

White was not alone in advancing the warfare thesis. Two decades prior to White, John William Draper, a chemist with very strong interests in history had embraced the warfare thesis in his book *History of the Conflict Between Religion and Science*. White, however, called attention to a major difference between his approach and that of Draper. White believed the conflict was between science and *dogmatic* theology while Draper believed the conflict to be between science and religion, particularly the Catholic religion. The term *dogmatic* is critical in the work of White as it refers to an epistemology based on the authority of strict Biblical literalism and tradition. For White, the conflict was not just about substantive issues; it was also about the methodologies of science and religion.

Before discussing criticisms of the warfare thesis, it must be noted that the identities of antagonists remain as a substantive and historiographic problem. For example, it can be argued, in line with White's thinking, that historical and contemporary conflicts have been between science and conservative dogmatic theologies rather than with religion broadly considered. It has also been argued that conflicts are between scientism and religion. Epistemic scientism, according to Mikael Stenmark, is the position that "only science can confer genuine (in contrast to apparent) knowledge about reality … Everything outside science is taken as a matter of mere belief and subjective opinions."[53] Polemic attacks on religion treated categorically, for example by "new atheists" such as Richard Dawkins, Sam Harris, and Christopher Hitchens, are sometimes cited as examples of scientism.[54] Others have argued that the battle is between reason and faith, a battle that according to Russell Shorto "may be the chronic fever of modernity."[55] There are, however, as noted by philosopher Donald Crosby vexing, but deeply significant ambiguities and complexities in the roles of faith and reason in secular life as well as in religion. He also contends that each critically depends on and is informed by the other.[56]

Those who challenge the warfare metaphor have documented a veritable catalog of historical errors and distortions in the works of White, Draper, and Russell.[57] Detailed historical scholarship has clearly demonstrated misrepresentations of St. Augustine and other church fathers on such matters as the role of revelation as a means of assessing truth, the doctrine of a spherical earth, and the location of the earth in the immediate solar system. Errors of warfare theorists have resulted in strong charges that White and Draper are "master mythmakers" and that their accounts "are more propaganda than history."[58]

Though historical errors and distortions in the works of Draper, Russell, and White are well documented, it is nevertheless possible that their larger interpretive conclusions are sometimes valid even in the face of recognized errors in detail. History includes empirical components such as original formal documents, letters, and other archival materials as well as interpretive or explanatory components. The interpretive components are arguably more problematic for the historian than the empirical components. It is possible that a single error in an empirical detail could foreclose on the possibility of a believable interpretation, but neither does scrupulous attention to empirical details guarantee believable interpretive work. A historian can be error prone with respect to empirically based data, but advance valid interpretations of a larger picture. Examples abound in historical studies. The correspondent for the Chicago Tribune relayed the story of Lincoln's Gettysburg address to the Tribune, but there were numerous errors in the details of the communication. The spirit of Lincoln's address was nevertheless accurately captured by the communication to the *Tribune*.[59] The work of the correspondent, by later standards of communication including audio and visual recording devices and advanced copies of speeches, was deficient, but by existing standards and difficulties in 1863, the empirical work, though flawed, was acceptable. Errors in detail did not mask the overall sense of Lincoln's address.

Historians, like other scholars, are not always careful to avoid the fallacy of composition; the idea that what is true of the parts must be true of the whole. The fallacy of composition is illustrated in current debates on climate change. The common claim that a local cold spell is evidence against global warming is countered with the reminder that "local is not necessarily global." A wider frame of reference reveals truths easily lost or distorted by pedantic scruples or in an overly narrow focus on local details. The interpretation of a historical event is not necessarily undermined by the identification of an error or even a succession of errors in the details associated with the event. Historians, like scholars in all disciplines, must hold themselves accountable to high standards of scholarship and to accuracy in relaying the fine details of their work, but they are no less accountable for assuring that their interpretive framing is driven with careful attention to the part–whole problem. Early warfare theorists have been roundly and appropriately chastised for errors in the details of their work, but the persistent force of the larger intellectual geography and composition of their claims persists and is manifested in public opinion, current conflicts over evolution, and in the titles of scholarly works such as Harold Attridge's book *The Religion and Science Debate: Why Does it Continue?*

The Complexity Thesis: Appreciative and Critical Comments

John Hedley Brooke pointed out that categorical beliefs in an "antithesis between science, conceived as a body of unassailable facts, and religion, conceived as a set of unverifiable beliefs, is assuredly simplistic."[60] Brooke was one of the first to emphasize the diversity of the relations between science and religion. Clearly, the warfare thesis as a singular or one-dimensional way to characterize the relations of science and religion is unworthy of serious scholars. In his book *Science and Faith*, philosopher and theologian John F. Haught draws helpful distinctions between *conflict* and *contrast*. The softer term *contrast* is more likely to encourage intellectual work on possibilities of convergence.[61] An alternative to the warfare thesis, what David B. Wilson refers to as the complexity thesis, is a manifestation of the "new history" designed to enhance and correct earlier historical narratives. In the words of Wilson, complexity is manifested in the "numerous combinations of scientific and religious ideas, which to be fully understood, [requires] delineation of their social and political settings."[62] The new history rejects the whig approach to history in favor of more rigorous scholarship deeply tuned to external relations along with presumably greater meta-level awareness of the work of the historian. The new history emphasizes facticity where facts are regarded not necessarily as transcripts of reality, but simply as those things that obstinately reoccur. There is also an emphasis, as in the sciences, on more manageable, focused, narrowly defined historical problems. Wilson, however observes, correctly we think, that the "Pursuit of complexity could produce ever narrower studies that are void of generalization."[63] A closely related problem, as noted earlier, is that obsession with ever finer detail can result in histories of things that are untrue. Examples abound.

For example, in earlier warfare literature there are claims, embellished with rich emotional imagery, that Galileo was imprisoned by the church. Recent scholarship however, has demonstrated that the imprisonment of Galileo is a widespread myth that has persisted for over 350 years. According to Maurice Finocchiaro the assumption of imprisonment was reasonable, at least for more than a century after the trial, but definitive evidence against imprisonment surfaced about 150 years after the trial.[64] The evidence demonstrates that during trial proceedings Galileo was spared the usual incarceration in jail cells and put up in seclusion in quarters that, for that day, might be regarded as luxurious. Neither did Galileo go to jail following the trial and condemnation. Rather, he was sentenced to live out the rest of his life under house arrest in his villa near Florence.

Those who embrace the complexity thesis and who stress the "reasonable" or unusually "benign" actions of the church claim a victory of sorts against the warfare thesis in their demonstration that Galileo did not literally go to jail. The claims of imprisonment of Galileo by warfare theorists from Voltaire to White are demonstrated to be exaggerations or simply wrong. But nagging questions remain. Careful scholarly research demonstrating the "kindly" action of the church corrects the historical narrative but opens the door to questions about deeper meanings of imprisonment. What was Galileo experiencing with respect to the intellectual and physical constraints he faced? Attention to external contextual relations is important, but consideration of Galileo's experience is a fundamental empirical requirement we may expect the historian to address. Emphasis on externality alone or on the complexity of external contextual matters should not be allowed to marginalize or mask attention to the role of individual experiences in the larger interpretive scheme.

Galileo's perspectives on his intellectual imprisonment are clear. As noted earlier, he spoke of "the lying mask of religion [and] this war against me that continually restrains me and undercuts me in all directions."[65] He was particularly outraged at restraints that forbid him to respond to his critics even when they made egregious errors in their discussions of his work. Galileo clearly believed he had been placed in a cruel and uncompromising intellectual prison that restrained him as he said "in all directions."

Furthermore, in his abjuration, he was forced to swear he would never again say anything verbally or in writing in support of the hated belief in a literal sun-centered planetary system. The bare fact that Galileo did not go to jail fails to capture the pain of intellectual confinement that forbade continued work on a problem that for so many years had been at the very center of Galileo's personal and scholarly life. Given a choice of a literal jail with rights to pursue the work he loved vs. the oppressive restrictions imposed by the Inquisition, he might well have preferred the former. Further, there was his humiliation that he was forced to perjure himself and the knowledge of direct orders from inquisitors that his earlier works could not be reprinted and new works on heliocentrism could not be published. The confinement and isolation of Galileo was physical, social, occupational, and intellectual. Carefully detailed historical demonstration that Galileo did not literally go to jail softens the actions of "the church." However, such a demonstration without due regard to more psychological matters, can, like the warfare thesis, deform and narrow appreciation and understanding of what happened to Galileo personally and to his scientific work. Galileo was confined and placed in an intellectual prison; these aspects of the historical narrative should not be neglected. The literalist claim that he did not go to jail is true, but at a more appropriate level of abstraction, it is not true.

The complexity thesis is also illustrated in research that casts serious doubt on earlier claims of warfare theorists that Galileo suffered physical torture at the hands of the Inquisition. It is highly unlikely that physical torture was actually employed against the aging Galileo.[66] Nevertheless, he was *threatened* with torture. In his book *God's Jury: The Inquisition and the Making of the Modern World*,

Cullen Murphy concludes "It is a mistake to assume that duress is absent when its instruments of torture are out of sight."[67] Furthermore, one can be tortured by questioning, by anticipation, suspense, uncertainty, and unexplained delays, all of which were tools of the Inquisition and most of which were used against Galileo. Galileo understood the seriousness of the charges against him and their possible consequences; he was aware too that physical torture was a legal tool of the Inquisition. An additional source of duress was associated with judicial procedures marked, in his words, by "calumnies, scams, strategems, and deceptions that were used in Rome … to cloud the vision of the authorities."[68] To declare, as earlier warfare theorists did, that Galileo was physically tortured is mistaken. Yet it is equally a distortion of history to deny that he was physically tortured without emphasizing the extreme duress he was under as a result of the Inquisition's techniques of intimidation. It is likely true that Galileo was not physically tortured, but this amounts to an abridgment that simplifies and thins the actions of official religious authorities, betrays an anemic appreciation for the meaning of torture, and distorts the historical narrative.

Another claim by warfare theorists that is now disputed is that there were terrifying consequences associated with the new Copernican cosmic architecture. Humans were demoted from their comfortable stationary home in the very center of the cosmos, but did the demotion have emotional consequences? Philosopher Carlton Berenda in his book *World Visions and the Image of Man* spoke of the pain of a lost heritage and the inevitability of strong relations between the way we view ourselves and the way we view our world. Questions in a new radically different geo-kinetic sun centered environment were inevitable though they were slow to develop. What does it mean to be in this seemingly impersonal abstract world on a moving planet that is simply one among many and no longer center stage? The displacement could hardly be inconsequential; where now was the abode of God, and how could it be that "up" is no longer "up," but "out?" Berenda points out "if the grossly material earth can be counted among the heavenly bodies, then *the heavenly bodies can be considered as grossly material.*"[69] Where then was the spiritual realm once so secure? Would morality be fatally undermined in the new seemingly unstable structure? If we can no longer trust the Bible, church authorities, or traditions in matters of cosmic architecture how can we trust them in other matters more directly pertinent to our lives?

Recently some historians have argued that there is no evidence for negative emotional fallout associated with the new heliocentrism. Dennis Danielson claims that the emotional fallout case widely argued by previous scholars, mainly warfare theorists, is another example of a fabrication and a myth. Danielson points to the paucity of evidence that heliocentric views had any disturbing emotional effect on people.[70] But the masses of common people who did not read or write could not leave records of their feelings about the new worldview. The absence of evidence, in this case, cannot be taken to mean that common people were emotionally neutral about the radical shift in worldviews. This is a common problem that confronts the historian. How much weight should be given to reasonable inference vs. data, or in this case, reasonable inference in the absence of data?

In the absence of written records, we can only infer how common people felt about the new cosmic architecture. However, much of the literature on heliocentrism written by the educated elite is hardly dispassionate or calmly intellectual or objective. What comparisons then, can be inferred between the clear-cut emotional concerns of the intellectual elite and those of common people? Were leading intellectuals fearful that common illiterate people would be scandalized when they grasped the significance of the new worldview?[71] To scandalize is to invoke affect in the form of fear, outrage, shock, or dismay. Church authorities clearly feared both the intellectual and emotional consequences of heliocentrism. The official condemnation of Galileo drips with emotional invective and outrage that go well beyond the intellectual legal requirements of the document. Reasonable scholars have abundant reasons to infer that heliocentrism had devastating consequences for existing belief systems and that such consequences were not restricted to the intellectual elite. The new heliocentrism not only contradicted sacred scriptures but struck at the heart of the long held, comfortable, and narcissistic belief that humans are located in the center of the universe. Such a dislocation could hardly be inconsequential.

The three examples just reviewed suggest that larger truths can be disfigured or lost altogether in the assemblage of microscopic detail. Contemporary historians of science, in the pursuit of detail and complexity, have worked to challenge the claims of the warfare thesis and to some extent have been successful. But we may now ask whether some of the claims of contemporary historians are as sweeping and categorical as the claims of those who supported the warfare thesis? Can the warfare thesis be dismissed as nothing but propaganda and myth making or would it be more plausible to acknowledge instances of conflict historically and, in the present, that in fact rise to the level of intellectual warfare? Is it credible to claim that there has never been intellectual warfare between scientists and theologians? Those who most adamantly oppose the warfare thesis nevertheless acknowledge its persistence. Otherwise, why spend so much time attempting to combat what has ostensibly been discredited? Finally, is it consistent with complexity theory to declare, as some do, that the warfare thesis resulted simply and primarily from the 19th century work of Draper and White?

*****

Unfortunately, too many scholars have left it to their readers to discern the meanings of intellectual warfare. We have suggested ten criteria to be used as a means of thinking about intellectual warfare. Most of these criteria have played out, historically and in the present, in many of the interactions between science and religion. Historians who portrayed relations between the two entities in terms of the warfare metaphor have not been entirely incorrect, but they have overgeneralized and thus advanced a simplistic and distorted viewpoint. More recent historians have advocated what has come to be known as the complexity thesis marked by careful scholarly analysis of the contextual details of the interactions between science and religion. Complexity theorists have demonstrated a much more nuanced and pluralistic account of the highly variable relations between science and religion. Their accounts however, have also resulted in distortions and simplifications as demonstrated in this chapter with examples from the Galileo case. Obsessive attention to detail, while important in its own right, sometimes masks larger truths. Further, it is clear that earlier historians such as Andrew Dickson White made numerous errors in the details of their historical narratives. But some of the complexity theorists have treated White and his work in a categorical fashion and overlooked or misrepresented important larger truths conveyed in the spirit of his classic work.

We strongly agree that there is no identifiable singularity that can reasonably be applied to assessments of the relations between science and religion. Unfortunately, extreme claims are encountered in the literatures of warfare theorists and complexity theorists. In what follows, we will encounter examples of intellectual warfare as understood in terms of the criteria we have advanced. We will also encounter milder tensions, irritations, accommodations, compromises, and cooperation in the dynamic centrifugal and centripetal forces that characterize the relations between science and religion.

Notes

1 Earlier versions of this chapter were published by the senior author in *The Midwest Quarterly* (2008, 49, 343–357) and as the Wallace Russell Memorial Lecture at the American Psychological Association, Honolulu, Hawaii, August, 2013.
2 Alfred North Whitehead, *Science and the Modern World* (New York: The Free Press, 1967), 182.
3 David Lindberg, "Natural Adversaries?" *Christian History* 21, No. 4, (November 2002), 45.
4 John W. Draper, *History of the Conflict Between Religion and Science* (London: Kegan Paul, Trench Thrübner, 1874).
5 Andrew Dickson White, *A History of the Warfare of Science with Theology in Christendom* (New York: Prometheus Books, 1993).
6 Bertrand Russell, *Religion and Science* (New York: Oxford University Press, 1997).
7 Michael Ruse, "Introduction," in *Religion and Science*, by Bertrand Russell (New York: Oxford University Press, 1997), x.
8 Jerry A. Coyne, *Faith vs. Fact: Why Science and Religion are Incompatible* (New York: Viking, 2015).
9 Keith Thompson, "Introduction," *The Religion and Science Debate: Why Does It Continue?* ed. Harold W. Attridge (New Haven, CT: Yale University Press, 2009), 2.
10 Rodney Stark, *For the Glory of God* (Princeton, NJ: Princeton University Press, 2003), 123.
11 Jonathan Sacks, *The Great Partnership: Science, Religion, and the Search for Meaning* (New York: Schocken, 2011).
12 Lawrence Principe, *Science and Religion* DVD-ROM (Chantilly, VA: The Teaching Company, 2006). See Lecture number 2.
13 See, for example, Section III titled "Religion and Science in Conflict," in *Science and Religion: Are They Compatible?* ed. Paul Kurtz (Amherst, NY: Prometheus Books, 2003),

129–187. Also see Susan Haack, *Defending Science within Reason* (Amherst, NY: Prometheus Books, 2003). See particularly, Chapter 10 titled Point of Honor, 265–297.
14 Nancy K. Frankenberry, *The Faith of Scientists in Their Own Words* (Princeton, NJ: Princeton University Press, 2008).
15 Samuel Butler, *Erewhom Revisited* (New York: E. P. Dutton, 1920), 151.
16 Deepak Chopra and Leonard Mlodinow, *War of the Worldviews: Science vs. Spirituality* (New York: Harmony Books, 2011).
17 Kenan B. Osborne and Ki Wook Min, *Science and Religion: Fifty Years After Vatican II* (Eugene, OR: Wipf & Stock, 2014).
18 Fraser Watts and Kevin Dutton (eds.), *Why the Science and Religion Dialogue Matters: Voices from the International Society for Science and Religion* (West Conshohocken, PA: Templeton Foundation Press, 2006).
19 Edward J. Larson, *The Creation–Evolution Debate* (Athens, GA: University of Georgia Press, 2008), 38.
20 Ibid., 38–39.
21 Karen Armstrong, *Fields of Blood: Religion and the History of Violence* (New York: Alfred A. Knopf, 2014), 4.
22 Ronald L. Numbers, *The Creationists: The Evolution of Scientific Creationism* (New York: Alfred A. Knopf, 1992).
23 White, *A History of the Warfare*, see pp. 84, 91, 362, and 372 in Volume 1, and pp. 49, 91, 95, 194, and 282 in Volume 2.
24 Haack, *Defending Science*, 267.
25 There are exceptions in liberal and progressive religious communities, but such exceptions are not common in the majority of faith communities.
26 See, for example, Brian Vickers, "Bacon and Rhetoric," in *The Cambridge Companion to Bacon*, ed. Markku Peltonen (New York: Cambridge University Press, 1996), 222–227.
27 William James, *The Meaning of Truth* (Cambridge, MA: Harvard University Press, 1975), 125.
28 Richard P. Feynman, "The Value of Science," in *Frontiers of Science*, ed. Lee A. Dubridge (New York: Basic Books, 1958), 260–267.
29 William James, *The Will to Believe* (Cambridge, MA: Harvard University Press, 1979), Chapter 1. See also Jonathan Haidt, *The Righteous Mind: Why Good People are Divided by Politics and Religion* (New York: Pantheon Books, 2012).
30 See I. Bernard Cohen, "Isaac Newton," in *Lives in Science: A Scientific American Book*, ed. Dennis Flanagan (New York: Simon and Schuster, 1957), 26–27.
31 See Loren C. Eiseley, "Charles Darwin," in *Lives in Science: A Scientific American Book*, ed. Dennis Flanagan (New York: Simon and Schuster, 1957), 204.
32 See Richard I. Evans, *B. F. Skinner: The Man and His Ideas* (New York: E. P. Dutton, & Co., Inc. 1968), 104. Also see Robert D. Nye, *The Legacy of B. F. Skinner: Concepts and Perspectives, Controversies and Misunderstandings* (Pacific Grove, CA: Brooks/Cole, 1992), 9.
33 *Christian History*, November, 21, No. 4, 2002.
34 René Descartes to Marin Mersenne, April 1634 in *Descartes' Philosophical Letters*, ed. Anthony Kenny (Oxford: Clarendon Press, 1970), 26.
35 Ibid.
36 Giorgio de Santillana, *The Crime of Galileo* (Chicago: University of Chicago Press, 1955), 310. The oath that Galileo was forced to sign is also available in numerous places online.
37 Ibid., 324.
38 Donald Wayne Viney, "Teilhard: Le Philosophe malgré l'Église," in *Recovering Teilhard's Fire*, ed. Kathleen Duffy (Philadelphia: St. Joseph's University Press, 2010), 69.
39 Ibid., 71.

40 Ibid., 76.
41 Ibid., 81.
42 On the other hand, Darwinian evolution raises troublesome questions for standard church dogmas such as the separate and special creation of human beings and their essential qualitative separation from the rest of the animal kingdom. The monogenic position that the entire human family has descended from a single couple also runs counter to scientific thought. There remains much to be clarified regarding claims of reconciliation between evolutionary thought and Catholic theology.
43 John Caiazza, "The Evolution Versus Religion Controversy: How Two Mystiques Devolved Into Politics," *Modern Age* 47, No. 2 (Spring 2005), 108.
44 Stark, *For the Glory of God*, 147.
45 Ibid., 14.
46 Herbert Butterfield, *The Whig Interpretation of History* (New York: Norton, 1931).
47 William Cronon, "Two Cheers for the Whig Interpretation of History," *Perspectives on History: The News Magazine of the American Historical Association* 50, No. 6 (September, 2012).
48 David. B. Wilson, "The Historiography of Science and Religion," in *Science and Religion: A Historical Introduction*, ed. Gary B. Ferngren (Baltimore, MD: The Johns Hopkins Press, 2002), 26.
49 Amy Harmon, "A Teacher on the Front Line as Faith and Science Clash," *New York Times*, August 24, 2008.
50 Kenneth R. Miller, "An Idea that Provoked, but Didn't Deliver," in *Intelligent Design: Science or Religion? Critical Perspectives*, eds. Robert M. Baird and Stuart E. Rosenbaum (Amherst, NY: Prometheus Books, 2007), 46.
51 See Joel Achenbach, "The Age of Disbelief," *National Geographic* 227, No. 3 (March 2015), 34–47.
52 Barbara Forrest, "Intelligent Design: Creationism's Trojan Horse," in *Intelligent Design: Science or Religion? Critical Perspectives*, eds. Robert M. Baird and Stuart E. Rosenbaum (Amherst, NY: Prometheus Books, 2007), 100.
53 Mikael Stenmark, "Science and the Limits of Knowledge," in *Clashes of Knowledge: Orthodoxies and Heterodoxies in Science and Religion*, eds. Peter Meusburger, Michael Welker, and Edgar Wunder (New York: Springer and Klaus Tschira Gemeinnützige GmbH, 2008), 113.
54 For example, see Alister McGrath, *Dawkins' God: Genes, Memes, and the Meaning of Life* (Malden, MA: Blackwell Publishing, 2005); Richard Dawkins, *The God Delusion* (New York: Houghton Mifflin, 2006); Sam Harris, *The End of Faith: Religion, Terror and the Future of Reason* (New York: W. W. Norton & Co. 2004); and Christopher Hitchens, *God Is Not Great: How Religion Poisons Everything* (New York: Hachette Book Group, 2007).
55 Russell Shorto, *Descartes' Bones: A Skeletal History of the Conflict Between Faith and Reason* (New York: Doubleday, 2008), 79.
56 Personal communication. For a detailed treatment, see Donald A. Crosby, *Faith and Reason: Their Roles in Religious and Secular Life* (Albany, NY: State University of New York Press, 2011).
57 Principe, "Science and Religion," 2006 (see Lecture No. 2).
58 Ronald L. Numbers (ed.), *Galileo Goes to Jail and other Myths About Science and Religion* (Cambridge, MA: Harvard University Press, 2009), 6.
59 Eric Zorn, "Dateline Gettysburg: The Tribune Regrets the (Minor) Errors," Chicago: *Chicago Tribune*. The byline of Zorn's article headed a column in the *Tribune* published November 21, 1863, http://articles.chicagotribune.com/2013-11-17/news/ct-gettysburg-lincoln-anniversary-zorn-1117-zorn-20131117_1_abraham-lincoln-book-shop-four-score-gettysburg-address (Accessed November 14, 2016).
60 John Hedley Brooke, *Science and Religion: Some Historical Perspectives* (New York: Cambridge University Press, 1991), 6.

61 John F. Haught, *Science and Faith: A New Introduction* (New York: Paulist Press, 2012).
62 David B. Wilson, "The Historiography of Science and Religion," 24.
63 Ibid., 26.
64 Maurice A. Finocchiaro, "That Galileo was Imprisoned and Tortured for Advocating Copernicanism," in *Galileo Goes to Jail and Other Myths About Science and Religion*, ed. Ronald L. Numbers (Cambridge, MA: Harvard University Press, 2009), 73.
65 Wade Rowland, *Galileo's Mistake: A New Look at the Epic Confrontation Between Galileo and the Church* (New York: Arcade Publishing, 2001), 279.
66 Finocchiaro, *Galileo Goes to Jail*, 68–78.
67 Cullen Murphy, *God's Jury: The Inquisition and the Making of the Modern World* (New York: Houghton Mifflin Harcourt, 2012), 89.
68 Maurice A. Finocchiaro, *Retrying Galileo: 1633–1992* (Berkeley, CA: University of California Press, 2005), 59–60.
69 Carlton W. Berenda, *World Visions and the Image of Man* (New York: Vintage Press, 1965), 84.
70 Dennis R. Danielson, "That Copernicanism Demoted Humans from the Center of the Cosmos," in *Galileo Goes to Jail and other Myths About Science and Religion*, ed. Ronald L. Numbers (Cambridge, MA: Harvard University Press, 2009), 50–58.
71 Finocchiaro, *Retrying Galileo*, 119.

2

THE PROBLEM OF KNOWLEDGE

> *But man, proud man,*
> *Drest in a little briefe authorite,*
> *Most ignorant of what he's most assur'd,*
> *(His glassie Essence) like an angry Ape*
> *Plaies such phantastique tricks before high heaven,*
> *As makes the Angels weepe.*[1]
>
> Experiences which are out of line with the teachings of Scripture must always be renounced as fallacious.
> The Bible has a monopoly on truth.[2]

Classical comparisons between religion and science explore such topical areas as the age of the earth, the architecture of the heavens, evolution, the origin of language, and the ethics of loans of interest. Contemporary comparisons include additional topics such as embryonic stem-cell research, sexual orientation, population and birth control issues, and climate change. Explorations of such substantive topics are informative, but there is an entirely different kind of comparison between science and religion, possibly the most important, but too often neglected in classical and contemporary works. The focus of this comparison is on methodological differences encountered in the activities and work of practitioners of religion and science. What are the methods employed in support of the truth claims offered by scientists and by religious leaders as they go about their work? In this chapter we focus on a comparison of the epistemic building blocks and normative practices commonly encountered in the sciences and in various faith traditions.

Epistemology

Jonathan Rauch, in his book *Kindly Inquisitors*, has jokingly declared that use of the term "'epistemology' at a cocktail party is a sure way to clear a room."[3] The term sounds heavy and it is heavy, referring as it does to the study of the nature, sources, and limits of human knowledge. Rauch is correct that epistemology does not lend itself to the kind of light-hearted intellectual fare commonly encountered in cocktail conversation. Epistemology includes, among other things, the methods employed in claims about knowledge and herein is its relevance not only to science and religion, but to all intellectual endeavors. There may be no subject as relevant to human welfare as epistemology and yet it is a subject too easily neglected or avoided altogether. Neglect and avoidance are motivated at least partly by denial because thoughtful and honest reflection confronts us at every turn with the admission that we are all beggars when it comes to the problem of knowledge. Serious study is relevant however because all academic fields include traditions, assumptions, methodological prescriptions, and orthodoxies. Students in schools of law devote much of their time to learning standard legal methods and procedures that will later play pivotal roles in the truth claims offered in courts of law. Theology students also devote hours of study to the methodologies designed to provide support for their knowledge claims. Students in the sciences devote long hours to the mastery of the scientific methods and increasingly complicated tools designed to contribute to the knowledge industry. It is clear that methods of knowing vary from one discipline to the next so discussion of science and religion is incomplete without a consideration of epistemological issues.

One way to understand differences and similarities between science and religion is to examine their respective treatments of topical areas commonly explored in epistemological studies. In what follows we outline some of the roles of curiosity, doubt, authority, reason, and experience as they have played out in religion and in science.

Curiosity

Curiosity is a fundamental building block in the origin, construction, and growth of all intellectual endeavors. The absence of curiosity undermines learning and creativity by leading to passivity, fatalism, and intellectual stagnation. But what is the role of curiosity in science and in religion and how has curiosity been regarded in the histories of these two endeavors? Curiosity reflects a desire or need to know or to understand. Infants appear to have an inborn inquisitive orientation as they focus attention on any novel object or event. Words such as *why*, *what*, and *how* develop as a natural part of the vocabularies of young children. In modern times, the nurturing of curiosity is central to general education as well as the development of in-depth knowledge in areas of special interest. Unfortunately, the nurturing of curiosity is not always, and has not always been a value. In the Western world, curiosity in some religious traditions was regarded as a mark of vanity, as a dangerous sin, or even as the downfall of humankind. According to Furcht and Hoffman in *The Stem Cell Dilemma* "There was no place for curiosity in the lockdown mindset of the Middle Ages."[4] The familiar story of Adam and Eve was often interpreted as a comment on the dangers of curiosity. The forbidden fruit is from the tree of knowledge of good and evil and the "fall of human beings" was often attributed to Eve's curiosity. In memorable lines Robert Browning characterized a common viewpoint in his poem "A Woman's Last Word."

> Where the apple reddens,
> Never Pry—
> Lest we lose our Edens,
> Eve and I.[5]

The fear associated with curiosity is illustrated in the words of John Milton from his work *Paradise Lost*.

> Sollicit not thy thoughts with matters hid,
> Leave them to God above, Him serve and feare.[6]

The term *feare* is significant in Milton's lines because it is often fear that subverts the development of curiosity. Fear is fed by beliefs that curiosity goes against the very word of God because sacred scriptures warn of the foolishness of curiosity about worldly matters. For example, I Corinthians 1:20 warns "God made foolish the wisdom of this world." The Qur'an in Surah 5:101 counsels believers to avoid "questions about things which if declared to you may trouble you." In Surah 6:32 it declares "This world's life is naught but a play and an idle sport." Why would one develop curiosity about life in a world characterized in terms of play or idle sport? It was often assumed that human pride was the motive for curiosity, and that the fruits for understanding the things of this world would be worthless or even dangerous. The negative or even fearful approach to curiosity prevailed for centuries and contributed to the stagnation, devaluation, and suppression of human worldly knowledge.

Peter Harrison, in a helpful article on curiosity and forbidden knowledge in early modern England, pointed out that it was Francis Bacon, one of the early founders of the enlightenment and the scientific revolution, who contributed to a reversal of attitudes toward curiosity in the West.[7] In view of the long history of deeply entrenched negative attitudes toward curiosity, Bacon (1561–1626) had to proceed with appropriate caution because radically new ideas in the 16th and 17th centuries could be met with the most severe punishment including imprisonment or even execution. Accordingly, Bacon's first cautious step was to express agreement with those who saw curiosity as a potential sin, even referring once to his own writings as "fragments of conceits."[8] Bacon argued, however, that the fruits of curiosity manifested in new practical discoveries could result in the reduction of suffering and the advancement of Christian charity. In other words, it was the way curiosity was used in the new sciences to serve others that was important. Ian Box notes that Bacon's moral position was "that love of others should prevail over love of self and by extension that public good is higher than private."[9] While Bacon was attempting to provide a nuanced philosophical defense of curiosity, Galileo working independently in Italy was already demonstrating unrelenting curiosity in his work with the telescope as he uncovered growing support for the feasibility of a sun centered solar system. Other scientists and philosophers who followed Bacon and Galileo demonstrated the freedom to embrace the new orientation toward curiosity so that what was once a vice was gradually transformed into a virtue. The changing status of curiosity, though seldom appreciated, is one of the great intellectual achievements of the early enlightenment in the West.

Curiosity and Science

Philip Ball, in his book *Curiosity: How Science Became Interested in Everything*, provides a detailed treatment of the changing fortunes of curiosity and how modernity has been shaped by the capacity to explore an increasing range of questions.[10] Curiosity is now considered as a virtue central to scientific discovery and is carefully nurtured in scientific laboratories and classes. In classrooms and in science fair projects students are rewarded, not just for the rigor of their thought or their mastery of technicalities, or the ability to memorize and mechanically recite received materials, but for the innovative or heuristic qualities of their ideas. The same is true of thesis and dissertation projects at the graduate level where there is a strong emphasis on creativity and originality. Nobel Prizes as well as other major awards are based on innovative, cutting edge or breakthrough studies that bring about major changes in our understanding of the world. Such awards are especially abundant in societies and cultures that encourage free and open inquiry in all intellectual arenas. It is doubtful science could have flourished in the West without the nurturing of more friendly attitudes toward curiosity that surfaced in the enlightenment. It is also noteworthy that curiosity in the modern era was not restricted to scientific questions alone. New developments in art, music, religion, government, economics, philosophy, medicine, and politics may well be attributable to the changing fortunes of curiosity. We may ask also whether the restriction or forbidding of questions in any arena of thought doesn't undermine creativity and innovation in other arenas of thought? The opposite may also be true; the unleashing of curiosity in any area of inquiry may well spill over into other areas.

Curiosity and Religion

Curiosity has had a more tenuous status in the history of religion though it is now enfranchised and even celebrated in most moderate to liberal religious cultures. For example, such cultures in the Christian tradition fully endorse the higher criticism of the Bible and believe that such criticism can enhance and deepen the quest for an authentic and meaningful spirituality. There are other contemporary religious cultures however, even at the outset of the 21st century, that display intense anxiety over modernity with its emphasis on unfettered and open inquiry motivated by the extension of curiosity into all intellectual arenas. Such inquiry in the sciences and technology, and in other disciplines such as history where the modern emphasis is on a critical as opposed to an exclusively celebratory approach to the past, constitutes a threat to the comfort provided by stability, permanence, certitude, and the unmovable foundations promised by some religious traditions. To be sure, there may be questions in all disciplinary areas that provoke fear and there is always the nagging fear of the disapproval of significant authorities. Increasingly however, in the modern world, such questions are met with intense honest and open public debate rather than suppression by authorities.

Curiosity is seriously undermined in religious and educational cultures that focus on extensive memory work, blind repetition, or robotic recitation of masses of material that must be unquestioned or accepted uncritically in a lock-step fashion. Numbing rote memory work is sometimes necessary but can also stifle independent and productive creative thought and can compromise the legitimate authority of the individual just as it can underscore, reinforce, and enhance the authority of an institution, a book, a tradition, or a charismatic leader.

Ultimately the status of curiosity may also rest on theories about the nature of truth. In his novel, *The Name of the Rose*, Umberto Eco captures old attitudes toward truth and knowledge in a sermon by a monk named Jorge who argues that there is no such thing as real progress. Jorge tells his colleagues that all truth has already been set forth in works by the "prophets, by the evangelists, by the fathers and the doctors."[11] Proper study then is to be found with eyes reverted to the past to recapture the truths that are canned, frozen, or properly embalmed. Jorge vigorously condemned the pride that leads to the foolish quest for new truths. But in rebuttal, it is clear that truth is not absolutely frozen in the past, rather truth is dynamic as illustrated in continuing and genuine ongoing additions and subtractions that contribute to the quality of life and to the growth and development of the meanings of things. Even in the moral arena new truths continually challenge older ideas. There is no better example of the evolution of morality than in the history of ideas about punishment.[12] Punishments that were once widely accepted are now viewed as inhumane, barbaric, uncivilized, and unthinkable. In earlier times, a woman caught in adultery could be stoned to death and the rules with respect to the size of the stones and distance between the accused and the crowd were such as to assure a slow and miserable death. Wives who scolded too much could be placed in the dunking stool and repeatedly plunged under water, those who went to sleep in church could be placed in stocks, and those guilty of such "crimes" as witchcraft, gambling, or drunkenness could be placed in the pillory. The belief that truth is static comes with a steep price including stale and shopworn views of reality, anachronistic religious practices, and stagnation of technology and science.

The status of curiosity also has implications for theories of the self. Curiosity will inevitably be regarded as an intolerable threat if the self is a mere instrument of authority or a means by which long held traditions are promulgated. But if the individual male or female is regarded as a genuine agent, as a potential unique source of novelty and invention, as something of intrinsic value, then mere training, memory work, and parrot-like repetition of received truths will take a back seat to the nurturing of critical thinking and genuine liberal education. The distinction between mere robotic training and memory work, which, to be sure, are necessary in some contexts, and critical thinking, which is important in all contexts, must be carefully and continuously monitored. For centuries, the West labored under a whole set of false beliefs about so-called natural or even supernaturally imposed gender inequalities. The cost of the suppression of full intellectual and practical participation in the life of the mind for half the world's population came with an incalculable cost as proven by the breakthrough work of a host of famous women such as Marie Curie, Florence Nightingale, Dorothea Dix, Leta Stetter Hollingworth, and Margaret Sanger.

Furcht and Hoffman, in their book *The Stem Cell Dilemma*, tell the story of Leonardo da Vinci who happened upon a cave on a hillside in Tuscany.[13] The cave serves as a metaphor to contrast the tensions between fear and hope. Should one enter the cave in the hope of finding unexpected treasures or should one remain on the outside for fear of potential dangers that might lurk in the cave? The tension is real for masses of people everywhere as manifested by deep concerns over topical areas such as stem cell research, teaching evolution in public schools and experiments in particle accelerators. As noted earlier, those in moderate to liberal religious traditions are at peace with curiosity and with well-established scientific discoveries. Others who embrace fundamentalist or conservative beliefs are more likely to be unwilling to enter the cave. We turn now to another development in the history of ideas that has proven to be of vital importance to the knowledge industry and that also highlights some important differences between science and many but not all religious organizations.

Skepticism and Doubt

The French skeptical philosopher, Michel de Montaigne (1553–1592) was possibly the most influential European scholar of his day. Indeed, historians Will and Ariel Durant made the claim that Montaigne's "influence pervaded three centuries and four continents."[14] Montaigne was particularly outraged at the senseless carnage resulting from 16th century religious wars between Protestants and Catholics. He argued that presumption and arrogance are original human maladies that foster unjustified beliefs, bloodshed, and war. Most humans are unaware of what they don't know, yet they are willing to fight and kill in defense of those things they have never subjected to critical analysis. Montaigne lamented the role religion played in human violence contending that, at its best, religion was made to "extirpate vices; [but] it covers them, fosters them, incites them."[15]

Montaigne noted the ease with which we are controlled by arbitrary authority and the vulnerability of belief systems to emotional control. He understood how the misuse of language contributes to interpersonal and international conflicts. In fact, he believed many of the world's problems are grammatical. He called attention to the ease with which sensory information is distorted and how reason can so easily be conditioned by prejudices and a priori assumptions. Montaigne noted that "scientific truths" mutate over time and that the finest philosophical minds the world has produced disagree on almost everything.

The works of Montaigne suggest that true humility is not so much a matter of denigrating the ego; rather humility includes that rare capacity to admit the possibility of error, to willingly suffer a kind of epistemological vertigo informed by continued critical analysis of the foundations of knowledge claims. If there is a virtue to be found anywhere it is in the capacity to doubt. Montaigne's philosophy calls for a careful analysis of the role of doubt in all intellectual activities including science and religion.

The Role of Doubt in Science

The importance of doubt in science was set forth by two of the early founders of modern scientific methodology, both of whom were deeply influenced by Montaigne's work. René Descartes and Francis Bacon, in response to the bleak implications of Montaigne's skepticism, hoped to restore faith in the possibility of genuine knowledge, but both of these luminaries agreed that doubt is an important starting point in human intellectual activities. Bacon understood that an honest quest for knowledge could lead to appropriate self-doubt or to a mind that "first distrusts and then despises itself."[16] He also argued that the major task in any inquiry is "first to lay aside received opinions and notions; and second, to refrain the mind for a time from the highest generalizations."[17] Bacon's ideal is a kind of openness that is made possible by the initial suspension of judgment and by the capacity to doubt old prejudices and biases or what he called "received opinions."

In his *Discourse on Method* René Descartes established procedural rules for the conduct of intellectual inquiry. His first rule was "never accept anything as true unless it is so clear and distinct as to be immune from doubt."[18] Descartes experimented with radical doubt wherein he pushed doubt to the limits by doubting everything he could. He found he could doubt all kinds of things such as the existence of God, the existence of the physical world, and the existence of other people, but the one thing he could not doubt was the fact that he was doubting and this, for Descartes, was a clear and distinct idea. What is important is that, like Bacon, Descartes agreed on the importance, even the centrality of doubt in intellectual inquiry, but then, like Bacon, he sought to move beyond doubt to a positive program that embraces the possibility of genuine knowledge.

The role of doubt from the time of Bacon and Descartes has continued to play a central role in scientific epistemology. The capacity to doubt is a virtue instilled in students as a part of scientific education and as a continuing reminder that the most assured conclusions may be challenged by new data that have been informed by variables that were overlooked in previous research. Doubt undercuts arrogance and fosters humility by serving as a constant reminder that the whole knowledge enterprise is an ever-changing fragile process that continues to open new horizons. Peter Berger and Anton Zijderveld, in their book *In Praise of Doubt*, argue that doubt opens us to alternative perspectives and "can lead to an increase in tolerance."[19] Doubt raises suspicion, that nothing is concluded once and for all. There will inevitably be additions and subtractions. Concepts of infallibility, permanence, and immutability are foreign to critical thinking. Doubt has been a powerful source of innovation in all disciplines as illustrated by Jennifer Michael Hecht in an extensive work titled *Doubt: A History*.[20]

The Role of Doubt in Religion

The place of doubt is less clear in most religious traditions than it is in science. Historically, doubt has been viewed as the enemy of faith, as a mark of weakness, the source of disbelief, or even as the work of the devil. Sermons on the problem of doubt often feature the Biblical story of Thomas (John 20: 24–29) one of the 12 disciples of Jesus. Thomas let it be known he would not believe in the resurrection unless he could personally touch the wounds resulting from the crucifixion. According to the account in the book of John, Thomas' doubt turned to belief when he was allowed to touch the wounds. Jesus then said "Thomas, because thou has seen me thou hast believed: blessed are they that have not seen, and yet have believed" (John, 20: 29). The doubt that Thomas initially displayed has often been presented to convey a negative character trait. The opening passages of the Qur'an make the claim that this is a book and a guide and there is no doubt in it. The status of doubt in religion is perhaps changing in the modern world where unexamined faith is openly challenged and where the virtues and success of doubt in scientific work are increasingly recognized. Further, moderate to liberal religious organizations now view doubt in positive terms as an honest, open, and desirable dimension of the faith journey. Robert Wennberg's book *Faith at the Edge: A Book for Doubters*, is an example of an emerging treatment of doubt in a great many religious organizations.[21] In other religious organizations, doubt continues to be treated as a vice and as a threat to authority.

The balance between belief and doubt remains as a perennial challenge in all intellectual arenas and in personal character development. An excess of doubt results in negativity or paralyzing cynicism in contrast with the credulity and gullibility associated with unchecked belief. Either extreme freezes intellectual activity.

Authority

The word *authority* is derived from the Latin *Auctoritas* meaning compelling influence, or command. Masses of people the world over place their trust in the words of authority as a basis for their truth claims. In fact, authority, for better or for worse, is likely the single most dominant epistemic foundation upon which masses of human beings, the world over, build their lives and explain their worlds. Sources of authority include: parents, tribes, iconic or charismatic individuals, books regarded as sacred, institutions, political parties, traditions, political or religious documents, and scientific discoveries. Sometimes direct revelation from a supernatural being is claimed as a source of authority but, historically, and even in the present day, there are very few people who make this kind of claim. Such a claim, for most of us, is questionable because we do not personally experience the revelation. Thomas Paine, in his *Age of Reason*, argued that a revelation to a given person is revelation to that person only. "When he tells it to a second person, a second to a third, a third to a fourth, and so on, it ceases to be a revelation to all those persons. It is revelation to the first person only, and *hearsay* to every other, and, consequently, they are not obliged to believe it."[22]

Authority as a way of knowing and understanding is ubiquitous and, in some respects practical, but it is also vulnerable to the most egregious abuses. The long history of the abusive use of authority in some religious institutions has continued unabated into the 20th and 21st centuries. Jim Jones and his People's Temple Organization provides one of the most tragic examples of authoritarian control resulting in the deaths of hundreds of people. Jones was a highly charismatic leader and founder of a political-religious organization known as the People's Temple. Jones preached a Marxist ideology integrated into a religious context. Criticism of his movement in Indiana and later in San Francisco motivated Jones to move his organization to a remote region of Guyana in South America where he established a community known as Jonestown.

Continuing complaints about Jones' coercive tactics included evidence that it was difficult or even dangerous to try to leave Jonestown. These complaints contributed to an investigation led by San Francisco Congressman Leo Ryan along with a group of reporters. Following the investigation, Ryan and his team attempted to leave Jonestown on November 18, 1978, but as they reached the small airstrip where their planes were parked they were assaulted with firearms by some of the militant members of Jones' organization. Several members of the team including Ryan lost their lives. Jones, who was addicted to drugs and who had become increasingly paranoid, realized the consequences of killing a congressman as well as other members of the visiting team. Accordingly, he initiated what would become the largest mass murder and suicide episode in recent history. On his demand, many members voluntarily consumed a beverage that had been laced with cyanide. Some of the members had to be coerced to drink. As a result, over 900 people including Jones and a large number of children lost their lives that day. The Jonestown tragedy as well as tragedies set in motion by other charismatic religious leaders such as David Koresh and Major Applewhite prompt questions about the marks of abusive authoritarian control. Possible examples include:

1. Threats of death for members who leave or threaten to leave an organization.
2. Threats of retaliation or even death for any criticism, including humorous criticism of the organization and/or its founders and leaders.
3. Physical isolation. Jim Jones epitomized this tactic by moving his constituency to a remote area of Guyana.
4. Intellectual isolation illustrated by restriction of reading materials and control of other media sources or the forbidding of specified constituents such as women from full participation in all aspects of the organization.
5. Sexual privileges for the leader or leaders of a group.
6. Extensive use of fear, guilt, and terror as control techniques.
7. Emphasis on robotic-like recitations and extensive memory work as opposed to genuine creative effort on the part of the community of believers.
8. Rigid control of how time is used by the constituency. The old saying "Idle hands are the devil's workshop" applies here. It is better to fill the day with menial or repetitive tasks and meaningless meetings rather than to allow time for reflection and genuine thought.
9. Strict control of homogenous grooming criteria and dress codes. If the intellectual landscape is completely flat and if everybody looks the same, there is little room for gifted individuals to stand out or to express progressive thoughts that might challenge the status quo.
10. Emphasis is on the great intellectual, spiritual, and social distance that separates authoritarian institutions or their leaders from the followers. Such perceived distance underscores the virtues of conformity, obedience, deference, duty, and submission. Eric Hoffer, in his classic little book *The True Believer*, offered the opinion that "The less justified a man is in claiming excellence for his own self, the more ready is he to claim all excellence for his nation, his religion, his race or his holy cause."[23]

The Role of Authority in Science

Though scientists may quote other scientists and thus use their colleagues as practical or provisional authorities, there is always an underlying general suspicion of authority in scientific epistemology. Indeed, it could be argued that all authority in science is merely provisional. When authority is used, it is to be checked and verified by other means. No one has the final say! It is a virtue in science to question authority and to test the predictions derived from authoritative scientific theories. There is recognition that the conclusions of the most celebrated of scientists are up for grabs and vulnerable to convincing contradictory data. Accordingly, scientific claims are open to change and sometimes quick to change. A certain spirit of epistemological anarchy is a mark of health in scientific circles. Nothing is immutable, infallible, ironclad, or written in stone for all time and for all circumstances. It is accepted or rather expected that there will forever be a different interpretation, a fresh perspective, a whole new organization of the facts, or even debate about what counts as a fact. Pedestalized authority is contrary to the very spirit of science. But why is this the case? Most scientists have a deep appreciation for the fact that authorities in all specialty areas may disagree with each other, that authorities in the past have often been wrong, and that authority which cannot be consistently and rigorously checked provides a sandy foundation for truth claims.

It can be argued that methodology itself serves as an authority in the sciences but while this may be partly true, scientific methods are not frozen in time; rather they expand and evolve as new instruments open up previously unimagined ways to observe nature and as new quantitative methods of analysis permit deeper and more sensitive ways to treat observational data. The invention of new observation techniques such as the telescope, microscope, X-rays, Cat-scans, and other imaging tools forever changed our understandings of the world as well as our ways of doing science.

The evolution of scientific methods over time deserves further comment and raises questions as to whether there is such a thing as *the* scientific method. Percy Williams Bridgman, a Nobel laureate in physics, argued that "there is no scientific method as such."[24] Bridgman was referring to the idea that there are a great variety of methods employed by scientists and that methodologies vary from one scientific field to the next and from one individual scientist to the next. Peter. B. Medawar (1915–1987) echoed the same theme in his book *The Limits of Science* where he noted that "There is indeed no such thing as 'the' scientific method. A scientist uses a very great variety of stratagems ... [and] no procedure of discovery can be logically scripted."[25] Stephen Brush, in a thoughtful article titled "Should the History of Science be Rated X?" demonstrates the evolution of scientific practices and methods over time.[26] He observes correctly that knowledge of this evolution may undercut any idealized notions about the permanence of scientific methodology. What scientists share in common is the knowledge that their procedures and methods must be open to replication. The results of important scientific studies will inevitably be checked by other studies and any repeated failure to replicate is the kiss of death in science. Authority is thereby diffused.

The Role of Authority in Religion

Authority in religion is much more complex and variable than in science. One of the major issues in religion centers on the locus of authority. For example, some religious organizations embrace the belief that the locus of authority should reside in the individual believer. Such belief is often friendly to scientific approaches to authority. Others locate authority in tradition and the institution of the Church, as in Catholicism; the Bible as interpreted by the individual, as in many mainline Protestant churches; the Bible in itself (*sui generis*) as in many fundamentalist Protestant churches; the Qur'an as subjected to hermeneutics as in moderate approaches to Islam; or the Qur'an in itself (*sui generis*) as in conservative Islamic traditions. Another point of contention centers on whether authority is taken to be absolute and irrefutable as in most fundamentalist organizations or provisional and context dependent as in more liberal organizations. The latter approach is more likely to be encountered in those progressive traditions that have made peace with scientific approaches to authority.

One of the vexing issues in conservative religious communities centers on whether hermeneutics or interpretive studies are unwarranted because of the belief that holy books speak with absolute clarity and are wholly without error on all major doctrinal issues. Thus, the claim is that any reasonable person can read the text and cannot possibly miss its meaning. The absolute clarity of the text in itself, the *sui generis* approach, however, runs into difficulties when passages in holy books contradict each other. For example, according to II Kings 8:26, Ahaziah was 22 years old when he began to reign, but according to II Chronicles 22:2, Ahaziah was 42 years old when he began to reign. Time and again, Bible stories are repeated and often there are discrepancies between two accounts of the same event. How are such descrepancies explained by those who believe the Bible to be an infallible and inerrant authority? The problem is explored both empathically and critically by Kathleen C. Boone in her helpful book *The Bible Tells Them So*.[27] Boone points out that those who believe in the inerrancy of scripture often concede that no translation of the Bible is inerrant because there are inevitably errors of translation and errors made by copyists. According to the inerrantists it is the original autographs that are inerrant and authoritative. The problem is that there are no known extant autographs for any of the books of the Bible. How then can one know that the autographs are inerrant?

Donald Viney argues that there are some additional problems because some of the autographs were themselves translations.[28] For example, Viney notes that Jesus spoke in the Aramaic language, but the written record was not in Aramaic. The first written accounts of his message are translations into Greek. In Mark 15:34 "Jesus cried out with a loud voice saying Eloi, Eloi, lama sabachthani." This statement in Aramaic is interpreted in Greek as "My God, My God, why has thou forsaken me?" So the autograph is a translation. Viney also points out that "the quotations of the Hebrew scriptures in the new testament are not taken from the Hebrew originals, but from the Septuagint, the Greek translation of the Hebrew scriptures."[29] Again, some of the autographs were not based on the original language, but on translations from the original language.

Another set of problems has surfaced with respect to the complete consistency and thus the absolute authority of the Qur'an. It is often asserted by Islamic scholars that the contemporary official versions of the Muslim holy book are entirely consistent with the earliest versions. This claim has been disputed by other Islamic scholars who claim to have found discrepancies between the earliest extant versions of the Qur'an and contemporary official versions.[30] A larger question for faith communities surfaces about whether authority is undermined when inconsistencies are discovered in holy books. Meanings of words inevitably change with new discoveries so that an original meaning may become blurred or even lost in contemporary cultures. For example, words such as *sunset* or *sunrise* are understood in entirely different ways in older geocentric vs. modern heliocentric worldviews.

Clearly, there are striking if not irreconcilable differences between science and the vast majority of religious organizations on the role of authority in the determination of truth. Authority in science is provisional and vulnerable. It is the duty of scientists to question and rigorously test the claims of authority. Authority in some religious organizations can also be regarded as provisional, but more often it is regarded as sacred or even infallible. Authority also manifests itself in different ways in the sociology of science compared with the sociology of religion. For example, a Pope in the Catholic faith, an Imam in the Islamic faith or a charismatic Protestant minister may have authority, influence, and power within their religious organizations that far exceeds any authority attributed to scientific leaders.

Further, as noted in Chapter 1, science and religion vary dramatically with respect to the ways emotions are recruited in support of belief content. Scientists become emotionally involved when the predictions of favorite theories fail, but in the end it is understood that reliable hard-core empirical evidence may dictate the modification or even the demise of favored theories. The extreme visceral nature of many religious beliefs, especially those based on absolute authority, is clearly illustrated in anger and massive street demonstrations, litigation, hateful rhetoric, threats against property and persons, and actual assassinations. The study and pursuit of a measured and reasonable moderation remains as a modern epistemic challenge.

Reason

The term *reason*, closely related to terms such as *logic* and *rationality*, refers to mental processes by which conclusions or explanations are drawn from premises, data, or propositions. Actions and thoughts that are rational or reasonable are deeply tuned to the demands of formal logic and to the demands and limitations imposed by physical and social context. This does not mean that reasonable or rational behavior is always the preferred behavior in every situation. In certain extreme situations an irrational choice with a low probability of success may be strongly preferable to all reasonable or rational alternatives. In some cases, what we call a "leap of faith" may be more desirable than blinkered logical alternatives. Parents who put their own lives in immediate grave peril or almost certain death to save a child provide examples that are not at all uncommon.

The term *reason* does not refer to an easily scripted single process that always follows the same set of rules. For example, deductive reasoning moves from a whole to a part or from a general proposition to a specific individual instance. If all men are mortal and if Socrates is a man, then Socrates is mortal. There is continuity among the three ideas; they fit together or even belong together in a linear chain. Another kind of reasoning, inductive or inferential reasoning, moves from a limited sample to a larger population. If a new drug reduces anxiety in an experimental trial with a sample of patients, and if the rules of inference are carefully followed, then we may conclude that there is a probability that the drug will be effective in treating the larger population. Such a controlled study on the relationship between a drug and anxiety reduction uncovers a connection or a pattern that was not previously understood. Francis Bacon believed that such studies could expand knowledge in all intellectual arenas and thus contribute to a whole new era in fields such as: medicine, physics, physiology, psychology, chemistry, communication, and transportation. Bacon also believed that centuries of stagnation resulted from excessive reliance on authority and tradition.

The Role of Reason in Science

Both deductive and inductive reasoning are employed in scientific activities. When scientists test hypotheses they deduce consequences that are subsequently explored in an experiment. The experiment itself generates data based on a limited sample of observations. Statistical tests then yield probabilities associated with the inferred consequences if the hypothesis is true. Sometimes the focus is on the inferred consequences of a null hypothesis. The focus in this case is on the expected consequences if the hypothesis is false. Inferences are then drawn about the population based on the results of an experiment with a limited sample. The population refers to all cases that are similar to the cases studied in the limited sample. There is always the possibility of error.

The Role of Reason in Religion

The status of reason in religion has been a source of contention from earliest times to the present. Thomas Aquinas, the greatest theologian since Augustine and perhaps the foremost Aristotelian scholar in his day, was committed to a reconciliation of faith and reason. Though he believed there are revealed truths that are not known through reason, he nevertheless elevated the role of reason in theological work. In the words of Richard Marius, "Aquinas believed that we can infer all sorts of things about God by reason alone."[31] Many of the products of such inferences however, have been subjected to severe criticism.[32] In contrast with Aquinas, Martin Luther believed that reason is toxic in matters of faith. Luther accepted the role of reason in everyday life and very likely would have no objection to the way reason has been employed in science. Nevertheless, he believed that where faith is concerned, reason could be destructive or serve as the devil's tool to mislead the faithful. The Wesleyan tradition of the Methodist church took a more moderate approach in arguing that we know God through the Bible, experience, tradition, and reason. The Bible was primary in this Wesleyan quadrilateral, but Wesley nevertheless, embraced a rather broad epistemology.[33] The contrasting positions of Aquinas, Luther, and Wesley are still encountered in major religious organizations. Clearly, the role of reason in religion is not as clear-cut as it is in science.

Experience

The complex meanings of the term *experience* are illustrated by a host of synonyms such as consciousness, attention, awareness, empiricism, acquaintance, observation, know-how, understanding, and wisdom, to name a few. The complexity is amplified by the fact that major technical philosophical systems are organized around the centrality of experience. Experience is also complex because it is associated with so many different things tied to the senses, emotions, and desires. Experience includes, but is not limited to, memorial, intuitive, learned, relational, judgmental, and inquisitive processes. It is, in a way, the world as revealed through the multitude of sources to which we can respond, but it also includes our responses, interpretations, and evaluations of the things we encounter. Experience is fundamental and foundational, yet difficult to grasp. Without it, and without the conscious awareness with which it is so closely tied, there is nothing. Basic epistemological questions center on the role of experience in knowledge, the limitations of experience, and, for present purposes, the different roles of experience in science and in religion.

A science of the senses in modern history has uncovered some of the limitations or boundaries of sensate experiences. We now know there are vast stretches of the physical world unavailable to the unaided senses and we suspect even greater stretches remaining beyond the current capabilities of our most advanced technologies. In addition to the limitations of the senses, there are additional constraints on experience that raise questions about its purity and fidelity. Early psychologists, following the lead of chemistry, engaged in a quest for the elements of experience. Other psychologists rejected the idea of elements arguing that experience is more like a stream, always surrounded and always moving. An element is supposedly something pure and unadulterated that stands alone. Consider a new-born baby given its first taste of a liquid. The baby experiences a sensation that might be regarded as pure in that there are no previous associates. But is the experience pure? If the item is sweet, the baby smiles, if there is a hint of bitterness, the baby grimaces and draws back.[34] In other words, the sensation is not a pure awareness of presence, rather that first sensation is shot through with affective qualities. Moreover, the first taste will be different depending on whether the baby, at the time of the taste, is comfortable and secure or agitated. An expression such as "pure pain" is fraught with difficulties because, while pain is cognitive, it is also affective through and through and associated with all sorts of adjectives such as tearing, burning, periodic, excruciating, etc.

Another constraint on experience surfaces in attempts to distinguish levels of awareness. Sensory physiologists and psychologists have often distinguished between sensation—mere awareness of an event vs. perception—interpretation or identification of a sensory event. Perception involves organization, association, and some degree of acquaintance or familiarity with an event whereas a pure sensation refers to a mere "thatness" unnamed and simply present but not identified. Finally, the term *concept* has been used to identify a larger more abstract organization that goes beyond the simple organizational qualities of perception. A concept involves classification such that numerous lower level items can be included in a larger pattern or system. We seek patterns as a way to understand or make sense of things. Concepts are selective and often used to reduce complexity and the messy ambiguities encountered in the ordinary pluralistic flow of experience. Thus, while concepts simplify, they may also constrain experience by leaving out things regarded as irrelevant, tangential, or extraneous. The American philosopher and psychologist William James, concerned about the constraining effects of concepts, warned that "we *carve out* order by leaving the disorderly parts out."[35] James worried that concepts sometimes serve as blinders resulting in simplistic, categorical, and truncated visions of the world. Concepts are too often the stuff of extremist mentalities or ideologies marked by oversimplification, presumption, and blind certitude.

There are additional constraints on experience such as drugs, hormonal variations, neurological anomalies, sensory deficiencies, extreme conditions such as warfare, the nature of social and cultural connections, health and disease, material culture, nutrition, and the accidents of life. Blindness to such constraints is a perennial challenge to social and individual growth and well-being. For example, symptoms often appear naked in experience and beyond comprehension until a higher level of awareness uncovers previously unknown causes. Any number of "mental events" surface from organic conditions or from a vast collection of forces below the level of awareness. Nietzsche was correct when he observed "we knowers are unknown to ourselves."[36] Another problem is the temptation to take unexamined experience naively as a reflection of the way things are or as a mirror of external reality, but experience does not exist in a vacuum. Experience, informed about itself, is a painful challenge to education because such information is a threat to human presumption and ideology. We turn now to experience as a way of knowing in science and in religion.

The Role of Experience in Science

Francis Bacon, as an early philosopher of science, celebrated the superiority of observation and experience over the authority, tradition, and dogmatism that had prevailed for centuries. The centrality of experience informed by observation is the single most distinguishing epistemological feature of the sciences. Nevertheless, observational activities in science are constrained and disciplined by explicit guiding methodologies and requirements. When individual observations under specified conditions are replicated, they may be entered provisionally as a part of the body of knowledge of a particular scientific discipline. Experience plays a central role in the sciences, but it must be harnessed, disciplined, constantly checked, and its conditions must be explicit and subject to replication.

The Role of Experience in Religion

There are paradoxical tensions between science and religion over the role of experience in matters of knowledge. These tensions must not be neglected in any study of the relations between science and religion. Science valorizes its controlled empirical traditions that emphasize observation and experience in matters of knowledge, but compared with science, many faith communities are open to a much greater range of experiences. For example, mystical experiences have served as foundational building blocks in some of the major world religions. Moses, Mohammed, and Joseph Smith all experienced what they and millions of their followers have regarded as direct revelations from God. In some religious traditions, mystical experiences of saints, miracles, and visions are regarded as informative about the nature of unseen realities. Visitations from angelic or demonic forces, speaking in tongues, and visual or auditory messages have often been regarded as hallmarks of the authentic religious life.

What is the blinkered scientist or the neutral bystander to make of such radical openness to all sorts of experiences? One answer has surfaced with social and behavioral scientists who have turned the spotlight of science on the nature, conditions, and claims of those who have had paranormal or mystical experiences. William James was one of the most important pioneers in the study of the experiences of the saints and mystics. His classic book *The Varieties of Religious Experience* was rich in its descriptions of such experiences and raised numerous questions about their nature.[37] One important question concerns the extent to which mystical experiences transcend cultural influences. It is clear that Christians are likely to have visions of Jesus, the Virgin Mary, or one of the saints while Muslims are likely to have visions of the Prophet or Allah. The observer on the outside of a belief system must always consider whether the claims of a mystical vision will withstand careful and detailed scrutiny or provide verifiable information about the world.

There are major differences between and within various religious traditions about the role of experience in matters of knowledge. Protestants were deeply committed to "The individual priesthood of the believer." The idea was that each individual has direct access to God through prayer, meditation, and confession without the need for any institutional mediator. Martin Luther argued that each believer has direct access to God along with a responsibility to study scripture and share it with others. The Protestant movement was augmented by the increased availability of the Bible via the printing press. The immediate result was a new emphasis on the individual and individual experience. Though there was ostensibly a new freedom in theological matters, Protestants were often not free to read Catholic literature and censorship was widespread in both Protestant and Catholic communities.[38] Nevertheless, the Reformation and the enlightenment witnessed the growth of a new emphasis on individual experience in matters of knowledge.

Catholics believed that an overemphasis on individual experience would result in a hodgepodge or jumble of theologies resulting in a proliferation of churches that could serve to fractionate Christianity. That indeed is what happened following the Protestant Reformation. The debate continues over the value of a strong central authority vs. more individualistic, pluralistic, and democratic organizations where every interpretation of scripture is up for grabs and no one has the final say on doctrines or church policy.

Individual experience is constrained by boundary conditions in religion and in science. In most religions there are orthodoxies, creeds, and traditions that place limits on the knowledge claims of the individual. In science there are methodological and substantive constraints that narrow the latitude of individual activity. On the substantive side there are questions such as the existence of God that simply cannot be clearly addressed or answered via scientific methodology. There are also all sorts of questions that are "out of bounds" or out of the reach of religious or scientific ways of knowing and practices. Nevertheless, the authority of individual experience is arguably more variable from one religion to the next than in science.

What Can We Know?

Thomas Teo, in an article on critical psychology, asks his readers to engage in a thought experiment.[39] "Assume you were born and raised in a country very different from your own—would your subjectivity still be the same as it is now?" In a related question, he asks his readers to assume they "were born in the 5th century—would you think, feel, want, and do the same things you now do?" Assume a negative answer to each question, but now ask yourself whether it is possible to avoid radical subjectivity—a kind of solipsism in which unique personal experience is the only reality. It is clear there are personal experiences or subjectivities that cannot be articulated or objectivized, but there are also compelling and obdurate objectivities that appear to run naked and that influence all of us in highly similar ways. There are commonalities in the machinery of the nervous system even if our experiences are highly variable. There are geometric principles and physical and chemical bonds and connections that strongly suggest that some of our experiences are of the same things even if such things are surrounded and tinctured by a penumbra of subjectivity. We are individuals, but we are not radically and indissolubly isolated from each other or from the world.

René Descartes found assurance in the idea that our thinking presupposes the truth of our existence. We may also be assured that our thinking is never completely isolated from the world of which we are a part or from the thinking of others. There are many shared practical truths that reliably work on a day-to-day basis. Still, whether we are theists, atheists, scientists—whatever identity or system we may claim, we are not reasonably justified in claiming we grasp the whole of things. Neither is there any system of thought, scientific or religious, with such a grasp. The world is far from finished. There are new additions and old errors everywhere that must be considered in ever-changing pictures of the world. We are reduced to fragmentary knowledge sufficient to provide practical but partial anchorages. The study of epistemology is a prescription for humility.

*****

Rivka Galchen claimed that "Science is as powerful epistemologically as it is weak politically."[40] By contrast, religion has often been as powerful politically, as it is weak epistemologically. Clearly, there have been and continue to be conspicuous epistemological differences between science and many, if not most, faith traditions. Specifically, there have been major discrepancies between science and religion with respect to the roles and uses of curiosity, doubt, authority, reason, and personal experience. Pioneers such as Montaigne, Bacon, and Descartes championed the values of doubt, curiosity, personal experience, and reason. Such values provided the intellectual roots for enlightenment philosophy and the scientific revolution. The roles of experience, reason, hermeneutics, and critical treatments of sacred texts also found their way into many faith traditions and thereby broadened and thickened theological perspectives.

A major obligation in every discipline is to identify persistent epistemological pathologies. One example is found in scientism, or the belief that strict scientific methodology is the only way to know anything and that science is applicable to every possible topical area. Another example is encountered in many parts of the world where there are still proscriptions against curiosity and doubt. One need not look far to find blind allegiance to authority, fear of reason, attempts to control the flow of information, and irrational certitude. There is nevertheless hope for growth in the development of deeper epistemological awareness in an age marked by an explosion of information and the growth of critical commentary on every imaginable subject.

Notes

1 William Shakespeare, *Measure for Measure: An Old-Spelling and Old-Meaning Edition*, ed. Ernst Leisi (New York: Hafner, 1964), 98.
2 Quoted in Carl Sagan, *The Demon Haunted World: Science as a Candle in the Dark* (New York: Ballantine Books, 1996), 129.

3 Jonathan Rauch, *Kindly Inquisitors* (Chicago, IL: University of Chicago Press, 1994), 35.
4 Leo Furcht and William Hoffman, *The Stem Cell Dilemma* (New York: Arcade Publishing, 2008), lviii.
5 Robert Browning, "A Woman's Last Word," in *Robert Browning's Poetry*, eds. James F. Loucks and Andrew Stauffer (New York: W. W. Norton & Company, 2007), 147.
6 John Milton, *Paradise Lost* (Franklin Center, PA: The Franklin Library, 1979). Quote from Book 9, 205.
7 Peter Harrison, "Curiosity, Forbidden Knowledge, and the Reformation of Natural Philosophy in Early Modern England," *ISIS* 92, No. 2 (June 2001), 265–290.
8 Francis Bacon, a letter to his brother, January 30, 1597, in *Francis Bacon: The Temper of a Man*, by Catherine Drinker Bowen (Boston: Atlantic Monthly Press, 1963), 88.
9 Ian Box, "Bacon's Moral Philosophy," in *The Cambridge Companion to Bacon*, ed. Markku Peltonen (New York: Cambridge University Press, 1966), 265.
10 Philip Ball, *Curiosity: How Science Became Interested in Everything* (Chicago, IL: University of Chicago Press, 2012).
11 Umberto Eco, *The Name of the Rose* (New York: Harcourt, Brace & Co., 1980), 399–400.
12 See, for example, Alice Morse Earle, *Curious Punishments of Bygone Days* (Detroit: Singing Tree Press, 1968).
13 Furcht and Hoffman, *The Stem Cell Dilemma*, lxiii.
14 Will Durant and Ariel Durant, *The Story of Civilization: Part VII, The Age of Reason Begins* (New York: Simon and Schuster, 1961), 413.
15 Michel de Montaigne, "Apology for Raimond Sebond," in *The Complete Essays of Montaigne*, Vol. 2, ed. Donald M. Frame (Garden City, NY: Anchor and Doubleday, 1960), 120.
16 Francis Bacon, *The New Organon and Related Writings* (New York: Liberal Arts Press, 1960), 103.
17 Ibid., 120.
18 John Cottingham, Robert Stoothoff and Dugald Murdoch, *The Philosophical Writings of Descartes*, 2 vols (Cambridge: Cambridge University Press, 1984–1985), Vol. 1, 120.
19 Peter Berger and Anton Zijderveld, *In Praise of Doubt: How to Have Convictions Without Becoming a Fanatic* (New York: HarperCollins, 2009), 29.
20 Jennifer Michael Hecht, *Doubt: A History* (New York: HarperCollins, 2004).
21 Robert N. Wennberg, *Faith at the Edge: A Book for Doubters* (Grand Rapids, MI: William B. Eerdmans, 2009).
22 Thomas Paine, "The Age of Reason," in *Common Sense and Other Writings*, Introduction and Notes by Joyce Appleby (New York: Barnes & Noble Classics, 2005), 259.
23 Eric Hoffer, *The True Believer* (New York: Mentor, 1951), 23.
24 Percy W. Bridgman, *Reflections of a Physicist* (New York: Philosophical Library, 1955), 416.
25 Peter B. Medawar, *The Limits of Science* (New York: Harper & Row, 1984), 51.
26 Stephen Brush, "Should the History of Science be Rated X?" *Science* 183, No. 4130 (March, 1974), 1164–1172.
27 Kathleen C. Boone, *The Bible Tells Them So* (Albany, NY: State University of New York Press, 1989).
28 Donald Wayne Viney, *A Philosopher Looks at the Bible* (Pittsburg. KS: Friends of Timmons Chapel, 1992), 12.
29 Ibid.
30 See, for example, Samuel Green, "The Different Arabic Versions of the Qur'an," http://www.answering-islam.org/Green/seven.htm (Accessed July 6, 2015).
31 Richard Marius, *Martin Luther: The Christian Between God and Death* (Cambridge, MA: Harvard University Press, 1999), 37.
32 See, for example, William James, *The Varieties of Religious Experience* (New York: Routledge, 2002), 340–342.

33 See, for example, the article "Wesleyan Quadrilateral" in Wikipedia, http://en.wikipedia.org/wiki/Wesleyan_Quadrilateral (Accessed July 6, 2015).
34 Diana Rosenstein and Harriet Oster, "Differential Facial Responses to Four Basic Tastes in Newborns," in *What the Face Reveals: Basic and Applied Studies of Spontaneous Expression*, eds. Paul Ekman and Erika L. Rosenberg (New York: Oxford University Press, 2005), 303.
35 William James, *A Pluralistic Universe* (Lincoln: University of Nebraska Press, 1996), 9.
36 Friedrich Nietzsche, *The Genealogy of Morals* (New York: Anchor, 1956), 149.
37 James, *The Varieties of Religious Experience*.
38 See Paul F. Grendler, "Printing and Censorship," in *The Cambridge History of Renaissance Philosophy*, ed. Charles B. Schmitt (New York: Cambridge University Press, 1988), 44–45.
39 Thomas Teo, "Critical Psychology: A Geography of Intellectual Engagement and Resistance," *American Psychologist* 70, No. 3 (April 2015), 245.
40 Rivka Galchen, "Weather Underground: The Arrival of Man-Made Earthquakes," *The New Yorker* (April 13, 2015), 40.

3

THE PROBLEM OF CAUSALITY

> *No forces other than the common physical-chemical ones are active within the organism.*[1]
>
> *The soul is the prime and chief cause of local motion in the body.*[2]

There may be no theoretical or practical problem that has stirred greater interest in practitioners of science and religion than the problem of causality. The theoretical-philosophical side of the problem has a long history, and there are excellent summaries of the works of various luminaries who have contributed to this extensive literature.[3] The practical side of the problem highlights how various explanations of causality play out in day to day living. In many respects, causality is a social-psychological problem that serves as a reminder that beliefs and attitudes are shaped by historical and cultural contexts. In fact, a major branch of social psychology known as Attribution theory explores the various ways people attribute causes to themselves, others, and the external world.[4] Attribution theory has also been applied specifically to religious phenomena and to some of the technical features of research in the psychology of religion.[5] Attributions about causal forces obviously may tell us more about ourselves than about the nature of the external world. The focus of this chapter will be on the everyday practical dimensions of the problem of causality in science and religion and how these practical dimensions are manifested in other fields such as education, medicine, and the law.

What is it that makes things happen or that produces effects? Is there a supreme being who is the cause of all things including those things humans may regard as evil? Are there supernatural forces other than God such as devils or demons that cause major mischievous effects in our world? Are there guardian angels that seek to protect us from evil? Is prayer a causal force that does real measurable work in the world? Do all events result exclusively from the operation of natural forces? Do some things result from sheer chance so that blame cannot be assessed? Do human beings have the kind of free will that renders some of their behavior unpredictable, or are there universal laws of causation that apply to human beings? How have beliefs about causality changed over the past two to three hundred years?

This last question is especially important as it calls attention to dynamic and ever-changing perspectives on how things operate. For example, in earlier periods of history it was not uncommon to attribute unfortunate weather events such as hailstorms or windstorms to malevolent forces such as demons or witches.[6] In our day, a meteorologist who explained a storm as the result of demonic forces instead of the interplay of high and low pressure centers, the jet stream, or variations in humidity would be unlikely to hold on to her job. For centuries, human and animal infirmities were sometimes attributed to possession by demons, but now a physician who explained an infirmity in such a manner would be shunned and would undoubtedly lose his license. As late as the 19th and early 20th century, some psychiatrists and scientists insisted that personality characteristics are determined by the shape of the skull.[7] In that same time period several well-known and respected scientists argued that women were naturally subordinate to men and intellectually inferior.[8] A similar claim has a long history in many of the world's religious traditions except that the subordination of women was often attributed to supernatural designs and intentions.[9] Clearly, human beliefs about causality have changed and mutated with the passage of time. Such changes are evident in the history of every field of endeavor including science, religion, technology, political science, and economics.

A practical illustration of the problem of causality is encountered in litigation involving parents who, for religious reasons, withhold medical treatment from their sick children. The religious freedom of the parents, particularly their freedom to practice their religion without government interference, is thus pitted against child welfare issues resulting in vexing social, legal, and philosophical dilemmas. Lawmakers in a number of states have struggled with these dilemmas as they have worked to draft responsible legislation that protects children but also respects the freedom of parents. Some of the problems at the interface of religion, science, and the law are illustrated in a handbook by James John Jurinski titled *Religion on Trial*.[10] Jurinski, for example, reviews the legal, religious, and scientific technicalities associated with parents who, for religious reasons, employ faith healing instead of standard scientifically based medical treatment for their sick children. If the child dies should the parents be held legally accountable? If parents have appealed to the will of God to save their child, how does the state review parents' actions without reviewing parents' religions? What responsibilities does the legal system have to protect children who may or may not be believers but are not of a legal age to make their own independent care decisions?

An illustration is encountered in the case of Amanda Bates, a 13-year-old Colorado girl who died from complications associated with diabetes.[11] Amanda's parents had dropped out of high school and belonged to a religious organization known as Church of the First Born. The church, like many other religious organizations, takes a literal approach to the large number of scriptures that portray healing as a reward for faith and diligent prayer. For example, in the book of James the following advice is provided for the faithful:

> Is any among you sick? Let him call for the elders of the church; and let them pray over him, anointing him with oil in the name of the Lord: and the prayer of faith shall save him that is sick, and the Lord shall raise him up; and if he have committed sins, it shall be forgiven him.
>
> (James, 5: 14–16)

This advice was carried out in the case of Amanda Bates, but she died in the agony of gangrene, caused by a condition that would have easily yielded to standard medical treatment.

How can courts navigate the complex legal and moral obligations to protect children and at the same time avoid government judgments of religious beliefs? Unlike many courts in other parts of the world, U.S. civil and criminal courts do not presume to evaluate the validity of human attempts to invoke divine healing. In the case of Amanda Bates, the judge had to balance calls to sentence her parents more severely for the painful death of their child while maintaining consideration of their religious freedom. The judge also had to consider protections of the other children in the large Bates family, as well as other minors throughout this small religious community that consistently chooses faith healing over Western medicine. There had been reported suspicious deaths of 11 other children in this community. In attempts to balance these factors, the trial judge lamented the limited legal power to protect the children in this complex situation. The parents of Amanda Bates were given 20 years of probation and sentenced to 1300 hours of community service, 100 hours for each of Amanda's 13 years. Additionally, they were required to enroll their other children in Medicaid. At the heart of these tensions we find different perceptions of the causes, and therefore also the prevention, of illness, suffering, and death.

Tensions between some forms of religious faith and medical science are also encountered in the related problems of people who refuse blood transfusions for religious reasons even though they may recognize that blood transfusions save lives. In some cases, courts have had to sort through decisions about causes of death. When Gwendolyn Rozier died after refusing a blood transfusion after complications from a kidney transplant, her heirs sued her physicians, alleging that physicians knew she was a Jehovah's Witness and that her physicians were negligent by failing to take steps to prevent her need for a blood transfusion following the procedure. One judge argued that the court's decision did not reflect on religion but rather that her death resulted from choices made by her and supported by her family.[12] Though cases like that of Amanda Bates and Gwendolyn Rozier make the news on a regular basis, they by no means can be taken as representative of Christian thought. Most Christians, while believing in the efficacy of prayer, have nevertheless made peace with standard medical views of causality. Indeed, the overwhelming majority of people of faith employ prayer *and* modern medicine and see no problems or contradictions in combining natural and transnatural explanations of causality. The efficacy of prayer, however, has not been and is not without controversy so we turn now to an examination of the controversy over prayer as a causal force.

Debates about Prayer as a Causal Force

The term *prayer* refers to a formal or informal address to God or another being presumed to possess supernatural powers. Among other goals, prayers include petitions or requests for changes that would result in improvements in the well-being of an individual or group. Prayer is also a vehicle for the expression of praise, thanksgiving, complaint, requests for forgiveness, or strength to face a problem. Prayers may also reflect simply a sincere desire or concern and may even end in a question.[13] For example, the psalmist (Psalms 89: 46) asks "How long, Lord? wilt thou hide thyself forever? shall thy wrath burn like fire?"

Prayer has traditionally been viewed in most religious cultures as a powerful causal force. Some believe that prayers may produce effects on physical forces, on other people, or on God. The idea that prayer somehow changes God is problematic in the sense that some classic theologies stress the perfection and immutability of God. Is the perfection of God somehow compromised if God can be moved through prayer from one position to a second position that conforms to human wishes or needs? Wasn't God's first position perfect in all of its dimensions and consequences?

Those who believe in prayer disagree about the modes or forms it should take. Some believe prayers should be spontaneous while others employ highly scripted or even "canned" repetitive prayers uttered in a mechanical fashion. Some believe group prayers are more successful or even commanding as a causal force compared with individual prayers (Matt. 18: 19–20). Others stress the importance of individual prayers in secret as in the admonition of Jesus to avoid public prayers and to pray in private (Matt. 6: 5–6). Some religions stress the importance of praying at certain times of the day, orienting in a specific direction, or assuming specific postures or varieties of movements during the act of prayer. In some religious cultures men and women are separated when they pray so that all the men pray together and all the women pray together. The salutation is also important and hinges on the particular God or Gods that are addressed.

Attempts to open public meetings (e.g., sporting events, classes in schools, political meetings) with prayers are controversial partly because of disagreements over who offers the prayer, to whom it is addressed, and even stronger disagreements over the ideal content of the prayer.[14] For example, should the prayer come from a Catholic, Protestant, Mormon, Jew, Muslim, or some other religious group? It is of interest that there are now online prayers in various languages such as Latin, English, French, German, etc. and prayers designed for specific religious traditions such as Catholic or Protestant prayers. A highly controversial type of prayer, the imprecatory prayer involves requests that the deity inflict some harm or even death upon an enemy. Such negative prayers for destruction are common throughout the Bible and other early religious texts and traditions, but they are not absent in some religious traditions at the outset of the 21st century.[15]

The efficacy of prayer as a causal force has been the subject of continuous interest and debate. William James, the American psychologist and philosopher, argued that prayer "is a process wherein work is really done, and spiritual energy flows in and produces effects, psychological or material, within the phenomenal world."[16] Such a friendly pragmatic approach admits that real causal efficacy may be subjective, having effects only on the person uttering the prayer or on the individual or group for whom the prayer is offered. But, according to James, such effects are real and are not properly or adequately understood by reductionist claims that prayer and other religious experiences are "nothing but" an overflow of the action of neurological machinery.[17] James finds no way to rigorously test the claims of those who believe or the claims of those who disbelieve in the possible material or objective effects of prayer. For James, it is enough that prayer, whether its effects be subjective or objective, does real work in the world. It has been argued that a rigorous or "scientific" test of the material effects of prayer is problematic because such a test necessarily involves the cooperation of deity.

Others with a materialist scientific orientation have been less generous than William James in their appraisal of the effects of prayer.[18] The best-known early example is found in a proposal by physicist John Tyndall (1820–1893) of a quantitative "scientific" analysis of prayer. Tyndall was one of the pioneers in the study of thermal radiation so he was particularly interested in whether there is actual measurable physical energy resulting from prayer. Specifically, he proposed that a group of patients with a known disease in a particular hospital and with known mortality rates become the objects of special prayers of healing. Mortality rates of these patients would then be compared with the mortality rates of other patients with the same disease. These "control" patients would be from comparable hospitals but would not have the organized prayerful efforts directed in their behalf. This proposal predictably inflamed critics. Some of Tyndall's detractors appealed to divine causation and held prayer meetings to pray for Tyndall himself.

Following a number of charges and countercharges by scientists and theologians, Francis Galton announced that he had already collected naturalistic observations on the efficacy of prayer.[19] Galton had compared his assumptions about the recipients of prayer with the actual life expectancies of people in various occupational groups. He assumed that there were more prayers on behalf of missionaries than for most others, and he found that missionaries to foreign lands had some of the highest mortality rates and shortest lifespans. Galton also observed that clergy, despite his assumption that they received more prayer, did not have significantly longer lives than doctors and lawyers. In short, Galton believed that his naturalistic observations failed to reveal a significant effect of prayer.

Prayer studies based on contemporary rigorous scientific methods that include double-blind experiments continue to find their way into scientific journals and popular literature.[20] Double-blind experiments include sophisticated coding procedures that prevent researchers and participants from knowing who receives a treatment, in this case prayer, and who is in various control groups (e.g., those receiving no prayer or those who think they are receiving prayer, but in fact are not). Results, to say the least, are contradictory and confusing. There are studies that report positive or beneficial effects of prayer and studies that fail to find such effects. A short summary of the results of prayer studies is set forth by Victor Stenger in his book *God: The Failed Hypothesis*.[21] There is also continuing disagreement about whether topics such as prayer fall outside the boundaries of legitimate scientific methodology. Do such studies include unstated assumptions about the nature and operations of a higher power assuming the existence of such a power? If there are hidden or untenable assumptions about the operations of a higher power would it then be possible to study the question or understand the nature of the variance and discrepancies encountered in prayer studies? This last statement is underscored by a reminder again of the various kinds of prayers and the possible subtleties of the effects they may produce. Thus any attempt to measure the effects of prayer should be carefully nuanced and tuned to the type of prayer that is offered and to the locus of the presumed or intended effect. We turn now to one attempt to simplify the problem of causality by attributing all causes to one source, namely God. As we will see however, the attempt comes along with a host of problems of its own.

God as the Exclusive Cause of All Things

In view of the apparent complexity of causality, it is understandable that there would be attempts to simplify the topic by searching for a single causal source as the basis for all things. Such a position is encountered in a classic book titled *The Incoherence of the Philosophers* written about 1095 by the Islamic scholar and mystic Al-Ghazali. Richard Rubenstein, in his book *Aristotle's Children*, relays a common interpretation of Al-Ghazali that "God, not nature, produces every effect."[22] Al-Ghazali's work conveys the idea that causality is an illusion created by humans. Specific concrete examples of things that are not naturally causal are set forth in his book "for example, the quenching of thirst, and drinking, satiety and eating, burning and contact with fire, light and the appearance of the sun, death and decapitation, healing and the drinking of medicine, the purging of the bowels and the using of a purgative, and so on."[23] Al-Ghazali argues that the connection of all these things and everything else "is due to the prior decree of God."[24]

There are extensive theological and philosophical problems associated with the idea that God is the direct or indirect single causal force for every event that has or ever will take place in the world. Is there no such thing as real chance or genuine randomness? How are we to account for the problem of evil? Simply stated, if God is omniscient, omnipotent, and omnibenevolent (i.e., all-knowing, all-powerful, and all-loving) and if God therefore has perfect knowledge, unlimited power, and a perfect desire to make things good, how then is there evil in the world?[25] These questions are especially relevant when bad things happen to good people or to innocent people or infants. How exactly is God separated from, or somehow intertwined with, historical and present atrocities?

Further, if God is the cause of every single event that ever occurs, are we then to conclude that nothing at all can have its real origin in human thought or action? The Qur'an notes that it is Allah who causes error and that there are those who are created for hell (Surah 6: 39 and 7: 178–179). At the same time, those who disbelieve shall be responsible for their disbelief (Surah 30:44). Clearly, the problem of causation now leads us into a bewildering intellectual if not emotional jungle. The same set of problems surfaces in Christian theology when belief in the complete and perfect foreknowledge of God comes up against the belief that humans have the power to choose. If God's knowledge of the future is real knowledge, then a human choice could not possibly contradict the foreknowledge of God; do humans make any real choices or must choices be illusions? Is God's very knowledge causative? Could an event be avoided, if God knows absolutely that the event will take place? Could a human make a choice that would surprise God? Indeed, could a perfect all-knowing God be surprised? These are abstract questions that simultaneously raise very practical questions in our daily lives. How do we interpret the choices of others? Should we perceive only the will of God in all actions by all people, or do we attribute choices and causal influence to humans?

Some theologians have attempted to deal with the problem by introducing the distinction between the permissive will of God and the perfect will of God. In the first case, God permits things to happen but does not approve of them. When the perfect will of God is employed, events happen inexorably as God wills. The distinction between the permissive will of God and the perfect will of God may however turn out to be a distinction without a distinction. That is, even if God's permissive will permits an action that violates God's perfect will, God's absolute knowledge and foreknowledge would discern the outcome of the action before it happened. Simply stated, with the three characteristics of God's perfection discussed previously, God always knows exactly what will happen and God always has the foreknowledge and power to make events happen or to change events. Otherwise God would not have absolute knowledge or would relinquish absolute power and would thus suffer a limitation or limitations that would be unacceptable to many theologians. For many, the definition of the perfection of God requires God to have complete causal control over all things.

Let us turn now from exclusively supernatural explanations of causality to exclusively natural or scientific approaches to the topic. As we have seen there are problems with supernatural explanations, but there are also issues, disagreements, and problems with naturalistic explanations of causality.

Scientific or Naturalistic Approaches to Causality

The first epigraph at the beginning of this chapter captures a powerful naturalistic sentiment in which human action is understood in purely naturalistic terms. Some of the most creative work on naturalistic approaches to causality came from the pen of Aristotle who separated natural causes into four general categories. According to Aristotle things do what they do partly on the basis of their material nature. He referred to this type of causation as the *material cause*. To use a modern example of Aristotle's position, an airplane made of the wrong materials would not fly. One reason for heavier than air flight is that the airplane is made of materials that are extremely strong, yet relatively light. A second kind of causation is illustrated in Aristotle's belief that events take place because of physical forces that immediately precede and act on them. For example, domino A falls against domino B, and domino B falls over. Thus domino A has a causal effect on domino B. Aristotle referred to this kind of cause as the *efficient cause*. Aristotle's efficient cause is close in meaning to ordinary understandings of causality. An event that reliably precedes another event is commonly viewed as the cause of the subsequent event. Thus, a light shined into the pupil of the eye is viewed as the cause for the contraction of the pupil or the force of the physician's rubber hammer is viewed as the cause of the knee reflex.

Aristotle identified another kind of causality and referred to it is as the *formal cause*. The formal cause refers to shapes or forms that are necessary to proper action, identification, or function. For example, if the wings, the fuselage, or the tail assembly of an airplane were not of the proper shape or form, the airplane would not fly. The airplane could be made of the proper materials (material cause), and it could have sufficient power (efficient cause), but if the shape did not conform to the basic principles of aerodynamics the plane would not fly. Shapes or forms are central to the very identity of much of what we encounter in the natural world. The shape or the formal characteristics of a sculpture may immediately suggest its likeness to a given person or object. The shape of a natural event such as a tornado identifies the type of storm it is and the likely functions it will perform. More simply, unless dominoes have rectangular forms that balance precariously on one narrow edge, the previous demonstration of efficient cause with dominoes would not be possible.

Still another kind of causality identified by Aristotle was the *final cause*. The final cause refers to the purpose or the end for which a thing exists. Synonyms for final causation include *purpose* and *teleology*, terms that also refer to inherent or intrinsic designs. We might say it is the purpose of an automobile to provide transportation, the purpose of a seed is to grow into a specific type of plant, or the purpose of a dog to bark at a stranger. Terms such as *teleology* and *final causality* are controversial in the physical sciences. Indeed, one is unlikely to encounter explanations based on final causality in sciences such as physics and chemistry. Scientists in these disciplines typically believe they can provide adequate explanations in their disciplines on the basis of material, efficient, and formal causation. An atmospheric scientist, for example, might explain a hurricane or tornado in terms of material, efficient, and formal causes (e.g., via the moisture carried by the storm, wind speeds that cause destruction, and the shape of the funnel cloud, respectively) but deny that such storms contain any inherent, intrinsic, or particular purpose. Similarly, a geologist would not likely talk about the purpose of a volcano or the purpose of an earthquake.

Teleology or final causes are also controversial in the life sciences and in the behavioral sciences. In fact, many of the early behaviorists such as Albert Weiss, Clark Hull, and Ivan Pavlov attempted to explain human and animal behavior strictly in terms of material, efficient, and formal causes. These theorists understood the common usage of terms such as *purpose, intention,* or even *insight.* They believed, however, that such terms are extremely "loose" and that so-called *purposes* or *intentions* are themselves conditioned or may be unpacked or broken down by "more elementary objective primary principles."[26] Other early behaviorists such as Edward Chase Tolman believed that the life sciences and behavioral sciences should not necessarily model themselves after physics and chemistry. Tolman believed that adequate explanations of animal and human behavior would necessarily involve terms such as *intention* and *purpose*.[27]

There are other complications associated with teleology and teleological explanations. When Aristotle talked about final causes, he was referring to inherent or intrinsic purposes built into the nature of things. Aristotle's *intrinsic teleology* reflected his view of "built in" natural purposes, as when a seed grows into a tree or a puppy grows into a dog. As we have seen, the idea of inherent purposes in scientific phenomena is not without problems, but a variation on Aristotle's concept of final causation encountered in some theologies is even more problematic. The theological variation holds that things do what they do in order to fulfill the wishes or the purposes of a deity. We can refer to his variation as *extrinsic teleology*. In the Western Medieval worldview, humans were the center of all creation, and God created things for the sake of humans. For example, in this worldview, sheep exist for divine purposes outside of themselves to provide humans with clothes and food. More common contemporary examples include perceptions of divine purpose in some large events. For example, is a hurricane in a given place at a given time the result of some act or purpose of a deity, or is the locus, direction, and velocity of a hurricane best explained in terms of the natural laws discovered in the science of meteorology? Herein, we encounter major differences in the sciences and in some forms of religion and these differences must not be neglected in any comparison of science and religion.

The Growth of Tensions between Naturalistic and Supernatural Explanations

In *A History of the End of the World*, Rabinsky and Wiseman call attention to tensions between supernatural and naturalistic explanations of the plagues of the 14th century.[28] On the one hand, masses of people believed the plague was sent by God as punishment or as a means of correcting human errors. Such a view is an example of what we referred to as extrinsic teleology, reflecting God's purposes for humans and nature. At the same time there were growing doubts about the effectiveness of prayer to stop the disease because the clergy and other church workers were infected as often or sometimes more often than other people. If the plague had truly been sent by God, why wouldn't there be some protection for God's dedicated workers? The worldview, based on extrinsic teleology, shaped perceptions of the disease. That is, the plague *must* surely reflect the purposes of God, and understanding of these purposes was necessary to appease or to otherwise appeal to God in order to stop the plague. As an added difficulty, there was also growing practical knowledge that the plague was contagious as there were clear signs that it spread from one person to another. Thus some degree of natural control of the disease was possible via isolation, sterilization, and general cleanliness. These limited remedies raised theological as well as practical questions. Could natural preventative methods somehow circumvent the will of God? Clearly such a question was troublesome as it called for the difficult task of reconciling naturalistic and supernatural explanations.

There were other developments throughout the modern period (from approximately 1600) that highlighted differences between naturalistic and supernatural explanations of common events. For example, early work on mortality statistics proved troublesome. The Qur'an in Surahs 3:156 and 57:2 notes that it is Allah who causes death. Indeed, because Allah controls all things (Surah 4:85) there is no cause of death outside of Allah. Christians have also embraced the idea that the appointed time of death is set by God (see Matthew 10:30). The French naturalist Comte de Buffon (1707–1788), however, called attention to lawful and natural explanations for mortality. Buffon pointed out that in the mid-18th century approximately one-half of all children died by the age of three. Small pox was the great killer, but children were vulnerable to a number of other infectious diseases. Infections, in an age before the development of antibiotics, also claimed a great number of lives. A simple scratch could result in death, as could food poisoning or the family well. Buffon noted that children who survived should be thankful for being favored by God, but then he pointed out that there was a greater chance of survival in France than in England. How would English scholars perceive God's will when faced with these international differences? Would French scholars perceive God's will differently? How do these differences in outcomes and perspectives reflect the purposes of God? The tension between a supernatural explanation wherein the child is "favored by God" and a natural geographic explanation is clearly fraught with difficulties.

Other tensions between supernatural and natural explanations for physical phenomena surfaced in the 18th century. The causes of natural disasters such as hurricanes, floods, volcanoes, and tornadoes were fiercely debated. Such debates continue in some quarters into the 21st century with Hurricane Katrina providing an example of an outpouring of answers to the question why? Katrina, one of the deadliest hurricanes in the history of the United States, caused unprecedented damage in New Orleans in 2005. Meteorologists and other scientists explained it simply as the result of natural forces within a weather pattern that will inevitably repeat itself with the passage of time. Others argued for a teleological basis for the hurricane placing blame in a wide variety of areas and practices such as nightclubs, brothels, and abortion clinics.[29] We turn now to one of the most interesting problems associated with questions of causality.

Determinism and Free Will

No treatment of the problem of causality would be complete without a consideration of the tensions between determinism and free will and the ways these philosophical worldviews play out in science and religion. Determinism emphasizes the idea that "for everything that ever happens there are conditions such that, given them, nothing else could happen."[30] A central principle of determinism is captured in the Latin expression *causa æquat effectum*, referring literally to the equality or even identity of cause and effect. That is, if A causes B, then A = B. The American psychologist and philosopher William James argues that this principle means "Each moment of the universe must contain all the causes of which the next moment contains effects, or to put it with extreme concision, it is plain that each moment in its totality causes the next moment."[31] Such a position implies a complete collection of known and unknown, but potentially knowable, connections that bridge and rigidly account for successive events in time. The idea of a universe connected through and through with no loose play anywhere has been embraced by some members of both scientific and religious communities, but, as we will see, the basis or origin of a completely connected or hard-wired universe is different for science than for religion.

On the scientific side one encounters luminaries such as Albert Einstein, B. F. Skinner, and Sigmund Freud who have argued in defense of strict natural determinism based on the regularities observed in the universe. Scientific determinists agree that many, perhaps most, causes are hidden from immediate view, but for many scholars this invisibility provides the challenge and excitement of scientific activity. Such a perspective implies a kind of meliorism or optimism because of the human capacity to discover previously hidden causes. Thus, the world is potentially knowable. Einstein's claims that "God is subtle, but he is not malicious" and "God does not play dice with the world" can be interpreted to mean that intellectual work is extremely challenging but the world is inherently knowable.[32] Discovery of new causes expands understanding and serves as the basis for ameliorative actions.

Determinism in religion is often based on assumed attributes of God including sovereignty (complete independence), omnipotence (infinite power), omniscience (infinite knowledge), and immutability (unchanging qualities). As discussed previously, a God with infinite knowledge is not limited by time and thus knows the outcome of all things before they happen. Such a belief is often associated with the controversial doctrine of predestination, the idea that God has determined in advance who will be rewarded and who will be punished in an afterlife. As noted previously, if God's knowledge is real knowledge such that people cannot do otherwise, it can be argued that God's advanced knowledge of all outcomes in the world, including the destiny of souls, is causal because God's true knowledge of outcomes could not be violated. God's pervasive knowledge along with the associated doctrine of predestination is clearly encountered in Islamic and Christian traditions and scriptures. The Westminster confession of faith in the Christian tradition states that "some men and angels are predestined to everlasting life; and others foreordained to everlasting death."[33] A comparable idea is encountered in the Qur'an when it says "whom Allah pleases He causes to err, and whom he pleases he puts on the right way" (Surah 6:39).

A thoughtful critique of strict determinism and of predestination is encountered in a difficult question raised by William James. How are we to "meet a world foredone, with no possibilities left in it?"[34] Does a world foredone by God imply a kind of mechanical lock-step inevitability that forecloses completely on any possible beneficial outcome of human efforts even for their personal destinies and would belief in such a world undermine scientific and other kinds of intellectual inquiry by encouraging passivity or fatalism? It was suggested earlier that scientific determinism, following Einstein's claim that "God is clever, but not malicious," can be regarded as a hopeful doctrine because an understanding of the regularities of nature serves as a basis for intervention and the manipulation of nature for human purposes. On the other hand, according to strict determinism, scientists could not be truly free to intervene in anything because scientists themselves are products of inexorable forces in a mechanical chain of events. No credit can be accorded to any individual or to any single event in the chain as each link in the chain did what it had to do. In a rigidly deterministic worldview, heroes and villains do not exist. This position was illustrated in the claim of Herbert Spencer that "historical change is due solely to physical, biological and cultural circumstances and is completely independent of personal control."[35] James's question "What does it mean to face a world foredone with no possibilities left in it?" remains highly relevant in both scientific and religious traditions.

Those who believe in free will, whether from scientific or religious perspectives, deny that humans are reduced in every situation to the status of mere spectators where all events are dictated in advance by forces beyond our control. There are events, perhaps even most events, that are independent of human control, but those who believe in free will argue in defense of genuinely new ideas and real causal efficacy that originate within the world of human consciousness. Those who endorse free will believe that inventive human intellectual processes sometimes cross a threshold that supersedes all previous known causal connections in a manner that opens the door to unanticipated new beginnings. Humans can consider alternatives, anticipate outcomes associated with each alternative, weigh the complexities and desirability of various outcomes, and sometimes act in ways that, for better or worse, defy all previous anticipations. Human cognitive processes are such that the past does not always provide an adequate explanation for what happens in the immediate present or in the future. We sometimes, perhaps rarely, make things happen, so the world can forever be different for the presence of a single human being. Thus, causal forces do not always proceed from the outside world, but sometimes from within. Proponents of free will can believe in a great deal of causality from without, but in addition to the myriad and reliable connections encountered at almost every turn they believe in the possibility of genuine novelty, indetermination, and real chance. This last point underscores the idea that determinism is an absolutistic philosophy because, if determinism is true, there can be no real chance, indeterminism, or genuine novelty anywhere. Belief in free will, by contrast, is more pluralistic as it accepts the abundance of causal regularities in the world that make science and engineering possible, but also finds loose play and opportunities for genuine and unique human causal interventions in the flow of events.

There are many examples of beliefs in free will in theology, but one of the most direct treatments of the position was set forth very clearly in a sermon entitled "Free Grace" first preached in 1791 by John Wesley, the founder of Methodism. In his sermon, Wesley argued that those who embraced predestination represent "God as worse than the devil."[36] Wesley argued further that scriptures that seem to imply predestination should simply be classified with many other scriptures the meanings of which are unknown.[37] In defense of free will, Wesley called attention to scriptures that stress the mercy of God such as II Peter 3:9 that states that God is "not willing that any should perish."[38]

The problem that surfaces in much of the literature on predestination and free will is that true freedom of choice may come at the price of a limited or self-limited God while predestination reduces humans to automata that live out their lives in accordance with the inexorable pre-set decrees of God. The intellectual and emotional tensions between predestination and free will are nowhere better illustrated than in a work by Jules Lequyer entitled "The Dialogue of the Predestinate and the Reprobate."[39] The reprobate is a cleric who has lived a virtuous life, but by means of a dream that permits him to see the future he finds that he falls into sin and will ultimately dwell in hell. The predestinate, also a cleric, has lived a degenerate life, but also via a dream that reveals the future, finds that he will be saved and dwell with God. Following their dreams, the clerics engage in a lengthy emotionally wrenching conversation about their eternal prospects. They explore the understandable philosophical and emotional questions about predestination and free will. The dialogue underscores Lequyer's doubts about attempts to reconcile free will with predestination. If one's fate is irrevocably decreed by God beforehand or even prior to one's existence, then we encounter, in the words of one helpful commentary, "The Nightmare of Necessity."[40]

If strict necessity is a nightmare, belief in free will also presents a challenge, particularly to science. The limitations of science are highlighted if strict causality or lawful statistical regularity cannot be assumed in all arenas of inquiry. From a pragmatic standpoint, however, few scientists believe they will ever be able to account for all the variation in natural events. Thus, some degree of spontaneity need not serve as a serious impediment to significant advances in scientific understanding because there will forever be unexplained variance. Further, most scientists probably believe their ideas and their work can make a genuine difference in the world, particularly with hope to change the world. Thus, belief in some degree of free will, however limited, may be problematic for science on the theoretical side, but is of little practical importance to the day-to-day work of scientists and others.[41]

The free will–determinism issue is by no means a purely abstract theoretical issue. It is a practical issue that plays out in religious, scientific, philosophical, and legal contexts. Consider the unfortunate legal case of David Garabedian. Garabedian had always been a mild mannered and gentle young man. He took a job with a lawn maintenance firm that required, among other things, that he mix the ingredients of a pesticide containing the chemical carbaryl. Carbaryl is one of the principal components of nerve gas and is known to produce clearly demonstrable behavioral symptoms such as slobbering, nightmares, headaches, burning in the eyes, urinary urgency, and violent outbursts. Carbaryl also produces strong neurological effects. For example, it interferes with an enzyme that clears away acetycholine at the synapse. An excess of acetylcholine in the hypothalamus can result in overwhelming rage.

Garabedian had been breathing carbaryl over a period of several days and experiencing all of the associated symptoms. Then while working on the yard of a customer, he suddenly felt an overwhelming urge to urinate. Seeing no place to relieve himself, he urinated beside the customer's house. Unfortunately, the customer observed the event, confronted Garabedian and gave him a shove during a verbal exchange that followed. Gerabedian experienced a sudden surge of rage and initiated an attack that resulted in the death of the customer.

Subsequent legal arguments swirled around the neurochemical explanation of Garabedian's sudden and uncharacteristic violent attack and the contention of the prosecution lawyers that he used his free will to kill the home owner. In the end, the jury was unconvinced by the expert witnesses for the defense who clearly laid out the scientific evidence on the effects of carbaryl.

The case is tragic on many counts; tragic for the home owner and her family and for David Garabedian and his family. What is the explanation for the murder? It is understandable that the family members of the home-owner would be unable to accept the chemical interpretation, but would the crime have occurred without the presence of carbaryl in the overall equation? The urinary urgency may well have been brought on by the carbaryl. The rage was uncharacteristic for David Garabedian, but why was he unable to marshal inhibitory mechanisms that could have checked the outburst? Was the murder an act of free will?

There is one form of argument that surely should be rejected by anyone who thinks clearly about the situation. According to the argument, often employed in courts of law, other people exposed to unfortunate proximate causes (in this case, the breathing of carbaryl) do not commit violent crimes. Accordingly, (1) Garabedian should somehow be like these other people and (2) there is something in the essential character, something deeply flawed, rooted in the "will" of the defendant that trumped all other causal forces and that merits retributive punishment. What is wrong with such reasoning? First, one may ask whether anyone is truly "like" anyone else? Even identical twins, despite their common genetic likeness, are vastly different simply as the result of the abundance of unique events in their lives, differential learning experiences, different friendships, accidents, etc. If there is one bit of unconscious or biochemical uniqueness anywhere in the enormously complicated neurochemical system, then the argument that the accused should be like all those who would not have committed the crime falls apart, must be added to a list of logical fallacies, and is unworthy of serious thinkers.

The dilemmas, however, remain and questions outnumber answers. Did the lawn company take appropriate measures to protect its employees from the demonstrated effects of carbaryl? What is the most meaningful consequence for the defendant and those who have grieved and suffered as the result of the episode? There are obvious multiple causes for the tragedy; what weight should be given to the known causes? It is of interest that because of a multitude of relevant scientific discoveries, the questions that surface in modern times far outnumber those that could have been raised in earlier periods of history. In earlier periods, the defendant would likely have been quickly dispatched to the gallows or worse and that would have settled the matter once and for all. The continuing march of science into the machinery of the brain and the inner life of the person is forever changing the ways we think about the nature of human experience and behavior along with the ways we think about longstanding judicial and religious assumptions and beliefs. The concept of an autonomous mental entity that somehow transcends all natural causal forces was, for long periods, sacrosanct, but that is no longer the case.

It should be noted that there is an extensive literature seeking a middle way or a compatibilism between determinism and free will. Continuing intense controversies over the polar positions, however, suggest that to date there has been no major broadly recognized reconciliation between the two positions. A rapidly expanding and evolving contemporary literature on free will and determinism includes new arguments based on research in the neurosciences along with behavioral research exploring implications associated with beliefs in free will and determinism.[42] Some scholars have called attention to an important distinction between freedom and free will. Freedoms of the press, the right to vote, to express opinions, or to move from place to place are presumably compatible with determinism. There are also intrapsychic freedoms such as freedom from compulsions, fears, or anxieties. Sigmund Freud was a thoroughgoing determinist, but was deeply interested in exploring meanings of personal and political freedoms. He worried that religion had too often curtailed human freedom.[43]

Science and religion are not always at odds on free will and determinism. There are faith communities that favor beliefs in free will and others that stress a kind of hard determinism based on the theoretical foreknowledge of God. Scientists stress naturalistic causation, but many scientists reject the hard-wired Newtonian view of the world and favor the possibility of free will based on quantum indeterminism along with chaos and complexity theory. Scientific and religious grounds for believing in free will or determinism may be different, but there can still be agreement with the practical conclusions of either of the two positions.[44]

*****

Because of its philosophical and scientific complexities, the term *cause* is often avoided in scientific literature where one may encounter terms such as *correlation, permissible generalization, invariable sequence,* or *observable regularity.* Even so, assessment of what we commonly refer to as causality is indispensable in daily life whether the setting be a courtroom, the scene of a traffic accident, attempts in an emergency room to understand the source of pain, the work of educators to understand and predict academic success, or the work of a mechanic to diagnose the basis of engine failure. Attempts to tease out causal influences are encountered at every turn. Furthermore, attributions of causality to supernatural forces vs. naturalistic forces account for major discrepancies between scientific and most religious orientations and explanations. Such discrepancies are manifested in very complex ways in social, cultural, and personal ways and should be explored in greater detail in empirical and analytic studies of human beliefs about causality. The consequences of such beliefs are highly relevant to daily life, the ways we adapt to our complex world, and to human influences in a world that is increasingly fragile. In the next chapter, we continue our investigation of causality by exploring beliefs in angels and demons as active causal forces. As we will see, such beliefs are more common in the 21st century than might be expected.

Notes

1 Part of an oath attributed to several students studying with Johannes Müller in the 19th century. See Michael Wertheimer, *A Brief History of Psychology*, 5th ed. (New York: Psychology Press, 2011), 64.

2 Heinrich Kramer and James Sprenger, *Malleus Maleficarum* (New York: Dover, 1971), 107.
3 For example, a brief scholarly discussion of theoretical approaches to causality can be found in a chapter by John Henry, "Causality," in *The History of Science and Religion in the Western Tradition: An Encyclopedia*, ed. Gary B. Ferngren (New York: Garland Publishing, 2000), 31–37. Another helpful overview of the problem of causality is by Michael Tooler, "Causation: Metaphysical Issues," in *Encyclopedia of Philosophy*, Vol. 2, 2nd ed., ed. Donald M. Borchart (Detroit: Thompson/Gale, 2006), 95–103.
4 For a brief overview of attribution theory see Bertram F. Malle, "Attribution Theories: How People Make Sense of Behavior," in *Theories in Social Psychology*, ed. Derek Chadee (Malden, MA: Wiley-Blackwell, 2011), 72–95. Also see Joachim I. Krueger, "Attribution Theory," in *Encyclopedia of Social Psychology*, Vol. 1, eds. Roy F. Baumeister and Kathleen D. Vohs (New York: Oxford University Press, 2000), 320–325.
5 For a technical overview of attribution theory and its role in research see Ann Taves, *Religious Experience Reconsidered: A Building Block Approach to the Study of Religion and Other Special Things* (Princeton, NJ: Princeton University Press, 2009). For applications of attribution theory specifically to research in the psychology of religion see Bernard Spilka, Phillip Shaver, and Lee A. Kirkpatrick, "A General Attribution Theory for the Psychology of Religion," *Journal for the Scientific Study of Religion* 24, No. 1, (March 1985), 1–20. Also see Bernard Spilka and Daniel N. McIntosh, "Attribution Theory and Religious Experience," in *Handbook of Religious Experience*, ed. Ralph W. W. Hood Jr. (Birmingham, AL: Religious Education Press, 1995), 421–445.
6 Kramer and Sprenger, *Malleus*. See especially Part II, Chapter 9.
7 William Douglas Woody and Wayne Viney, *A History of Psychology: Emergence of Science and Applications*, 6th ed. (New York: Routledge, 2017), 184–185.
8 Carol Tavris, *The Mismeasure of Woman: Why Women Are Not The Better Sex, The Inferior Sex, or The Opposite Sex* (New York: Simon and Schuster; 1992). Also see Ellen B. Bratten and Wayne Viney, "Some late Nineteenth-Century Perspectives on Sex and Emotional Expression," *Psychological Reports* 86 (April 2000), 575–585.
9 For example, see The Qur'an 4:34; for a short review of Biblical justifications of sexism across history, see Peter J. Gomes, *The Good Book: Reading the Bible with Mind and Heart* (New York: Harper Collins, 1996).
10 James John Jurinski, *Religion on Trial: A Handbook with Cases, Laws, and Documents* (Santa Barbara, CA: ABC Clio, Inc., 2004).
11 Nancy Lofholm, "Couple Gets 20 Years Probation," *The Denver Post*, November 9, 2001.
12 See Khalil AlHajal, "Doctors Not Liable for Death of Jehovah's Witness who Refused Blood Transfusion, Court Rules," http://www.mlive.com/news/detroit/index.ssf/2014/01/doctors_not_liable_for_death_o.html Posted January 10, 2014 (Accessed October 1, 2014).
13 A Kansas farm-hand was disarmed as he heard his red-faced teary-eyed boss scream out a streak of expletives followed by the question "My God, why can't human beings learn to settle their differences without going to war?" The boss had just heard the news about the outbreak of the Korean War. The boss, not normally a religious man, had just addressed God with a question. The farm-hand later came to the conclusion that he had just heard a kind of prayer more direct and sincere than any he had ever heard in church.
14 Bruce J. Dierenfield, *The Battle over School Prayer: How Engel v. Vitale Changed America* (Lawrence, KS: University Press of Kansas, 2007).
15 Tiffany Stanley, "Praying for Bad Things to Happen to Bad People," *The Salt Lake Tribune*, July 1, 2009. For a brief example of how prayers for destruction can be implicit in other prayers, see Mark Twain, "The War Prayer," in *The Complete Essays of Mark Twain*, ed. Charles Neider (Garden City, NY: Doubleday, 1963), 679–682.

16 William James, *The Varieties of Religious Experience* (New York: Routledge, 2002), 375.
17 For a careful analysis of James's pragmatic approach to religion see James Cresswell, "Can Religion and Psychology Get Along? Toward a Pragmatic Cultural Psychology of Religion That Includes Meaning and Experience," *Journal of Theoretical and Philosophical Psychology* 34, No. 2 (May, 2014), 133–145. Also see Brent Slife and J. Reber, "Is there a Pervasive Implicit Bias Against Theism in Psychology?" *Journal of Theoretical and Philosophical Psychology* 29 (2009), 63–79.
18 See Stephen G. Brush, "The Prayer Test," *American Scientist* 62, No. 5 (September–October 1974), 561–563.
19 Ibid., 562.
20 Bernard Spilka and Kevin L. Ladd, *The Psychology of Prayer: A Scientific Approach* (New York: The Guilford Press, 2013).
21 Victor J. Stenger, *God, The Failed Hypothesis* (New York: Prometheus Books, 2008), 94–102.
22 Richard E. Rubenstein, *Aristotle's Children: How Christians, Muslims, and Jews Rediscovered Ancient Wisdom and Illuminated the Dark Ages* (New York: Harcourt, 2003), 85.
23 Al-Ghazali, *The Incoherence of the Philosophers* (Provo, UT: Brigham Young University Press, 2000), 166.
24 Ibid.
25 Godfried Wilhelm von Leibniz argued from his belief in these attributes of God that God knows what the best possible world can be, is powerful enough to create the best possible world, and wants the best possible world. Therefore, Leibniz concludes, this *must be* the best of all possible worlds. See Godfried Wilhelm von Leibniz, *Theodicy: Essays on the Goodness of God, the Freedom of Man and the Origin of Evil*, ed. Austin M. Farrer, trans. E. M. Huggard (New York: Cosimo Classics, 2010). A classical critic of this view is Voltaire, who in his book *Candide* satirizes Leibniz with the character Professor Pangloss who famously maintains in the face of repeated disasters that the world must be perfect. See Voltaire, *Candide*, trans. Robert M. Adams (New York: Norton, 1991).
26 Clark Hull, *Principles of Behavior* (New York: D. Appleton-Century, 1943), 26.
27 See Ernest R. Hilgard and Gordon H. Bower, *Theories of Learning*, 3rd ed. (New York: Appleton-Century-Crofts, 1966). See Chapter 7.
28 Yuri Rubinsky and Ian Wiseman, *A History of the End of the World* (New York: Quill, 1982). See also Frederic J. Baumgartner, *Longing for the End: A History of Millennialism in Western Civilization* (New York: Palgrave, 1999).
29 See Richard Owen, "Katrina – Controversial Prelate Now a Bishop," *The Times* (London), February 2, 2009.
30 Richard Taylor, "Determinism," in *The Encyclopedia of Philosophy*, Vol. 2, ed. Paul Edwards (New York: Macmillan, 1967), 359.
31 William James, *Some Problems of Philosophy* (Lincoln, NE: University of Nebraska Press, 1996), 192.
32 Ronald W. Clark, *Einstein: The Life and Times* (New York: World Publishing Company, 1971), 19.
33 Westminster Assembly, *The Westminster Confession of Faith* (Charleston, SC: Forgotten Books, 2007). See Chapter 3.
34 William James, letter to Shadworth H. Hodgson, 1885, in *Letters of William James*, Vol. 1, Henry James (ed.), (Boston, MA: The Atlantic Monthly Press, 1920), 245.
35 William James, *The Will to Believe* (Cambridge, MA: Harvard University Press, 1979), 164.
36 John Wesley, "Free Grace," in *Classics of Protestantism*, ed. Vergilius Ferm (New York: Philosophical Library, 1959), 176.
37 Ibid.
38 Ibid., 178.

39 See Donald Wayne Viney (ed. and trans.), *Translation of the Works of Jules Lequyer* (Queenston, Ontario: The Edwin Mellen Press, 1998), 51–160.
40 Donald Wayne Viney, "The Nightmare of Necessity: Jules Lequyer's Dialogue of the Predestinate and the Reprobate," *The Journal for the Association of the Interdisciplinary Study of the Arts* 5, No. 1 (Autumn 1999), 19–32.
41 Vohs and Schooler demonstrated that beliefs in free will and determinism affect behavior. When they assigned students to read a passage in support of determinism, students, in a subsequent task, were more likely to cheat; similarly, when students read a passage in support of free will, they were less likely to cheat. Katherine D. Vohs and Jonathan W. Schooler, "The Value of Believing in Free Will: Encouraging a Belief in Determinism Increases Cheating," *Psychological Science* 19, No. 1 (January 2008), 49–54.
42 See Robert Kane, *A Contemporary Introduction to Free Will* (New York: Oxford University Press, 2005). Kane provides a helpful overview of early 21st century perspectives and research on free will and determinism.
43 Wayne Viney and Elizabeth Parker, "Necessity as a Nightmare or as a Pathway to Freedom: Freud's Dilemma, a Human Dilemma," *Psychoanalytic Psychology* 33 (2016), 299–311.
44 Robert Kane, *A Contemporary Introduction*, see Chapter 12 for a discussion of Free Will and Modern Science.

4

CAUSALITY CONTINUED

Angels and Demons

> *The devil as a roaring lion, walketh about, seeking whom he may devour.*[1]
>
> *Where there is doubt, there is freedom.*[2]

The previous chapter explored differences between supernatural and naturalistic approaches to causality. This chapter will focus more exclusively on supernatural explanations with emphasis on the resilience of beliefs in demonological forces. There is obviously no place in science per se for belief in demons, but as we will see, there is widespread belief in demons as well as angels. Such belief commands our attention if we are to honestly explore differences between science and various religious beliefs. We focus first on why, in a scientific age, do beliefs in demons and angels persist?

Persistence of Belief in Angels and Demons

Popular belief in angels and demons as causal forces is by no means a relic of the past. According to a survey by the Pew Research Center "Nearly seven-in-ten Americans (68%) believe that angels and demons are active in the world."[3] According to a Harris poll conducted in 2007 more Americans (62%) believe in the Devil than in Darwin (42%).[4] Beliefs in literal demons and abstract evil forces are not limited to the United States, but are encountered in many parts of the world. In an article published in 2015 in the *New Republic* Joseph P. Laycock speaks of "A Demonic Renaissance."[5] He notes that beliefs in demonic forces are by no means esoteric even if they constitute a mystery to those of a scientific persuasion. We believe there are numerous reasons for such beliefs.

Influence of Sacred Scriptures

One source for belief in demons is encountered in the sacred texts of major religions. Beliefs in literal evil entities or actual personages are fostered in the sacred literatures including canonical texts in Hebrew, Zoroastrian, Christian, Hindu, and Islamic traditions. The opening pages of the Qur'an and the Bible quickly introduce the reader to the tensions between God and the forces of evil that include fallen angels and other mysterious beings that work mischief and vie for the loyalty of human beings. Sacred literatures, taken as the actual literal word of God, are coercive and intimidating even when they stretch credulity, violate logic, or undermine what is known in ordinary experience. Moreover, many religious leaders and institutions emphasize the literal truth and authenticity of the scriptures as keys to understanding the real world.

Furthermore, in many cases, the faithful are forbidden to entertain doubts or to employ critical treatment of scriptures. Thus, long standing claims, clearly at variance with ordinary experience, science, reason, and logic are perpetuated.

Need for Control

Belief in the presence of demonic forces inevitably leads to urgent needs for control of their activities and influence. Strategies for control include prayers, sacrifices, rituals, various appeasements, and exorcism. There is strong contemporary interest in the control of demonic forces as manifested in the use of exorcism in both conservative Protestant and Catholic churches. In the introduction to his book, *Exorcism and the Church Militant*, Fr. Thomas Euteneuer contends that recent interest in the occult means the church will soon be inundated with requests for exorcism.[6] Euteneuer's claim is based on the belief that some occult practices encourage demon possession and that the church must then be prepared to deal with requests for intervention. A news release by Nick Pisa titled "Pope's Exorcist Squads Will Wage War on Satan," notes that Pope Benedict XVI authorized major increases in the number of trained exorcists so that each Diocese would have adequate numbers of practitioners to deal with anticipated increases in requests for exorcisms.[7]

Exorcism, literally to bind by oath, refers to elaborate ceremonies that include actions and procedures such as kissing the cross, sprinkling of holy water, recitation of scriptures, incantations, and prayers designed to cast demons out of persons or objects. Catholic exorcism ceremonies are much more structured and controlled than Protestant exorcisms. In his book, *Exorcism and the Church Militant*, Euteneuer provides an informative chapter on the Catholic approach to the conduct of an exorcism.[8] The nature of the ceremony in fundamentalist Protestantism depends entirely on the procedures preferred by the individual exorcist. Roman Catholic exorcisms are guided by tradition and a scripted set of procedures that include advanced approval by church authorities, although in practice there exists some degree of variation in exorcisms in the Roman Catholic tradition.[9] There are a variety of videos of exorcisms available on line including an interesting version of an Islamic exorcism.[10]

Obviously, possession by demons is not a recognized diagnostic category in scientific, neurological, psychiatric, or psychological literature. Herein, lies a major difference between the scientific community and those in faith communities who take sacred texts such as the Bible or the Qur'an literally. The Bible and the Qur'an specifically include a great many references to supernatural forces that work against human interests. While many Christian churches continue to embrace prayer as a causal force, most do not recognize or practice exorcism. Many mainstream churches view demonology and exorcism as relics of the past. Given widespread continuing popular and fundamentalist religious opinion, however, demonology is a topic that cannot be neglected in discussions of science and religion.

Ignorance of Natural Causality

Another reason for beliefs in exorcism is encountered in the marked absence of knowledge of natural causes. In the absence of such knowledge it is understandable that beneficent or malevolent events would be regarded as the work of supernatural friendly or unfriendly entities such as angels or demons. Tendencies to personify causal forces occurred partly because unknown and indifferent natural causes were beyond comprehension. The discovery of the nervous system, of chemical elements, low and high pressure gradients, and of a myriad of mechanical laws gradually provided alternative naturalistic explanations. There was understandable appeal afforded by a world populated with angels and demons who could possibly be appeased through proper acts of obeisance including prayers, confessions, negotiations, and rituals. The ritual control of demonic forces is illustrated by Christians when they make the sign of the cross as a means of protection. Ritual control is illustrated in the Hajj when Muslims throw stones or pebbles at walls as a means of rebuking evil or demonic forces.

Failures of Scientific Explanations

There is great promise in science, but science, like everything else, falls short in the face of senseless tragedy and death. There will always be things beyond comprehension that simply come along in their brutal naked presence and leave believers and non-believers alike with a sense of ineffable loss and despair. Sigmund Freud identified three major general forces we could regard as malevolent because they work against human happiness and well-being.[11] The first is the physical world that often rages against human interests both at the macro and micro levels. Floods, hurricanes, earthquakes, volcanoes, bacteria, and viruses take an annual toll incalculable in terms of the destruction, displacement, death, and misery they leave behind. The physical world sustains life, but also produces continuing multiple threats to well-being. Freud notes that it is a miracle that we live at all.

The second source of suffering, according to Freud, is our own body. We fight what Freud considered rather pitiable rear-guard actions to preserve health and youth, but despite our best efforts, we all ultimately suffer the same fate. Some of the most dramatic historical encounters between science and religion center on their differing explanations of the nature and causes of illness. In his book *Plagues and Peoples*, William H. McNeill notes "The doctrine that disease came from God could easily be interpreted to mean that it was impious to interfere with God's purposes by trying to take conscious precaution against disease."[12] McNeill also notes that early scientific approaches to medicine often resulted in as much harm as good, but that doctors "dealing with things of this world ... were more liable to empiric elaboration over time."[13] Scientific medicine focused on the material and efficient "things of this world." The results, in terms of understanding, prediction, and intervention, though nothing short of epic, do not always speak to our ultimate concerns.

Freud's third category was perhaps the most lethal of the three. We receive most of our satisfactions and love in our relations with other people, but ironically, other people also inflict more death and misery than all the natural disasters put together! When we think of wars, human greed, unequal distribution of goods, brutal dictators, dysfunctional families, the demand for subordination to irrational beliefs and practices, overcrowding, the history of brutal punishments, corrupt political systems, and all the various prejudices and narrow identities we embrace including religious hatreds, we cannot help but agree with Freud. It should come as no surprise that historically and even in the present scientific age, there is widespread belief in demons at work in the natural world and in other people.

There are accidents, tragedies, unexplained events, illnesses, injustice, and unfair practices at every turn in life. Human beings naturally seek ways to understand all the brokenness they encounter in their lives and the lives of others. Naturalistic or scientific explanations may provide solace and foster understanding, but not always. Thus, millions of people turn to beliefs in a world literally saturated by angelic and demonic forces.

Lure of Teleological and Ad Hoc Explanations

Eric Rogers, in his book *Physics for the Inquiring Mind*, set forth a thoughtful and somewhat humorous discussion on the utility and persistence of demonological explanations.[14] Rogers asks you to imagine yourself in a dialogue with Faustus on the subject of friction. Faustus speaks for demons and claims he can explain friction with demons as adequately as you can with the principles of physics. Imagine an object, say a brick, on a table top. You push the brick along the table and experience resistance or friction. Faustus claims the resistance is caused by invisible demons pushing against you and the brick. At one point in the conversation, you feel you have found the knock down argument. You point out that if you put oil on the table you experience less friction. Of course, says Faustus, oil drowns demons. The conversation goes on and again you feel victory is within your grasp:

> You: 'If I slide a brick along the table again and again, the friction is the same each time. Demons would be crushed in the first trip.'
> Faustus: 'Yes, but they multiply incredibly fast.'
> You: 'There are other laws of friction: for example, the drag is proportional to the pressure holding the surfaces together.'
> Faustus: 'The demons live in the pores of the surface: more pressure makes more of them rush out to push and be crushed. Demons act in just the right way to push and drag with the forces you find in your experiments.'

Notice that Faustus has an explanation, however flawed from a scientific point of view, for a sophisticated physical concept such as friction. His ad hoc explanation accounts for all the physical variations associated with friction. Clearly, demonological explanations have lost credibility when it comes to explaining physical phenomena such as changes in the weather, physical illness, and crop failures. Such is not the case however, when it comes to bizarre behaviors and ideas and this is partly because there are religious institutions and large numbers of their constituents and leaders who continue to teach and believe in demonic forces.

Though the psychological sciences have made enormous progress in evidence-based naturalistic explanations and treatments, how much easier would it be for Faustus to engage the psychologist or the psychiatrist when it comes to explaining unusual behaviors that to date do not yet yield to the exact kind of quantitative and physical analysis available to the physical scientist?[15] From a scientific standpoint, bizarre and unusual behaviors are explained in terms of conditioning, social and cultural contexts, neurotransmitter imbalances, and other neurological and chemical changes. Exorcists agree, but add that some behaviors are the result of possession by demons. Later, we will discuss tragedies associated with demonological explanations of behavior.

Religious Views on the Origin of Evil

As noted, sacred literature in many religions is filled with references to a universe of evil entities that interact in causal ways with human thoughts and activities. Belief in personified evil entities raises three difficult but fundamental questions regarding the existence of these entities: What was their origin? What is the reason for their existence? What is the range of their activities? Additional complicated questions also arise: If there is a plurality of evil entities, what is their social organization? What is their relation to God? How are believers to discern when an event has a natural basis and when it has a supernatural basis? For many faith communities, this last question is loaded with practical implications. For example, how does one treat cognitive disorganization, bizarre behaviors, emotional misery, or unwanted intrusions in the stream of experience? Does one seek clinical psychological help, or does one seek supernatural intervention? The answers to these questions rest on assumptions about the causes of unwanted experiences and behaviors.

There is little agreement from one religion to the next regarding the origin of evil entities, but most address the question. The Qur'an, for example, in Surah 15 beginning with verse 26 notes that Allah "created man of clay that gives forth sound, of mud fashioned in shape." Surah 96, verse 2 declares that the Lord "created man from a clot." Some scholars believe this verse refers to a blood clot.[16] Verse 27 in Surah 15 declares that the Jinn had been created earlier out of intensely hot fire. The term *Jinn* (plural is *Jinni*) and the term *angels* are sometimes used interchangeably. Following the creation of man, Allah ordered the angels, who had been created earlier, to bow down, prostrate themselves, and show obeisance to the man. The angels bowed down, but one angel named Iblis refused to bow down because he believed he was better than Adam. After all, Iblis was made of fire while Adam was brought forth from more lowly materials. Iblis was cast out by Allah but granted respite until the end times. During his respite, his goal is to "lie in wait" for humans in order to dissuade them from following the straight path (see Surah 15: 27–43).

A great many Christians and Jews believe the devil is a kind of metaphor used to explain natural and human forces that work against goodness and the well-being of humankind. Others, perhaps a majority of the Christian community, believe that scriptures that refer to the devil should be taken literally. The origin of the devil is problematic for all faith traditions. According to Elaine Pagels, the idea of Satan as almost like God is a little more than 2000 years old in Western culture.[17]

Beyond scholarly or historical questions, how do those who believe in the devil account for the devil's origin, particularly, as discussed in the previous chapter, if God must be by nature omniscient, omnipotent, and omnibenevolent? As William James asked "How—if perfection be the source, should there be Imperfection?"[18] The problem of evil, as discussed in the preceding chapter, raises legitimate questions that are not fully addressed in Biblical literature. Donald Viney calls attention to the fact that many of our ideas about angels and demons came not so much from the Bible but from theologians. He notes that Augustine believed that "God created a hierarchy of angels, or pure bodiless spirits, prior to creating humans. The angels, like the humans that would follow them, were endowed with intellect and will. The highest of the angels, Satan, turned away from God and this encouraged other angels to do the same."[19] Thus, there were good and bad angels, the latter becoming the demonic forces that would inflict pain and misery on earth. If the origin of demons is problematic, the way they accomplish their work is even more problematic.

The Work of Demons

As noted earlier, demons and angels have been employed historically as explanations for a host of events including fair and foul weather. Robert Reilly noted that some Arab press releases announced that Hurricane Katrina was "a wind of torment" and "a soldier of Allah" sent as a punishment to America.[20] He also noted that for a brief period in the 1980s "weather forecasts were quietly suspended by the Pakistani media, although they were later reinstated."[21] The suspension likely resulted from the apparent disconnect between the techniques of modern meteorology and belief in demonic forces as the cause of weather phenomena. Yet, the growing reliability, accuracy, and practical value of predictions based exclusively on naturalistic assumptions are increasingly difficult to challenge, as are the difficulties of exchanging these for demonological interventions. One can imagine the turmoil in modern air travel without the widespread and complex meteorological support system. Nevertheless, the ever-increasing accuracy of scientific predictions of such phenomena as the weather, eruption of volcanoes, the efficacy of vaccinations or even ultra-sound predictions about the sex of a baby or medical predictions about internal bodily states based on highly detailed scientific imaging systems, constitutes a threat to those who downplay the role of natural causation. Still, for all the demonstrable progress in purely naturalistic approaches to causation, one encounters continued reference to transnatural explanations of all kinds of events. For example, American conservative minister Pat Robertson, in a television broadcast on his 700 Club, blamed the devastating January 2010 Earthquake in Haiti on a pact that earlier Haitians made with the devil.[22] For centuries, lightning strikes were viewed as a tool of God to punish sin.

The *Malleus Maleficarum*

The most famous or, depending on one's point of view, notorious manual for treating and explaining the work of demons and witches is the *Malleus Maleficarum* (the Hammer against Witches) first published in 1486 by Dominican Monks Heinrich Kramer and James Sprenger.[23] Kramer and Sprenger were professors of theology and had been assigned as Inquisitors to northern Germany. The publication of the *Malleus* followed a communication of Pope Innocent VIII released in December of 1484, in which he observed that many persons in northern Germany had abandoned themselves to witchcraft and devils resulting, among other things, in still-births, crop failures, sores, diseases, and sexual dysfunction. The Pope warned of strong retaliation from the church including "excommunication, suspension, interdict, and yet more terrible penalties, censures, and punishment" for any person, regardless of rank who sought in any way to interfere with the work of Kramer and Sprenger.[24] Little wonder the Inquisition persisted or even thrived into the early Modern period in the early 1600s.

The *Malleus* itself is divided into three major sections. The first deals with difficult theological questions centering on how it is possible there could be devils in the first place and how they could be endowed with the causal power to influence so many events in the natural order. If God is the Creator of all things, and if God is truly Sovereign, omnipotent, omniscient, just, and benevolent, how could there be any evil causal force whatsoever with the powers to bring about the calamities attributed to witches and devils? This collection of questions is challenging for any monotheistic religion embracing the concept of an omnipotent God. Almost a third of the *Malleus* is a complicated theological treatise attempting to deal with these questions from a Catholic perspective. Kramer and Sprenger conclude, among other things, that witchcraft requires "the devil, a witch, and the permission of Almighty God."[25] In their worldview, God permits, but does not wish evil to occur, even though God's existence and God's permission are necessary for witchcraft. In the worldview of Kramer and Sprenger, the centrality of these tensions between supernatural good and supernatural evil cannot be underestimated. For example, the *Malleus* opens with questions of the necessity of belief in demonology and witchcraft for Christianity. They conclude that these beliefs are central and that claims that demons or witches do not exist "manifestly savors of heresy."[26]

Despite the inseparability of supernatural good and supernatural evil for Kramer and Sprenger, when evil does occur it is somehow for the perfection of the world. They note that "good things are more highly commendable, are more pleasing and laudable, when they are compared with bad things; and authority can be quoted in support of this."[27] They go on to note that the attributes of God's wisdom, justice and goodness are more easily discerned in the contrast between evil and goodness. They also note that the devil is tormented when he discovers that "God uses all evil for the glory of His name, for the commendation of the Faith, for the purgation of the elect, and for the acquisition of merit."[28]

The second part of the *Malleus* turns to descriptions of how devils and witches go about their work: how they stir up tempests and hailstorms, interfere with procreation, how they afflict animals and crops and how they bewitch people. This is the part of the *Malleus* that deals directly with questions about causality. The second part of the *Malleus* also describes specific causal remedies prescribed by the church for the interference and prevention of demonological influence. This section includes references that clearly relate to behaviors that would now be viewed as evidence of psychological-medical disorders. For example, they discuss the power of witches to "prevent erection of the member which is accommodated to fructification" and to prevent ejaculation.[29]

The second part of the *Malleus* opens by calling attention to three classes of people "blessed by God whom that detestable race [of demons] cannot injure with witchcraft."[30] These three include: prosecutors and judges who administer justice, members of the church who are especially diligent in using church approved methods to fortify themselves against witchcraft, and those who are especially blessed by holy angels. In their worldview, supernatural forces also provide protection from demons.

According to the *Malleus* a mere touch from a witch or a devil is sometimes sufficient to be the cause of an unfortunate event. For example, Kramer and Sprenger tell of a pregnant woman who had been warned by her midwife not to leave her dwelling and to avoid all contact or conversation with a woman suspected of being a witch. The pregnant woman later did go out and accidentally encountered the suspected witch who immediately laid both of her hands on the woman's stomach. Instantly the pregnant woman felt pain. She returned to her dwelling and informed the midwife of what had happened. The midwife told her that the baby was now dead. At delivery, the dead baby came out in pieces. Kramer and Sprenger note "this great affliction was permitted by God to punish [the pregnant woman's] husband, whose duty it was to bring witches to justice and avenge their injuries to the Creator."[31]

The means by which an unfortunate event is brought about often involves complicated physical and verbal procedures presumed to have strong causal effects in the physical world. For example, Kramer and Sprenger tell of a procedure whereby a black cock is taken to a crossroads, sacrificed, and tossed into the air. In response, a devil stirs up the air and, with "the permission of the living God, sends down hailstones and lightnings."[32] Another method used to bring on storms involved the transport of water by a witch to a field. A hole is dug and filled with the water provided by the witch. A storm is caused when the witch stirs the water and calls upon the name of the devil.[33] Kramer and Sprenger continually warn the readers of the *Malleus* to reject superstitious explanations for the events they describe. They believed the procedures they identified had real and demonstrable causal influence.

The third part of the *Malleus* sets forth the legal procedures by which ecclesiastical and civil courts initiated and conducted trials. Three methods were identified for initiating legal proceedings. The first method is for one person to make an accusation and to testify in court in a manner that proves the truth of the accusation. Failure of the accuser to prove the case could result in danger to the welfare of the accuser. Although Kramer and Sprenger reject mortal enemies of the accused as witnesses, they recommend admitting evidence from enemies under certain conditions.[34] The second method is for one person to file an accusation against someone suspected of witchcraft. The accuser however may refuse to appear in court to help prove the case. Kramer and Sprenger support this method on the grounds that the person accused of witchcraft may indeed be a witch and could with a mere look or touch bring great calamity into the life of an accuser or informer. The third method, referred to as an inquisition, requires no accuser or informer. Where there was general suspicion that witches or demonological forces were operating in a given place, a judge or inquisitor could simply announce or post a warning that an inquisition would be initiated within a 12-day period. People were admonished to come forward if they had any reason (e.g., damage to crops, death of an animal, injury to a person) to suspect anyone of being involved in witchcraft. The primary goal during an inquisition is a voluntary confession from the suspected witch.

Once accused, it was a near impossibility for a defendant to win a case. One reason is that torture or the threat of torture was viewed by the church and the legal system as a legitimate means of extracting a confession.[35] Torture techniques included thumb screws, surgical extraction of the tongue, extraction of finger nails or toe nails, and the rack, which was used as a method of stretching the victim thereby inflicting excruciating, unimaginable pain. Though there were many variations on the structure of the rack, most included a rectangle about the size of a bed designed for one person. The rack was equipped with cylindrical shaped rollers with ropes or chains that could be attached to the roller and tied to the victim's extremities (e.g., ankles and wrists). A crank attached to a gear and a ratchet was attached to the ropes and was turned very slowly in the process of interrogation. As the victim was stretched the joints were first hyper-extended, then dislocated, or pulled completely apart. Tendons could be stretched beyond any possibility of repair. Little wonder most victims broke under the torture and told the inquisitors whatever they wanted to hear.

Inquisitors employed methods of investigation that would today be viewed as unequivocal examples of torture. For example, in trial by red hot iron the defendant was required to attempt to lift and carry a red hot iron block for a certain distance. An innocent suspect was expected to be able to do so without burns or with no more than minimal injury; God would surely not allow the innocent to suffer, and injury was a sign of guilt. Although, in the words of Kramer and Sprenger, "a miraculous effect is looked for," they present trial by ordeal as a valid and reliable method to determine guilt.[36] Despite the emphasis on torture, they warned extensively of the risk of false confessions, and they provided several safeguards against false confession. For example, the suspect who confesses during torture must confess again without being tortured.[37] Of course, the suspect knows that recanting the confession is likely to lead to additional torture, but this safeguard met their standards.

Though some cultures continue to employ torture, especially for those accused of crimes such as terrorism and treason, the efficacy of torture remains a legal, strategic, and ethical question.[38] Torture, wherever it is used, is justified by some political and religious leaders and by those in charge of its administration.[39] Typical justifications for the use of torture include the following: "without torture we would not have gained the information we need," "it is prescribed by holy writ," "it uncovers the names of other offenders and sends a stern message to other would-be offenders," "it purifies the populace (the screams of the victims on the rack or in the fires signify the release of demons from the minds and bodies of the accused—the severe mission of God is being fulfilled)." Despite data that suggest rapport building leads to better intelligence,[40] torture has a long legal and cultural history that extends into the present.[41]

The *Malleus* points out that a person accused of witchcraft may have an advocate, but it is the judge rather than the accused who chooses the advocate. The advocate was to have been an even-handed honorable man. The advocate, however, is not free in the trial to engage in oratorical tricks and he must be very circumspect and careful not to defend an error "for in that case he would be more damnably guilty than the witches themselves."[42] Little wonder, Witch trial "advocates" largely failed in their attempts to fairly represent the defendant.

The Demise of Demonology

Michael Streeter notes that "just as there was no precise date for the start of the burning times or witch craze, so there was no precise time at which they ended."[43] There are, however, identifiable forces that contributed to growing doubts about the very existence of demons, the validity of methods attributed to witches, judicial procedures in witch trials, and the use of extreme torture techniques in witch trials. As noted at the outset of this chapter however, demonology is not a relic of the past, but it has been largely exorcised in areas such as meteorology, medicine, and geology. It persists however, in many religious beliefs and practices as an attempt to explain bizarre behaviors. With the advances of the brain and cognitive sciences, there are now alternative naturalistic explanations for such behaviors that in time may well threaten remaining demonological explanations. In what follows, we explore the growth of some of the ideas that challenged common beliefs about witches and demons.

Early Modern Medicine

Johann Weyer (1515–1588) was a Dutch physician, an early pioneer in psychiatry, and one of the first to speak out specifically against the *Malleus Maleficarum* and the witch trials of his day. Weyer's best known work was *De Praestigiis Daemonum* "On the Illusions of the Demons," or "Concerning Deceptive Demons."[44] Sigmund Freud considered *De Praestigiis Daemonum* as one of the ten most important books in the history of psychoanalysis, possibly because Weyer anticipated some of the concepts (e.g., unconscious processes, repression, importance of dreams, and possible sexual interest of court officials in the women they prosecuted) that would later become a part of the psychoanalytic movement.[45] Indeed, sprinkled throughout the *Praestigiis*, one encounters ideas about unconscious processes, repression, the importance of dreams, and suggestibility.

As a product of the 16th century, Weyer accepted the idea that there were demons, but he denied that demons have the extensive powers attributed to them in the *Malleus*. It is not particularly surprising that Weyer retained a belief in demons; many of the early pioneers in science and philosophy continued to believe in the demons as well as magic, alchemy, and astrology. Weyer was deeply concerned about the use of torture as a means of extracting confessions and about the biased judicial procedures advanced in the *Malleus*. He also realized that many of those convicted of witchcraft struggled with mental illness.

Weyer was outraged that faulty religious, judicial, and investigatory philosophies had been responsible for the brutalities associated with the witch trials. He went so far as to say that the "accusers are the special slaves of the Devil; some may call them diviners, but for me they shall stand as the real evildoers."[46] Such a statement was extremely dangerous in the social and religious context of the 16th century. Indeed, the *Praestigiis* was placed on the Catholic Index of Forbidden Books and anybody caught reading Weyer's work was threatened with excommunication.[47] The *Praestigiis* was translated into numerous languages and went through several editions, but its immediate influence was apparently negligible, possibly because of fear of retaliation for supporters of the work and for the fact that it planted the seeds of doubt about the religious mentality undergirding the witchhunts. One of Weyer's greatest contributions was his insistence that medical specialists and not just legal and religious officials should be consulted in the assessment of suspected witches.[48]

Mechanization and Advances in Measurement

Early modern scientists such as Newton, Kepler, and Galileo demonstrated the quantitative nature of phenomena such as the motions of planets, the speed of falling bodies, and the laws of optics. Kirsch calls attention to the irony that *pricking* as a method for diagnosing demon possession was introduced in 1609, the same year Kepler published his theory that planets in our solar system move in ellipses around the sun.[49] A common belief was that true witches had small patches of skin insensitive to pain. Thus, the accused was stuck in a variety of locations with a sharp needle or pin. The accused was assumed to be a witch if an insensitive location could be identified. Since pain receptors are distributed very unevenly, it was not unlikely that an insensitive spot especially in dorsal parts of the body could be identified.

There were other advances in measurement that were highly relevant to demonological theories. For centuries it was believed that "The soul is the prime and chief cause of local motion in the body."[50] The 17th century however, witnessed new and more precise explanations of animate motion. Such naturalistic explanations were fed by growing interest in the intricate movements of mechanical inventions such as toys, clocks, and windmills that were caused by the controlled release of energy generated by running water, weights, or spiral "wind-up" springs. Inventive combinations of power sources, along with the use of gears, ratchets, wheels, and pulleys demonstrated that complex mechanical movements are the result of material, efficient, and formal causes. There was no need to posit any kind of ghost or demon in the machine to explain movement. In the early modern period, there was growing speculation that human movements in all their variety and intricacy, were also mediated by purely natural processes. Such beliefs challenged the necessity of demonology to explain motion in particular, and human behavior in general.

Thomas Hobbes (1588–1679), one of the first modern thinkers to advance a mechanistic explanation of motion declared that "The heart is a spring, the nerves are strings, the joints are wheels giving motion to the whole body."[51] René Descartes, however, wanted to know the specifics so he turned to "the book of the world" to explore anatomy and to conduct dissections and vivisections. He had been motivated partly by the increasingly intricate movements observed in the mechanical inventions of his day. Based on his observations, Descartes came to the conclusion that animate motion in animals and humans could be largely explained on the basis of natural processes unfolding in the central and peripheral nervous system.[52] Descartes believed that animals were machines without souls. By contrast, he believed humans possess a rational soul that mediated complex deliberative and higher cognitive processes. Nevertheless, most human movements, like animal movements, were mechanical.

Descartes set forth several testable hypotheses that would help set the intellectual agenda in physiology for the next two or three centuries, and we return to these in detail in Chapter 5. Though all of his hypotheses eventually proved wrong, they served to motivate other scientists to go to their laboratories. Thanks partly to René Descartes, the science of neurology was born, and this science is important and relevant because neurological explanations often conflicted with demonological explanations.

An Increasingly Skeptical Scholarly Community

Weyer was not alone in planting doubts about torture, the judicial procedures employed in the Inquisition, the powers of demons, and the religious beliefs that supported the witch hunts. Ann Barstow points out that "as early as 1489 ... the Swiss lawyer Ulric Molitor denied that witches cause illness or impotence, fly through the air to the sabbat, or are impregnated by the devil." Barstow notes further that Reginald Scott, a pioneer in empirical approaches to agriculture, challenged almost all the early modern beliefs about witches and even called attention to the idea that "woman-hatred [was] at the heart of the trials."[53] Uta Ranke-Heinemann called attention to the heroic stance of "Jesuit Friedrich von Spee, who despite the danger that he himself might be burned to death, argued against the trials."[54] The seeds of skepticism about the witch craze, though isolated and slow to catch on, had been planted by a small number of forward looking scholars.

A more pervasive kind of skepticism surfaced in the work of the French philosopher Michel de Montaigne. Montaigne, troubled by the religious wars of his day between Protestants and Catholics, turned his attention to the problems of epistemology with a special focus on how it is that people can feel so much certitude about their beliefs, particularly beliefs for which certitude is at best elusive. In a devastating critique of human beliefs and pretensions, Montaigne argued for the development of a kind of hypersensitivity to the shaky foundations of human knowledge.[55] He called attention to the limitations of the senses, lazy enslavement to habits, the effects of emotions on beliefs, and the powerful influence of social, religious, and cultural contexts. It is noteworthy, according to Montaigne, that when we compare ourselves to animals we do not always fare so well. It may turn out that dogs are more loyal than humans and that birds are better parents. Humans are unique in the animal kingdom for the shallow yet carefully developed and organized excuses we give for killing each other.[56] Montaigne asks nothing less than that we honestly confront ourselves with serious questions about what we really know. Is our so-called knowledge based merely on authority or on tradition? Can we trust reason or is reason itself conditioned by more fundamental intellectual habits of thought? Perhaps it is arrogance or pretension that is the fundamental human fault. Durant and Durant underscore Montaigne's importance because his skepticism "caught on" and deeply influenced other scholars, particularly Francis Bacon, and René Descartes, two of the founders of modern scientific thought in the early 1600s.[57]

The most direct and bold assault on belief in demons came from the rationalist philosopher Benedict Spinoza (1632–1677). Spinoza argued that such beliefs were naïve, superstitious, and complete nonsense. Spinoza embraced a coalescence between radical monotheism and monistic naturalism. God is one with nature and nature is one with God and there are no other intervening forces or entities such as demons, angels, ghosts, etc. Spinoza's philosophy opened the door to a thoroughgoing naturalistic psychology free from the operation of all transnatural forces whether they are presumed to be good or evil. For Spinoza, God was immanent in nature; not transcendent or radically other than nature. When humans study nature, they are studying God. If God is truly omnipotent and omnipresent, how could there be any other force. According to Spinoza, demons are nothing more than products of human imagination. Further, belief in demons has caused great mischief in the world.

The intellectual atmosphere was slowly shifting from a near exclusive emphasis on theological matters to a new interest in science and philosophy. There was less and less emphasis on demons partly because of a growing suspicion that demons, unlike the new physiology and neurology, do not really explain much, if anything. If there are demons, how, in specific detail, to they enter a body, where do they reside, how does the energy of a non-natural entity interact with the energetic system of a natural entity? The devastating and tragic personal, social, and cultural effects of the witch-hunts may also have contributed to a new openness to the promises of the scientific revolution. Still, for all the theoretical and practical problems associated with beliefs in demons as causal forces, such beliefs persist unabated in a scientific age and may even be enjoying a comeback in terms of the numbers of believers.

*****

Donald Viney calls attention to Voltaire's claim that "Never has there been a more universal empire than that of the devil."[58] Substantiation for such a claim is encountered in surprisingly widespread beliefs in the operation of demonic forces at the outset of the 21st century and the propagation of such beliefs by political leaders and major religious institutions with worldwide influence. Euteneuer has argued "In today's day and age, Satan is growing exponentially more powerful due to the enormity of human sinfulness," and goes on to note "Occult forces have been unleashed into our modern world like the emptying of a demonic Pandora's Box of unclean spirits."[59] Herein, lies a major and incommensurable difference, between science with its emphasis on the clear demonstrable effects of identifiable natural causes and those political and religious organizations that continue to promote beliefs in occult forces that cannot be captured by canonical scientific methodologies. A battle of worldviews in many quarters continues unabated.

Notes

1 See 1 Peter 5:8.
2 A Latin Proverb, quoted by Carl Sagan, *The Demon Haunted World: Science as a Candle in the Dark* (New York: Ballantine Books, 1996), 402.
3 Jacqueline L. Salmon, "Most Americans Believe in Higher Power, Poll Finds," *The Washington Post*, June 24, 2008.
4 Ed Stoddard, "Poll Finds more Americans Believe in Devil than Darwin," Posted November 29, 2007, http://uk.reuters.com/article/iduKN2922875820071129 (Accessed July 7, 2015).
5 Joseph P. Laycock, "Why are Exorcisms as Popular as Ever," Posted December 28, 2015, http://new republic.com/article/26607/exorcisms/popular/ever (Accessed January 1, 2016).
6 Thomas Euteneuer, *Exorcism and the Church Militant* (San Francisco: Ignatius, 2010), xxxii.
7 Nick Pisa, "Pope's Exorcist Squads Will Wage War on Satan," Posted December 29, 2007, http://www.dailymail.co.uk/news/article-504969/Popes-exorcist-squads-wage-war-Satan.html (Accessed January 1, 2016).
8 Euteneur, *Exorcism*, Chapter 6.
9 Michael W. Cuneo, *American Exorcism: Expelling Demons in the Land of Plenty* (New York: Broadway Books, 2001).
10 Isham Zulkipli, "Islamic Exorcism," Posted June 7, 2006, http://youtube.com/watch?v=YTEshwPppFM (Accessed July 7, 2015).
11 Sigmund Freud, *Civilization and its Discontents*, in *The Standard Edition of the Complete Psychological Works of Sigmund Freud*, ed. J. Strachey (London: Hogarth Press, 1961), Vol. 9, 55–145.
12 William H. McNeill, *Plagues and Peoples* (New York: History Book Club, 1976), 236.
13 Ibid., 237.
14 Eric M. Rogers, *Physics For the Inquiring Mind: The Methods, Nature, and Philosophy of the Physical Sciences* (Princeton, NJ: Princeton University Press, 1960), 344.
15 These differences have led Barney Beins to refer to physics and related fields as the hard sciences and to psychology and related fields as "the difficult sciences." Barney Beins, "Skeptical but Not Cynical: The Importance of Critical Thinking" (Harry Kirke Wolfe Distinguished Lecture, American Psychological Association presented at the April, 2014 meeting of the Rocky Mountain Psychological Association, Salt Lake City, UT).
16 Stephen Prothero, *God is Not One: The Eight Rival Religions that Run the World – and Why Their Differences Matter* (New York: HarperCollins, 2010), 41.

17 Elaine Pagels, *The Origin of Satan* (New York: Random House, 1995).
18 William James, *Some Problems of Philosophy* (Lincoln, NE: University of Nebraska Press, 1996), 138.
19 Donald Wayne Viney, *On Exorcising Demonology* (Unpublished manuscript, 2016).
20 Robert R. Reilly, *The Closing of the Muslim Mind* (Wilmington, DE: Robert R. Reilly, 2010), 114.
21 Ibid., 67.
22 Michael Santo, "Pat Robertson on Haiti Earthquake: Caused by Pact with the Devil," http://www.huliq.com/3257/90436/pat-robertson-haiti-earthquake-caused-pact-devil (Accessed May 18, 2016).
23 Heinrich Kramer and James Sprenger, *Malleus Maleficarum* (New York: Dover, 1971).
24 Ibid., xliv–xlv.
25 Ibid., 1.
26 Ibid.
27 Ibid., 85.
28 Ibid.
29 Ibid., 117–118.
30 Ibid., 89.
31 Ibid., 118.
32 Ibid., 148.
33 Ibid., 149.
34 Ibid., 221–222.
35 Peter De Rosa, *Vicars of Christ: The Dark Side of the Papacy* (New York: Crown, 1988), 443.
36 Ibid., 234
37 Ibid., 226.
38 Archival, experimental, and meta-analytic data strongly suggest that torture leads to resistance and falsehood rather that to high-quality information. See Herbert Wray, "The Science of Interrogation: Rapport, not Torture," http://www.psychologicalscience.org/index.php/news/were-only-human/the-science-of-interrogation-rapport-not-torture.html (Accessed March 20, 2015). The ethical debates about the participation of psychologists have generated debate and ethical failures; see the clear position of the American Psychological Association regarding psychologists' participation in enhanced interrogation techniques at American Psychological Association, "Position on Ethics and Interrogations." http://www.apa.org/ethics/programs/position/ (Accessed May 20, 2015).
39 See Sara Fischer, "Cheney Has No Regrets: I Would Do it Again in a Minute," http://www.cnn.com/2014/12/14/politics/dick-cheney-torture-report-meet-the-press/ (Accessed May 20, 2015). It is of interest that perceptions of treatment of suspected terrorists, including waterboarding, varied by religion. According to a December 11–14, 2014 *Washington Post–ABC News* Poll, White Evangelical Christians were less likely than nonreligious respondents to define treatment of terrorists as torture (39% and 72%, respectively defined treatment as torture); similarly, 69% of white Evangelical Christians believe this treatment was justified, compared to 41% of nonreligious respondents. See K. Pete, "Christians more Supportive of Torture than Non-Religious Americans," Posted December 16, 2014, http://www.democraticunderground.com/10025968626 (Accessed August 17, 2016).
40 Pär Anders Granhag, Aldert Vrij, and Christian A. Meissner, "Information Gathering in Law Enforcement and Intelligence Settings: Advancing Theory and Practice," *Applied Cognitive Psychology* 28, No. 6 (November–December, 2014), 815–816.
41 Jean Kellaway, *The History of Torture and Execution: From Early Civilization through Medieval Times to the Present* (Ludlow, UK: Thalamus Publishing, 2000).
42 Kramer and Sprenger, *Malleus*, 218.

43 Michael Streeter, *Witchcraft: A Secret History* (Hauppauge, NY: Quarto, Inc., 2002), 128.
44 Johann Weyer, *De Praestigiis Daemonum*, in *Witches, Devils, and Doctors in the Renaissance*, ed. George Mora (Binghamton, NY: Center for Medieval & Renaissance Studies, State University of New York at Binghamton, 1991), 324.
45 See Ernest Jones, *The Life and Work of Sigmund Freud*, Vol. 3 (New York: Basic Books, 1957), 422.
46 Johann Weyer, *De Praestigiis*, 324.
47 Ibid. In an introduction to *De Praestigiis Daemonum*, Mora et al. provide a very helpful overview of the life and times of Weyer. The section in the introduction on Weyer and Psychiatry (lxiii–lxxix) is especially useful. See especially lxix.
48 Ibid., lxxiv.
49 Irving Kirsch, "Demonology and the Rise of Science: An Example of the Misperception of Historical Data," *Journal of the History of the Behavioral Sciences* 14, No. 2 (April 1978), 155.
50 Kramer and Sprenger, *Malleus*, 107.
51 Bernard Peach, "Leviathan," in *World Philosophy Essays-Reviews of 225 Major Works*, Vol. 2, ed. Frank N. McGill (Englewood Cliffs, NJ: Salem Press, 1982), 839–846.
52 For more details on the specifics of Descartes' theory of movement see William Douglas Woody and Wayne Viney, *A History of Psychology: Emergence of Science and Applications*, 6th ed. (New York: Routledge, 2017), 175–177. Also see Julian Jaynes, "The Problem of Animate Motion in the Seventeenth Century," in *Historical Conceptions of Psychology*, eds. Mary Henle, Julian Jaynes, and John J. Sullivan (New York: Springer, 1973), 166–179.
53 Anne Llewellyn Barstow, *Witchcraze: A New History of the European Witch Hunts* (San Francisco: HarperCollins, 1994), 176–177.
54 Uta Ranke-Heinemann, *Eunuchs for the Kingdom of Heaven: Women Sexuality and the Catholic Church* (New York: Penguin, 1990), 230.
55 Michel de Montaigne, "Apology for Raimond Sebond," in *The Complete Essays of Montaigne*, Vol. 2, trans. Donald M. Frame (Garden City, NY: Doubleday, 1960).
56 Ibid.
57 Will Durant and Ariel Durant, *The Story of Civilization: Part VII The Age of Reason Begins* (New York: Simon & Schuster, 1961).
58 Donald Wayne Viney, *On Exorcising Demonology* (Unpublished Manuscript) 1.
59 Thomas Euteneuer, *Exorcism and the Church Militant*. See pages xxvi–xxxii.

5

SOUL AND BODY

> The heart is a spring, the nerves are strings, the joints are wheels
> Giving motion to the whole body.[1]
>
> It is the Nature of the body to be moved, as to place, directly by a spiritual nature.[2]

A chapter on soul and body underscores sharply contrasting conceptual schemes and incommensurable languages encountered in science and religion. Scientists, working within the constraints of naturalism, do not employ the word *soul* as a legitimate explanatory concept, but *soul* is ubiquitous in the languages of most faith communities and is generally taken as a real nonmaterial entity. Further, various concepts of the soul are central to a host of serious religious practices and understandings. Perhaps soul and body represent parallel universes of discourse without workable bridges. Stephen J. Gould spoke of science and religion as non-overlapping magisteria (NOMA).[3] Magisteria refers to an intellectual domain in which there is legitimate practical and theoretical teaching authority. According to NOMA, science and religion, and body and soul are thus parallel and each is legitimate in its own right.

Materialism and Idealism

In an article on Body and Soul, Mark Edmundson asks an interesting question: "Does the body still exist if we do not have souls?"[4] The question harks back to the contention by the Roman philosopher Plotinus (AD 205–270) that "Soul is not in the universe, on the contrary the universe is in the Soul."[5] The claim of Plotinus and the meanings of Edmundson's question are unpacked partly by a distinction between idealism and materialism. Idealism is the philosophical position that reality, as we know it in conscious experience, is of a mental nature. What Plotinus is saying is that things that are knowable, including knowledge of the physical world and knowledge of our body cannot be external to conscious mental processes. In other words, everything begins in conscious awareness—"the universe is in the soul." If there were no experience, no conscious awareness, there would be no world, no body. The materialist position, by contrast is that all real things are composed of matter in its various arrangements and movements. Thus, vague terms such as *mind* or *soul* are in fact nothing more than brain or brain processes. According to this position, mental processes are entirely dependent upon the workings of the brain.

What then can be gained by including a chapter on soul and body? As we proceed, it will be clear that there have been, and are, boundary issues between the two domains and these issues are difficult to ignore. Further, there is a history of encroachments of one domain into the other and competition, with practical consequences, for the legitimacy of specific explanatory schemes. This chapter opens with an exploration of the problem of motion. We then turn to an unlikely subject, the problem of the instantiation or infusion of the soul into the body. This is not a legitimate scientific topic, but scientific research in embryology has some surprising implications for older religious views on the problems of instantiation. The chapter closes with a brief examination of some surprisingly relevant tensions over the origins of sexuality.

The Problem of Motion

In the *Malleus Maleficarum* (the Hammer against Witches), Heinrich Kramer and James Sprenger, following the lead of Aristotle, note "it is the nature of the body to be moved, as to place, directly by a spiritual nature."[6] They express agreement with the commonly held belief of their day that even "the highest bodies, that is, the stars, are moved by spiritual essences."[7] So far as humans are concerned, Kramer and Sprenger claimed "the soul is the prime and chief cause of local motion in the body."[8] This view was echoed as late as the 18th century in vague claims that the soul is "the motor-power or life force of the human machine" along with even stronger claims that "the rational soul was the cause of all reflex or involuntary movements."[9] One of the most obvious things one can say about a corpse is that something has departed from it. What is that something? Is it the spirit, the soul, some unknown animating force? The term *psyche* derived from the Greek language was typically translated as spirit, mind, air, or soul. The term *air* is a reminder of another obvious characteristic of a corpse in that respiration or air has departed from the body. The inexplicable psyche, typically associated with mental activities such as consciousness and reflective self-awareness, intention, perception, memory, and sentience, was often invoked as an explanation for animate motion but the specific means by which such motion is generated remained shrouded in mystery. The early Greek philosopher Thales was troubled by the problem of motion. Was there a mechanical basis for movement or was there an animistic or unobservable spiritual force that accounts for movement? Thales apparently wondered whether magnets, because of their attractive and repulsive moving powers, possess some kind of soul.[10] Of course, motion, according to many religious views, is but the tip of the iceberg in the potential activities and powers of the soul.

The term *soul*, so prevalent in religious literature, often served as a translation of psyche. Such a translation follows many classical conventions. It is not surprising that European religious scholars in the Middle Ages translated the Greek word *psyche* as "soul"; such translations clearly fit their religious worldview. Later translators recognized the cognitive nature of psyche and were likely to translate it as mind or consciousness. Because science has moved into selected but limited domains explained by religious concepts of the soul, we attempt to minimize confusion across these domains, and therefore we translate the term *psyche* as "soul". Such a translation is employed simply as a means of contrasting and comparing scientific and religious explanations of selected phenomena. The term *soul*, as used in this chapter, is not intended as a reference to any detailed treatment of the topic encountered in specific religious orientations or denominations.

Histories of concepts of the soul explore questions such as its metaphysical nature, its destiny following the death of the body, the time of its instantiation in the body, its relation to mental activities, and its role in the motion of the body. The first two questions are clearly beyond the sphere and scope of science but there are scientific discoveries that now compete with explanations based on earlier religious concepts of the soul. The following materials will explore scientific contributions to the problem of motion that grew out of early experiments in neurology. In a word, we will see that the domain of the soul has been challenged or perhaps shrunk with the growth of selected scientific discoveries. Herein is a captivating and little recognized or understood arena for some of the most challenging and vexing tensions between science and religion, an arena that must not be neglected if we are to understand the history of relations between science and religion.

Mechanistic Approaches to Motion

For centuries animate motion was explained in terms of the operation of the soul, but such explanations have been challenged by the slow and measured development of purely mechanistic explanations of movement. Furthermore, early neurological research has extended those mechanistic perspectives to human and animal life. As noted earlier, science as it is understood in its classic pragmatic and paradigmatic expressions, does not consider animating spiritual or other supernatural forces that cannot be clearly tied to explicit identifiable connections in a chain of material events. Simply stated, there is not a scientific tool to confirm or evaluate the supernatural. Such a limitation does not rule out the existence of a spiritual realm; it simply assumes that such a realm is incompatible within the constraints of scientific methodology. The attitudes encountered in science are illustrated in a story William James told about the famous physicist James Clerk Maxwell. Even as a child, Maxwell would interrupt anybody offering a vague explanation with "Yes, but I want you to tell me the particular go of it."[11] Such a remarkable statement from a child captures the scientific spirit in a most economical manner. Early proto neurologists also wanted to know the particular go of it when it came to the problem of human and animal movement. Explanations of motion, as a product of the operation of a soul, are vague and unacceptable to those who love specific details or who want to know the specific detailed go of things.

René Descartes (1596–1650) was one of the first of the modern thinkers to become obsessed with the tensions between mechanistic explanations of movement and explanations based on non-material entities. His classic dualistic mind–brain position, known as interactionism, assumed the existence of an extended body *res extensa* and an un-extended thinking substance *res cogitans* (mind or soul). These two realities presumably interact in a way that appeals to common sense. Thinking appears to precede and direct movement. Additionally, events in the physical system such as an injury to the body influence mental processes. Though such a two-way interaction satisfies the requirements of naïve day-to-day experience, Descartes, like James Clerk Maxwell, wanted to know the "the particular go of it." Descartes' theory of the interaction of the soul and body raises some thorny issues. How does something that is only physical interact with something that is only mental? Where does this interaction occur? Descartes was fascinated with the details associated with these questions and his curiosity led him from the world of books to the world of the laboratory.

In an article titled "The Problem of Animate Motion in the Seventeenth Century," Julian Jaynes notes that Descartes was captivated by the automaticity or apparent "self-induced movement" of primitive moving toys, machines, and clocks.[12] In Descartes' day, there was a growing fascination with the building of ever more complex and entertaining statue-like figures capable of surprising movements and gestures. Such movements were made possible by the development of mechanisms and materials permitting the slow release of stored energy as in wind-up springs and other mechanical means. It was the age of the development of the pendulum clock and the invention of ever more complicated and versatile gears, belts, pulleys, and other means of transferring energy. Primitive hydraulic systems based on pressurized water running through pipes could be used to activate vanes or blades pitched at an appropriate angle such as the blades of a windmill. Water, wind, weights, and wind-up springs were used as sources of energy to drive increasingly intricate toys such as dancing dolls, moving statues, and machines that sometimes had practical utility. For example, windmills had long been used for pumping water or grinding grain, but now there were ever increasingly complex variations and extensions of some of the technologies used in the windmill.

According to Jaynes, Descartes was particularly captivated by artistically crafted statues installed in the grottos and fountains of the Royal Gardens in Paris. In his "Treatise on Man," Descartes marveled that the force of water moving under pressure through pipes is sufficient to drive the mechanisms that produced the elaborate movements of the statues.[13] Descartes believed that the mechanisms in human-made machines were uncovering the secrets of the hand of God in animal and human motion.[14] To be sure, the works of God as revealed in the intricacies of animal and human motion were far better crafted, and were more artistic, refined, and smooth than the crude movements observed in human-made machines.[15] Nevertheless, Descartes believed there were productive analogies between the workings of animal and human bodies and the mechanisms of moving machines. Thus, he allowed his imagination to be guided by possible continuities that might reveal the handiwork of God in one of the great mysteries of nature—how to account for animate motion.

Descartes studied major works on anatomy available to him in the early 1600s. He also conducted his own research on animal anatomy and physiology, observing connections between the brain, the spinal cord, and the rest of the body. Could it be that nerves or bundles of axons visible to the naked eye functioned somewhat like the water pipes in moving statues? Perhaps there were connections between all the nerves of the body and the ventricles or cavities in the brain that could possibly serve as storage tanks providing highly refined fluids that function much as the water in the pipes of moving statues. Descartes thought of these refined fluids as "animal spirits" that consist of miniscule extremely fast particles that move through the nerves like a fine wind. He compared the fine wind to the wind provided by the bellows of an organ that activates the mechanisms and structures in the pipes of the organ to produce music. Descartes believed there were fine strings that ran through the length of nerves and that there were valves at critical junctures that could be opened or closed via the strings or animal spirits to produce a great range of movements.

The complete picture of Descartes' mechanistic theory of movement is less important for our purposes here than the implications of his theory for comparisons of animals and humans and for the research programs that were subsequently generated by his assertions and predictions.[16] Essentially, Descartes' ideas proved wrong, but he inspired generations of scientists who followed him. His theories generated testable hypotheses that drove the next two generations of physiological research. The following are among his assertions and predictions:

1. A flexed muscle grows in mass because animal spirits flow from the ventricles of the brain through the nerve into the muscle. Thus, the apparent increase in size of the flexed muscle is attributable to its inflation by animal spirits.
2. Animals do not have pineal glands; this claim fit Descartes' assumptions that animals are purely mechanical, that only humans have souls, and therefore only humans need to have a place for the mind to interact with the body.

The pineal gland in humans, located roughly in the center of the head, is the only gland that is singular. All other glands exist in pairs. Thus, the pineal gland, because of its singularity and location was viewed as a habitation of the soul, though Descartes did not believe that the pineal gland was the exclusive locus for the operation of the soul in humans. He did say "when God unites a rational soul to this machine ... he will place its principal seat in the brain."[17]

3. The pineal gland in humans is richly supplied with nerves.
4. The pineal gland can move from side to side to send animal spirits through the nerves to the cortex in search of memories or associations.
5. The same nerve can handle both motor and sensory functions.
6. The speed of action within a nerve is almost instantaneous as when a string is pulled or extremely fast because of the flow of the rarefied animal spirits.

Descartes believed that all movement in animals is purely mechanical and many movements in humans are mechanical. Some movements in humans, however, result from the operation of *res cogitans*, the thinking substance that is closely tied to the pineal gland and that can be responsible for rational thought. If all movement in animals is mechanical, it follows that animals are mere machines without soul and comparable to the moving statues in the Royal Gardens. Descartes practiced dissection and vivisection claiming that animals, as machines, do not feel pain in the same way that humans do.[18] The cries and yelps of animals are but the rusty cogs or the stripped gears of a machine.

The Heuristic Value of Descartes' Theory

Some of the foregoing predictions or assertions are clearly subject to empirical tests and herein Descartes stands at the interface between religious and scientific explanations. In fact Descartes helped set the scientific agenda for the next 200 years as scholars from various disciplines set about the business of testing his claims. Nicolaus of Steno, sometimes known as Neils Stensen (1638–1682), a more accomplished anatomist than Descartes, quickly dismantled Descartes' assertions about the pineal gland. Animals do have pineal glands, the pineal gland is not richly supplied with nerves, and the pineal gland could not possibly move from side to side. Further, Stensen argued that concepts such as "animal spirits" are vague and unacceptable for science. Stensen brought the habitation of the soul in the pineal gland into question.[19] Another blow to Descartes' theory came later, when it was discovered that a pinealectomy might interfere with sleep patterns but is not fatal to intellectual or cognitive processes.

Further tests of Descartes' theory are encountered in the work of Jan Swammerdam (1637–1680). In his classic work *The Book of Nature*, he provided numerous clear demonstrations that a flexed muscle does not gain in mass.[20] Mass is simply redistributed in a flexed muscle. A muscle flexed under water does not displace any water. Swammerdam's demonstrations challenged Descartes' contention that a flexed muscle is filled with animal spirits.

There were additional problems. It had long been observed that movements in the form of reflex activity persist, in some cases, long after decapitation. In some animals such as turtles or snakes, and under some conditions, reflexes can be observed many hours following decapitation. If nervous conduction is extremely fast, why would post mortem reflexes persist for such lengthy periods?

Robert Whytt, following earlier experiments by Stephen Hales and Alexander Stuart, further demonstrated the role of the spinal cord in reflex activity. Whytt ran a hot wire through the length of the spinal cord of a decapitated frog. Immediately, all motion disappeared.[21] The outcome challenged Descartes' claim that the spinal cord is only a conduit for animal spirits.

As noted, Descartes proposed nearly instantaneous conduction from ventricles to muscles, but this claim could not be tested until the mid-19th century. The speed of conduction of a nervous impulse was finally measured in the 19th century by Hermann von Helmholtz (1821–1894) but the speed was much slower than anticipated. Today, the relatively slow speed of neural conduction is perceived as a central aspect of human and animal physiology; it remains difficult for readers in the 21st century to grasp the 19th century impact of Helmholtz's discovery. Edwin G. Boring declared that the work of Helmholtz had "brought the soul to time, as it were, measured what had been ineffable, actually captured the essential agent of mind in the toils of natural science."[22] Helmholtz made further contributions to mechanistic perspectives on movement when he argued for conservation of mass and energy in living systems as in other systems.[23] In other words, according to Helmholtz, there are no forces other than physical–chemical forces active in the living organism.

Descartes also believed a single nerve could mediate both motor and sensory functions, but it would later be discovered that motor and sensory functions were separate. A bundle of nerve axons may well include both sensory and motor nerves, but each individual nerve within the bundle is either motor or sensory.

In effect, Descartes was wrong on almost every count. But unlike earlier theorists, Descartes provided testable hypotheses for future generations of scholars. His productive errors were a powerful source of ideas and inspiration for subsequent researchers.

Descartes and his immediate successors increased the appetite of researchers for more intense investigations into the structure of the nervous system and the nature of animate motion. The 18th and 19th centuries witnessed a succession of discoveries that contributed to growing confidence that animal and human motion could be adequately explained by natural processes. Luigi Galvani (1737–1798), one of the pioneers in electrophysiology, demonstrated increased activity in frogs legs when the exposed nerves in the severed legs were activated by an electric charge. McHenry calls attention to increased and sometimes grotesque movements following electrical stimulation of the severed spine of criminals who had been decapitated.[24] During the French Revolution there had been numerous experiments on the heads and bodies of humans who had gone to their deaths on the guillotine. McHenry noted "The most telling effect of Galvani's work was its destruction of the outworn hypothesis of the nervous system's activation by the soul, by animal spirits, or by nerve fluid."[25]

The discovery of electrical activity in the nervous system fed growing beliefs in naturalism and, in the words of Rosenfield, "its bearings upon human physiology, no longer viewed animistically but as a science governed by normal laws of cause and effect."[26] Rosenfield, in her book *From Beast Machine to Man Machine*, details the discoveries in early scientific physiology and neurology that led to the dramatic new scientific alternatives to animism.[27] In 1757, just short of 100 years after the death of Descartes, Julien Offray de la Mettrie, in his book *Man a Machine*, challenged the idea that there was a qualitative gap between humans and the rest of the animal kingdom.[28] The mechanistic program initiated by Descartes for animals was now extended to humans. The 18th and 19th centuries witnessed an acceleration of discoveries on the relations of brain structures and their functions leading many researchers to the assumption that the mysteries of motion were best understood from a naturalistic perspective. Maybe there were no inherently unknowable energies, mystical entities, or mysterious forces responsible for the activities and behaviors of living creatures. The transition to such a conclusion was and still is extremely painful in many quarters, but the benefits and rewards, especially in the neurological and medical sciences, have been unprecedented.

The naturalistic accounts of movement do not negate the existence of possible transnatural realities such as the soul, but such accounts shrink the domain of the soul and suggest that motion, once explained in terms of the activities of the soul, can best be explained in terms of natural physical structures and functions. As noted previously, scientific findings can neither confirm nor deny the existence of supernatural entities. But, ongoing development of mechanistic explanations for movement has reduced the need to appeal to the supernatural as an explanation.

As an aside, Descartes' theory of animal and human motion is a case study in the vicissitudes of scientific methodology. Though Descartes' theory of animal and human motion proved wrong on almost every count, most of his assertions were stated in a form that made them amenable to empirical investigation. Empirical work showed clearly that animals do have pineal glands, that such glands are not richly supplied with nerves, that muscles could not possibly be inflated with animal spirits and so forth. A testable theory that fails to bear up under empirical scrutiny can nevertheless render an invaluable service to science by inspiring further research and providing motivation to pursue alternative theories. All scholars should strive to be so inspirationally wrong. Descartes' theory had heuristic value by generating an outpouring of work that provided the foundations for the new sciences of physiology and neurology.

Acceptance of naturalistic explanations in the life sciences may have been reinforced by 19th and 20th century successes in automation in the physical sciences and engineering. The 18th century was ushered in with the development of primitive steam engines. Major breakthroughs in steam engine technology, and most notably improvements by James Watt (1700–1800), led to the application of steam engines in boats, tractors, trains, and as power sources in factories.

The idea of automaticity has a long and dynamic ever-changing history. According to the *Oxford English Dictionary*, the word *auto* and the Medieval Latin word *automatus* refer to that which is self-induced or "by oneself." The term *automobile* (self-induced movement) captured the public imagination. A "horseless carriage" was almost beyond comprehension. Terms such as *autopsychic*, that which is induced by the spirit, mind, or soul, and *autochthonous*, from native soil, are encountered in early philosophical and theological literature. By the 18th century however, the term *auto*, increasingly referred to physical movement generated purely by identifiable natural processes. The die had been cast for strengthening similar understandings of movement in the life sciences. The term *auto* was increasingly used as a prefix for scientific terms such as automobile, *automatic, automatism, automation, autonomous*, and so forth.

The credibility of mechanical and scientific accounts of motion may also have been fed by rapid developments in artistic animation in the 19th and 20th centuries. Still life art was the norm from the earliest beginnings of art, but in the 19th century artists were experimenting with methods for the creation of the illusion of movement by presenting a rapid succession of simple pictures each occupying slightly different locations. Some of the earliest methods included "flip pages," a collection of flexible pages containing simple figures each drawn in slightly different locations from page to page. As one flipped rapidly through the pages, it appeared as if the simple figure moved from one location to another. The invention of the stroboscope in the early 1800s provided vastly improved techniques for the production of apparent motion. Apparent motion captured the public imagination and resulted in unprecedented advances in the entertainment industry. Nowhere is this better illustrated than in the Walt Disney's productions of Mickey Mouse movies and his classic production of *Snow White and the Seven Dwarfs*. Animation had entered a new era with talking figures and life-like story lines. Here was movement without classic notions of the soul, but "with soul" conceived in a more metaphoric sense.

A final note on Descartes is important and relevant to the overall theme of this book. Cottingham, Stoothoff, and Murdoch call attention to the wrenching emotional difficulties associated with his personal intellectual journey.[29] Descartes was a devout Catholic, eager to support his church and its teachings. At the same time, his love of reason and of clear and distinct ideas; in a word, his love of truth, brought him into conflict between the demands of his faith and the requirements and demands of reason and observation. His work underscored the challenge in reconciling religious and naturalistic accounts of human motion. There continue to be discoveries in neurology, psychology, and other brain sciences that challenge the role of the soul in the operation of mental processes. In a word, the domain of the soul has been limited by the growth of selected scientific discoveries. Herein, is a captivating and little recognized or understood arena for some of the most challenging and vexing tensions between science and religion. It is an arena that must not be neglected in informed discussions of the relations between science and religion.

The Problem of Instantiation

Belief in a soul that is a separate entity infused into the body and that possibly survives the death of the body results in numerous issues in faith communities. Ostensibly, such issues are of little significance to scientists as scientists and yet, as we have already seen, scientific discoveries sometimes have unintended implications for religious beliefs. In religious literature, one encounters a history of extensive debates about how and when the soul is instantiated or placed inside the body. The terms *besoul*, to be endowed with a soul, or *ensoul*, to infuse a soul into a body, have been common in religious literature. Surprisingly there are specific discoveries coming out of embryology and cloning studies that are relevant to old religious issues.

Some of the early theologians including St. Thomas Aquinas followed Aristotle's belief in successive animation (the belief that the soul is infused in the body sometime after conception) as opposed to simultaneous animation (the belief that the soul is infused at the moment of fertilization). Peter De Rosa calls attention to ancient beliefs that the embryo goes through stages from vegetative to animal and finally to human. He notes further that "the embryo became human at forty days for the male and eighty days for the female."[30] In recent years it has been assumed in many quarters that the soul is infused into the body at conception (when the sperm fertilizes the egg).

Psychogeny, literally the study of the origin of the soul, includes questions about the entrance of the soul into the body. Perspectives on psychogeny also include questions beyond the scope of science about the origin, locus, and nature of the soul prior to its union with the body. For example, before a soul is placed into a body does it have some residence and if so where does it reside? Further, by what means is a soul transferred from one location to another and once in the body, where does it reside? The term may not be acceptable to some theologians who believe that souls are gendered. Later, we will address that issue. In what follows, we will restrict our discussion to theories or assumptions about when instantiation takes place along with the discoveries in embryology that are relevant to that question.

Psychogenic Identity Theory

One theory of simultaneous animation is known as psychogenic identity theory. According to this theory there is a formal identity between the fertilized egg in the womb and the later fully self-conscious adult. The term *identity* cannot, of course, refer to any kind of one-to-one correspondence. The mature adult has linguistic, social, cultural, and psychological acquisitions that emerge gradually over time and that could not conceivably be tied, even loosely, to the fertilized egg. Identity in this context is of a much weaker nature, referring simply to a numerical relationship (one soul and one body). Kuhse and Singer, in their work on embryo experimentation, identify a major problem in the following way: "the zygote that gave rise to me and I, the adult, are not the same individual—the former is a unicellular being totally devoid of consciousness, whereas I am a conscious being consisting of many millions of cells."[31] Though identity theory enjoys widespread acceptance, it is not without troubling problems that could not easily have been anticipated prior to the development of modern scientific work, especially in the field of embryology.

As noted, psychogenic identity theory is associated with simultaneous animation so that the soul is infused when the egg is fertilized by the sperm. At that point, according to the theory, there is one soul and one body. We now know however, that cell division begins quickly after fertilization and that each of the early stem cells has omnipotentiality sometimes referred to as totopotentiality. Thus, any cell in the developing morula or blastocyst (the primitive colony of cells) is capable of serving as the building block for any body organ. It is also known that early in cell division, say somewhere around the sixth day, it is possible to cut the colony of cells in half and produce identical twins. This sometimes occurs naturally, but it is possible now to do it surgically.[32] Prior to such a surgical division, the colony of cells can be characterized as one soul infused at conception and one body, but now on the sixth day after conception, we surgically cut the colony in half so that there will be two bodies that can grow into fully developed offspring. One may now ask whether both bodies have souls and, if so, it appears that the second soul would have to be infused after conception supporting the theory of successive animation. The existence of a second soul in this situation argues against the contention that conception is the exclusive time of instantiation. This whole line of argument is by no means trivial as it bears significantly on deeply divisive contemporary moral issues and some church doctrines with strong theoretical and practical implications.

There are not only scientific and religious questions. The timing of instantiation sits at the heart of the current policy and legal debates about some forms of birth control. For example, Bob Beauprez, a 2014 gubernatorial candidate in Colorado, stated his opposition to state funding for IUDs, a form of birth control that blocks implantation of a fertilized egg in the uterus.[33] Beauprez referred to IUDs as aborifacients, devices that end a pregnancy after it has occurred. The American College of Obstetricians and Gynecologists, along with the U.S. Federal Drug Administration, defines IUDs as contraceptives that prevent rather than end pregnancy. This dispute rests on definitions of pregnancy and conception which in turn center on questions of timing and instantiation.

Another challenge with simultaneous animation encountered in psychogenic identity theory is illustrated in the occurrence of chimeras. In such cases, there are two colonies of cells developing simultaneously, but separately in the uterus; these two blastocysts could become fraternal twins, but with chimeras something else happens. The two colonies of cells, each presumably with a psyche or soul, float together and fuse to become a single individual with two sets of chromosomes. According to psychogenic identity theory, the two individual colonies of cells were animated (besouled) at conception so from a numerical standpoint there are two souls and two bodies. In some cases, however, the two morulas float together and fuse to become one organism known as a chimera. If the chimera represents one soul and one body, it is by no means inconsequential to ask what happened to the second soul? The theoretical question is highly significant and requires an honest answer partly because of the extreme intensity of the commitment in some quarters to the absolute truth of simultaneous animation and identity theory.

Psychogenic Emergentism

Another approach to questions of psychogeny surfacing out of belief in successive animation is psychogenic emergentism, the belief that souls develop gradually along with the development of the body. In other words, there may be very little spirit or soul present prior to the development of a heart beat or consciousness, but with time there are distinct features emerging that bespeak of a spirited or conscious being. The point is illustrated further in the awareness of a newborn compared with the awareness of say, a four month old baby who now focuses intently on objects in the environment, recognizes faces, laughs, coos, and imitates. Psychogenic emergentism, as opposed to psychogenic identity theory, argues that animation is not instantaneous and certainly not simultaneous with the union of two physical entities: the sperm and the egg. Some psychogenic emergentists may argue for primitive psyche to emerge with a fertilized egg; others may argue that an egg and a sperm each possesses, and maintains boundaries and their own internal states and that each entity has some primitive psyche before conception. In contrast with psychogenic identity theory, psychogenic emergentism postulates that there are literally millions of acquisitions in prenatal and postnatal development including language development, culture, socialization, education, aptitudes, religious and political contexts, and geography that define us and that in the end reflect the inner person, the definition of who we are. According to psychogenic emergentism, the soul can grow with the body and, to extend these ideas to their logical conclusions, can fade with dementia, injury, or other events.

Clearly there are different moral and religious implications associated with psychogenic identity theory and emergentism.[34] Briefly, by definition, psychogenic identity theory equates the moral status of a fertilized egg with that of a fully conscious human being with long held and deep ties to friends and family members including children, spouses, and others. These beliefs have important practical consequences. In some religions, belief and practice dictates preference for the life status of the fertilized egg over that of the fully sentient mother. In some religions there is a strongly held belief that a baby who dies prior to baptism is in danger of eternal damnation. Accordingly, debates over complicated deliveries have raged around the extent to which a mother's life should be put at risk to assure, not that her baby will live and thrive, but that her baby may survive at least long enough to be baptized.[35] Unlike psychogenic identity theorists, psychogenic emergentists value acquired biological complexities over the simplicities of the fertilized egg, but at the other end of life, a psychogenic emergentist can value elderly deteriorating adults less than adults in the noonday of their consciousness. As we stated elsewhere, "Psychogenic Emergentism runs the risk of reducing value and worth to their instrumental dimensions and ignoring their intrinsic dimensions."[36] There are vexing moral issues surrounding the instantiation issue for both psychogenic emergentists and psychogenic identity theorists so there is much work to be done to shed light on this extremely complicated problem. Perhaps neither side occupies the high moral ground.

The Origins of Sex and Gender

There was a major breakthrough in the scientific account of sex determination in 1905 when Nettie Maria Stevens (1861–1912) and Edmund Beecher Wilson (1856–1939) independently discovered the XY sex determination system that operates in humans and most animals. Their work was a major breakthrough in understanding the role of XX and XY chromosomes in the biological origins of the sex of offspring. The discoveries of Stevens and Wilson suggested a probabilistic and naturalistic basis for sex determination along with hints about future possibilities for parental control of the sex of offspring. Such work is in stark contrast with earlier theological debates about the role of soul in the determination of sex and gender.

There had been centuries of theological disputes about whether souls were gendered. Were there male and female souls and, if so, how does a gendered soul influence the development of the physical structures associated with males and females? Further, if the soul is an organizing principle in the determination of sex and gender, how are we to account for sex in animals that presumably are not besouled? Still another problem centered on the origins of people who are transgender, intersex, or who feel they are simply outside of male or female categories. Popular interest in gendered souls is manifested in extensive online discourses exploring a great range of theologies and problems such as whether a soul departing the body at death retains the sexual identity that it had in life. We mention these discourses simply to highlight another arena in which scientific and naturalistic explanations are in sharp contrast with a great many religious beliefs. We return in more detail to questions of sex and gender in Chapters 8, 9, and 10.

*****

Religious concepts such as spirit and soul are alien to scientific ways of thinking, but remain integral to the belief systems encountered in a great many faith communities. Science has extended and expanded its naturalistic investigations into arenas once regarded as the exclusive domain of the soul. As a result, naturalistic explanations now compete with longstanding religious views. This encroachment of science into territories once dominated by religion serves as a basis for increasing conflict or, on the other hand, for possible synthesis or creative accommodations.

For all their successes and benefits to date, the brain sciences have little more than scratched the surface of our understandings of the workings of that mysterious province we refer to variously as mind, soul, or spirit. We are spirited creatures and it often remains meaningful in literary, poetic, philosophical, psychological, social, and religious settings to speak of the mind or the soul. The meanings of these terms, however, are changing with the advance of science and are now increasingly understood at new and different levels of abstraction. If such terms have lost their status as specific entities, they nevertheless continue to point to and suggest emergent or transcending qualities not easily captured in the workshops of neuroscience where the focus is on the important underlying details of the machinery of the brain.

Notes

1 See Bernard Peach, "Leviathan," in *World Philosophy Essays Reviews of 225 Major Works*, Vol. 2, ed. Frank N. McGill (Englewood Cliffs, NJ: Salem Press, 1982), 839–846.
2 Heinrich Kramer and James Sprenger, *Malleus Maleficarum* (New York: Dover 1971), 107.
3 Stephen Jay Gould, *Rocks of Ages: Science and Religion in the Fullness of Life* (New York: Ballantine, 1999), esp. Chapter 2.
4 Mark Edmundson, "Body and Soul," *Hedgehog Review: Critical Reflections on Contemporary Culture* 17, No. 2 (Summer 2015), 38.
5 Plotinus, *The Enneads*, Vol. 5, trans. Stephen MacKenna (London: Faber and Faber, 1956), 411.
6 Kramer and Sprenger, *Malleus*, 107.
7 Ibid.
8 Ibid.
9 See Lawrence C. McHenry, Jr., *Garrison's History of Neurology* (Springfield, IL: Charles C. Thomas, 1969), see pp. 112 and 131.
10 Geoffrey Stephen Kirk and John Earl Raven, *The Presocratic Philosophers: A Critical History with a Selection of Texts* (Cambridge: Cambridge University Press, 1962), 96.
11 William James, *Pragmatism* (Cambridge, MA: Harvard University Press, 1975), 95.
12 Julian Jaynes, "The Problem of Animate Motion in the Seventeenth Century," in *Historical Conceptions of Psychology*, eds. Mary Henle, Julian Jaynes, and J. J. Sullivan (New York: Springer, 1973), 170.

13 René Descartes, "Treatise on Man," in *Philosophical Writings of Descartes*, Vol. 1, eds. John Cottingham, Robert Stoothoff, and Dugald Murdoch (Cambridge: Cambridge University Press, 1985), 100.
14 Ibid., 99.
15 Ibid.
16 More detailed accounts of Descartes' views are set forth in his "Treatise on Man" and in Jaynes' article on "The Problem of Animate Motion in the Seventeenth Century."
17 Descartes, "Treatise on Man", 102.
18 Domenico Bertoloni Meli, "Early Modern Experimentation on Live Animals," *Journal of the History of Biology* 46, No. 2 (Summer 2013), 199–226.
19 See William Douglas Woody and Wayne Viney, *A History of Psychology: Emergence of Science and Applications*, 6th ed. (New York: Routledge, 2017), 178.
20 Jan Swammerdam, *The Book of Nature*, trans. Thomas Flloyd (London: C. G. Seyffert, 1758).
21 Lawrence C. McHenry, *Garrison's History of Neurology* (Springfield, IL: Charles C. Thomas, 1969), 114.
22 Edwin G. Boring, *A History of Experimental Psychology*, 2nd ed. (New York: Appleton-Century-Crofts, 1950), 124.
23 Ibid., 127.
24 McHenry, *Garrison's History*, 124.
25 Ibid., 127.
26 Leonora Cohen Rosenfield, *From Beast Machine to Man Machine: Animal Soul in French Letters from Descartes to LaMettrie* (New York: Octagon, 1968), 29.
27 Ibid.
28 Julien Offray de la Mettrie, *Man a Machine* (LaSalle, IL: Open Court, 1912).
29 John Cottingham, Robert Stoothoff, and Dugald Murdoch (eds.), *The Philosophical Writings of Descartes*, Vol. 1 (Cambridge: Cambridge University Press, 1985), 79.
30 Peter De Rosa, *Vicars of Christ: The Dark Side of the Papacy* (New York: Crown Publishers, 1988), 374.
31 Helga Kuhse and Peter Singer, "Individuals, Humans and Persons: The Issue of Moral Status," in *Embryo Experimentation: Ethical, Legal and Social Issues*, eds. Peter Singer, Helga Kuhse, Stephen Buckle, Karen Dawson, and Pascal Kasimba (Cambridge: Cambridge University Press, 1993), 66.
32 In dairy cattle, morulas have been split as many as eight ways with each of the eight placed into a host cow. The result is eight genetically identical calves. See George. E. Seidel Jr. and R. Peter Elsden, *Embryo Transfer in Dairy Cattle* (Milwaukee, WI: Hoard & Sons, 1997).
33 John Frank, "Bob Beauprez's IUD Remark in Debate Generates Controversy," *Denver Post* (October 1, 2014).
34 For a discussion of moral implications of identity theory and emergentism see Wayne Viney and William Douglas Woody, "Psychogeny: A Neglected Dimension in Teaching the Mind–Brain Problem," *The Teaching of Psychology* 22, No. 3 (October 1995), 173–177.
35 Uta Ranke-Heinemann, *Ennuchs for the Kingdom of Heaven Women, Sexuality, and the Catholic Church* (New York: Penguin, 1991), 306–311.
36 Viney and Woody, "Psychogeny," 176.

6
EVOLUTION

> *I regard evolution to be the greatest menace to civilization in the world today.*[1]
>
> *Evolution is a fact, like apples falling out of trees.*[2]

At the outset of the 21st century evolution remains the subject of particularly widespread and often bitter tensions between scientific and selected but very large religious communities. These tensions are by no means benign and, as we will see, easily rise to the level of intellectual warfare as defined by the criteria outlined in Chapter 1. The intensity of the rhetoric over evolution is illustrated by Congressman and physician Paul Broun from Georgia who declared "all that stuff I was taught about evolution, and embryology, and the big bang theory, all that is lies straight from the pit of hell."[3] In their scholarly book *Evolution, Creationism, and the Battle to Control America's Classrooms*, Berkman and Plutzer repeatedly employ the language of warfare with expressions such as "battle of ideas," "hot war," "evolution-creation wars," and "front lines."[4] Berkman and Plutzer refer to court cases, curriculum control, and "assortive hiring" of teachers as marks of the conflict.[5] The intensity and breadth of contemporary conflicts over creationism and evolution undoubtedly feed the public perception of intellectual warfare between science and theology or science and religion far more than the early books embracing the warfare thesis by Stanley Draper and Andrew Dickson White.

Over 150 years have passed since the publication in 1859 of Charles Darwin's classic book *On the Origin of Species*. Though the great body of the scientific community is now informed and guided by evolution, widespread popular controversy still rages over the theory and its implications. Numerous public opinion polls continue to show that a majority (57% to 68%) of Americans prefer that creationism be taught in public schools along with evolution.[6] Several polls show that a significant minority of Americans (33% to 40%) favor teaching creationism instead of evolution.[7] Paul Froese and Christopher Bader, in their book *America's*

Four Gods, provide evidence that a clear majority of Americans who believe in authoritative or benevolent Gods emphatically reject the idea that humans have a common ancestry with other primates.[8] According to a Gallup Poll conducted in December of 2010, 52% of Republicans and 34% of Democrats believe God created humans in their present form within the last 10,000 years. Level of education also contributed to the variance in this survey. Forty-seven percent of those with a high school education or less, compared with 22% of those with post-graduate education, believed God had created humans in their present form within the last 10,000 years.[9]

Though conflict between scientists and selected Christian communities has been most visible in the United States, there is now growing evidence of tensions over evolution and religion in the Islamic faith. For example, Dr. Usama Hasan, despite his status as an Iman, Fellow of the Royal Astronomical Society, and physics lecturer, received death threats from Islamic conservatives following a lecture emphasizing compatibilities between evolution and the Islamic faith. Dr. Hasan was forced to express regrets and to issue retractions for some of the points he made in his lecture.[10] It will be recalled that death threats were among the marks of intellectual warfare outlined in Chapter 1. The growing number of websites devoted to Islam and evolution suggests that, like many Christians, Muslims are deeply divided over evolution and its implications. In general, many Muslim scholars contend that Muslims are free to believe in an old earth so long as the supremacy and activity of God is recognized in the overall direction of history. Herein, however, is the rub. Natural selection, embraced by Darwin and the great majority of scientists, emphasizes accidents, contingency, chance, and the centrality of identifiable natural causes in the flow of all biological and physical events. Richard Dawkins, citing an article in the *Guardian*, tells of Muslim medical students in London distributing leaflets critical of evolution.[11]

With growing interest in the Islamic world in the biomedical sciences, we may expect growing and often heated discussions of evolution and its implications for religious belief. Salman Hameed, a leading scholar on science in Muslim societies, has observed that many Muslims agree "the age of the earth does not lie in the Qur'an."[12] Accordingly, Muslims may be able to avoid battles over the age of the earth that continue to beset many American Christian communities. Hameed goes on, however, to note that the "vast majority of Muslims ... reject human evolution outright."[13] Such rejection is fueled by beliefs encountered in many Muslim as well as Christian traditions in a single act of creation resulting in a human form mirroring the image of God and thus assumed to be stable over time. Such beliefs clearly run counter to the evolutionary emphasis on ever-changing morphologies and functions resulting from chance mutations and genetic adaptations to environmental demands. In an article in *Science*, Hameed calls attention to Islamic groups that are informed by the Intelligent Design

Movement, but overall, as in the United States, there is considerable variability among Muslims regarding their stance on evolution and creation.[14]

In what follows, we explore the evidence of the warfare thesis in current creationist–evolution debates and then examine major substantive differences that may contribute to possible continuing intellectual warfare between creationist theories and evolutionary thought.

Evidence in Support of the Warfare Thesis

The marks of intellectual warfare in the creation–evolution controversy reveal a wide range of strategies including: demonstrations, sermons on college campuses against evolution, home schooling, legislative initiatives, judicial activities resulting from legislation, founding of private schools, creationists booths in county fairs, attempts to win membership on school boards sometimes through stealth tactics, and attempts to influence the selection of textbooks. Recent years have also witnessed the development of museums and dissemination of creationist pamphlets and other literature in national parks and public museums that dispute canonical scientific interpretations offered by secular institutions. In what follows, we briefly review some selected but clearly visible examples of these activities in the struggles between creationism and evolution.

Legislative and Judicial Activities

The classic early example of attempts to control via legislative and judicial activities is found in the Tennessee "Butler Act" passed on March 13, 1925. The act declared that it would be unlawful for teachers in publically supported schools "to teach any theory that denies the story of the Divine Creation of man as taught in the Bible, and to teach instead that man has descended from a lower order of animals."[15] Clearly the act, like many state legislative actions to follow, was intended to control educational activities through legislation.

The legal test of the restrictions imposed by the Butler Act played out in the well-known and celebrated Scopes trial in Dayton, Tennessee in the summer of 1925.[16] Tennessee science teacher John Scopes was accused of violating the Butler Act by teaching evolution in his high school science class. Scopes had been assured he would be defended by the America Civil Liberties Union and thus agreed to participate in a legal test of the law. The trial itself turned into a highly publicized national media circus event pitting Christian conservative and fundamentalist religious leaders against scientists and liberal religious leaders who saw no conflict between evolution and religion. The public appeal and glamor of the trial was enhanced all the more when popular politician William Jennings Bryan agreed to work with the prosecution. The drama reached a fever pitch when famous trial lawyer Clarence Darrow agreed to work with the defense.

The defense hoped to show that the Butler Act was unconstitutional because it favored a particular religious interpretation of human origins and thus violated the First Amendment and undermined the academic freedom of John Scopes. Judge John T. Raulston, however, imposed the narrowest possible interpretation of the purpose of the trial by restricting testimony to the bare essentials of the Butler Act focusing exclusively on whether Scopes had violated the requirements of the act. Accordingly, nationally and internationally known expert scientific witnesses for the defense were barred from testifying. The upshot was that Scopes was found guilty and fined one hundred dollars. A subsequent appeal to the Tennessee Supreme Court failed.[17] The Butler Act remained as a Tennessee state statute for 42 years until it was repealed in 1967 by Democratic Governor Buford Ellington.[18]

The trial itself reinforced the public perception of a deep and pervasive conflict between science and religion. It also energized legislative efforts in many other states to restrict or ban the teaching of evolution in tax-supported educational institutions. The trial also brought national and international publicity to Dayton, Tennessee, often characterizing the inhabitants of the town, along with much of the south, as willfully ignorant and anti-scientific. The publicity continues in museums in Dayton, in annual re-enactments of the trial, and in numerous stage and film reproductions of the so-called Scopes Monkey Trial.[19]

In 1928, just three years following the Tennessee Butler Act and the Scopes trial, the state of Arkansas passed a statute forbidding the teaching of human evolution in state supported public schools including tax-supported universities. The Arkansas law was unique in two ways: first it was initiated following the results of a general election held in June of 1928 and passed by nearly 60% of the voters.[20] Second, the constitutionality of the Arkansas law would ultimately find its way to the United States Supreme Court in a case known as *Epperson v. Arkansas*. The statute had been on the books for nearly 40 years before it was finally challenged. Susan Epperson, a high school biology teacher who was teaching at Little Rock High School in the 1965–1966 school year found herself caught between the restrictions of the long-standing state statute forbidding the teaching of human evolution and a textbook adopted by the school that included a chapter on evolution. As a result she filed suit with the assistance and financial support of several organizations including the American Civil Liberties Union (ACLU). She sought nothing less than the overturning of the statute forbidding the teaching of evolution. This was a bold move, especially in view of the fact that the statute had been initiated by a majority vote of the citizens of Arkansas. A lower court sided with Epperson, but the Arkansas Supreme Court overturned the ruling of the lower court. In 1968 The U.S. Supreme Court, hearing the case fully 40 years after the establishment of the Arkansas statue, came down with a landmark ruling. The Supreme Court found that the Arkansas statute was unconstitutional because it was clearly motivated by an agenda to favor a particular religious doctrine. The statute was thus at odds with the First Amendment of the Constitution because the state was clearly establishing a religious point of view.

The ruling of the U.S. Supreme Court in *Epperson vs. Arkansas* forced a change in the strategy of creationists. It was now clear that the courts would not uphold an outright ban on the teaching of evolution, so the new strategy focused on "equal time" or "balanced treatment" of evolution and creationism. Such "equal time" or "balanced treatment" was to be initiated in science classes. Immediately there were legal challenges resulting from legislation for "equal time." An early test was provided by *Daniel v. Waters*, argued before the 6th U.S. Circuit Court of Appeals in 1975. The court struck down a law in Tennessee requiring that theories of human origins set forth in biology textbooks used in tax supported public schools must include an equal emphasis on the Genesis account of creation. The court ruled that the law was a clear violation of the First Amendment. The law, as stated, elevated an account of human origins based on a single religious position and gave this account equal status with the large body of scientific research on the topic.

Twelve years following the ruling in *Epperson v. Arkansas*, the U.S. Supreme Court would once again enter the fray in a case known as *Edwards v. Aguillard*. The case centered on a Louisiana law that required balanced treatment of evolution and "creation science." The expression "creation science" was employed to lend credibility to creationism and to attempt to show that it is on equal scientific footing with evolution. According to the law, a classroom presentation of either of the two "scientific theories" (evolution or "creation science") must be accompanied by equal time devoted to the other theory. The Supreme Court treated the Louisiana law as a ruse designed to enfranchise a religious interpretation of human origins. In a seven to two decision, the court overturned the Louisiana law, though Chief Justice William Rehnquist and Associate Justice Antonin Scalia dissented from the majority opinion as they bought into the claim that the Louisiana proposal would protect academic freedom. Seventy-two Nobel Prize winners declared in an *Amicus Brief* that creation science is a religious and not a scientific position.[21]

The action of the court in *Epperson v. Arkansas* and in *Edwards v. Aguillard* contributed to another change in the strategy of the creationists. It was now clear that the courts would not ban the teaching of Darwinian evolution, nor would they support equal time or balanced treatment of evolution and creationism in science classes. The new strategy attempted to promote the more "neutral concept" of "intelligent design" in contrast with earlier expressions linking the origins of the world to a specific Christian or Biblical account. Intelligent design (ID) preserves the central vision of creationism with its emphasis on purpose and direction in nature, but avoided direct reference to the Bible or to a specific designer or creator. Intelligent design could, however, be construed as entirely consistent with religious views on the origin of the world. Predictably, a test of ID v. evolution with its emphasis on natural causality, would find its way into the courts.

A pivotal test case on evolution and ID surfaced following a 2004 decision by the Dover, Pennsylvania School District to require that information about ID be included as an alternative to evolution in ninth grade biology classes. Students were also to be exposed to materials that raised questions about the adequacy of evolutionary explanations. Six of nine members of the Dover Board of Education voted in favor of the requirement, but the remaining three members resigned in protest. Creationists who had no background in education or science temporarily filled the positions vacated by board members who resigned. Science teachers in the district refused to present the materials challenging evolution and in support of ID required by the Board of Education. As a result of the Board's action, 11 parents headed by Tammy Kitzmiller, a single mother, initiated legal proceedings. The parents were supported by the ACLU, Americans United for the Separation of Church and State, and by the Pepper Hamilton law firm. The case, known as *Kitzmiller et al. v. Dover School District*, was tried in the U.S. District Court for the Middle District of Pennsylvania before Judge John E. Jones, a Republican who had been appointed by George W. Bush.

It was clear from the beginning that the outcome of the trial would turn on whether ID theory was science or a derivative of creationism dressed in new language. In early discussions, conservative Dover School Board members repeatedly spoke of the need to teach creationism and to bring Christianity back to the classroom. However, as the agenda of the board members matured and as the possibility of a lawsuit appeared imminent, the language employed in meetings quickly shifted from "creationism" to ID. The term *creationism* would obviously suggest a narrow gauged religious theory and would thus be a violation of the first amendment. The abrupt change in language, however, presented insurmountable difficulties. Though the records of early Board meetings were destroyed, numerous witnesses and journalists who attended Board meetings reported on their observations that early discussions were laced with creationist language. Nevertheless, in trial, some of the Board members perjured themselves by denying they had ever used the term *creationism*.

The trial included some of the most prominent experts testifying in support of the plaintiffs and the defendants. Unlike the famous Scopes Monkey Trial, Judge Jones permitted the broadest possible legal approach to the problem. Michael J. Behe, professor of biochemistry at Lehigh University and well-known author of *Darwin's Black Box*, argued for intelligent design supported by his belief that some structures are too complex to have come about by blind chance or by natural selection. Kenneth Miller, professor of Biology at Brown University and author of *Finding Darwin's God*, provided alternative interpretations for Behe's complexity thesis and argued that ID is not science because it includes untestable hypothetical causes that operate outside the natural order of things. Edward Humes, in his book *Monkey Girl*, noted "The real star in this forty-day trial would be science" as there was a dazzling display of "transitional fossils" that refuted many of the claims of creationism.[22] Pivotal testimony was also provided by philosopher Barbara Forrest, co-author with biologist Paul R. Gross of *Creationism's Trojan Horse: The Wedge of Intelligent Design*. Forrest's testimony was devastating in many ways as it traced the political and religious roots of ID theory along with the strategies for using ID as a wedge to challenge evolution. Such testimony raises questions as to whether ID, as it is currently known, was really born in honest scientific work or was it basically born in, and motivated by, religious ideology.

The rulings of Judge Jones were set forth in a detailed and carefully constructed 139 page document issued on December 20, 2005.[23] Based on evidence presented at the trial, Judge Jones concluded, among other things, that the ID movement is a blatantly obvious offshoot of creationism, the ID policy set forth by the Dover School Board violated the establishment Clause of the U.S. Constitution, and that ID theory is not science. Jones took no position on the "true theory" of the origins of life, but restricted his conclusions to what is appropriate classroom content for science classes as judged by canonical scientific epistemology.

In a scathing indictment, Judge Jones concluded further

> The citizens of the Dover area were poorly served by the members of the Board who voted for the ID policy. It is Ironic that several of these individuals, who so staunchly and proudly touted their religious convictions in public, would time and again lie to cover their tracks and disguise the real purpose behind the ID policy.[24]

It was also pointed out that several of those who voted for the ID policy were abysmally ignorant regarding the details of ID theory.

In recognition of the depth of the emotions and the deep divisions within the Dover community and within the nation, Judge Jones predicted that those who disagreed with his ruling would accuse him of being an activist Judge.[25] He argued, however, that his was not an activist court and that the only activism associated with the case was that of the

> ill-informed faction on a school board, aided by a national public interest law firm eager to find a constitutional test case on ID, who in combination drove the Board to adopt an imprudent and ultimately unconstitutional policy. The breathtaking inanity of the Board's decision is evident when considered against the factual backdrop which has now been fully revealed through this trial.[26]

As he predicted, Jones was subsequently accused of egregious judicial errors.[27] Additionally, according to David Humes, author of *Monkey Girl*, Jones, in the aftermath of the trial, received "death threats from the zealots of the 'culture of life.'"[28] Lauri Lebo, in her book *The Devil in Dover* called attention to hate mail directed at Tammy Kitzmilller including death threats against her daughters.

Lebo further illustrated the breadth and intensity of feelings after the trial by calling attention to the strongly worded comments of conservatives such as Phyllis Schlafly, Bill O'Reilly, and Ann Coulter.[29] Following the election of a more moderate school board in Dover, Pat Robertson, as quoted by Lebo, said "If they have future problems in Dover, I recommend they call on Charles Darwin. Maybe he can help them."[30]

The foregoing materials represent a small sample of well-coordinated, shifting and creative strategies designed to weaken, destroy, or control evolutionary thought. As noted earlier, such activities constitute one important mark of intellectual warfare. As we shall see, however, the persistent efforts of creationists to confront evolution are by no means restricted to attempts to control classroom content in public schools. As we have seen, judicial rulings have not gone well for creationists in recent years. As a consequence one could reasonably conclude that the number of judicial confrontations might diminish in coming years, but there is evidence against such a conclusion. Simon Brown, in an article in *Church and State* has pointed to evidence of increasing pending anti-evolution legislation since 2010.[31] There may also be increases in efforts of creationists to establish private schools, theme parks, and privately supported museums. Another possibility is that there will be yet another change in the legal strategy of creationists including legislative requirements to simply point to possible weaknesses in evolutionary theory. Still another possible development is that the march of scientific knowledge will speak with such clear evidence that the issue, like earlier battles over geocentrism and heliocentrism, will gradually die out.

Educational Efforts

In recent years there have been continuing efforts to introduce creationist interpretations of natural phenomena in public schools and textbooks. In addition, creationists have attempted to influence museum displays, and to include their materials in the science sections of bookstores in national parks in the United States. An example was provided by controversy over the appropriate location for Tom Vail's book titled *Grand Canyon: A Different View*.[32] Vail's book, beautifully illustrated with color photographs by Charly Heavenrich, provides a creationist account of the origin and development of the Grand Canyon. Brief supportive sections by 23 creationists are included in the text. Technical arguments in support of creation theory are sparse, but Biblical verses and theological statements, some unrelated or only remotely related to evolution, abound throughout the book. There are also numerous comparisons between the beliefs of secular scientists and creationists. For example, one contributor, Tasman Walker observes, "Before we can properly understand geology, we need to know the earth's history. Unlike secular geologists, creationist geologists don't need to speculate about history because we accept the eyewitness accounts of past events, preserved in a reliable written record – the Bible."[33] One of the issues was whether Vail's book should be located in the science section of a bookstore run by the National Park Service. The presence of the book in the bookstore is not an issue, but it is argued that the book belonged possibly in an inspiration section because it contradicts canonical geological science by making the claim that the Grand Canyon was quickly carved out during Noah's flood.

There are numerous creationist museums in the United States, but the most ambitious museum project is encountered in the Creationist Museum located near Petersburg, Kentucky.[34] This 70,000 square foot facility, built at a cost of over 25 million dollars, incorporates state of the art displays, videos, workshops, virtual tours online, and a museum store. Displays provide a Biblically based history of the origins of life on earth including, among other things, beautifully crafted depictions of dinosaurs living side by side with human beings. The Bible does not specifically mention dinosaurs, but the presence of dinosaurs and humans in the same time frame is consistent with a literal six-day theory of creation. According to standard scientific chronology, dinosaurs lived and were extinguished long before the appearance of humans on earth. Further, many of the dinosaurs were highly mobile flesh-eating creatures; they would have been devastating co-inhabitants with humans. The Biblical interpretation promoted by the Museum, is that all creatures lived in perfect harmony in the prelapsarian era of the Garden of Eden. The term *prelapsarian* refers to an innocent sin-free world presumed to exist prior to the fall of human beings. Creationists assume that in that era, there was perfect harmony so that dinosaurs and other creatures that would later prove deadly to human life could co-exist in a cooperative and affirming way with human beings. Many believe the fall of human beings, as described in Genesis, ushered in a new era marked by tragedy, death, discord, extreme punishments including the pain and dangers of childbirth and the corruption of the physical, and biological worlds. According to the six-day creationist account, the dinosaurs prior to the fall of human beings would have been herbivores; following the fall however, they would have been carnivores whose presence would have constituted a formidable threat to human life. According to evolution, the idea of a prelapsarian era does not square with the fossil record with its display of fangs, claws, and evidence that animals were devouring other animals long before the appearance of humans on earth.

The Creationist Museum has been a source of conflict between Biblical literalists and scientists within the Christian community. Moderate to liberal Christians who reject strict Biblical literalism see the museum as an embarrassment and as an assault on truth. Biblical literalists see the museum as a source of truth and as a welcome alternative to the evolutionary message encountered in public secular museums. There are scientists who have complained that they are being demonized in some of the materials set forth in the museum.[35] Others have argued that the term *museum* is inappropriate and that the general character of the place is more like a Disney Theme Park.[36] There are very visible guards in the museum, but these may be necessary because there have been demonstrations and occasional unruly behaviors by visitors. Most museums present materials in a manner that promotes free inquiry and thoughtful contemplation, but the clear goal of the Creation Museum is to convert visitors by juxtaposing human reason and "the word of God." Workers in the museum believe that in any conflict between scripture and science, it is science that must be in error, because scripture is held to be the infallible word of God. Tensions may actually be amplified in years to come as the Creation Museum is now complemented by the nearby Noah's Ark theme park including a replica of Noah's Ark complete with claims that there were dinosaurs on board.

The Language of Warfare

Warfare, whether physical or intellectual in nature, inevitably includes cutting and intense emotional language that paints a grim picture of the intentions of the enemy. Edward J. Larson, in his book *Summer for the Gods* captures the war of words on both sides of the evolution–creation debate noting that William Jennings Bryan, in a fiery speech prior to the Dayton trial, observed that "The contest between evolution and Christianity is a duel to the death."[37] Larson also quotes Clarence Darrow, who noted that the goal of the Scopes trial was to "prove that America is founded on liberty and not on narrow, mean, intolerable and brainless prejudice of soul-less religious-maniacs."[38] It is a part of everyday experience to encounter claims that those who believe in evolution are fascists or communists bent on destroying American values. Creationists are often characterized as history deniers, narrow minded and either dense or willfully ignorant. The war of words continues. Berkman and Plutzer in their book *Evolution, Creationism, and the Battle to Control America's Classrooms* point out that "evolution in the classroom has been a hot war during the opening decade of the twenty-first century."[39]

Substantive Assumptions and Claims Compared

The clash between evolution and creationism is clearly evident in educational settings, popular literature, scholarly literature, and legal and judicial activities, but what about the substantive content of the two belief systems? Are there undiscovered bridges that point to the possibility of finding common ground or are the two systems simply incommensurable? In the materials that follow we briefly explore some of the more salient examples of substantive differences between evolution and creationism that appear to be diametrically opposed. The examples we have selected, along with many other possible examples, suggest that the warfare metaphor as it pertains to creationism and evolution is appropriate and likely to remain appropriate well into the future. We suspect that if there is common ground it would entail levels of abstraction unacceptable to either of the opposing parties.

Teleology

Teleology, as noted in Chapter 3, refers to purposes, end states, or goal directed activity. Though there is a vast literature on the theoretical problems associated with teleology in science, our focus here is on the practical ways teleology plays out in creationism and science.[40]

Creationist theories are marked by a strong emphasis on teleology. It is assumed that things happen for a purpose to fulfill the will of deity or to achieve specifiable or explicit end states. Everything is "for" some other thing. In the first chapter of Genesis in the 29th and 30th verses, God declares that herb bearing seeds and the fruit of trees are for food for humans and for other creatures. The Qur'an, in Surah 2:57 notes that clouds were made to provide shade. According to creationist theories, things are not typically created as ends-in-themselves, but as means to fulfill the needs or purposes of other things. There are no accidents; rather, everything is intricately related to every other thing in one-cosmic-and-purposeful-comprehensive-completeness. There are no exceptions; the tragedy, the brokenness, and all the pain encountered in this world, regardless of the origin of these things, still serve some purpose possibly known only by the Almighty. The Qur'an (Surah 10:61) assures believers that "there does not lie concealed from your Lord the weight of an atom in the earth or in the heaven." Christians are assured (Matthew 10:29) that "not a single sparrow falls to the ground without your father knowing it." Believers in the Christian tradition are assured further that the worst of calamities does not finally prevail because "all things work together for good to them that love God" (Romans 8:28).

Evolutionary science makes no such promise: indeed according to evolution there is real chance, risk, and accident in the battlegrounds of nature. Some things stand in stark nakedness and cannot be sanitized, rationalized, or easily understood in terms of human or divine purposes. In the *Origin*, Darwin expressed doubts about the explanatory utility of divine purposes by noting that some people believe that natural systems reveal "the plan of the Creator; but unless it be specified whether order in time and space, or what else is meant by the plan of the Creator, it seems to me that nothing is thus added to our knowledge."[41] Furthermore, detailed and technical scientific inquiry may be stifled or suppressed when events are simply "explained" as the result of divine purpose. Darwin worried that such "explanations" shed no real light on the workings of nature. It can also be added that further investigation may be impeded or regarded as unnecessary if "divine purpose" is accepted as an explanation for a natural event. Darwin believed there was great explanatory power in the identification of previously hidden specifiable natural causes of events. Such identification enhances real understanding and may even lead to possibilities for control.

Darwin, and many of his followers, found it difficult to reconcile divine purposes with all the apparent waste, misdirection, and suffering encountered not only in humans, but throughout the animal world. Darwin noted that all species produce more offspring than can possibly survive. In some cases as many as 99% never reach adulthood as they become victims of accidents, disease, starvation, or as prey for predators. Humans were not exempt. For centuries, one in two babies perished before reaching the age of three years.[42] Smallpox and the plague were among the greatest threats to human life and happiness. In the 1940s and 1950s there was a worldwide epidemic of poliomyelitis, a cruel disease leaving a great many of its victims paralyzed or otherwise disabled for life. In time, the viral antecedent of polio was discovered, vaccines were developed, and the epidemic subsided to the point that the disease has all but disappeared in many nations that have supported vaccination. Teleological interpretations of the pain and suffering raise deeply troubling, vexing, and perhaps unanswerable questions, and, in any case, provide no general amelioration or control, but the discovery of the viral antecedent of polio changed everything. Darwin was struck by the waste and the suffering he encountered throughout nature and what such waste and suffering implied for the economics of pleasure. It may be arguable whether evolutionary thought avoids the problem of teleology, but it is clear that science in general, including scientific evolution seeks to explain the world in terms of identifiable natural causes and to avoid teleological explanations.

Complexity

Another mark of creationist theories is their claim that there are "bewildering complexities" that could not possibly have come about by mere chance. The assumption is that nature, left to itself, produces only random or chaotic processes. Thus, a forward looking "intelligent designer" is a prerequisite to any real understanding of the kinds of complexities we observe in the natural world. This claim was pursued in considerable detail in *Kitzmiller v. Dover* with expert witnesses such as Michael Behe supporting the concept of "irreducible complexity" or the idea that intricacies and complexities in nature cannot be understood apart from the work of a designer.[43] Other experts such as Kenneth Miller dispute the claims of designer theories in favor of natural selection.[44] There is a vast literature on the complexity problem—a literature that appears to point to irreconcilable differences between creationism and evolution. Does nature, left to itself, produce chaos or are there primitive regularities that produce some degree of natural order that results in predictable sequences, segregation (as when oil is poured on water), patterns, attractions, repulsions, and combinations? Can primitive order then result in more complex organizations and patterns? Must design be imposed from the outside or is there genuine "requiredness," "fittingness," and order intrinsic in nature?

Mutability of Species

In the introduction to the *Origin*, Darwin was very clear in the expression of his doubt "that each species has been independently created."[45] Instead, he argued that species are mutable and are descendants of other species. Modification results from natural selection and thus, different animals and plants have lived at different times and have diverged in significant ways from their ancestors. There is extinction of species and the emergence of new species not present in the fossil record in earlier periods of natural history. In stark contrast, creationists assume strong continuities between current species and their counterparts in the Garden of Eden. Creationists can agree that there are obvious modifications resulting from environmental constraints or selective breeding in domesticated animals, but they argue that such modifications do not mask the continuities of species over time.

Authority

Aside from technical quarrels over geological, paleontological, biological, and other purely scientific matters, creationists and evolutionists remain deeply divided on epistemological matters. Most creationists accept the idea that there are "new truths" brought about by scientific investigations but such "new truths" must be consistent with or verify larger truths set forth in scriptures such as the Bible or the Qur'an. Creationists who are scriptural literalists believe that if science and scripture appear to provide contradictory information, it is science that must be questioned because scripture is authoritative in all matters. It can be argued that the most fundamental difference between creationists and evolutionists centers on the role of authority in matters of truth. As noted in Chapter 2, there is no person, book, or institution that has the final once-for-all say in science. Everything has to be repeatedly checked against the continuous flow of the best possible empirical evidence. Authority in scientific work is not contained, frozen, or immutable. Authority in science is provisional and that includes methodology as experimental methods and procedures are forever under the microscope by being carefully scrutinized in every publication. Methodology also grows with the development of new observational tools that provide ever-clearer pictures of the world. Science is thus a dynamic, growing, pragmatic, and publically open enterprise marked by a belief that new truths may challenge, replace, attenuate or adumbrate older truths. Scientific approaches to truth are fundamentally different from the approaches of scriptural literalists who believe their foremost responsibility is to what they regard as the literal revealed word of God.

This fundamental epistemological difference plays out decisively in the creation–evolution debates as it did earlier in debates over astronomy. The parallels between the debates over evolution and the debates over astronomy raise questions, among other things, over literal and metaphorical approaches to scriptures. In an earlier era, powerful religious leaders took scriptures literally when they rejected the new astronomy surfacing in the works of scientists such as Copernicus, Galileo, and Kepler. Nowhere is this better illustrated than in the actual condemnation of Galileo. The condemnation speaks of Galileo's "false opinion that the sun is the center of the world and immovable and that the earth is not the center of the world and moves." It goes on to declare that this is a "false doctrine" and "contrary to holy scripture."[46] According to scriptural astronomy taken literally, the sun moves (Joshua 10:12–13), and the earth does not move (1 Chronicles 16:30). What was once an emotionally charged debate has now cooled because specific scriptures once taken literally are now understood metaphorically.

The same thing happened with respect to loans at interest. Such loans, in Catholic and Protestant traditions were widely condemned and forbidden on threat of severe punishments. Ezekiel 18:5–13 is but one of many scriptures warning against loans at interest or increase. The scripture identifies "Lending at interest" as one of many "abominable things" that will result in severe punishments. In the 19th century there was increased awareness of the devastating and stagnating effects on economies when loans of interest are forbidden. Even Biblical literalists now conveniently and blithely ignore Scriptures that forbid such loans.[47]

Morality

Tensions between evolutionists and creationists are not simply intellectual, they are visceral affairs of the gut over issues of morality and honesty. The clash over the perceived moral implications of the two positions may be a stronger driving force than any of the quarrels over specific scientific and technical details. Creationists have often blamed evolution for communism, fascism, anti-Semitism, racism, sexism, and other "evils" that inevitably lead to the corruption of society. Evolutionists accuse creationists of dishonesty, willful ignorance, sensationalism, and authority-ridden patterns of thought that undermine science and technology with devastating consequences for future progress. One thing is certain, we cannot understand all the dimensions of the controversy without paying some attention to the moral problems that separate the two camps.

Darwin's moral sensitivities were shocked when the H.M.S. *Beagle* visited Tierra del Fuego at the tip of South America. In his diary he observed that the Fuegians had to spend almost all their time in the search for food and in defense against other surrounding tribes. He observed that

> the husband is to the wife a brutal master to a laborious slave. Was a more horrible deed ever perpetuated than that witnessed on the west coast by Byron who saw a wretched mother pick up her bleeding dying infant-boy whom her husband had mercilessly dashed on the rocks for dropping a basket of sea eggs![48]

The Fuegians enjoyed none of the benefits of civilized society; in Darwin's eyes their skills and behaviors were not far removed from the instincts of animals. In their biography, Adrian Desmond and James Moore observed that Darwin was "primed to accept [moral relativism] after the Beagle's visits to Tierra del Fuego and New Zealand."[49] He accepted the idea that moral values are learned, but at times he acted as if some things should be understood as intrinsically wrong. He experienced bitterness and outrage at some of the moral problems he encountered in supposedly civilized societies. He had a particular hatred of slavery that grew more intense on his journey as he contemplated the agony of the separation of slave families at auctions and as he witnessed the beatings of slaves. Such actions were often legal so there was little the onlooker could do. Following an incident of the beating of a slave boy, he remarked "I thank God, I shall never again visit a slave country ... These deeds [atrocities against slaves] are done and palliated by men who profess to love their neighbors as themselves, who believe in God, and pray his will be done on earth!"[50] The morality of Darwin sometimes exceeded the morality of those who claimed the high moral ground.

Darwin's personal morality was informed by unusual sensitivity and compassion for the suffering he encountered throughout the animal kingdom. The torturous death of his young daughter Annie filled Darwin with disdain for facile explanations of illness and death and reminded him of nature's apparent uncaring or even cruel disregard for the life of an individual. We are born, so we die, but Darwin could not reconcile the prolonged and agonizing death of a child with any theological formula. He puzzled over the utility of the hundreds of intestinal worms that can burrow into the bloodstream, or the wasp that lays its eggs inside the living flesh of a caterpillar. It was clear enough that the cruel suffering and death of some individuals was essential to the survival of others. The moral implications surfacing in his detailed studies of nature led him to doubt the received picture of a gracious, forgiving, friendly, beautiful, and harmonious world. It was rather an intense fight for survival lost in the early stages of life by the overwhelming majority of individuals in all species.

Desmond and Moore, in their biography pointed out that Darwin found common ground for a morality based on evolution and a morality based on the New Testament. Perhaps, both moralities are based on fear of the devastating consequences of immoral behavior; consequences in this life for the evolutionist and consequences in the next life for the Christian. Both sides can agree that provision for future well-being is a moral obligation.

*****

Sustained and emotionally charged confrontations between creationists and evolutionists mark this as possibly the most prominent of current issues separating the great bulk of the scientific community from very large and vocal segments of conservative faith communities. Though there are emerging deep divisions over topics such as homosexuality and embryonic stem cell research, these issues have yet to reach the fever pitch of conflict and strife manifested in ongoing social, organizational, political, educational, and judicial confrontations between creationists and evolutionists. Short of unforeseen breakthroughs in knowledge comparable to the clear demonstration of parallax in the earlier geocentric–heliocentric debates, it is unlikely the conflict will subside as the substantive differences and the assumptions encountered in evolution and creationism seem incommensurable.

Notes

1 Attributed to John Washington Butler, author of the 1925 Butler Act in Tennessee. Quoted in George E. Webb, *The Evolution Controversy in America* (Lexington, KY: University of Kentucky Press, 1994), 82.
2 Ibid., 235. The quote is attributed to Stephen Jay Gould.
3 Statement in an address at Liberty Baptist Church in Hartwell, Georgia, September 27, 2012, http://www.youtube.com/watch?v=rikEWuBrkHc (Accessed February 6, 2015).
4 Michael Berkman and Eric Plutzer, *Evolution, Creationism, and the Battle to Control America's Classrooms* (Boston, MA: Cambridge University Press, 2010).
5 Ibid., 6–7, 195–197.
6 Ibid., 37.
7 Ibid., 36.
8 Paul Froese and Christopher Bader, *America's Four Gods: What We Say about God and What That Says about Us* (New York: Oxford University Press, 2010), 90–91.
9 Frank Newport, "Four in 10 Americans Believe in Strict Creationism," in *The Gallup Poll: Public Opinion 2010*, ed. Frank Newport (New York: Rowman & Littlefield Publishers, Inc., 2011), 445–446.
10 Tom Peck and Jerome Taylor, "Scientist Imam Threatened over Darwinist Views," *The Independent* (London), March 5, 2011, 16.
11 Richard Dawkins, *The Greatest Show on Earth* (New York: The Free Press, 2009), 436.
12 Salman Hameed, "An Old Earth for All Muslims: But How Does Evolution Fit In?" *Earth* 56, No. 10 (October 2011), 79.
13 Ibid.
14 Salman Hameed, "Bracing for Islamic Creationism," *Science* 322, No. 5908 (December 2008), 1637–1638.
15 Tennessee Sixty-Fourth General Assembly. An Act Prohibiting the Teaching of Evolution Theory in all the Universities, Normals, and all other Public Schools of Tennessee, which Are Supported in Whole or in Part by the Public School Funds of the State, and to Provide Penalties for the Violations Thereof, *Public Acts of the State of Tennessee*, Chapter No. 27, (March 13, 1925) HB185. http://law2.umkc.edu/faculty/projects/ftrials/scopes/tennstat.htm (Accessed January 6, 2012).
16 Webb, *The Evolution Controversy*, 81–108.
17 *John Thomas Scopes v. The State of Tennessee*, 1927. http://law2.umkc.edu/faculty/projects/ftrials/scopes/statcase.htm (Accessed October 12, 2015).
18 Tennessee, Public Act, Chapter 237, No. 48. An Act to Repeal Section 498–1922, Tennessee Code Annotated, Prohibiting the Teaching of Evolution, 1967. http://law2.umkc.edu/faculty/projects/ftrials/scopes/tennstat.htm (Accessed January 7, 2012).
19 For example, see Stanley Kramer, dir., *Inherit the Wind*, DVD with Spencer Tracy, Fredric March, and Gene Kelly (Hollywood, CA: MGM Home Entertainment Inc., 2001).
20 Webb, *The Evolution Controversy*, 101–103.
21 *Edwards v. Aguillard*, 482 U.S. 578 (1987). A summary and an auditory transcript of the trial is available online at the Oyez Project at http://www.oyez.org/cases/1980–1989/1986/1986_85_1513 (Accessed January 26, 2012).
22 Edward Humes, *Monkey Girl: Evolution, Education, Religion, and the Battle for America's Soul* (New York: Harper Collins, 2007), 255.
23 *Kitzmiller v. Dover*, Tennessee (Middle District) 707 (2005).
24 Ibid., 137.
25 Ibid.
26 Ibid., 137–138.
27 Judge Jones was correct to anticipate criticism of his ruling. See, for example, David K. Dewolf, John G. West, Casey Luskin, and Jonathan Witt, *Traipsing into Evolution,*

Intelligent Design and the Kitzmiller v. Dover Decision (Seattle, WA: The Discovery Institute, 2006).
28 Humes, *Monkey Girl*, 345.
29 Lauri Lebo, *The Devil in Dover* (New York: New Press, 2008), 214.
30 Ibid., 180.
31 Simon Brown, "Creationism Crusade," *Church & State* 64 (February 2012), 4–5.
32 Tom Vail, *Grand Canyon: A Different View* (Green Forest, AZ: Master Books, 2006).
33 Ibid., 36.
34 Information on the Creation Museum is available at http://creationmuseum.org/
35 See June Kennerly "Paleontologists Brought to Tears, Laughter by Creation Museum," June 30, 2009 http://www.physorg.com/news165555744.html (Accessed January 8, 2012).
36 For example, see Paul Zachary Myers, "The Creation 'Museum.'" Posted August 10, 2009, http://scienceblogs.com/pharyngula/2009/08/10/the-creation-museum-1/ (Accessed November 14, 2016).
37 Edward J. Larson, *Summer for the Gods: The Scopes Trial and America's Continuing Debate over Science and Religion* (Cambridge, MA: Harvard University Press, 1997), 143.
38 Ibid., 146.
39 Berkman and Plutzer, *Evolution, Creationism, and the Battle*, 13.
40 For a more detailed treatment of the theoretical problems associated with teleology see Phil Dowe, *Galileo, Darwin, and Hawking* (Grand Rapids, MI: William B. Eerdmans, 2005), Chapter 5.
41 Charles Darwin, *On the Origin of Species* (London: The Folio Society, 2006), 328.
42 See Comte de Buffon, *Selections from Natural History General and Particular* (New York: Arno Press, 1977), Vol. 1, 393.
43 Michael J. Behe, *Darwin's Black Box: The Biochemical Challenge to Evolution* (New York: Simon & Schuster, 1996).
44 Kenneth Miller, "Expert Statement at the Dover, Pennsylvania Trial," in *Intelligent Design: Science or Religion*, eds. Robert M. Baird and Stuart E. Rosenbaum (Amherst, NY: Prometheus Books, 2007).
45 Darwin, *Origin*, xxxi.
46 Giorgio De Santillana, *The Crime of Galileo* (Chicago, IL: University of Chicago Press, 1955), 312–313.
47 For a detailed treatment of the history of loans on interest see Andrew Dickson White, *A History of the Warfare of Science with Theology in Christendom* (New York: Prometheus, 1993), Vol. 2, Chapter 19.
48 Charles Darwin, *Journal of Researches into the Natural History and Geology of the Countries Visited during the Voyage of the H.M.S. Beagle around the World under the Command of Capt. Fitzroy, R.N.* (New York: D. Appleton, 1897), 215–216.
49 Adrian Desmond and James Moore, *Darwin: The Life of a Tormented Evolutionist* (New York: W. W. Norton, 1991), 262.
50 Darwin, *Journal*, 499.

7

GALILEO AND THE CHURCH

> *In discussions of physical problems we ought to begin not from the authority of scriptural passages, but from sense-experience and necessary demonstrations.*[1]
>
> *The sun also arises and the sun goeth down and hasteth to the place where he arose.*[2]

The story of Galileo and the church is not just a story about disputes over the architecture of the solar system. It is a much richer story about the tragedies of certitude, conflicting methodologies, contested boundaries, shifting intellectual territories, and the interpretive work of historians. For centuries, church influence extended into virtually all philosophical, moral, legal, medical, and natural arenas. Church doctrines and practices were pervasive, largely settled, and authoritative. Theology was the "Queen of the Sciences" and thus served as a filter, a guide for legitimate inquiry, a set of regulative ideals, and the source of orthodox conclusions. The church had a long history as an intellectual and spiritual placeholder, but in the days of Galileo its privileged position had been slowly eroding.

Erosion was everywhere; a once proud institution was on the defensive. The Protestant Reformation had challenged the morality of church practices, such as the sale of indulgences, and what the Protestants regarded as significant departures of the Catholic Church from strict Biblical teachings. The earlier invention of the printing press was contributing to a larger reading public, a more informed laity, and a proliferation of new literary sources increasingly available to large audiences. People could read and interpret the Scriptures for themselves. In an attempt to restore church control of reading materials, Pope Paul IV in 1559 initiated the Index of Prohibited Books.[3] The Index listed books containing heretical ideas deemed dangerous to the faith or that were critical of Church doctrines or leaders. Just over 400 years later, Pope Paul VI in 1966 abolished the

Index. Another attempt to control printed material surfaced with the use of the imprimatur, a term literally signifying "permission to print." Prior to publication, church censors often screened manuscripts for doctrinal errors and heretical or unorthodox ideas. Church censors had the right to suppress the publication of manuscripts or to demand correction or removal of materials deemed dangerous to the faith. Nevertheless, with the advent of the printing press, the floodgates were open with a profusion of ideas that got past the gatekeepers and challenged old beliefs. For example, Miguel de Montaigne, in a famous essay entitled "Apology for Raimond Sebond," launched powerful condemnations of human presumption and arrogance.[4] Doubt, long regarded as a sin, was elevated by Montaigne as a virtue and obligation. Failure to doubt might even be regarded as intellectually reckless and as the fundamental cause of unjustified presumption and certitude. Not surprisingly, Montaigne's essay was placed on the Index of Forbidden Books.[5]

There were other intellectual developments surfacing at the time of the Galileo affair that challenged older ways of thinking and that are crucial to understanding the contest between Galileo and the Church. For example, Francis Bacon published his *Novum Organum Scientiarum* (New Instrument of Science) in 1620, 12 years prior to the publication of Galileo's famous *Dialogue Concerning the Two Chief World Systems*. Among other things, Bacon cataloged common errors; what he called Idols that undermine the discovery of truth. He identified excessive reliance on authority and tradition as Idols that blind us to important truths. Bacon called for a new empiricism that begins with doubt and proceeds with observation, data collection, and the construction of generalizations based on masses of data. Observation was enfranchised as a way of knowing or a means of discovery that promised a way out of years of stagnation and blind acceptance of authority, tradition, and dogma. Bacon would have approved the first epigraph at the beginning of this chapter.

The discovery of the new world across the Atlantic contributed to the growing epistemological changes by highlighting the value of exploration and observation and suggesting that there are unexpected new truths to be discovered in all arenas of life by empirical methods. It was increasingly difficult to regard truth as frozen, embalmed, or exclusively possessed and stored up by institutional authority. There were genuinely important practical truths about the world suggesting the need for a fresh expanding vision of how knowledge is acquired. New instruments such as the telescope also challenged the naïve realism that what there is to know can be known through the unaided senses. These, and many other developments put the church into a defensive posture and provide an important contextual backdrop for an informed assessment of the tensions between Galileo and Church leaders. Galileo stood at the headwaters of the development of rational-empirical methods that challenged traditional beliefs based on authority, tradition, and dogma. To be fair, there were significant numbers of church scholars deeply enthused about the promise of observational techniques, but throughout the Galileo affair, their voices were often drowned out by traditionalists and official declarations.

The Substantive Problem

For centuries, the earth had been regarded as flat, immovable, and as the center of the solar system. But from the 5th and 6th centuries BCE the intellectual elite understood that the earth was shaped as a sphere.[6] Such understandings however, may not have been quick to filter down to masses of people who could not read or write. Every period of history, including the present, witnesses the intransigence of superstition, myths, fables, and false beliefs. Astrology continues to flourish even in a literate and scientific age. Evolution is now canonical in all the sciences and yet, even in a literate world a century and a half after Darwin, a recent Gallup poll shows that over 40% of Americans believe that humans were created in their present form within the last 10,000 years.[7] In earlier ages, illiteracy was rampant and information sources were limited contributing to pervasive intellectual inertia and stagnation resulting in a particularly stubborn barrier to the communication of new truths as well as to long established older truths. One can construct a long list of luminaries who understood that the earth was a sphere, but it is not unreasonable to believe that illiterate peoples, isolated in their ignorance, had anxieties about bottomless pits and edges of the earth. Such anxieties may also have been perpetuated among illiterate peoples who had learned of sacred scriptures that spoke of "ends of the earth" (I Samuel 2:10, Job 28:24, Psalms 19:4–6) and the "four corners of the earth" (Ezekiel 7:2 and Revelation 7:1). Sacred scriptures, taken as the infallible word of God, continue to trump scientific views in the minds of masses of people. Jeffrey Burton Russell in his book, *Inventing the Flat Earth*, noted "the church fathers who tried to make the Bible a textbook for natural science were in the minority."[8] But the minority view among intellectual leaders may nevertheless have persisted for long periods as a majority view among the illiterate.

An earth-centered or geocentric worldview had wide appeal, partly because it agreed with naïve sensory data as revealed in the obvious "rising" and "setting" of the sun. The experience of the stability of the earth was also difficult to square with concepts of a moving earth. Of even greater importance, the geocentric worldview appeared to be consistent with the sacred scriptures. Evidence for a moving sun is provided by scriptures (Josh. 10:12–13, Hab. 3:11, and Eccles. 1:5). Evidence highlighting the stability or immovability of the earth is found in scriptures such as (I Chron. 16:30, Ps. 93:1, and Ps. 96:10). And, as noted above, the Bible speaks of the ends of the earth and the corners of the earth. Such scriptures, taken literally as they often were, are consistent with older beliefs in a flat and stable earth with literal edges and corners. The problem is compounded when scriptures are regarded as "read only texts" providing faithful word-for-word dictations from the Almighty. After all, God is no deceiver. Thus, any new belief about the earth in relation to the rest of the cosmic architecture faces a formidable nearly impenetrable barrier among illiterate peoples as well as significant minorities of literate Biblical literalists. Sacred scriptures, taken as absolute literal commands of God, serve easily as barriers to thoughtful consideration of the legitimate claims of observation and reason.

Nevertheless, prior to the work of Galileo, the leadership of the Catholic Church had tolerated the treatment of a sun-centered cosmos as an interesting hypothesis about the geometry of the solar system. Such a hypothesis might even have practical value if it resulted in improved calendars and better predictions about the behaviors of earth's neighbors. Problems slowly surfaced however as individual scholars expressed increasing skepticism about the ontological status of the long accepted earth centered view of the cosmos. There was clearly a troubling intellectual disconnect between the claims of sacred scriptures as interpreted by conservative theologians and the emerging new claims that the earth is no longer center stage, that it moves on its axis and circles the sun.

Nicholaus Copernicus

The idea of a sun-centered cosmos was not new, it had a long history dating from the 5th century BCE when various Greek scholars spoke of a central fire circled by the earth and other planets.[9] The prevailing earth-centered theory dates from 150 CE when Claudius Ptolemaeus (100–c.170 CE), known simply as Ptolemy, set forth a circular cosmology with earth at the center in his famous treatise known as the *Almagest* (roughly meaning "greatest"). This work served for centuries as an accepted guide to the structure of the solar system. The first serious systematic challenge to the Ptolemaic system slowly gained momentum in the 16th century following the publication in 1543 of Copernicus' revolutionary work titled *On the Revolutions of the Celestial Spheres*. This work, often referred to simply as the *Revolutions* is now recognized as a singular and transposing event in the history of science, philosophy, and religion. It marks the beginning of an intellectual revolution marked by a seismic break with a comfortable past. The troubling message of the *Revolutions* was that the earth is a planet rotating on its axis and revolving around the sun like the other planets.

Nicholaus Copernicus (1473–1543) is remembered not only with the eponymous term *Copernican* but for the enormous breadth and depth of his intellectual interests and accomplishments. Never married, he devoted himself unreservedly to the "life of the mind." As a student in Polish and Italian universities Copernicus distinguished himself in mathematics and astronomy. He spoke several languages, and earned a doctorate in Canon Law.[10] He was a student of Greek language and philosophy and a strong advocate of humanistic studies. As secretary for an influential uncle he was active in political and economic affairs, but always appropriated large windows of time to astronomy. His interest in heliocentrism was set forth early in the second decade of the 16th century in a collection of unpublished commentaries. Thus, the classic work on the *Revolutions* was based on decades of deliberation, but Copernicus realized the danger of going to press with a work so clearly at variance with the long accepted and comfortable earth-centered worldview. Accordingly, he delayed publication. Legend has it that a published copy of the *Revolutions* was placed in Copernicus' hands just prior to his death in 1543.

The claims in the *Revolutions* that the sun was the center of the cosmos and that the earth was an orbiting planet laid largely dormant for at least half a century following the death of Copernicus. David Wootton, in his book *Galileo: Watcher of the Skies* notes "In the first fifty years after the death of Copernicus, only four people published in support of the Copernican system."[11] The paucity of supporting published comment is understandable partly because the Copernican system didn't call for mere assimilation, but for radical intellectual revolution. Caution in the face of the dislocation and disruption of long-standing stable anchorages is admirable or even adaptive, but caution in this case may also have been based on the fear of the possible consequences of contradicting the claims of sacred Scriptures. Such fear had a realistic basis. In his book, *The Case of Galileo: A Closed Question?* Annibale Fantoli details the development and growth of the intense Scriptural controversy gradually developing after the publications of the *Revolutions*. The controversy culminated in the denunciation of Copernicus by Protestants such as Martin Luther and John Calvin and the later official announcement of the Catholic Church that the Copernican doctrine was contrary to Holy Scripture.[12] The claim was also made that Copernicanism could be "more harmful to the Holy Church than the writings of Luther and Calvin."[13]

Seventy-three years following the printing of Copernicus' *On the Revolutions*, the Congregation of the Index forbade its further publication pending necessary corrections. A formal decree in 1616 declared that belief in heliocentrism was a heresy. Dava Sobel, in his biographical study of Copernicus, suggested that "the condemndation of Copernicus's ideas ... probably served to make his book more popular."[14] Sobel documented a succession of editions of *On the Revolutions* following the decree of 1616. Sobel also noted that *On the Revolutions* was finally dropped from the Index of Prohibited Books in 1835 and that in 2008 a "First-edition copy of *On the Revolutions* sold at auction for more the $2 million."[15]

Galileo

The Copernican crisis would ultimately come to a head in the discoveries and later condemnation of Galileo Galilei (1564–1642) who is often heralded not only as the chief advocate of Copernicanism, but as the single most important pioneer in the development of scientific methodology, and in the claims of historians Will and Ariel Durant that "no man since Archimedes had ever done so much for physics."[16] Galileo, born in Pisa in 1564, was a precocious child evincing a great range of interests but always obsessed with the workings of mechanical objects. In 1581 he matriculated in the University of Pisa ostensibly to study medicine but he quickly discovered his preference for subjects such as mathematics, mechanics, and physics. He left the university after four years and prior to graduation in favor of several years of intense private study and tutoring in mathematics and other subjects of choice. A three-year period of teaching mathematics at the University of Pisa beginning in 1589 was followed by a position as Chair of Mathematics from 1592 to 1610 at the University of Padua. These early years were filled with notable inventions and achievements in the fields of physics and mechanics. Galileo was celebrated for his extensive work on the movements of the pendulum and the closely related work on the speeds of free falling objects. He invented a hydrostatic balance, assisted Evangelista Torricelli in the development of the first barometer, clarified the relations of pitch and vibrations and set forth fundamental distinctions between the subject matters of physics (solidity, motion, extension, number and figure) and what would later capture the attention of psychologists (colors, sounds, odors, and tastes). These distinctions, known respectively as primary qualities and secondary qualities, would be developed later by scholars such as John Locke and René Descartes. Galileo anticipated the possibility that the subject matters of the discipline that would later be called psychology would ultimately prove to be quantifiable. It is a mistake to think of Galileo simply as an astronomer, but this is the work for which he is most clearly remembered and to which we must now turn.

    Galileo assembled his first telescope in 1609, but many years prior to that, possibly as early as 1590 he was beginning to favor the Copernican worldview.[17] His early observations through the telescope raised both epistemological and substantive questions. The epistemological questions are difficult to grasp over four centuries later in an age that has witnessed previously unimaginable augmentations and prosthetics for all sensory systems. But in the 17th century the telescope was a fundamentally new tool that was nothing short of disruptive and deeply troubling. The prophets, seers, fathers, evangelists, and sages who had lived for centuries without this tool were obviously blind to fundamental realities and truths that existed everywhere beyond the reach of their unaided senses. This new instrument uncovered the disturbing observational limitations of previously pedestalized and revered leaders who had issued prescriptions about what to believe and how to live. If there were fundamentally new realities and truths uncovered by this instrument, then how much faith should we place in the more truncated visions of those who had gone before us? Little wonder there were suspicions and questions about this new instrument. Was it a source of deception or even diabolical? Was it faithful in its representations of objects invisible to the naked eye? The latter question was answered easily enough in empirical demonstrations that distant objects viewed through the telescope in terrestrial settings were congruent with subsequent close inspections of those objects.

    When Galileo pointed his telescopes to the night skies, a whole new set of disturbing questions arose. The first question was obvious. Even if it is clearly demonstrated that the telescope provides faithful representations of distant terrestrial objects, what assurance is there that it does the same for distant objects in space? There was no direct empirical test as there was for earthbound objects. Maybe there is an unknown medium in space that distorts the images provided by the telescope. Still, the demonstrations of the reliability and faithfulness of telescopic observations in terrestrial settings were enough to encourage optimism about its usefulness as a revolutionary and valuable new tool for the astronomer.

When Galileo first trained his telescope on the moon he affirmed what he already believed; namely, that the surface of the moon was not perfect and clear as proclaimed by most geostatic theorists from the time of Aristotle. The telescope revealed a moon like the earth, covered with mountains, valleys, and craters, along with additional irregularities. If the surface of the moon was somewhat like the surface of the earth, perhaps the same might be true of more distant objects. The very thought challenged beliefs in the special status of the supposedly perfect "crystalline spheres" roaming the heavens and so dear to the hearts and minds of those who valorized the heavens as qualitatively superior to this lowly earth.

Galileo's disturbing discoveries continued. Early in 1610 he discovered the moons of Jupiter. As noted by David Wootton, "here was the first direct evidence that the cosmos did not consist of an array of heavenly bodies all of which orbited around a common center, the earth."[18] Late in 1610 Galileo provided telescopic evidence that Venus goes through phases in a manner somewhat comparable to the phases of the moon. While this observation did not absolutely prove the truth of heliocentrism, it did falsify the geocentric theory of Ptolemy and demonstrated that Venus circles the sun. In 1611 Galileo affirmed the observations of sunspots reported earlier by other astronomers. The existence of sunspots and their intense activity helped undermine earlier beliefs in the static perfection of the sun. Evidence was rapidly mounting against geocentric cosmology. Indeed, the evidence marshaled by Galileo should have been sufficient to temper the claims of the geocentrists. Still, as noted by David Lindberg, "Galileo's telescopic observations certainly did not demonstrate the truth of the heliocentric model."[19] It was commonly understood by scholars that such proof was dependent on a demonstration of stellar parallax, but astrometrics in Galileo's day were not sufficiently advanced for such a difficult task.

Simple parallax is demonstrated by retinal disparity meaning that slightly different images of objects are recorded by each eye. Fixate on the index finger held up in front of your eyes. Now close one eye and then the other and you will notice that an object behind the index finger appears to be in different locations depending on which eye is open. Stereopsis or binocular vision results in humans from the fact that the eyes occupy different lateral locations on the face. Stellar parallax is much more difficult to demonstrate, but think about the earth circling the sun and also turning on its axis as opposed to being in a stationary location. A telescopic observation of a distant object (comparable in this example with your index finger) can be made in relation to a still more distant object. Now, six months later when the earth has travelled half way around the sun, the telescope can once again be trained on the same distant object in relation to the more distant object. Parallax is demonstrated when the relation between the two objects appears to have changed as a function of the different lateral locations of the earth. Such a demonstration provided the evidence of the revolutions of the earth around the sun that Galileo could not provide.

Mathematicians and other scholars in Galileo's day understood that a demonstration of parallax was necessary as a means of supporting the heliocentric model. It can be claimed that the absence of such a demonstration is the reason scholars refused to accept the Copernican system. Such a claim however is beset with problems. Scholars apparently wanted to believe, to use a familiar phrase, that the absence of evidence is evidence of absence. But the same scholars who understood the importance of parallax must also have understood the limitations of the available tools for measuring it along with the fact that there had been very few attempts at such measurement. Where the quest for evidence has been limited, and where the exploratory tools are inadequate, it may be more reasonable to assume that the absence of evidence is not necessarily evidence of absence. Some scholars may have claimed that the absence of demonstrated parallax was the reason for their rejection of heliocentrism, but historians can reasonably be skeptical of such claims. The relevant literature reveals other reasons for the rejection of the Copernican system, including emotional reasons and reasons based on authority.

The Telescope and the Concerns of Church Leaders

It is commonly agreed that glassmakers and lens grinders in the Netherlands discovered the telescope, but its subsequent refinement by Galileo along with his demonstrations of its pragmatic value were revolutionary and mark the beginnings of a new era in human history. The telescope and later the microscope generated new ways to observe and to think about the locus and boundaries of human knowledge. The new worlds uncovered by the telescope and the microscope diminished the traditionalist mystique and enhanced the value of information gleaned from investigations conducted in the present. A major lesson of the Galileo affair is that knowledge is not something stored up from the past, static and possessed, but must now be regarded as on-going, dynamic, and mutating. As noted at the beginning of this chapter, the Galileo affair was not simply about the architecture of the cosmos, it was about methodology and the locus, metamorphosis, reach, and limits of knowledge.

"The Church" in Galileo's day has often been understood as a monolithic entity because its leaders or leader could make unequivocal, formal, official, legal, and binding pronouncements on a great range of subjects. Such an understanding of the church however, is not without problems and these problems are illustrated in the Galileo case. For example, there were strong disagreements among high-ranking church officials and scholars over heliocentric and geocentric worldviews. Sermons were preached against and in favor of Copernican cosmology and there were intense disputes about differences and compatibilities between the Bible and Copernicus. On one hand, it is a mistake to think of "the church" as representing a single, consistent, or homogeneous viewpoint. On the other hand, there were official legal declarations by Church authorities that were definitive. A historical focus on the complexities of the tensions within the church, including all those who were friendly to Galileo, can diminish or obscure the negative effects of the official actions of the church, but exclusive attention to the official actions and final outcomes fails to do justice to the extensive complexities surrounding the Galileo affair. In what follows, the emphasis will be on selected pivotal developments in the relations between Galileo and the official declarations of the Church.

Galileo's preference for Copernican cosmology was becoming increasingly visible to church authorities from the late 1590s and clearly obvious in 1610 when he published the *Starry Messenger*. In that same year he was honored with a life-time appointment as Chief Mathematician at the University of Pisa. Just short of a year later Cardinal Robert Bellarmine, after looking through Galileo's telescope, asked the mathematicians of the Roman College if they could confirm the observations Galileo had set forth in the *Starry Messenger*. Observations of the existence of multitudes of stars invisible to the naked eye, the phases of Venus, the moons of Jupiter, and the irregularities of the moon's surface were largely confirmed. The mathematicians made it clear however, that they did not necessarily agree with Galileo's interpretations of his findings.

In 1615 Dominican friars Niccolo Lorini and Tommaso Caccini approached the Roman Inquisition with charges against Galileo and his followers. Among many charges Galileo was accused of rejecting miracles, belief in a vacuum, and disrespect for the scriptures. The Inquisitors found that most of the charges against Galileo were not supported, but they had also been asked to rule on whether Copernican theory was a heresy. Witnesses for and against Galileo and Copernican theory were called to testify before a special set of consultants to the Inquisition who were asked to rule on the movement of the earth and relative locations of the earth and the sun. Early in 1616 the team of consultants came back to the Inquisition issuing a decree that belief in a sun-centered world is absurd and heretical and belief in the movement of the earth is also absurd and that such beliefs are contrary to divine scriptures and dangerous to the Catholic faith.[20] Clearly, the decree of the consultants, with its references to the scriptures, demonstrates that it is a mistake to downplay the role of epistemic differences between Biblical literalism and naturalistic observations in the Galileo affair. The inquisitors recommended that Galileo be warned to abandon his support for the Copernican worldview. In February of 1616 Cardinal Bellarmine immediately summoned Galileo to his residence where he administered the warning that henceforth Galileo was not to hold or defend the Copernican heresy. Cardinal

Bellarmine undoubtedly issued the warning with sincerity and enthusiasm because he believed Copernicanism, taken literally, was in danger of "injuring our holy faith and rendering the holy scriptures false."[21] Within a month following the warning of Galileo, the Congregation of the Index forbade the publication of Copernicus' *Revolutions* until it had been properly corrected. The corrections were finally set forth in 1620.

In 1623 Cardinal Maffeo Barberini (1568–1644) was elected pope and took the title Urban VIII. This was a significant development because Barberini, as Cardinal, had always supported Galileo. The next year Galileo visited Rome where he enjoyed numerous visits with Urban VIII. In an apparent relaxation of the earlier restrictions imposed by Bellarmine in 1616, the Pope restored Galileo's right to explore and write about Copernican theory on the condition that the theory always be treated as a mathematical hypothesis rather than as an ontological claim. Late in 1624, following Pope Urban's assurances, Galileo initiated work on the *Dialogue Concerning the Two Chief World Systems*, the book that would ultimately lead to his Inquisition trial and condemnation. The *Dialogue* was finished six years later in April of 1630 and published in February of 1632. As suggested by the title, the book was published as a dialogue among three protagonists: two philosophers and a nobleman. The philosophers are Salviati who speaks for Galileo and heliocentrism, Simplicio who speaks for the geocentric view embraced by most of the theologians, and Sagredo, the nobleman who simply seeks the truth. The name Simplicio already prejudices the case implying as it does that the defender of the geocentric view is, to use contemporary language, a simpleton. Simplicio sets up arguments that Salivati easily defeats. For example, Simplicio repeats the Aristotelian position that the surface of heavenly bodies are pure and crystalline. Salviati, of course can argue from the telescopic observations of the surface of the moon. But Galileo goes a step further and demonstrates that the surface of a crystalline moon would reflect light in a very different way from what we normally observe. Simplicio is repeatedly and soundly defeated to the point of embarrassment.

Needless to say, church authorities were deeply offended not only by the bias they found in the way the arguments were set up, but by the choice of the demeaning term *Simplicio*, a term that could obviously have been intended for members of the Roman hierarchy including the Pope himself. Clearly, the use of the term was one of many demonstrations of Galileo's political and social insensitivities. But in the *Dialogue* Galileo forgot, or was temperamentally unable, to speak as a politician. He was speaking as a deeply committed scholar who believed the geocentrists, as reflected in the arguments of Simplicio, were intellectually irresponsible in their failure to recognize that the demonstration of the phases of Venus falsified their Ptolemaic theory, even if it did not provide knock down proof of heliocentrism.

Shortly after the publication of the *Dialogue* Pope Urban VIII prohibited its distribution and appointed a special commission to examine it for possible heresies and for possible violation of the earlier warning issued in 1624 that Galileo was to treat heliocentrism merely as a mathematical hypothesis. By late summer of 1632 the special commission had submitted a devastating conclusion that Galileo had clearly exceeded the boundaries imposed earlier by the Pope. As a consequence, the Pope referred the matter to the Inquisition. He personally presided over deliberations that ended with the decision to issue a summons for Galileo to come to Rome where he would ultimately stand trial. This would be the beginning of the end of Galileo's public attempts to support the new sun-centered view of the world.

In October of 1632 Galileo received the summons to appear before the Inquisition in Rome. In the hopes of gaining a more convenient and friendly atmosphere for the trial, Galileo requested that it be moved from Rome to Florence. The Inquisition rejected the request with a threat that failure to voluntarily comply with their orders would result in the use of force. In December of 1632, three physicians sent written verification to Rome that the 68-year-old Galileo was too sick to travel. The Inquisition rejected the claims of the physicians and once again threatened the use of force to move Galileo to Rome. As an aside, Galileo was in fact, plagued by a rash of severe health problems, including the possibility of Syphilis.[22] He also suffered irregular heartbeat, insomnia, gout, numerous pains possibly from arthritis, depression, and repeated respiratory problems associated with fevers. It is unlikely the aging Galileo or his physicians were using his illness as a ruse to avoid the trip to Rome.

The Inquisition Trial

Early in 1633 Galileo arrived in Rome where he was housed in comfortable quarters, but forbidden social contacts without approval of the Inquisition. Galileo was interrogated by the Inquisitors in three sessions over a period stretching from April 12 to June 22. Testimony during this period was also gathered from officials who had examined the *Dialogue*. It was commonly understood that defendants interrogated by the Inquisition were under threat of torture. The Inquisition, established by Pope Gregory IX in 1232, served as an official judicial branch of the church. Pope Innocent IV, in 1252 allowed torture to become a tool of the Inquisition.[23] Because of his eminence, age, and poor health it is unlikely Galileo would have been subjected to physical torture, but as noted in Chapter 1, the threat of torture should not be downplayed because the threat of torture is torture of a psychological nature and can have devastating consequences.

The trial was not about the substance of the arguments presented in the *Dialogue*. Rather, the focus was on whether Galileo failed to obey the orders delivered by Cardinal Bellarmine in 1624 and whether the *Dialogue* in fact had defended Copernican theory. Galileo had cleverly written his book in the form of a dialogue that in the words of John Gribbin, was "a neat way to teach unconventional (or in this case, heretical) ideas without exactly endorsing them."[24]

The arguments for and against are presumably those of the protagonists and not necessarily those of the author. Any claim of Galileo's neutrality however was doomed to fail, because in other works and in letters Galileo had clearly placed himself in the Copernican camp. For example, in a letter to the Grand Duchess Christina of Tuscany, written in 1615, Galileo clearly identified himself with the Copernican system and noted that if the church leaders wished to suppress the new cosmology it would "be necessary not only to prohibit the book of Copernicus and the writings of other authors who follow the same opinion, but to ban the whole science of astronomy."[25] Further, the arguments in the *Dialogue* prejudiced the case in favor of the Copernican system.

On the first day of the trial major questions surfaced on the legitimacy of treating heliocentrism as a mathematical hypothesis. Galileo submitted a letter to the Inquisitors he had received from Cardinal Bellarmine summarizing the injunction the Cardinal had communicated to him in 1624. There was nothing in the letter that would prohibit the treatment of Copernicanism provisionally. But some of the fine details of that letter were at variance with a mysterious unsigned memo introduced in the trial by the Inquisition panel. The memo had apparently been stored since 1624 in the Holy Office of the Commissary General. It also summarized the meeting between Bellarmine and Galileo in 1624. The upshot of that memo, possibly written by a clerk, was an absolute restriction against any verbal or written defense of Copernican theory. Discrepancies between the two documents, along with irregularities associated with the memo from the Office of the Commissary General, are summarized by Blackwell in his overview of the trial.[26]

Pope Urban VIII had been unaware of the little known memo that had presumably been residing in the Holy Office of the Commissary General since 1624. Thus, Urban's relaxation of the restrictions on Galileo were at variance with the stringent prohibitions contained in the mysterious memo. The Pope was enraged because he believed Galileo had deceived him by failing to mention the absolute restrictions set forth in the memo from the Holy Office. It is possible, even likely, that Galileo had not seen the memo prior to his trial. The Pope was also angered over the disrespectful nature of the arguments for geocentrism set forth in the *Dialogue*.

The first day of the trial ended in a quagmire of contradictory evidence and this may have contributed to uncertainties about the outcome. There was little doubt Galileo was in violation of the letter and the spirit of the proscriptions against defending Copernicanism, but there were tensions over a proper course of action in view of the irreconcilable differences between the two major trial documents. The final outcome very likely hinged on what took place in the several days between the first and second sessions of the trial. Cardinal Francesco Barberini (1597–1679), nephew of the Pope, met with Galileo to discuss the gravity of his situation and to propose a plea bargain. A lighter sentence would result if Galileo would "plead guilty not to defending Copernicanism, but to a lesser charge of appearing to do so."²⁷ Galileo was in a no-win situation. If he continued to fight, he could easily have been consigned to torture and a cruel death and this possibility may have been communicated to him by Barberini in the meeting between the two trial sessions. By yielding, Galileo would perjure himself and sacrifice integrity. The latter was the lesser of two evils because he was led to believe a lighter sentence might amount to little more than a slap on the hands.

Thus, on the second day of the trial, Galileo played the game. He testified he had overstated the case for heliocentrism in the *Dialogue* and then he perjured himself by telling the Inquisitors he fully embraced the geocentric model and all the teachings of the Church regarding the shape of the cosmos. Earlier, in letters to friends, he had argued that certain Biblical passages concerning the natural world should not be taken literally. It was clear, as noted in the first epigraph heading this chapter, he had sided with the truths of naturalistic observations when such observations could not be reconciled with the literal sense of scriptures. Theologians were understandably offended that a mere layman in the interpretation of scripture should dare to encroach upon their territories. But during the trial, Galileo was now at pains to assure the Inquisitors that he was a good Catholic who fully embraced all the teachings of the Church including official interpretations of the Holy Scriptures.

The guilty plea included a recantation ultimately signed by Galileo on June 22, 1633. In the recantation ceremony, Galileo dressed as a penitent and with hands on the Bible, was forced to declare he had always believed and in the future would continue to believe everything taught by the Catholic Church, that he must abandon belief in a moving earth and a sun-centered universe, that he now must "abjure, curse, and detest" his errors, that he must promise not to say or write anything in the future that would arouse suspicion against him, that he would faithfully carry out any assigned penances, that he would denounce any heretic or person suspected of heresy to the Holy Office, and that should he fail on any of these promises, he would turn himself in and suffer the penalties prescribed by the Sacred Canons of the Church. Galileo's book was burned in front of him and he was informed that his sentence would include imprisonment for an indefinite period at the pleasure of the Pope.

Galileo was deeply embittered when the actual sentence was handed down. The plea bargain had been violated by a sentence far greater than anything he might have reasonably anticipated. Moreover, a final summation of the trial was filled with contradictions and outright falsehoods. Galileo felt he was the victim of chicanery and lies. Some of the members of the Congregation of the Inquisition may have agreed because three of the ten members of the panel including Cardinal Barberini did not sign the final trial documents.

Following the trial Galileo was isolated in the Villa Medici near the Vatican and later transferred to Siena near his home in Florence. Finally, he was allowed to live out his remaining days under house arrest at his Villa in Arcetri in the hills south of Florence. As noted in Chapter 1, Galileo was not placed in the "dungeons of the Inquisition," but he was placed in an intellectual prison and in relative social detention. Church authorities controlled visitation rights and Galileo was warned against any further research or discussion regarding Copernican cosmology. His work on Copernicanism was banned and some of those who had supported him were punished. For example, Wootton notes that Orazio Grassi, a Jesuit mathematician, was sent into exile, presumably for defending Galileo.[28] This was an example of vigorous efforts to convey to other scholars that the Copernican system was a dangerous heresy and therefore off limits.

Galileo was allowed to work on other scientific problems and must have received some satisfaction in 1635 when a Latin translation of the *Dialogue* was published in Strasburg. In his years of detention, he had few ways to discern the status of his work. Would all the attempts at suppression relegate his works to obscurity or could his works somehow survive? Amidst his worries, Galileo nevertheless continued to work on problems that were presumably acceptable to the Inquisition. He worked on a treatise on machines, ways to accurately assess longitude and latitude, and an early version of a pendulum clock. He also assimilated the results of over 30 years of largely original work on two new sciences—the science of motion and the strength of materials. The title *Discourses and Mathematical Demonstrations Concerning Two New Sciences Pertaining to Mechanics and Local Motion* often appears simply as *Dialogues Concerning Two New Sciences*. The book was written in the form of a dialogue with the same three protagonists employed in the earlier work on astronomy. Galileo considered this to be his most important work as it dealt with the basic sciences of motion and mechanics. It is a work that, along with Galileo's epistemological innovations, establishes him as the founder of modern physical science.

Publication of any new work had been forbidden, but the man so broken and lifeless at the end of his trial slowly rediscovered his bearings and regained some of his earlier fighting spirit even under the constraints of house arrest and declining health. He hoped to find a way to publish in Venice, then in Vienna, and finally in Paris. These attempts were unsuccessful where there were fears of the long arm of the Inquisition. The *Dialogue Concerning Two New Sciences* was finally spirited out of Italy and a subterfuge was employed making it appear that Galileo was innocent of violating the restriction of the Inquisition against publication of any new work. The manuscript finally wound up in Protestant Holland where it was published in 1638 in Leiden, South Holland. In the dedication, Galileo sent a not-so-subtle message to the Pope and to the Inquisition. He spoke of the "ill-fortune which has followed my other books" and his hope that this work might be saved from oblivion and someday be useful to those who could intelligently follow its message.[29] The use of the term *intelligently* carried a strong message. By 1638 Galileo had lost vision in both eyes. As a consequence of his blindness and failing health he petitioned the Inquisition to be released from his isolation and the restrictions of his sentence. His petition was denied. He died in Arcetri in

January of 1642 just short of his 78th birthday. He had served most of the last decade of his life under house arrest.

Historiography Revisited

There is extensive variability in historical treatments of the Galileo affair, perhaps as much variability as in treatments of the American Civil War. Historians, like all scholars, have personal, political, and religious identities difficult to neutralize and typically resistant to data that contradict presuppositions. One may hope that a historical narrative is data-driven in the sense that its descriptive qualities are as true as possible to the established chronology and characteristics of events. The personal identities the historian brings to an investigation, however, are not irrelevant to the final interpretive conclusions. Some scholars may wish to discover the one true history that settles things, but such a wish may be profoundly a-historical. Abraham Lincoln was correct when he said "history is not history unless it is the truth."[30] But there are many truths known and unknown, truths mutate as research uncovers new materials, errors are discovered, interpretive work is ongoing and dynamic, history is written and re-written. One may hope a given history is simply as true as it can be at a given time.

Historians who feel empathy for the plight of the church in the 15th and 16th centuries provide helpful perspectives. Church leaders were products of a time and a culture and the trusted representatives of the oldest and most powerful institution of the day. As noted earlier, it was an institution literally under siege and clearly on the defensive. The clergy were typically the leading academics and scholars of the day, guardians of a worldview and methodologies that had "stood the test of time." Moreover, it was a worldview that was hallowed and revered for its perceived consistency with the very word of God and with all that was sacred and holy. One could hardly expect moderation or tolerance for new ideas regarded as destructive or possibly toxic for the presumably veridical moral and intellectual structures of the church. And yet, in spite of everything, church leaders were willing to allow the Copernican theory to be treated as a hypothesis. They can be valorized for such tolerance as they displayed and their genuine interest in new telescopic discoveries.

History written with deep feelings for a besieged institution also has merit in the light of the difficulties presented by Galileo himself. As noted earlier, Galileo was no politician. He could be impatient, garrulous, mercurial, insensitive, and deceitful. Further, he did not provide knock down proof for heliocentrism and yet he projected an image of himself as vastly superior to other scholars. His presumption, arrogance, and certitude were bound to provoke hostility in even the most patient of his contemporaries and authorities. With more convincing evidence the church would have been forced to be more conciliatory, but in view of the most robust contextual understanding, church authorities, even in view of their substantive errors, can be defended for such prudence and moderation as they were able to muster.

It is also evident that historians, especially those writing in the 19th century might feel a deeper identity with Galileo than with the church. The 19th and 20th centuries witnessed a new and growing emphasis on the individual, especially in capitalist countries. Ralph Waldo Emerson, in his essay "Self Reliance," celebrated individuals such as Jesus, Martin Luther, John Wesley, John Fox, and John Milton as he argued that "all history resolves itself very easily into the biography of a few stout and earnest persons."[31] William James, a champion of individualism, argued that "the bigger the unit you deal with, the hollower, the more brutal, the more mendacious is the life displayed" and he went on to speak of "the eternal forces of truth which always work in the individual and immediately unsuccessful way, under-dogs always, til history comes, after they are long dead, and puts them on the top."[32] Such a statement could easily be construed as a legitimate characterization of the relations between Galileo and the Church, but James was making a more generic claim. In an article "The Importance of Individuals" and another titled "Great Men and Their Environment," James chided deterministic historians who downplay or neglect the roles of individuals in historical change.[33] Scholars such as James and Emerson were impatient with the inertia, inflexibility, dishonesties, and constraining effects endemic in social institutions and organizations. Modern scholars in the tradition of Emerson and James could hardly ignore the defiant transformative power apparent in the work of individual social reformers such as Mary Wollstonecraft, John Stuart Mill, Alice Paul, Margaret Sanger, and Martin Luther King Jr. Such highly visible leaders shook the foundations of conventional practices and were key in the acceleration of social reforms. History written without appreciative attention to the contributions of such individuals is anemic at best. The same goes for scientific thinkers such as Copernicus, Galileo, Newton, Leuwenhoek, Darwin, Currie, and Einstein.

Histories of the Galileo affair can sometimes be differentiated in terms of their emphasis on the individual vs. emphasis on the complexities of context. Subtle apologetic preoccupations can be found in both approaches. Earlier histories and historians have been roundly criticized for overemphasizing the role of individuals in historical change. More recent historical scholarship has focused on context, but the dimensions of context are bewildering in their complexity as they include material, technical, political, religious, philosophical, aesthetic, geographic, and economic considerations. Galileo's work itself provides a new context for the problems of descriptive astronomy and physics. It is a near impossibility to capture the multidimensional complexities of context either in historical events or, for that matter, in the present. What is the context of the present? There is another problem; context is sometimes treated as if it were static. That is not the case. Context is dynamic, changing, and elusive. Galileo's social and intellectual contexts were anything but stable and he clearly failed to fully grasp the meanings of transitions in his contexts. It is important to grasp as much context as possible in historical narratives, but it is overly promissory to claim an adequate account of the complexity or effect of context. It is assumed that a detailed and deep grasp of context promotes understanding, but Richard Cohen sounds a cautionary note in his reminder that "to understand is almost to justify."[34]

Galileo was the most visible player in the transition from an "age of faith" to a new age in which science would become a dominant if not the dominant force. John D. Caputo notes "the medieval philosophers once described reason as capax dei, a capacity for God, finite capacity for the infinite."[35] But with the revolutionary work of luminaries such as Galileo, Descartes, and Bacon there was a new practical emphasis on observation and experiment as tools for properly identifying and explaining the works of God in nature. Earlier, it could be argued that "only through the word of God can the works of God be known." But Galileo was asking for a seismic shift in the meaning and locus of "the word of God." With Galileo, the "word of God" must now be regarded as an open book, large as the heavens, owned by no one in particular, stored in no institution or holy text, and subject to ongoing additions, surprises, and revisions. Knowledge of the natural world could no longer be excluded as a part of the word of God or be regarded as contained, frozen, or bottled up in any book or institution. There was no legitimate historical or pre-existing filter to screen out unauthorized or unexpected innovations. Galileo cannot be understood apart from his pivotal role in challenging the epistemic authority and credibility of the church.

It was inevitable that legal action would be initiated to silence the man whose claims and methods amounted to a dangerous incursion into sacred territories long regarded as the exclusive possessions of the church. Though there were progressive scholars within the church who were sympathetic with Galileo, the official church could not afford to concede the substantive claims and methodological innovations surfacing out of the work of Galileo. At the outset of this chapter we spoke of the difficulties confronting the church in the 15th and 16th centuries. The nature of the reaction of the church against Galileo has sometimes been tied to these difficulties and specifically to the tensions the church was experiencing as a result of the Protestant Reformation with its emphasis on Biblical literalism. We seriously doubt however whether an untroubled church would have been any more tolerant of Galileo. The proximate cause for his trial and condemnation, as revealed in his recantation, centered on the striking conflict between Church interpretations of Biblical teachings and Galileo's interpretation of his naturalistic observations. Biblical literalists were outraged at what they regarded as the audacious heretical claims of Galileo. It took only a credible formal complaint filed with the Holy Office of the Inquisition to initiate a process. If Niccolo Lorini and Tommaso Caccini had not filed a formal complaint with the Inquisition in 1615, another would almost certainly have followed.

*****

The short-term outcome of the Galileo trial is in marked contrast with the long-term results. The suppression of the works of Copernicus and Galileo could not possibly hold in the face of mounting evidence in their favor and in an increasingly diverse and expanding world of ideas. There was growing appreciation for the successes associated with the new methodologies pioneered by Galileo along with growing suspicion of the adequacy of older scholastic techniques for understanding the works of nature. The sun-centered model Galileo was forced to repudiate in his recantation ultimately prevailed though many details remained to be worked out at the time of his death. It would now be up to the church to recant the position it had defended and the mistakes that had been made by the Inquisition. Recantations by individuals can work quickly; not so with institutional recantations. In 1741, nearly 100 years after the death of Galileo, Pope Benedict XIV permitted the publication of the complete works of Galileo with some modifications of the *Dialogue*. In 1939 Pope Pius XII praised Galileo's contributions and his ability to overcome obstacles. In 1992 Pope John Paul II expressed regret over the mistakes made by the Inquisition. The science has been settled; the history is anything but settled.

Notes

1 Galileo Galilei, Letter to Madame Christina of Lorraine, Grand Duchess of Tuscany, 1615. Inters.org/Galilei-Madame-Christina-Lorraine (Accessed July 3, 2015).
2 Ecclesiastes 1:5.
3 See Peter De Rosa, *Vicars of Christ: The Dark Side of the Papacy* (New York: Crown, 1988), 445.
4 Michele de Montaigne, "Apology for Raimond Sebond," in *The Complete Essays of Montaigne*, Vol. 2, trans. Donald M. Frame (Garden City, NY: Doubleday, 1960), 112–308.
5 *The New Catholic Encyclopedia*, 2nd ed., s.v. "Montaigne."
6 See Jeffrey Burton Russell, *Inventing the Flat Earth: Columbus and Modern Historians* (New York: Praeger, 1991), esp. Chapter 1.
7 The Gallup poll: Public Opinion 2012, *In U.S. 46% Hold Creationist Views of Human Origins* (New York: Rowman & Littlefield, 2014), 241.
8 Russell, *Inventing the Flat Earth*, 74.
9 John Gribbin, *History of Western Science* (London: The Folio Society, 2006), 7.
10 Dava Sobel, *A More Perfect Heaven: How Copernicus Revolutionized the Cosmos* (New York: Walker, 2011), esp. Chapter 1.
11 David Wootton, *Galileo: Watcher of the Skies* (New Haven, CT: Yale University Press, 2010), 53.
12 Annibale Fantoli, *The Case of Galileo: A Closed Question?* (Notre Dame, IN: University of Notre Dame Press, 2012), esp. Chapters 2, 3, and 4.
13 Maurice A. Finocchiaro, *Retrying Galileo 1633–1992* (Berkeley, CA: University of California Press, 2005), 72.
14 Sobel, *A More Perfect Heaven*, 226.
15 Ibid., 245.
16 Will Durant and Ariel Durant, *The Story of Civilization VII: The Age of Reason Begins* (New York: Simon and Schuster, 1961), 603.
17 Annibale Fantoli, *Galileo: For Copernicanism and the Church*, 2nd ed. (Notre Dame, IN: University of Notre Dame Press, 1996), 61.
18 Wootton, *Galileo: Watcher of the Skies*, 102.

19 David Lindberg, "Galileo, the Church, and the Cosmos," in *When Science and Christianity Meet*, eds. David C. Lindberg and Ronald L. Numbers (Chicago, IL: University of Chicago Press, 2003), 42.
20 Richard J. Blackwell, *Behind the Scenes of the Galileo Trial* (Notre Dame, IN: University of Notre Dame Press, 2000), 4.
21 Robert Bellarmine, Letter on Galileo's Theories April 12, 1615. http://sourcebooks.fordham.edu/mod/1615bellarmine-letter.asp (Accessed November 14, 2016).
22 See John L. Heilbron, *Galileo* (New York: Oxford University Press, 2010), 161–162.
23 Peter De Rosa, *Vicars of Christ*, 443.
24 John Gribbin, *History of Western Science 1543–2001* (London: The Folio Society, 2006), 106.
25 Galileo, Letter to the Grand Duchess Christiana of Tuscany, 1615. www.fordham.edu/halsall/mod/galileo-tuscany.asp (Accessed May 19, 2015).
26 Blackwell, *Behind the Scenes*, 6
27 Wootton, *Galileo, Watcher of the Skies*, 222.
28 Ibid., 225.
29 Galileo, From the Dedication in *Dialogues Concerning Two New Sciences*, https//ebooks.adelaide.edu.au/g/Galileo/dialogues/complete.html (Accessed July 12, 2015).
30 Letter from Abraham Lincoln to H. W. Herndon, 1856, ed. Arthur H. Shaw, *The Lincoln Encyclopedia: The Spoken and Written Words of A. Lincoln Arranged for Ready Reference* (New York: The Macmillan Co., 1950), 149.
31 Ralph Waldo Emerson, "Self Reliance," in *The Works of Ralph Waldo Emerson in One Volume* (Roslyn, NY: Black's Readers Service, no date), 103.
32 William James, Letter to Mrs. Henry Whitman, 1899, ed. Henry James, *The Letters of William James*, Vol. 2 (Boston: The Atlantic Monthly Press, 1920), 90.
33 Both articles are available in William James, *The Will to Believe* (Cambridge, MA: Harvard University Press, 1979).
34 Richard Cohen, "There is no Why Here," Editorial in *The New York Times*, Tuesday September 30, 2014, p. A23.
35 John D. Caputo, *Philosophy and Theology* (Nashville, TN: Abingdon Press, 2006), 26.

8

ADVANCES IN UNDERSTANDING OF THE ORIGINS OF SEX

The Lord has made everything for its purpose.[1]

We are all too ready to forget that in fact everything to do with our life is chance, from our origin out of the meeting of spermatozoon and ovum onwards.[2]

An examination of major reference sources underscores the multiple meanings of the term *sex*. For example, one of the meanings in *The Oxford English Dictionary* is that sex is "Either of the two main categories (male and female) into which humans and many other living things are divided on the basis of their reproductive functions." Another definition in an earlier version of the *Oxford English Dictionary* is that sex is the "Quality in respect of being male or female." There are numerous problems with both definitions, but they effectively highlight two distinctively different approaches to the subject. The first definition points to common distinctions based on organic, biological, or morphological structures associated with various species used as a means of identifying individuals as male or female. The second definition suggests a more psychological approach to the topic. According to this definition, sex refers to experiential or phenomenal qualities including feelings, beliefs, and attitudes associated with being male or female. *The Oxford English Dictionary* also explores additional meanings including sex as the act of intercourse or sex as a transitive verb as in the sexing of animals, i.e., the dividing and separation of males and females common in the practice of animal husbandry.

Multiple concepts of sex inform, cut across, and weave into almost every other intellectual endeavor including: morality and ethics, biology, chemistry, religious beliefs, economics, sociology, psychology, aesthetics, and philosophy. There is no "totality," "coherent specificity," or "easy singularity" where sex is concerned and nowhere do we encounter greater challenges to the ways we theorize and conceptualize the meanings of "similarity" and "difference." Ambiguities abound and have been multiplied by modern laboratory studies, social movements, demographic redistributions, and attempts to challenge and reshape earlier political, social, economic, and religious boundaries.

The early history of sex was understandably dominated by religious views and by religious prescriptions for sexual ethics including strict specifications for the roles of women and men.[3] Such roles and ethical guidelines were typically dualistic and developed in the context of abysmal ignorance of biological fundamentals and of the complexities, ambiguities, and varieties of natural human object attachments. Patty Sotirin, in a discussion of the philosophy of Gilles Deleuze, speaks of "an 'in-between' to all of the most pernicious dualisms that constitute us as subjects and that give significance to our most fundamental relationships."[4] The "in-between," and the "beyond," suppressed, denied, or hidden for centuries, have exploded into contemporary awareness to challenge long held assumptions, practices, and ethical structures about strict dichotomous roles for males and females. But changing territories and new boundaries resulting from naturalistic and scientific discoveries, evolving political landscapes, and expanding ideas of spirituality are not easily assimilated into earlier ways of thinking.

A rigorous science of sex was a relatively late development surfacing with the growth of empirical and naturalistic philosophies, careful anatomical studies, and the introduction of research tools such as the microscope. Reference to a "science of sex" does not imply, however, that there had not been careful observational studies and imaginative and sometimes productive theoretical work on reproduction and sex dating back to the Greeks and earlier periods of history.[5] Aristotle, in particular, in his *De Generatione Animalium* explored a great variety of questions such as the origin of males and females, the causes of birth defects, reproduction in viviparous and ovoviviparous animals, metamorphic stages, and the relative roles played by male and female generative materials. Aristotle's work on reproduction, sex, and embryology set the intellectual agenda for centuries. Subsequent scholars such as Aurelius Augustine, Thomas Aquinas, and Paracelsus were among the many who extended and amplified Aristotle's productive work. Though the major focus of this chapter will be on selected biological studies, beginning with the discovery of sperm, there will be occasional references to the works of earlier background studies that provide context for understanding modern developments.

Selected Biological Studies

The discovery of sperm cells in the late 17th century resulted in new theories and interpretive complications for both religious and scientific scholars. The focus, in what follows, will be on the questions, puzzling implications, and the imaginative theories growing out of the new worlds revealed by microscopy. The microscope, no less than the telescope, and their continuing refinements, contributed to an intellectual revolution whose reach continues to grow with implications that sometimes remain beyond our grasp. Jane Maienschein, in her book *Embryos Under the Microscope*, speaks of the radically different and confusing perspectives afforded by microscopically observed embryos vs. the more hypothetical embryos we can only imagine without the aid of the microscope.[6] The same confusion came about with the first microscopic observations of sperm cells.

The earliest microscopic observations of sperm cells in the late 17th century resulted in heated debates about these "small animals" swimming about in seminal fluids. They were clearly living things, but what were they and what role did they play, if any, in reproduction? In her book *The Ovary of Eve: Egg and Sperm and Preformation*, Clara Pinto-Correia revisits the questions that followed the discovery of sperm. If sperm were little animals: "What did they eat? Did they have intestines? ... Did they have a soul?"[7] Why were there so many of them?

The discovery of sperm also resulted in heated debates about their role in reproduction. If humans were made in the image of God, how could it be that, like other animals, we would come from a lowly worm-like animal? Perhaps these little animals had nothing to do with reproduction, but were somewhat akin to bacteria swimming about in the seminal fluids of the male. Wasn't it reasonable to believe that the real agent of reproduction was something more singular in nature and of a much finer more rarefied quality yet to be discovered in the seminal fluid?

Experiments in the early 19th century by Jean-Louis Prévost and Jean-Baptiste Dumas strongly suggested however, that it was in fact the little worm-like animals that were essential to fertilization.[8] Prévost and Dumas called attention to the existence of sperm in a great variety of animals. They also noted that sperm that lacked motility, such as those encountered in immature animals, were incapable of negotiating their way through the liquid matrix to the egg. In a series of experiments, Prévost and Dumas clearly demonstrated that various impediments to sperm motility interfered with fertilization. For example, a series of filter papers inserted between sperm and egg reduced the number of sperm available to reach an egg. The probability of the fertilization of an egg was a negative function of the number of filters. Prévost and Dumas also demonstrated that sperm in a solution subjected to an electric current were incapable of fertilizing an egg. Elizabeth Gasking noted that experiments conducted by Prévost and Dumas "constituted a genuine and successful attempt to put the facts of generation on a firm basis of observation and experiment."[9] Following the work of Prévost and Dumas, there was little question that it was these little animals that were essential to the fertilization of the egg.

Another question centered on problems associated with the sheer numbers of sperm. If they were the vital agents of reproduction and if only one little animal was necessary to fertilize an egg, what happened to all the rest following insemination? Genuine reproductive potential in each of millions of sperm raises troublesome questions about the meaning of all the waste that occurred, even in sexual intercourse that led to successful conception. This question was and remains particularly troublesome in some religious circles partly because of the religious and philosophical implications of the story of Onan in the 38th chapter of Genesis. According to Levirate traditions, Onan was obligated to marry Tamar, the wife of his deceased brother. Onan knew that his offspring with Tamar would not legally be his. So, when he performed his sexual duties with Tamar, he withdrew prematurely and spilled his seed on the ground. Now, God was angered and slew Onan. But what was Onan's sin?

Religious scholars have filled volumes with perplexing theological debate about this question. Surprisingly, the discovery of sperm activated and complicated matters. Prior to discussing the complications arising from the discovery of sperm, it will be informative to mention at least three of the classic arguments regarding Onan's sin. One argument centers on possible economic selfishness. A male offspring from Onan and Tamar would be Onan's brother's child and would reduce Onan's own inheritance from Judah, Onan's father. Another possibility is that Onan's sin is simply his stubborn failure to obey Levirate law. The interpretation that has been most common in Christian and some Jewish traditions and that is clearly tied to subsequent ethical prohibitions is that it is the actual spilling of the seed that is the sin.

This interpretation appears most consistent with Deuteronomy 25:11–12. If two men are in a fight and if the wife of one of the men enters the fight and takes hold of the private parts of the man fighting with her husband, then her hand shall be cut off and there is to be no pity for her. The source of the seed of the combatant is clearly of greater value than the hand of the woman defending her partner; the source of the male seed is not to be violated or compromised. The sin of wasting seed became a theological obsession throughout history and continues to prevail in many religious traditions into the 21st century. But the discoveries of science revealed that the greatest waste, a waste of almost unimaginable extent, is encountered in nature itself. There are over 250 million sperm in a typical emission and very few emissions result in fertilization. The order of magnitude of waste must now be understood on an astronomical scale.

The seriousness of waste is illustrated in the various treatments of masturbation in Western religious traditions. Thomas Aquinas viewed masturbation as a sin against nature. Pinto-Correia notes that the Franciscan Monk Benedicti was concerned about the nature of the fantasies that occur during masturbation.[10] The object of desire was always a source of fascination among theologians. It was thought that some fantasies, just as some behaviors, are more sinful than others. Ranke-Heinemann, for example, speaks of theological debates about "whether the sin [of sex] was greater with a beautiful woman or with an ugly one."[11] The history of punishments for masturbation include: threats of mortal death, eternal damnation, beatings, castration, and the creation of a variety of highly imaginative painful restraints that prevented access to the offending organs. There were also suggestions for reducing the number of involuntary nocturnal emissions. A string might be tied to the male member at bedtime, pulling the member back between the legs. Then the string was run up the back side and attached to the neck of the potential dreamer. Now, an erection would be painful both to the male member and to the neck.[12] Medical literature, as late as the 20th century, reinforced and amplified religious views on the evils of masturbation. It was argued that the practice could corrupt body and mind and result in blindness, lethargy, stupidity, insanity, and every variety of moral turpitude. *The New Catholic Encyclopedia* softens the stance of the church on masturbation by acknowledging empirical research and differing opinions while continuing to insist that the practice "is seriously inordinate and, if voluntary and knowing, sinful."[13] These views carry political consequences as well; Jocelyn Elders, briefly United States Surgeon General, lost her position in 1994 over her support for masturbation.[14]

Obsession with waste and concern that waste was sinful are reasonable in the context of earlier periods of history. The mechanisms of reproduction were poorly understood; populations were stressed by disease, wars, and other hazards; life was short; the birth process itself was a major source of premature death for women; and death rates of infants and children were high. McLaughlin notes that in the Middle Ages, infant mortality was "in the order of one or even two in three."[15] Small pox, other childhood diseases, infections in an age prior to antibiotics, wells, and medical overdoses all contributed to premature infant deaths. It is understandable that ethical structures were designed to address the problems of the day. The goal of sex was reproduction and survival. Any circumvention of these goals such as the waste of seed via masturbation, homosexuality, abortion, birth control, or sex for any reason other than reproduction were regarded as sinful or even punishable by death. But now the morality of those old ethical-religious structures is increasingly being called to question in an age of burgeoning population growth, malnutrition and massive starvation, changing age demographics marked by longer and longer life spans, greatly enhanced safety for women in child birth, increasingly high probabilities of infant survival, diminishing natural resources, and accelerating pollution and degradation of water, land, and air.

Ecological perspectives demand recognition that ethical and moral structures adaptive in one context can be toxic or fatal in another context. On the other hand, older truths, often regarded as sacred and absolutely fixed, often foreclose on the possibility of finding easy transitions or engaging in meaningful discussions of temporal differentiation and difference. The history of evolving attitudes toward topics such as family size, birth control, abortion, homosexuality, and masturbation illustrates the agonies of a lost or fading heritage. Herein we encounter keys to understanding striking theoretical and practical differences between scientific discoveries and political and religious conservative philosophies. Survival itself and quality of life are at the heart of disputes that persist to the present day.

Ovists vs. Spermists

The discovery of sperm opened up another debate regarding human and animal origins. The debate, with puzzling religious consequences, centered on the primacy of the egg vs. the sperm, was illustrated in opposing intellectual camps known as ovists and spermists. The egg, because of its size in birds and some reptiles had been known and studied for many centuries prior to the discovery of the sperm. There was widespread belief that all life has its origin in the egg and that mammals, like birds and reptiles, come from eggs. One problem was that no one had observed a mammalian egg until the 19th century. In 1826, Karl Ernst von Baer (1792–1876), a Russian biologist working with numerous mammals such as dogs, rabbits, and cats, published an account of his observation of the egg of a dog. With careful microscopic observations, von Baer was able to differentiate the egg from the Graffian follicle. Others were able to repeat the observation. There had been a race to discover a mammalian egg from the time of the discovery of the sperm. The difficulty is understandable in view of the extremely small size of mammalian eggs. The egg of a human is about the size of a period made by a sharp lead pencil. Nevertheless, a remarkable event in the history of the observation of human eggs was filmed by Dr. Jacques Donnez in 2008 when he spotted the birth of an egg during a hysterectomy on a 45-year-old woman. Dr. Donnez was able to magnify and photograph the egg as it emerged from the ovarian follicle. The egg surfaced and separated itself from the follicle in a period from 12 to 15 minutes.[16]

The identification of eggs and sperm re-introduced long standing perplexing questions about the relative roles of male and female gametes in the reproductive process. As noted, the eggs of birds and some amphibians had been observed for centuries so their importance was well understood, but if God created Adam first, surely his seed would have primacy. What was the nature of the generative material in the egg and in the sperm, and what was the nature of the force or forces that set those materials in motion? According to ovists, the male simply activated what was already there, already preformed in the egg. Such a position was reasonable in the context of available knowledge. Following the discovery of the sperm, however, there were now stronger claims that the egg served only to provide a nutritive environment for the sperm. Spermists called attention to the vigorous activity of the sperm and to the apparently passive qualities of the egg. Ovists celebrated the majesty, dignity, and quiet qualities of the egg – it was the worthy candidate to be the chief player in life processes. Spermists, by contrast, spoke of the vigor and life-like qualities in the searching movements of the sperm. Surely the egg was nothing more than a passive, nutritive receptacle for the life forces clearly present in the sperm. As an aside, it is interesting to call attention to the attribution of gendered qualities to microscopic gametes. For participants in this debate, gender is apparently everywhere from the macroscopic world of Mars and Venus to the microscopic world of egg and sperm.

As noted, ovists often insisted that the organism to be was already preformed in the egg. The term *preformed* opens our inquiry into a major 17th century issue that persists in various forms to the present – preformationism and epigenesis. Did the sperm do anything more than activate what was already there in the egg or was the organism already preformed in the sperm rather than the egg?

Preformationism

Preformationism is a theory of origins long embraced by scholars from scientific, philosophical, and religious traditions. Simply stated, preformation in its strongest form means that an organism once existed in miniature and that development is simply expansion, growth, or amplification of what is already present in the gamete. There are highly imaginative drawings of homunculi (extremely minute persons) thought to be encased inside the egg or the sperm. Infinite divisibility suggested the possibility of infinite miniaturization. Thus, a Homunculus was thought to contain all the preformed ancestors of its past, dating back to the very beginnings of life. Russian dolls provide an apt metaphor for the implications of preformationism. The ever-smaller miniature homunculi may even possess all the parasites and bugs (unimaginable diminutives) that beset the organism. Thus, creation was an all-at-once act and not a continuing, on-going or emerging process from undifferentiated or seemingly indifferent parts. Everything was there in the gamete of the primordial ancestor – the ovary of Eve or the seed of Adam.

The philosopher Gottfried Wilhelm von Leibniz (1646–1716) was a strong advocate of preformationism. Donald Rutherford, in his book *Leibniz and the Rational Order of Nature*, notes that Leibniz believed in "the panorganic structure of the universe: the idea that matter is everywhere composed of organisms enveloped within organisms ad infinitum."[17] As a co-discoverer of the calculus, Leibniz was accustomed to thinking in terms of infinitesimals; objects or units of time so small as to be unmeasurable. He could easily imagine preformed minuscule individuals existing in the germ plasm dating back to the beginnings of the world.

Hints of preformationism are evident in an old Mormon hymn that refers to a primordial mother and a previous existence in a heavenly sphere from which one is now estranged but hopes to return.[18] Thus, existence on earth is transient and purposeful but without memory for an earlier existence in a different sphere. The unfolding from pre-existence in extreme miniaturization implied a remarkable continuity of present, past, and future along with a possible purpose for each individual part of the entire sequence. Preformationism was consistent with many religious doctrines but also received support from philosophers and naturalists. The philosopher Nicholas Malebranche argued it was reasonable to believe in "infinite trees inside one single germ."[19] Preformation implies that each of us had two births, a birth in the beginning and another birth when it was our time in the great chain of being to enter this temporary habitat that we now occupy. An all-knowing God knew each of us in the beginning. It follows that the succession moves forward as well as backward. Current offspring, and their future offspring and so on, were also known at the beginning and the whole chain will proceed from a fixed beginning to a fixed end. The end is as fixed as the beginning. The reach of creation; the continuity of past, present, and future; and the meaningful place of each individual in the sequence served as sources of wonder and comfort.

As noted, strict preformation implies regression and progression of ever smaller gametes enclosed in ever smaller containers all the way back to the first parents and all the way forward in time until the end. This implies that creation was complete in the beginning, a position amounting to a radical determinism or a pre-determinism foreclosing on the possibility that any given sperm following a sexual episode might fertilize an egg. Questions abound. Why then, so many sperm? If everything is set in motion in the beginning, is there any role for chance in reproduction? A rigid lock-step series also raises questions about the origin of still-births and children born with an atypical appearance or with deformities, what earlier scholars referred to as monsters. Were these deformities really there and built in at the outset of the entire creative process? Children born with unfortunate anomalies have always constituted a theoretical and moral problem for religious leaders who believe that foreknowledge is among God's attributes. For science, such anomalies amount to a different set of theoretical problems along with a strong emphasis on practical problems associated with possible technological intervention.

Pinto-Correia called attention to claims that children with deformities are not necessarily an embarrassment to preformationism because there is no reason to suppose God would not program some selected catastrophes into the historic succession of events.[20] Thus, what humans regard as the problem of evil at the macro level is already preprogrammed into selective entries in the unfolding microscopic chain of events. Preformation then, is not necessarily inconsistent with the existence of children or other creatures who are poorly adapted or malformed. Perhaps they serve some larger purpose unknown to us. That's a long standing and currently common religious explanation, but the theoretical, moral, and practical problems remain.

As noted earlier, preformationists were divided on whether preformation was in the egg or the sperm. There is a vast literature on the tensions and spirited arguments set forth by the two camps. Neither camp, however, could adequately explain the obvious mix of the phenotypic characteristics of both parents in their offspring. Such a mix implies development of organisms from a complex interaction of separate parts. Neither the egg nor the sperm could have it all. Thus, we encounter a different approach to generation that lacks the historical continuities suggested in preformation and that comes with a new set of problems of its own.

Epigenesis

According to the theory of epigenesis, each organism is genuinely new as an emergent from a complex interaction of the male and female gametes in the context of an environment that contributes in its own ways to final outcomes. Broadly speaking, the environment may be nurturing and friendly or deficient in required resources. Epigenetic theory rejects the idea of a mechanical unfolding of a highly organized, pre-differentiated, and preformed individual organism. The deterministic characteristics of preformationism are replaced by a probabilistic approach to genesis in which the whole is dependent on a complicated accretion and assemblage of multifaceted parts.

Aristotle and Descartes were among the most important precursors of the epigenesists, though neither used the term. Aristotle believed the male seed served as the efficient cause to activate the material cause already present in the egg. The formal cause was to be found in the finer details of the male and female gametes. Aristotle's teleology is also consistent with epigenetic theory. Purpose, for Aristotle, is immanent in the natural processes of reproduction, not something imposed from outside as presumed in preformation theory. In other words, Aristotle believed in an intrinsic teleology found in nature itself as opposed to an extrinsic teleology in which end-states are pre-determined by deity.

Epigenesis was initially rejected partly because of concern over how so many parts, apparently foreign or indifferent to each other, could find their way together to form a highly organized being. Leibniz argued that mechanical systems by themselves could not possibly produce a complex organism unless there was some pre-existing organization. He believed that such organization was of a divine nature.[21] Development is thus mere augmentation of what is already there. Concern based on questions about the origins of complexity have been ameliorated somewhat by the development of cell theory and the discovery of DNA. Still, the specific details on the origins of order and complexity and the possibilities of spontaneous organization from parts ostensibly blind to each other remain as a curiosity. What are the specific means by which order comes about not only in living materials but in the inorganic world as well?

Epigenesis has become less of a mystery in the context of discoveries that parts of natural systems are not necessarily indifferent or blind to other parts. Indeed, part processes and functions may often be coerced by the presence and nature of other parts and by the dynamic structural characteristics of the whole. The part–whole problem and its manifestations from physics to psychology became an obsession with the founders of Gestalt psychology. Michael Wertheimer notes that Gestalt theorists argued that natural processes, left to themselves, do not necessarily result in disorder. "If one places a drop of oil or mercury in water it becomes a spheroid by its own dynamic properties, not by any mold into which it is poured; the dynamic self-distribution of forces results in the spherical form of the globule: these forces come from within."[22] If salt is poured into water, salt crystals with all sorts of interesting patterns will gradually result from the mix. Stuart A. Kauffman, in his book *The Origins of Order: Self-Organization and Selection in Evolution*, points to apparent spontaneous order in the inorganic world. Like Wertheimer, Kauffman calls attention to the behavior of oil in water, but notes that what takes place at that level is without the benefit of a Darwinian type of natural selection. This suggests a more fundamental order inherent in the mix of primitive inorganic elements and compounds. Kauffman notes that "snowflakes assume their evanescent sixfold symmetry for spare physicochemical reasons" and ponders "how such self-ordering may mingle with Darwin's mechanism of evolution – natural selection – to permit or, better, to produce what we see."[23]

Wolfgang Köhler argues that classic deterministic machine theory excludes "any dynamic interrelations among the parts of a field, such a field can be put together in any arbitrarily chosen fashion. In a mere mosaic each element is entirely indifferent to the nature of its neighbors."[24] Köhler argues that natural physical organizations are not necessarily mere mosaics and thus "not insensitive to the characteristics of other facts in their neighborhood."[25] In the natural world there are genuine intimacies among the parts of a field, but these intimacies are easily missed if attention is directed exclusively to part processes, to mere hook-ups or wired connections. Wertheimer notes that "The qualities of the whole determine the characteristics of the parts; what a part has to be is determined by its place, role, and function in the whole of which it is a part."[26]

Epigenetic theory is understood more clearly in the context of changing paradigms in the sciences. Theoretical physicist Fritjof Capra argued that the new paradigm is marked by a shift from the part to the whole. "In the new paradigm, the relationship between the parts and the whole is reversed. The properties of the parts can be understood only from the dynamics of the whole."[27] The reach and the radical nature of the new paradigm is captured by Wertheimer in the claim that

> the whole is psychologically, logically, epistemologically, and ontologically prior to its parts. A whole is not only more than the sum of its parts, it is entirely different from a sum of its parts: thinking in terms of a sum does violence to the very nature of the dynamics of genuine wholes.[28]

A whole that is entirely different from or radically other than a mere summation of parts implies the possibility of corrigible arrangements and emergent novelty that in the words of philosopher Donald A. Crosby in his book *Novelty* "is an outcome of complexity, of movement over time from simpler to more elaborate forms of being."[29] These more elaborate forms of being are encountered across the spectrum from quantum phenomena such as quantum entanglement and quantum superposition to the emergent qualities of compounds, to the formation of an individual organism.

Expansion of Possibilities for Human Control

In her book, *Embryos Under the Microscope: The Diverging Meanings of Life*, Jane Maienschein explores a great range of possibilities for the manipulation and control of development.[30] She calls attention to current research that assumes a combination of "both epigenetic development and a predeterministic starting point that decides some features but only influences others."[31] In other words, a weak form of preformation based on the influence of genes and chromosomes is coupled with epigenetic features including, among other things, all the complexities of intrauterine life. As noted earlier, children who are stillborn or born with deformities constitute a theoretical problem for strong forms of preformation theory. According to epigensis, the problem is primarily pragmatic. Mutations in the generative material, genuine accidents, or toxicities in the environment that result in deformities may be subject to corrective interventions. There is heuristic value in regarding deformities as accidents in the assemblage of parts. Intervention and prevention are increasingly possible when the source of an accident or genetic anomaly can be identified. For example, about 1 in 4000 women have defective mitochondrial DNA that results in tragic birth defects and painful early deaths of children. Mitochondrial DNA or mtDNA is always passed from the mother to the child and is different from the DNA that produces all the noticeable physical characteristics such as eye and hair color. The mtDNA is basically an energy source and has been compared to the battery of an automobile. It is now possible for scientists to extract all the genetic material from the egg of a mother with defective mtDNA. The extracted genetic material is then transferred into a donor egg from a mother with healthy mtDNA. The original genetic material from this egg is removed, but the mtDNA remains. The result is a healthy egg with the genetic material from the mother to be, coupled with the mtDNA from the egg of the donor mother. The healthy egg is then fertilized and implanted in the woman who desires to carry a baby free from defective mtDNA. The procedure has been carried out on various healthy primates and, of this writing, will likely be approved for humans.

The procedure, of course, is highly controversial. The resulting child has three parents and is thus a clear exhibit of epigenetic theory and the possibilities for human control of genesis. If the child is female, she will later pass on the genetic modification to the next generation and so on for generations to come. One of the major concerns is that the procedure is a first step in the development of designer babies. Another concern is that scientists will make some kind of mistake in the transfer process and thus create uncontrollable genetic mutations that could persist for generations. There are, to be sure, important moral issues to be debated, but our concern here is with the more theoretical questions about the nature of the origins of life.

The origin of males and females has also been a source of confusion, at least until the discovery of chromosomes. According to preformation theories in their more radical form, the sequence of males and females in any family line must have been set in motion at the beginning. But again, why did offspring, whether male or female, display so clearly the physical characteristics of mothers and fathers? Explanations of the origins of males and females had a long and interesting history. Males were likely to reside on the right side of the body and females resided on the left. If a woman desired a male child she should lie on her right side during copulation. A man who desires a male child should tie a string around his left testicle prior to having conjugal relations. If a woman feels quickening on the right side of her body she is likely carrying a boy, if quickening is on the left side, it is a girl. The circle was commonly viewed as the most perfect geometric shape. Eggs that were more circular in shape were more likely to produce males, those that were more elongated were more likely to produce females. The greater the heat of the passion of the male in a sexual episode, the greater the chances of producing a boy. It follows that older men are less excitable and colder than younger men and thus more likely to produce a girl. An older man who desires a boy should take steps to avoid sex on a cold night. Clearly, there has always been tension between fixed providential theories of the origins of life and human desires for control. Nowhere is this tension more clearly evident than in the literature on family planning and birth control.

Birth Control

Theological problems surfacing out of the extension of science into the sexual arena are repeatedly illustrated in the history of birth control. There have always been compelling needs and desires for control over reproductive functions. Women with severely compromised health conditions such as tuberculosis or diabetes have in all times understood that another pregnancy could threaten their lives and the well-being of their existing children. Accordingly, desperate control efforts are found in the literatures of almost all the major cultures of antiquity. Remedies such as crocodile dung, honey, cedar oil, frankincense, elephant dung, fermented acacia, and imaginative varieties of gummy substances have been used in various combinations throughout history in attempts to kill the male seed or prevent its transport.

The divergent adaptive needs of males and females complicate the birth control picture in decisive ways. Historically, males, free from the multitude of potentially fatal risks of pregnancy and childbirth, have been focused largely if not exclusively on the propagation of offspring. Moreover, organizations and institutions controlled by all male hierarchies initiate and propagate policies favorable to male interests. Females, in contrast with males, must face the discomforts and demanding work of pregnancy, the pain and risks of delivery, and primary responsibility for the requirements of sustenance of life for offspring. Little wonder history provides overwhelming evidence of a continuing intense quest for control over reproductive functions. Unfortunately, reliable control measures did not surface until the 20th century, and most of these measures faced stiff and sometimes frenzied resistance as evidenced by restrictive laws, legal battles, moral imperatives, demonstrations and marches, disputes about sex education, and an abundance of slogans such as "war on women," "war on science," or "war on religion."

In the early years of the 20th century, Margaret Sanger (1883–1966), a nurse and reformer, developed an obsession with birth control following the early death of her mother who had suffered through 18 pregnancies and 11 deliveries of children all of whom weighed over 10 pounds at birth.[32] Sanger believed her mother's early death at age 48 was the result of her sexual servitude. Sanger's interests were also fed by her personal observations that large families are almost always poor while smaller families enjoy greater economic stability. Her interest peaked when she made an emergency visit to the home of one Sadie Sachs who was in critical condition following an attempted self-induced abortion. Following successful medical intervention, Sadie was spared, but pleaded for birth control information. She already had more children than she could support, but birth control information was sparse and often illegal. Months later, Sanger was called back to the home of Sadie Sachs; this time a self-induced abortion proved fatal.[33] Subsequently, Sanger became the most visible activist for reproductive choice. In one of her attempts to shape public awareness, Sanger published a book titled *Motherhood in Bondage*. The book included hundreds of letters written by girls and women detailing the agonizing and sometimes fatal effects of a brittle one-size-fits-all system insensitive to the complexities of individual situations.[34]

Among the chief impediments to birth control information in the United States was The Comstock Law named after conservative activist and crusader Anthony Comstock (1844–1915). In 1873, Comstock persuaded the United States Congress to pass sweeping legislation criminalizing virtually every activity associated with reproductive choice. With the Comstock Law, it was no longer legal to produce, reproduce, own, distribute, publicize, or transport information about medical procedures, techniques, devices, or drugs that might interfere with conception or result in abortion. The law went so far as to forbid the use of the United States Postal Service as a way to convey information about reproductive issues. Comstock used his various positions as a United States Postal Inspector, founding member of the New York Society for the Suppression of Vice, and a leader in the Young Men's Christian Association (YMCA) to threaten, monitor, and prosecute anybody who violated the law. As a result, doctors, nurses, teachers, and other professionals were frozen in fear as they faced imprisonment and fines for any infraction of the law.

Comstock became a zealot for the causes he embraced. He viewed himself as a champion of the youth, a "weeder of God's garden," and as the chief guardian of America's morality. He bragged that he had "convicted persons enough to fill a passenger train of sixty one coaches [and that he had] destroyed 160 tons of obscene literature."[35] He apparently felt little or no remorse that he drove as many as 15 people to suicide.[36] Comstock also launched attacks on what he regarded as obscenity in the arts including novels, plays, magazines, paintings, and sculptures. He conflated obscenity with birth control information and with illustrations in medical texts. According to Broun and Leech "In making the arts dangerous, he made them glamorous."[37] Comstock openly admitted that he used clever tricks, subterfuge, deception, chicanery, and outright lies to secure confessions and convictions.[38] In his view, a successful outcome trumped methodology in the battle against the devil and evil. As an aside, it should be pointed out that the authoritarian and moralistic atmosphere created by religious and political crusaders such as Anthony Comstock was a highly visible part of the social context for Andrew Dickson White as he worked on his classic *History of the Warfare of Science with Theology in Christendom*.

In spite of the multitude of restrictive moral prescriptions in early 20th century America, there were steady scientific and political developments chipping away at the problem of sexual and reproductive servitude experienced by most women. In the 1950s William Masters and Virginia Johnson initiated laboratory studies on actual sexual behaviors and responses of men and women. Initially, they worked with volunteer prostitutes and later with hundreds of community volunteers. Their discoveries on such topics as the nature of orgasms, vaginal lubrication, and the nature of sexual arousal captured public interest as they challenged standard myths about sexuality. Shortly after World War II, Alfred Charles Kinsey published books on male and female sexuality based on extensive data he had collected via questionnaires and interviews. He found that "people were much friskier than they cared to admit, with 85 percent confessing to premarital sex, 50 percent acknowledging extramarital affairs, and almost everyone saying they masturbated."[39]

The empirical methods of Masters and Johnson and Kinsey, along with the growing public awareness of the work of Sigmund Freud, sharpened public curiosity about a subject that hitherto had been off limits or that had been relegated to and dominated by the dictates of religious and political authority. Margaret Sanger welcomed the advance of knowledge about human sexuality based on scientific methods, but was troubled that available contraceptive measures were unreliable, awkward, and overly dependent on the cooperation of males. Sanger knew that a better world for women could not be achieved without the development of a reliable mechanism, procedure, or a drug controlled exclusively by women and for women. Early in her career as a reformer, she had hoped to achieve her dreams for women via educational and information reforms. In that spirit, and in violation of the restrictive Comstock laws, she had opened the first birth control clinic in the United States knowing it would fail. It did. She was arrested and spent 30 days in jail, but she achieved a political victory of sorts. The public became increasingly aware of the vast chasm between cold abstract generalizations and ideologies embraced in many religious organizations compared with the concrete realities of individual lived experiences of women. Long lines of desperate women showed up at Sanger's clinic with chilling stories about their personal dilemmas. Sanger encountered case after case of wrenching stories such as poor women with large undernourished families, life threatening health conditions, and uncooperative husbands diagnosed with venereal diseases such as syphilis. Such women longed for accurate information on how to prevent another pregnancy.

Sanger's most ambitious dream was for the development of a readily available, inexpensive, and reliable birth control pill for women. The dream seemed little more than a mere fantasy wish, but an unlikely combination of a zealous reformer, a wealthy widow, an eccentric biologist, and a Catholic medical doctor would turn the dream to a reality. Margaret Sanger, of course was the zealous reformer who in 1950 met Gregory Pincus, a biologist with deep interests in reproductive processes. Unlike many of the leading biological scientists of his day, Pincus believed in the theoretical and practical possibility of the development of a birth control pill for women. His meeting with Sanger in 1950 marked the beginning of a lengthy collaboration between the scientist and the reformer. Years of tedious experiments on animals including numerous failures and successes were extremely expensive and could have never been accomplished without the extensive financial support of Katharine McCormick, a powerful player in the suffrage movement and, in the words of Jonathan Eig, committed to the idea that "Without birth control, any woman might become a prisoner to her husband, a mere breeder."[40] The success of Pincus with animal experiments would need to be followed up by human trials and this called for the cooperation of the medical community. John Rock was a respected doctor and devout Roman Catholic who believed that babies have a right to be wanted, that bourgeoning populations constituted one of the greatest threats to all humanity, and that the Catholic Church would ultimately change its position on birth control.[41] Because of his Catholicism, Sanger didn't really trust John Rock or want him on the team, but he would ultimately prove to be a valuable force in the development and promotion of birth control. The history of contraception would forever change because of the persistence of the collaborative efforts of these four key players and many others along with the risky commitment of Searle Drugs to release the first oral contraceptive in 1960 under the label Enovid. Literally millions of women world-wide now make regular use of the original pill and its successors such as RU 486.

Intense and bitter conflicts over birth control and family planning remain highly visible in the opening decades of the 21st century. The conflict is manifested in public demonstrations, legislative and judicial activities, budgetary and funding priorities, and disagreements over educational content for young people. Deep divisions between conservative and progressive forces are driven by concerns about the dangers inherent in burgeoning population growth, theological theories over the nature of besoulment and personhood, and questions about the moral rights and autonomy of women in the noon day of their awareness compared with the moral rights and claims of the fertilized egg or the developing embryo.

Birth Control as an Example of the Warfare Hypothesis

We return now to a fundamental question. To what extent do the continuing tensions over birth control illustrate a conflict between science and religion? A careful examination of the literature on the topic suggests the validity of the claim of Vern L. Bullough that "there is not a conflict between science and religion, but there is often a conflict between religion and science."[42] The science of birth control as reflected in the work of Gregory Pincus was motivated largely by curiosity about natural reproductive processes. John Rock was similarly motivated, but he was also driven by moral and social concerns associated with overpopulation and the right of every child to be a wanted child. As noted earlier, he believed his Catholic Church would ultimately change its position about birth control and population issues. He did not believe he was at war with his church. The remarkable discoveries of Pincus and Rock came under the critical scrutiny of religious leaders with mixed results. In some faith communities there was acceptance or even welcoming of birth control via the pill, but in other faith communities there have been, and continue to be, fiery sermons, intense and continuing legislative and judicial activities, demonstrations, threats and actual attacks against birth control centers, abortion providers, and the burning of clinical facilities. These activities almost always have a religious basis.

In his book *Godly Seed: American Evangelicals Confront Birth Control, 1873–1973*, Alan Carlson notes that "laws suppressing birth control information in American history were pure products of Evangelical Protestant fervor; nary a single Roman Catholic was involved."[43] Such a claim may seem counterintuitive in the 21st century as Catholic opposition to most forms of birth control has become more visible. But Carlson demonstrates that opposition to birth control in the early 20th century was led by Protestants and was manifested in the passing of laws such as the Comstock Law that criminalized almost all activity associated with birth control. Official Catholic opposition to birth control became more visible in America with the development of the pill and the Papal encyclical *Humanae Vitae* issued by Pope Paul VI in 1968.

After the pill was introduced in 1960, John Rock arguably became the most visible advocate for its use. Assured of the safety of the pill, and its health and social benefits, Rock worked tirelessly giving speeches, writing articles, appearing on radio and television shows, and, in general, attempting to convince his church the time had come for a re-appraisal of the moral questions surrounding birth control. In 1963 Rock published a book titled *The Time Has Come: A Catholic Doctor's Proposals to End the Battle Over Birth Control*. In her book *The Pill, John Rock, and the Church*, Loretta McLaughlin points out that Rock's book was published in numerous languages and "was perceived as exactly what it was, a head-on challenge to the Holy See in Rome."[44] There was massive public support for Rock's arguments and position, including strong support among the Catholic laity and a great many Catholic leaders. Some high level Catholic leaders believed the Church had been on the wrong side of history and that it could ill afford another "Galileo affair."

The work of Pincus and Rock caught the Church off guard. The pill did not destroy sperm, neither did it destroy the egg. It simply extended the "safe period" in the woman's natural cycle. Rock argued that the pill could be logically viewed as a natural extension of the rhythm method approved by the church. Conservative Catholic leaders were not buying Rock's conclusions partly because, with the pill, the extension of the "safe period" was now under the control of the woman. Such leaders engaged in *ad hominem* attacks against Rock viewing him as a "moral rapist" or suggesting that contraception amounted to murder.[45] Progressive Catholics, including a great number of priests, agreed with Rock's arguments but were fearful of going public with their agreement.[46] Rock, almost single handedly, exposed a troubling popular international awareness of major fault lines in Catholic practices and theology. It was no longer possible for the Holy See to ignore the growing controversy and the deep divisions among its leaders.

In 1964, Pope Paul VI called for a special committee of church leaders to reexamine the long-standing theological constraints on birth control. As noted earlier, there were deep divisions among Catholic leaders. Progressives strongly favored John Rock's position but conservatives were adamant in their opposition to any change in church policy. Finally, Paul VI came down on the side of the conservatives in 1968 when he issued the encyclical letter dealing with the regulation of birth and titled *Humanae Vitae*. The Pope informed the faithful that the magisterium is competent to interpret natural moral law. He reiterated his strict opposition to artificial birth control methods but encouraged scientists, especially Catholic scientists, to conduct research on chaste methods for the limitation and spacing of offspring. Such research would presumably affirm the "truths" of the Church's positions on the transmission of life as well as its position on proper expressions of marital love.

The Pope was unprepared for the unprecedented angry response manifested in defiant reaction to the encyclical by many church leaders along with massive numbers of Catholic laity. Progressive priests ignored the Pope's position by simply "looking the other way" when it came to birth control. There were fierce published rebuttals against the Church's position and a 2012 Gallup Poll showed that 82% of Catholics compared with 90% of non-Catholics approve of birth control.[47] Pope Paul apparently got the message because as noted by Loretta McLaughlin he "never pressed further for its acceptance, or took disciplinary action against any clergy who opposed it."[48]

Warfare is an apt term for some women who experience wrenching personal conflicts between the demands of their faith and their individual life conditions that counsel strongly and rationally against pregnancy. John Rock is also an example of one who must have experienced warfare as he was caught between his Catholic faith and his conviction that the church was wrong about birth control and insufficiently tuned to the dangers of overpopulation. In the end, Rock found it increasingly difficult to attend mass.

The language of warfare in popular and scholarly literature continues in these opening years of the 21st century and is not without justification because there is intense intellectual warfare over birth control and abortion. The warfare is brought partly by scientific discoveries and techniques and those who are committed to conservative theologies based on the authority of sacred traditions and literalist approaches to sacred scriptures. Progressives believe the high moral ground is owned by those whose faith includes the judicious use of the fruits of scientific discoveries.

*****

Though there were tensions between scientific and religious treatments of new discoveries in the micro world, they did not rise to the level of the tensions that surfaced in the explorations of the heavens. There is, for example, no conflict that approached the level associated with tensions over geocentric and heliocentric worldviews and the trial of Galileo or the condemnation of his works. Nevertheless, the microscope had joined the telescope in the promotion of an expanding worldview that challenged old assumptions and certainties. Religious leaders were especially perplexed over the prodigious waste of nature in the reproductive process. Rigid proscriptions to guard against waste such as opposition to birth control and condemnation of homosexuality and masturbation were increasingly called into question both by scientific discoveries and by radically shifting social and environmental contexts.

Further, differences between science and religion where sex is concerned may be playing out in modern tensions over evolution. Darwin's first technical point regarding evolution is that all organisms produce more offspring than can possibly survive. He was deeply aware of the enormous waste in nature. As a former theology student, he was at a loss to explain the waste and the brutality he encountered in nature. Another of Darwin's technical points is that some organismic variants are, by chance, better adapted in some niches. The role of chance in macro evolution and in microscopic human origins as opposed to divine predetermination is a continuing source of tension between creationists and evolutionists. Human control, particularly the control of women, in reproductive processes vs. the moral prescriptions of many faith communities, remains a hotly debated and controversial contemporary issue.

Notes

1 Proverbs 16:4 (RSV).
2 Sigmund Freud, "Leonardo Da Vinci and a Memory of his Childhood," in *The Standard Edition of the Complete Psychological Works of Sigmund Freud*, Vol. 11, ed. and trans. James Strachey (London: Hogarth Press, 1957), 137.
3 See, for example, Uta Ranke-Heinemann, *Eunuchs for the Kingdom of Heaven: Women, Sexuality and the Catholic Church* (New York: Penguin Books, 1990). A major focus is on celibacy and its effects on prescriptive roles for women and men.
4 Patty Sotirin, "Becoming-woman," in *Gilles Deleuze: Key Concepts*, ed. Charles J. Stivale (Ithaca, NY: McGill-Queen's University Press, 2005), 107.
5 We agree with Lorraine Daston and Elizabeth Lunbeck that the distinctions between "observation" and "experiment" are often fuzzy. There were "geniuses of observation" long before the advent of science. See Lorraine Daston and Elizabeth Lunbeck (eds.), *Histories of Scientific Observation* (Chicago, IL: University of Chicago Press, 2011), 1–9.

6 Jane Maienschein, *Embryos Under the Microscope: The Diverging Meanings of Life* (Cambridge, MA: Harvard University Press, 2014).
7 Clara Pinto-Correia, *The Ovary of Eve: Egg and Sperm and Preformation* (Chicago, IL: University of Chicago Press, 1997), 66.
8 See Elizabeth B. Gasking, *Investigations into Generation 1651–1828*. (Baltimore: The Johns Hopkins Press, 1967), 140–147.
9 Ibid., 143.
10 Pinto-Correia, *The Ovary*, 81.
11 Ranke-Heinemann, *Eunuchs*, 159.
12 Pinto-Correia, *The Ovary*, 86–87.
13 *The New Catholic Encyclopedia*, 2nd ed., s.v. "Masturbation."
14 Douglas Jehl, "Surgeon General Forced to Resign by White House," *New York Times* (December 10, 1994), http://www.nytimes.com/1994/12/10/us/surgeon-general-forced-to-resign-by-white-house.html (Accessed August 24, 2016).
15 Mary Martin McLaughlin, "Survivors and Surrogates," in *The History of Childhood*, ed. Lloyd Demause (New York: The Psychohistory Press, 1974), 111.
16 BBC News. "Ovulation Moment Caught on Camera," posted June 11, 2008, www.bbc.co.uk/2/hi/7447942.stm (Accessed November 14, 2016).
17 Donald Rutherford, *Leibniz and the Rational Order of Nature* (New York: Cambridge University Press, 1995), 201.
18 Eliza R. Snow (Lyrics), James McGranahan (Composer), "O My Father," in *Hymns: The Church of Jesus Christ of Latter-Day Saints* (Salt Lake City, UT: Deseret Book Company, 1978), 139.
19 Quoted in Pinto-Correia, *The Ovary*, 19.
20 Ibid., 181.
21 Rutherford, *Leibniz and the Rational Order*, 201–202.
22 Michael Wertheimer, *A Brief History of Psychology*, 5th ed. (New York: Psychology Press, 2011), 184.
23 Stuart A. Kauffman, *The Origin of Order: Self-Organization and Selection in Evolution* (New York: Oxford University Press, 1970), xiii.
24 Wolfgang Köhler, *Gestalt Psychology* (New York: Liveright, 1970), 115.
25 Ibid.
26 Wertheimer, *A Brief History*, 136.
27 Fritjof Capra, "The Role of Physics in the Current Change of Paradigms," in *The World View of Contemporary Physics*, ed. Richard F. Kitchener (Albany, NY: State University of New York Press, 1988), 147.
28 Michael Wertheimer, "Gestalt Theory, Holistic Psychologies, and Max Wertheimer," *Personale Psychologie: Beitraege zur Geschichte, Theorie und Therapie*, ed. Günther Bittner (Göttingen: C. J. Hogrefe, 1983), 32–49.
29 Donald A. Crosby, *Novelty* (New York: Lexington Books, 2005), 49.
30 Jane Maienschein, *Embryos Under the Microscope*. See, especially, Chapters 6–8.
31 Ibid., 30.
32 Jean H. Baker, *Margaret Sanger: A Life of Passion* (New York: Hill and Wang, 2011), 10.
33 Ibid., 49–51. It is not known whether the Sadie Sachs story refers to a literal person or whether it represents a composite of several typical cases. Either way, the message is the same.
34 Margaret Sanger, *Motherhood in Bondage* (Columbus, OH: Ohio State University Press, 2000).
35 Haygood Broun and Margaret Leech, *Anthony Comstock: Roundsman for the Lord* (New York: Albert & Charles Boni, 1927), 15–16.
36 Ibid., 212.
37 Ibid., 15.
38 Ibid., 159.

39 Jonathan Eig, *The Birth of the Pill: How Four Crusaders Reinvented Sex and Launched a Revolution* (New York: W. E. Norton & Company, 2012), 5. This book provides an excellent non-technical overview of the development of the birth control pill from the early work of Pincus on the effects of progesterone on ovulation in rabbits and rats, to human trials, to the production of Enovid by Searl.
40 Ibid., 94.
41 Margaret Marsh and Wanda Ronner, *The Fertility Doctor: John Rock and the Reproductive Revolution* (Baltimore: The Johns Hopkins University Press, 2008), 247–277.
42 Vern L. Bullough, "Science and Religion in Historical Perspective," in *Science and Religion: Are They Compatible?* ed. Paul Kurtz (Amherst, NY: Prometheus Books, 2003), 131.
43 Allan Carlson, *Godly Seed: American Evangelicals Confront Birth Control, 1873–1973* (New Brunswick, NJ: Transaction Publishers, 2012), 15.
44 Loretta McLaughlin, *The Pill, John Rock, and the Church* (Boston: Little, Brown and Company, 1982), 159.
45 Ibid., 164.
46 Marsh and Ronner, *The Fertility Doctor*, 237.
47 *The Gallup Poll*, 2012, "Americans Including Catholics, Say Birth Control Is OK," 227–228,
48 McLaughlin, *The Pill*, 191.

9

WOMEN AND MEN

Scientific and Religious Perspectives

> *Thy desire shall be to thy husband, and he shall rule over thee.*[1]
>
> *The sexual divide is the most persistent and arguably the deepest divide in the world today.*[2]

Reference sources such as *The Catholic Encyclopedia* and the *Encyclopedia of Mormonism* include informative descriptions of the nature and role of women from the perspectives of their faith traditions. Such descriptions typically document and celebrate the unique qualities and importance of women, the extensive and expanding opportunities enjoyed by women, and the many ways in which women and men are regarded as equals within their particular religious organizations. Leaders in most religious traditions, whether they be Muslim, Protestant, Mormon, or Catholic, present themselves as liberators, champions, and protectors of women.

An alternative conception is that the bulk of the major world religious organizations are patriarchal and well-known for the limiting and sometimes uncompromising prescriptions for the "proper place" of women in both religious and secular settings. In particular, leadership positions in most religious administrative hierarchies are male hegemonies. It is not prejudicial to call attention to rigid restrictions placed on leadership possibilities for women in the administrative hierarchies of large conservative religious organizations. In such organizations, women rarely occupy pulpits with the authority enjoyed by men or participate on equal footing with men in high-level deliberations on matters of policy or doctrine. Religiously based sexual apartheid continues to be a straightforward truth at the outset of the 21st century. The reasons offered by all male hierarchies for the separation of sexual spheres are often packaged in the language of theology and/or various interpretations of history and myth. It is not unreasonable however, to suspect deeper psychological, cultural, and philosophical influences at work in the entrenched and widespread discrimination.

Full participation and leadership positions are increasingly available to women in liberal to moderate religious organizations that are trailblazers in matters of religious equality for women, but such organizations pale in size compared to those that practice the many forms of gender discrimination. Further, even in liberal religious organizations, women earn less money than men for the same quality of work and promotions may come at a slower rate.

Science and religion have not really been different regarding the full participation of women in all levels of their substantive, organizational, and administrative work. Women have had to deal with social and financial barriers and a climate of gender bias in many scientific disciplines. Women have been and remain underrepresented in many college-level science courses and in the scientific work force. This is especially true in the physical sciences and engineering. Gender bias in science and religion is not surprising when it is remembered that both disciplines grew up in the historical context of essentialist philosophies that emphasized robust irremediable natural or created kinds. It is important therefore to focus attention on the role essentialism has played in science and religion.

Essentialism

For centuries males and females were viewed as created or natural kinds, easily categorized, clearly delineated in terms of structural and functional characteristics, and as existing in their present forms from the beginnings of time. This view can be characterized as a type of *essentialism*, a term referring to the fundamental unambiguous intrinsic nature or character of something or that which makes a thing what it is.[3] Essentialist views of males and females are reflected in the earliest religious literature and the holy books of some of the world's major religions. For example, according to the second chapter of Genesis, man was created or formed by God from the dust of the earth. After the creation of man, God created plant life followed by animal life including all the beasts of the fields and the fowl of the air. Later, woman was created and designed as a companion, partner, or helper fitted to man's needs. The essential differences between men and women were thus clearly delineated and created by a higher power for different but complementary purposes.

There were at least seven major ideas in early Biblical literature with far-reaching consequences for the status of women: first, the male was created prior to the woman; second, man received the breath of life directly from God and therefore woman received this breath only indirectly through man; third, by naming the animals, the male was an active participant in creation; fourth, the woman was created specifically for the man as a companion or a helper; fifth, the first woman was deceived by Satan and thus responsible for the fall of man; sixth, the first three events were ordered and approved by God, the highest power in the universe, and were thus regarded by believers as a set of incontrovertible truths. A final consequence for women is that they are condemned to enhanced pain in childbirth and subjection to their husbands. Some of these ideas set forth in Genesis are mirrored in later Biblical literature as in First Timothy 2: 11–15 where the reader is reminded that man was created first and that it was woman who was first deceived in the Garden of Eden. That same passage holds that women should learn in silence and with all submission and that they should not be allowed to teach or to have authority over men. On the other hand, the letters of the Apostle Paul often emphasize and approve the active roles of women in the early church. Women could prophesy, pray, and even serve in positions of leadership. Nevertheless, there is ambivalence regarding women in Paul's letters as evidenced by his requirement that women cover their heads to show their subservience.[4]

Essentialist philosophy is also set forth in the Qur'an (Surah 4:34), which says "men are the maintainers of women" and that the good woman is obedient and that the woman who is guilty of desertion should first be admonished and then isolated. If admonition and isolation do not result in the desired effect, the woman may be subjected to corporal punishment. The Qur'an in Surah 24:31 also commands believing women to cast down their looks, to wear head coverings, and not to display their ornaments except to family members.

The presumed essential liabilities of women were magnified in the works of some of the most important documents and leaders in the early Christian church. Clement of Alexandria, speaking of women, maintained that "the very consciousness of their own nature must evoke feelings of shame."[5] Clement goes on to say that women, outside of their houses, should be completely veiled. The book of Ecclesiasticus in the Apocrypha declares that "Woman is the origin of sin, and it is through her that we all die" (25:24). It goes on to declare, "A silent wife is a gift from the Lord" (26:12). Though the Apocrypha is not accepted by all Christians, the aforementioned quotations are consistent with many of the teachings of the church fathers. Tertullian, who lived in the latter part of the 2nd and early part of the 3rd centuries, displayed strongly ambivalent beliefs about women and their role in the church. He praised "righteous women," women who were martyrs, and virgins. He even accepted the idea that women could sometimes speak prophetically. At the same time, Tertullian set forth some of the strongest condemnations of women ever written: "*You* are the devil's gateway … the first foresaker of the divine law … because of *your* punishment, that is, death, even the Son of God had to die."[6] Tertullian believed that women should be veiled, that they had one rib fewer than men (presumably because God took a rib from Adam to form Eve). Tertullian's highly variable observations about women provide grist for both apologists and polemicists. It is somewhat difficult to tease out his deepest personal beliefs because he was a product of a larger culture marked by strong beliefs in the subordination of women and was undoubtedly influenced by ideas comparable to those encountered in scriptures such as those cited above from the 25th chapter of Ecclesiasticus and from the 2nd chapter of First Timothy.

Essentialist views of males and females are ubiquitous in early Jewish, Christian, and Muslim religious traditions. Most cultures emphasized a seam between males and females that runs throughout much of the natural world. A virulent brand of religious essentialism is illustrated in the 13th century writings of celebrated scholars such as Albertus Magnus and Thomas Aquinas. Albertus Magnus, also known as Albert the Great, was the teacher of Thomas Aquinas, as well as a key figure in the development of scientific thought. He was lionized as another Aristotle because of the enormous breadth of his learning. Unfortunately, Albert also perpetuated many of the misogynist views of the Greeks and the early church fathers. According to Ranke-Heinemann, Albert should be regarded as the "Patron of Rapists" because of his claim that "The more a woman resist, the more she wants it."[7]

Essentialist thought is nowhere better illustrated than in the *Malleus Maleficarum* by Dominican monks Heinrich Kramer and James Sprenger. The *Malleus* served as a widely used handbook by Catholics and Protestants in the witchhunts during the Inquisition of the late Renaissance and early modern periods. Kramer and Sprenger argued that women were capable of "the greatest heights and lowest depths of goodness and vice." They agreed with other theologians "All wickedness is but little to the wickedness of a woman." Kramer and Sprenger contended that women are more credulous than men, more impressionable, "feebler both in mind and body," and that "Women are intellectually like children." They continue with a litany of the views of many of the theologians of the day declaring that women are more carnal than men, that "women have weak memories," that they are natural liars, and that they incline the "minds of men to inordinate passion."[8] Kramer and Sprenger argued that, in view of their natural weaknesses, it was little wonder that women were more vulnerable than men to the temptations of the devil. We can also conclude, that given the prejudices of the time, it is little wonder that women were far more likely than men to be tried for witchcraft, found guilty, and executed.

Essentialist views continue to be employed to justify the presumed spiritual distance between religious leaders and the laity. For example, lay ministers in the Catholic Church, many of whom are women, may engage in many activities including teaching, preaching, and visiting the sick. There is nevertheless, a common belief in a spiritual chasm that separates women from the priesthood. In the words of John Allen "the sacrament of holy orders produces an ontological change in the new priest … allowing him to stand in *persona Christi* while celebrating the sacraments. Lay ministry produces no such ontological change."[9] To be sure, the ordination of women in the Catholic Church remains as a highly contentious issue, but in practice, there are boundaries that bar women and other members of the laity from full participation in the hierarchical structure of the organization.

The Church of Jesus Christ of Latter-Day Saints also bars women from the priesthood. The strongly entrenched position of the church was dramatically illustrated in June of 2014 by the excommunication of Kate Kelly, an activist for gender equality in the Mormon Church.[10] Kelly was co-founder of "Ordain Women," an advocacy group challenging restrictions against the full participation of women in all church related activities. Kelly was accused by an all-male disciplinary council of the sin of apostasy. An apostate, sometimes considered as a traitor, is one who has renounced or abandoned former beliefs. Kelly insisted she is not an apostate, but she cannot abandon her opposition to gender apartheid where the priesthood is concerned.

Those who reject gender-based boundaries in church practices insist that such boundaries often have a political rather than a theological basis. Most excommunicates in the Mormon Church can be forgiven if they repent and renounce their errors. The errors, of course, may reside in church practices and doctrines, and in such cases, Mormons believe in the possibility of new revelation. In 1978, for example, church leaders believed they received new revelation regarding former beliefs about black skin and the roles of African American people in the church. Subsequently, African American men could be ordained as priests.

Problems with the subordination of women in religious organizations have become especially topical at the outset of the 21st century. Religious organizations ostensibly embrace and promote impeccable moral ideals. At the same time, there is increasing awareness that women are as educated and as spiritually astute as men. There is clearly increased resistance to patronizing attitudes that grow out of ideology. It can also be argued that there is a price to be paid for the suppression of the feminine voice in positions of spiritual leadership. Perspectives are inevitably lost and spiritual imperialism along with rigid and limiting boundaries are reinforced. Suppression of the female voice may also feed the perception that the highest reality (God) is actually masculine and best served by masculine perspectives. The suppression of the female voice in the pulpit is also likely to be as damaging to men as to women. For example, gendered entitlement of men may undermine sobered and disciplined self-appraisal and balanced interpretive studies of sacred literature.

Church Control

From its earliest beginnings, the Catholic Church developed doctrines pertinent to the philosophy and practice of sexual and gender issues. Church doctrines became authoritative, based as they were on scripture, apostolic tradition, cultural influences from the Greek and Roman periods, essentialism, and the presumed deep moral implications of sexual behavior. Church interest extended to both theoretical and practical matters. On the theoretical side Ranke-Heinemann calls attention to endless debates on such questions as to whether it is possible to have sex without sinning? If so, what was the recipe for sinless sex? Is there sin if the motive for coitus is nothing more than pure, dutiful, procreation? Did Adam and Eve have sex in the Garden of Eden? If not, what were the means of reproduction and propagation of the species? Did animals engage in sex, even if Adam and Eve did not?[11] These and other questions filled volumes set forth by a celibate hierarchy obsessed with what was forbidden in their own lives.

On the practical side, there were extensive rigorous demands for strict conformity to a long list of rules and regulations regarding sexual activities. There was to be no sexual coupling on Sundays or on any of a long list of holy days. Sex was always for procreation and not for pleasure. Based on common perceptions of the story of Onan (as we discussed in Chapter 8), birth control techniques including withdrawing or spilling of seed were strictly forbidden. As we will see later in this chapter, obsession with the presumed sinfulness of birth control persists in the opening decades of the 21st century. Thomas Aquinas believed humans must guard against the danger of blind bestial impulses in sexual activity. There were rules against sexual unions that imitate animal sex and penalties for deviations from strict religious rules. The confessional is obviously voluntary, but Priests were free to ask questions, to monitor conformity, and to impose penalties for disobedience.

Early "Scientific" and Secular Views: Essentialism Continued

The Scientific Revolution would be slow to witness the development of rigorous empirical studies of sex and gender, but as we saw in the previous chapter, challenges to essentialism quickly surfaced with the advent of empirical studies. Still, as late as the 19th and early 20th centuries it was common to find academicians, including scientists, who embraced an exclusively essentialist approach to males and females. Naturalistic essentialism, however, differed from the theological or supernatural essentialism described earlier. The essentialism encountered in the work of 19th and early 20th century scientists focused on differences presumed to be produced by natural biological processes. Such a naturalistic essentialism was evident in popular magazine articles, newspapers, and "scientific papers" where one encounters literally hundreds of articles emphasizing intrinsic or natural differences between males and females. As noted by Sandra Bem, "the biological accounts of male–female difference and male dominance that have emerged since the mid-nineteenth century have merely used the language of science, rather than the language of religion, to rationalize and legitimize the sexual status quo."[12]

Gustav Le Bon, one of the founders of social psychology, made the claim that the brains of women "are closer in size to those of gorillas than to the most developed of male brains."[13] Paul Broca, the famous French anatomist who discovered the speech projection area of the brain, conducted autopsies that revealed a difference of 181 grams in the weights of the brains of women (1,144 grams) compared with the brains of men (1,325 grams). Broca was confident that women were less intelligent than men and that the gap between male and female intelligence had been widening. His belief in a widening gap was based on evidence of smaller differences between prehistoric male and female skull capacity compared with greater differences in more recent male and female skulls.[14] It is clear there is a relationship between skull capacity and the size of the body but the meaning of the relationship has never been clear. Are large men with large cranial capacities more intelligent than smaller men with relatively small cranial capacities? Immanuel Kant, with a physical frame barely over five feet in height did not lack for intelligence. The smaller cranial capacity of women compared to that of men cannot be used as a basis for measuring intellectual capacity. Tragically, phrenology, though it provided more complex evaluations of skulls of women and men than did crainiometry, continued to exaggerate the perceived differences in abilities. For example, phrenologists Nelson Sizer and H. S. Drayton noted that it was common for women to appear to be brilliant, but they are "more showy than solid; very fond of variety, and therefore incapable of fixing the attention long on one subject, and so unfitted for pursuits that require abstraction."[15] Beyond brain size and skull shape, there were those who were not overly concerned about supposed deficiencies of women because, as noted by Francis Galton, "the female influence is inferior to that of the male in conveying ability."[16]

The supposed intellectual inferiority of women compared with men was not the only gender related topic in the mid to late 19th century. Respected leading figures also argued that women were emotionally less stable than men. T. S. Clouston, arguing from the pages of *Popular Science Monthly*, contended that women were slaves "of the instincts and emotions."[17] The well-known philosopher and sociologist Herbert Spencer claimed there had been an "earlier arrest of individual evolution in woman than in men, necessitated by the reservation of vital power to meet the cost of reproduction."[18] E. Van de Warker, speaking from the pages of *Popular Science Monthly*, claimed that because of hysteria, woman's "mind is always more or less disturbed."[19] Francis Galton claimed that women, compared with men, were more strongly influenced by some of their feelings and that "they are blinder partisans and more servile followers of custom."[20] Broca, Le Bon, Galton, and Spencer and others were well-known scholars speaking with apparent authority in popular and scientific sources. Their opinions not only perpetuated essentialist views of gender but also undoubtedly contributed to a self-fulfilling prophecy in all but the most self-confident, competent, and understandably angry women.

Sigmund Freud, one of the most influential psychologists of the 19th and 20th centuries viewed men and women as essentially different. For example, for children approximately three to five years of age, he postulated separate developmental processes for boys and girls, the Oedipus conflict and the Electra conflict respectively. Even though he was an atheist, Freud's psychoanalytic explanations of humans' desire for an ultimate God rest upon what he perceived to be a human wish defined in terms of masculine needs for a perfect father as manifested in the Oedipus conflict.[21] Freud's views of women were limited at best and odious at worst. Even Ernest Jones, Freud's biographer and confidant, noted "There is a healthy suspicion growing that men analysts have been led to adopt an unduly phallo-centric view of the problems in question, the importance of the female organs being correspondingly underestimated."[22] Despite these and other concerns about Freud's system of thought, he sometimes appeared to see beyond his own views. In *Future of an Illusion*, he defined an illusion not as an idea that is false, but as an idea rooted in wish fulfillment. Thus, illusions are beliefs that speak to our needs. Despite Freud's support for the cultural perceptions of essential differences between women and men, he argued that the idea of female intellectual inferiority is an illusion that he calls "disputable and its interpretation doubtful" and rooted in the wish fulfillment of the scholars who already perceive women as inferior.[23] Freud's views on women were largely consistent with common stereotypes in Victorian Vienna in the late 19th and early 20th centuries. Unfortunately, the acceptance of his views in some quarters propagated essentialist claims through the latter part of the 20th century.

Whether essentialism has a naturalistic or a religious basis, the practical moral and social consequences for women were and are devastating. There were widespread beliefs in the late 19th century that, with rare exceptions, women were incapable of meeting the intellectual requirements of a university education. The fierce debates about suffrage included strong claims that, because of their basic nature, women cared little about politics and would thus enter the voting booth filled with misinformation. It followed that voting privileges for women would undermine democracy. An article by then ex-President Grover Cleveland, published in *The Ladies Home Journal* offered the opinion that good women really didn't want to vote because they understood their divinely appointed roles.[24] In another article in *The Ladies Home Journal*, Cleveland made the claim that women's social clubs could be harmful by undermining the values of motherhood and wifehood.[25] In the religious arena, it is noteworthy that there were debates, even in relatively moderate churches, about the roles women could legitimately fill in worship services. For example, in the Congregational Church, shortly after the Civil War, there were debates about whether women should be allowed to assume leadership positions in worship services.[26] There were also strong denials that women were qualified to enter scientific fields. In an article titled "Women in Science" the claim was made that "There are no women of genius; when they become geniuses they are men."[27]

Precursors to a Science of Gender

For all the blind ignorance, willful ignorance, and misogynist rhetoric throughout history, there were voices crying in the wilderness for a radically new orientation toward males and females. It can be argued that Jesus represented a radical departure from some of the dominant sexual stereotypes of his day. In violation of the religious laws and practices of his day, he spoke to women in public, even foreign women (see John 4: 7–42). He approved of education for women (Luke 10:39), accepted women as travel companions (Luke 8: 1–3), and never once blamed women for the fall of man in the Garden of Eden, even discussing the co-creation of men and women as discussed previously. At considerable personal risk he directly violated the long established rule that those found guilty of adultery should be stoned to death (see Deuteronomy 22:22). According to John 8: 3–11, a woman caught in adultery was brought to Jesus. The religious leaders who caught the woman reminded Jesus of the established penalty of stoning. Jesus, in a clear and stunning reversal of long-standing Biblical practice, said, "Let him among you who is without sin, cast the first stone."[28]

An implicit challenge to many of the presumed gender differences embraced by early modern scholars was set forth in the work of the empirical philosopher John Locke (1632–1704). Locke argued that the mind at birth is as "white paper, void of all characteristics, without any ideas."[29] Locke's famous "blank slate" hypothesis had far-reaching implications for presumed gender differences and for education in general. Perhaps many of the so-called essential differences in men and women were attributable, not to inherent natural qualities or supernatural endowments, but to conditioning, culture, role expectations, and especially to differences in educational opportunities. The implication was that many of the presumed essential differences between women and men would disappear if the two sexes were on a level playing field with respect to educational opportunities. These ideas remained undeveloped in Western culture for decades following the work of John Locke.

Mary Wollstonecraft (1759–1797), one of the most visible reformers of the 18th century, seized on Locke's philosophy and set forth the implications of that philosophy for gender issues in her classic book *A Vindication of the Rights of Woman*.[30] In terms of its urgency, rhetorical intensity, and polemics, Wollstonecraft's *Vindication* can be compared to Jonathan Edwards' famous sermon "Sinners in the Hands of an Angry God." In her classic feminist manifesto, Wollstonecraft argued that women in the 18th century were treated as mere toys, robbed of educational opportunities and thus kept in a state of childish ignorance and acquiescence. She argued that women regarded as mere ornaments were robbed of real personhood and maintained in a state of perpetual social and economic dependence. She believed that the unequal and toxic cultural milieu was injurious not only for women but for men who were robbed of the rich companionship that could be provided by informed, educated, and interesting women.

Though Wollstonecraft suffered severe criticism from conventional and conservative forces, she was arguably the most important early pioneer in laying the groundwork for a re-examination of longstanding gender roles and for a science of sex and gender. Less than a century following the publication of the *Vindication*, John Stuart Mill published his book *The Subjection of Women*.[31] Mill argued that the subordination of one sex to another was wrong in itself and detrimental to all human improvement and progress. Mill found it difficult to imagine the damage to human advancement and the losses incurred when full participation in all cultural activities is denied to half the human race. Woody and Viney note that Mill boldly believed that "male chauvinism parades in the sciences as natural law or in religion as true theology based on divine ordinance."[32] Rejecting the weight of tradition, Mill argued for full voting privileges for women, equal educational opportunities, and what he called a "perfect equality" that would obviously include equality in religious leadership with balanced opportunities for women and men. As with Mary Wollstonecraft, Mill suffered hostility from forces dedicated to preserving traditions of the past.

Exclusivist Essentialism Challenged

Scholars such as John Locke, Mary Wollstonecraft, and John Stuart Mill provided a philosophical framework for new ways to think about differences between men and women. The upshot of their work was that some of the observed differences were attributable not to intrinsic, genetic, or biological qualities, but to the effects of the obvious restrictions on educational, political, vocational, and spiritual opportunities for women. The playing field was anything but equal. To level the playing field the philosophical work of Locke, Wollstonecraft, and Mill would now need to be supplemented by hard-core well-controlled empirical studies designed to provide data pertinent to the issues. Such studies commenced in the early 20th century and would weaken many of the claims of radical essentialism and help usher in major social changes. We argue, however, that naturalistic essentialism, though deeply entrenched, has been yielding more readily than religious essentialism to the results of empirical studies on the abilities of women and men. Religious essentialism, buttressed by the certitude associated with authority, sacred traditions, and presumed divine decree, has been slow to acquiesce even in the face of overwhelming contradictory evidence. But the evidence has continued to pile up and relentlessly chip away at exclusivist naturalistic essentialism and theological dogma. Opportunities for women slowly widened especially in the secular arena and educational institutions, but also in moderate to liberal religious organizations. Changes in secular and moderate to liberal religious arenas, however, have not been matched by comparable changes in those religious organizations that continue to embrace theological essentialism.

Emergence of a Science of Gender

An essentialist argument that worked very broadly against equal educational and political opportunities for women was encountered in what was known as the variability hypothesis. The earliest versions of the variability hypothesis consisted of the claim that women were more variable than men. Men were regarded as stable, reliable, consistent, and dependable whereas women were regarded as flighty, unstable, unreliable, and given to all sorts of inconsistencies. Following the work of Darwin however, variability became a virtue and a critical feature in selection and survival. Thus, in its later form, it was men who were regarded as highly variable while women tended toward the average and were all pretty much alike. In defense of the greater variability of men, it was noted that most of the world's criminals and saints were men. Further, most of the geniuses were men and there were more men among people with intellectual disabilities. These views clearly reflect current scholarship on in-group heterogeneity and out-group homogeneity, the common intergroup perception that *we*, whoever we are, are a diverse group of individuals while *they*, whoever they are, are very similar to each other.[33] One practical effect of the beliefs about limited variability in women was the assumption that there was a greater spread of intelligence in men than in women; this assumption was then employed to argue against higher education for women. Higher education was for the intellectually gifted and not for the average person. It was even argued that women would be unable to handle difficult subjects such as mathematics, chemistry, physics, or engineering. Such subjects might even have long-term debilitating effects on a woman's ability to function normally in society. If women were to be admitted to colleges they would need a special curriculum consisting of subjects to which they were naturally fitted such as cooking, child-care, and sewing. Early college curricula for women reflected these beliefs.

Evidence in support of the variability hypothesis was defended with the observation that it had been men who had excelled in legal and political arenas and men who had produced great art, music, literature, and science. The observation was superficially accurate but failed to parse the effects of variance in men and women attributable to unequal educational and vocational opportunities for women. In further support of the variability hypothesis, it was discovered that young boys compared with young girls were more likely to be diagnosed with developmental or intellectual disabilities. The problem with the comparison, however, was that young boys had far greater educational opportunities and faced higher expectations than young girls and were accordingly more likely to be diagnosed.

Though "scientific arguments" in favor of essentialist philosophy regarding sex were prominent in 19th century literature, it would also be the work of scientists and their colleagues that resulted in research that gradually challenged essentialist arguments. One of those scientists was Leta Stetter Hollingworth (1886–1939) who referred to the literature of her day comparing males and females as a "literature of opinion."[34] It was ironic that the "literature of opinion" had been supported and perpetuated by a long list of leading and respected scholars such as Frederick Nietzsche, Paul Broca, Herbert Spencer, Grover Cleveland, and Gustav Le Bon. Hollingworth argued that what was needed was a "literature of fact" based on well-controlled data-based experimental studies that provided careful disciplined comparisons.

Hollingworth called attention to early studies published in 1897 by Karl Pearson who found no reliable statistical evidence to support differential variability in males and females. In extensive studies, Pearson measured averages along with measures of variation in men and women and boys and girls ages 6 through 10. Measures covered a great range of structural and functional characteristics such as body weight, height, chest girth, strength of pull, strength of grip as measured by Regnier's dynamometer, length of long bones such as the femur, keenness of sight, and numerous cranial measures. Pearson's data came from several sources including: Francis Galton's work in anthropometry, Quetelet's *Anthropométrie*, and the Cambridge Anthropometry Committee.

The data, based on literally thousands of observations, raised serious questions about the variability hypothesis. Pearson found that on some measures females were very slightly more variable than men and on other measures men were slightly more variable than women, but overall there were no differences. Variability within groups was typically greater than variability between groups. One of Pearson's conclusions was that the "principle that man is more variable than woman must be put on one side as a pseudo-scientific superstition until it has been demonstrated in a more scientific manner than has hitherto been attempted."[35] He concluded further that "Those writers who find in this principle not only 'social and practical consequences of the widest significance' but an explanation of the peculiar characteristics of the 'whole of our human civilization' are scarcely to be trusted when they deal with the problems of sex."[36] The expression "social and practical consequences of the widest significance" undoubtedly referred to the use of the variability hypothesis as a pretext to bar women from college or to restrict their political and vocational opportunities.

Hollingworth viewed Pearson's studies as among the few that provided a "literature of fact," but there was a clear need for a study to address the potential contaminating effects of environmental influences. Accordingly, together with her colleague Helen Montague, Hollingworth conducted an experimental study based on 10 measures of 2000 new-born infants (1000 males and 1000 females) from the New York Infirmary for Women and Children.[37] According to the variability hypothesis, males are more variable than females in all things, including physical characteristics. Accordingly, measures of new-born babies should yield results demonstrating greater variability of boys compared with girls and such measures, unlike those collected by Pearson, would be less subject to possible environmental influences. Montague and Hollingworth included seven cranial measures in their study along with measures of height, weight, and circumference of shoulders. Premature babies, syphilitic babies, and twins were eliminated from their samples, and babies from upper middle-class homes were under represented in the study. A weakness of the study by contemporary standards is that there is no mention of whether those who administered the measures were "blind" with respect to the hypothesis or the sex of the babies. Measures were taken by a large number of attending physicians and that might have somewhat mitigated the danger of any constant errors attributable to the sex of the baby or knowledge of the hypothesis.

Montague and Hollingworth found no differences in variation on any of their ten measures of new-born males and females. They looked at average deviations, standard deviations, and ranges based on the data from all 20,000 observations. New-born boys were very slightly larger on the anatomical measures than new-born girls so Montague and Hollingworth used appropriate corrections for their measures of variability. A larger mean would likely be associated with a larger measure of variability so in accord with statistical adjustments suggested by Edward Lee Thorndike and Karl Pearson, average deviations and standard deviations were divided either by the mean or the square root of the mean. Some of the adjusted variability measures were exactly the same for boys and for girls. In fact, there were no differences in variations even without the statistical adjustments suggested by Thorndike and Pearson. This was ground-breaking research, devastating in its implications for what Hollingworth had called the literature of opinion.

The absence of inherent or natural differences in the variability of males and females undermined the rationale for keeping women out of college. Perhaps women were as variable as men not only in physical characteristics, but also in all things including intelligence, aptitudes, sensory and motor skills, and for our purposes in this work, we might add spirituality. If there were as many women as men in the high end of any performance curve, why not provide equal educational opportunities in all fields followed by equal vocational opportunities including law, medicine, mathematics, engineering, and religion? Isn't it after all an empirical question as to whether women could perform as well as men in all secular and church related vocations?

There was another myth prevalent in Hollingworth's day employed to defend restrictions on educational opportunities for women. In the words of Hollingworth, the claim was that, "Women, by virtue of the rhythm of their menstrual functions, experience regularly recurring interferences with the use of all of their abilities, and must be considered for a considerable part of each lunar period as invalids or semi-invalids."[38] Hollingworth explored this claim in her doctoral dissertation, titled "Functional Periodicity: An Experimental Study of the Mental and Motor Abilities of Women during Menstruation."[39] Her research included prolonged and rigorous examinations of topics such as memory, speed and accuracy of perception, steadiness, fatigability, and speed of learning of women in relation to their menstrual periods. She found no demonstrable influence of periodicity on the memorial, perceptual, or motor skills included in her battery of tests. Her study cast serious doubt on another common belief repeatedly encountered in the literature of opinion.

Hollingworth called attention to the minimal experimental work conducted in the early 20th century on average abilities of males and females. The upshot of the work that had been done was that variability within each sex was far greater than variability between the sexes. Men were slightly superior to women in speed of tapping, but women were slightly superior to men in selected memory tasks, but again, the differences were small. She quoted Edward Lee Thorndike who concluded: "The most important characteristic of [sex differences] is their small amount."[40] The experimental data were clearly challenging long-held armchair dogma and *a priori* assumptions regarding the abilities of women and men. Furthermore, public interest in the topic was high and fed by popular articles such as one by Rheta Childe Dorr published in *The New York Times Magazine* in 1915.[41] Dorr's article included a picture of Hollingworth and a summary of the work on variability with the suggestion that there is nothing in woman's nature that forecloses the possibility of achievement in an unimaginable range of vocational possibilities. History has clearly demonstrated that such a conclusion was prophetic.

The work of scientists such as Karl Pearson and Leta Stetter Hollingworth helped clear the way for expanded opportunities for women in all human arenas, but a variety of up-hill battles would remain based on the persistence of old attitudes. For example, empirical studies of "stereotype threat" demonstrate that entrenched negative perceptions may undermine performance of individuals and groups.[42] An illustration is provided by numerous studies that have demonstrated the effect of stereotype threat on women's performance in mathematics.[43] The dangers of stereotype threat apply to women and to men as well as to ethnic groups. There is no reason to believe that stereotype threat is not a powerful force in many faith communities with strong gender role expectations often based on belief in divine commands.

The Gender Continuum

The emphasis in this chapter has been on exclusive essentialist binary approaches to gender. The key term is *exclusive* because there are few who would deny the very real natural differences between males and females. Females have babies, men do not. Also, men on average are physically stronger. But for centuries, the deeply entrenched emphasis on natural differences stifled curiosity and inhibited more open and objective inquiries into the abilities of women and men. The supposed truth of gender differences was front-loaded; there was no need for empirical studies. Still, there had always been a realization that some men fit the stereotype of manhood better than others and some women were more feminine than others. There was overlap, but the extent of the overlap was underestimated. As noted in the previous chapter, there was also a clear awareness of biological ambiguities as in the presence of people who are intersex and animals that are hermaphrodites. Science, along with common sense, was discovering that sex is not always unambiguous and that the clear value-loaded dichotomous distinctions between males and females encountered in the history of religious and secular thought must now be replaced with a more nuanced approach.

Though there is comfort and economy in highly differentiated theological or natural kinds such as saint and sinner, intelligent and unintelligent, or male and female, early statisticians such as Francis Galton, Karl Pearson, and Jacques

Quetelet were discovering new and more challenging ways to think. In addition to binary classifications, some things, perhaps most things are distributed or strung out and best understood in terms of a continuum demonstrating, for example, degrees of intelligence and degrees of masculinity or femininity. "Exclusivist essentialism," whether in religion or science, was simplistic, historically blind to obvious complexities, and devastating in its implications for women and for men. Francis Galton was correct when he argued, "there is no bodily or mental attribute ... which cannot be gripped and consolidated into an ogive with a smooth outline."[44] The space between practical polar opposites could no longer be viewed as empty.

The New Emphasis on Similarities

Thanks to early advocates for equality such as Mary Wollstonecraft, John Stuart Mill, Karl Pearson, Helen Montague, and Leta Stetter Hollingworth, along with an explosion of public interest in women and their abilities fed by thousands of popular articles in newspapers and magazines, the late 20th century witnessed an acceleration of educational and vocational opportunities for women.[45] The abilities of women would now be tested in the give-and-take of the "real world." Furthermore, achievements of women would increasingly be tracked by normative statistical data. Surprisingly, the term *women* would not appear in the index of *The Statistical Abstract of the United States* until 1974. In that year, the single topic on women was the number of women employed in the Federal Government.[46] By 2011, the term *women* in the index was followed by over 120 subcategories or divisions within sub-categories.[47] In 1987, the term *education* was included as a sub-category under women. That edition provided data from a survey of college graduation numbers showing that 103,000 women had graduated from college in 1950 compared to 329,000 men.[48] By 1982, the number of women who graduated from college in all fields outnumbered the men for the first time in U.S. history; 480,000 to 473,000 respectively.[49] From that time, women who have earned bachelor's degrees have outnumbered men. In 2008, for example, the Statistical Abstract shows that 918,000 women earned bachelor's degrees compared to 681,000 men.[50] In that same year, 33,000 women earned doctorates compared with 32,000 men.[51]

There have also been dramatic changes in the number of advanced professional degrees earned by women. The changes are illustrated in the percentage of women earning professional degrees in the period from 1970 to 2008. Women, in 1970 earned 8.4% of medical doctorates in the United States compared with 49.3% by 2008. For doctorates in dentistry the change was even more dramatic. Women in 1970 earned less than 1% of the doctorates in dentistry compared with 44.5% in 2008. Statistics for women earning law degrees in that same period reflect a climb from 5.4% to 47%. Women earned 2.3 % of professional theological degrees in 1970 and 34.3% in 2008.[52]

Changes in other arenas are even more dramatic. Women were not allowed to participate in the ancient Olympic Games. Neither could they attend the games as spectators. Women were also barred from participating in the first modern Olympic Games held in Athens in 1896. Women participated in a limited way in the games in 1900 but over the strenuous objections of Baron Pierre de Coubertin, one of the chief organizers of the modern Olympics. Coubertin "abhorred the thought of women making fools of themselves by sweating in public. Until his death, he tenaciously attacked the 'regrettable impurity' that had infiltrated the games with women's participation."[53] There had been claims that participation of women would be uninteresting and thus fail to attract spectators, but once again, old prejudices and stereotypes were wrong. Women's events have increasingly stirred as much interest as men's events and illustrated levels of athleticism that could never have been imagined in earlier days. Women representing the United States in the 2012 Olympics, for the first time, outnumbered the men. Another first was accomplished by the entry of two women from Saudi Arabia, a country that as of 2017 still did not allow women to drive. Clearly there are remaining barriers and such barriers are more deeply entrenched in many religions than in science, but with increasing participation of women in science, engineering, space flight, corporate leadership, and sports, the barriers are falling.

A period of just over 100 years has witnessed one of the most remarkable intellectual revolutions in human history. Earlier claims that women were less intelligent than men, could not handle difficult subjects, had weaker memories, should not vote, or could not perform well in college or sporting events take their place among the most egregious flaws in the history of human reasoning. The exclusion of women in the highest levels of spiritual leadership in many faith traditions may someday also be regarded as an equally egregious flaw in the history of human reasoning and theological hermeneutics. The past underscores the tragic consequences of excessive reliance on authority and the resulting beliefs and attitudes undisciplined by reason, doubt, and vigilant observation. Expanding epistemic attitudes have clearly resulted in data that vindicate the early positions of pioneers and visionaries such as Mary Wollstonecraft, John Stuart Mill, Karl Pearson, and Leta Stetter Hollingworth.

Still, the religious suppression of educational opportunities for women remains in many parts of the world and is nowhere more tragically illustrated than in the case of Malala Yousafzai. An Islamic militant opposed to education for girls boarded a school bus in Pakistan where he opened fire wounding three children including Malala who was shot in the head. She miraculously survived the wound and achieved a remarkable recovery following restorative therapy in the UK. Subsequently, she has achieved international fame as one of the leading advocates for education for women. In 2014 she was the co-recipient of the Nobel Peace Prize, the youngest person and first Pakistani to receive the prize. Education for girls remains a contentious issue throughout many Middle Eastern and African countries.

Sex and Gender Outside of Categories

There is a rapidly growing awareness that sex and gender do not exist in clean categories. Even biological sex, which appears to break cleanly into males and females, has long been recognized as highly variable.[54] Genital variations that inspire physicians to call a specialist to evaluate a child's genitalia occur in approximately 1 of 1500 to 2000 live births in the United States.[55] This number, however, does not capture the wide human variability in sex, because it does not capture people with Klinefelter syndrome (men who have an additional X chromosome) or other genetic variations, and some people have intersex genitalia that are not readily identifiable at birth.[56] After reviewing United States' medical data 1955–1998 and using inclusive criteria for variations, scholars concluded that as many as 2% of live births led to a child with sexual variation of some kind.[57] Male and female are not clean categories of sex, and our prior failures to recognize sexual diversity are now playing out in court, for example, as military veterans who identify as intersex (i.e., neither biologically male nor female) have sued the U.S. State Department and other entities for recognition of their identity outside of male and female categories.[58]

Gender raises additional questions beyond biological sex. Through history, for both science and religions, biological sex (i.e., whether one is male or female) has been largely confounded with gender (i.e., whether one identifies as a man, a woman, or a gender outside of these categories) and viewed as an essential and categorical difference. In early conceptions of gender research, scholars assumed that male humans were men and that female humans were women. Even late 20th century studies started from this bipolar assumption. In recent decades, the study of gender has exploded, scientific support has challenged the existence of clean gender categories, and people now view themselves and their genders in a myriad of ways.[59] People who identify as transgendered or gender nonconforming are individuals whose gender identity or gender presentation does not match their biological sex as identified at birth.[60]

People who are transgendered or gender nonconforming have existed across cultures and history, yet both religious and scientific organizations have often devalued, pathologized, or otherwise rejected them. For example, the Hijras, born biologically male and living as women, have long historical roots in India, but they only recently received legal recognition as people who identify with a third gender.[61] Similarly, photographer Jill Peters documented Albanian Sworn Virgins, participants in a tradition that dates to the 15th century that allows women to live as men.[62] These individuals avoided arranged marriages common for young women, and they assumed the roles of men in society, including social functions as well as the walk, talk, and mannerisms of men. Many other examples exist throughout history, not only of people who are transgendered but, in many cases, of the powerful recognition and respect they receive in their communities. For example, many Native American cultures revered people who are called Two

Spirit, although this term conveyed and conveys many different ideas across highly diverse groups.[63]

Despite the abundance of these and other examples to challenge binary categories of gender, both science and religion have struggled to recognize the breadth of human experience. For an example that ended in a tragic clash of psychology and gender essentialism, Albert D. J. Cashire served as a Private in the Union Army, fought in many battles, and was active in veterans' causes after the war. A small, clean-shaven soldier who was able to help his comrades with sewing and laundry, he worked as a carpenter after the war. His life was changed, however, when he was struck by an automobile and broke his femur in 1911. The physicians who set his leg discovered that he was biologically female; despite his status as a combat veteran and his claims that he had a happy and healthy life as a man, he was forced to wear a dress as he lived the rest of his life incarcerated in an institution for people with psychological disorders.[64]

A scientific or religious framework that rests upon two rigid categories cannot adequately capture human experience. These changes have spread rapidly in recent years in the United States, not only in scientific studies but also in the larger culture. Caitlyn Jenner's decision to transition publicly to her identity as a woman as well as her willingness to provide interviews and challenge critics have radically reshaped these conversations and led to her runner-up status for *Time*'s person of the year for 2015.[65]

These tensions surrounding questions of gender identity exploded into the bathroom debates of 2016. When North Carolina passed legislation that required individuals to use bathrooms that correspond to their birth sex and prevented cities from passing related anti-discrimination measures, the federal Departments of Justice and Education responded with a joint letter in support of transgendered students' rights to use the bathroom that corresponds to their gender identity.[66] Not only have many politicians opposed the federal directive, but some religious leaders have pushed back strongly; a professor of Biblical studies at the Southern Baptist Theological Seminary argued that only two genders exist and that "the conflict has only just begun."[67] These issues have transcended religious and political arenas. When a national retailer announced that customers may use the bathroom that fits their gender identity, a boycott erupted with 1.4 million signatures; to resolve this conflict, the retailer plans to spend $20 million to upgrade all of its stores to include private bathrooms in an attempt to defuse the issue in a manner acceptable to both sides.[68] To support federal policies, the White House added a gender-neutral bathroom in April 2016, even as these debates raged across the United States.[69]

Questions about gender continue to move quickly. Never has a civil rights question about identity and discrimination gained such national traction and moved so quickly into the public consciousness. Across 2015 and 2016, these questions have gained prominence, and scientific support for people who identify outside of their biological gender has grown quickly and considerably. It remains unknown whether future scholars will view these years as a blink of accommodation before the clash of a larger war or as the start of accommodation and acceptance of human gender diversity.

*****

The warfare metaphor between science and theology as described in Chapter 1 is applicable to sexuality and gender in some of the same ways it has been in evolution. There have been and continue to be intense disagreements, amounting to intellectual warfare, within numerous faith traditions and between faith traditions and other interest groups on the roles and rights of women. Some of these disagreements are playing out in propaganda, large public demonstrations and legal battles over religious freedom vs. such topics as employment discrimination, in religious organizations that receive government funding, rules for protestors at abortion clinics, and funding for birth control. It would be a mistake to downplay the intensity of feelings expressed in epithets such as "war on women" or "war on religion." Many of the criteria outlined in Chapter 1 for defining intellectual warfare apply to the materials presented in this chapter.

Disagreements have undoubtedly been fueled partly by scientific discoveries that are clearly incompatible with traditional understandings of sex and gender. For example, if gender identities and sexual orientations are clearly not matters of choice, then the restrictive, value loaded, or punitive attitudes and measures of the past are no longer appropriate. Scientific research has resulted in widespread shifting and evolving public attitudes toward women and is clearly making inroads into the ways this topic is understood and treated within religious traditions. The circle of inclusion has widened and, in all probability, will continue to widen as reliance on authority is challenged by hard-core empirical evidence gathered from the achievements of women in the sciences, medicine, the business world, and education. It would be a sad comment if religious organizations turn out to be the last to unequivocally embrace the widening circle. The following chapter explores emerging scientific and religious views on sexual orientation.

Notes

1 Genesis 3:16.
2 Cynthia Fuchs Epstein, "Great Divides: The Cultural, Cognitive and Social Bases of the Global Subordination of Women," *American Sociological Review* 72, No. 1 (February 2007), 1–22.
3 For a discussion of essentialism see Ellen B. Bratten and Wayne Viney, "Some Late Nineteenth Century Perspectives on Sex and Emotional Expression," *Psychological Reports* 86 (April, 2000), 575–585.
4 For an informed discussion of the roles of women in the early church see Bart D. Ehrman, *Misquoting Jesus: The Story Behind Who Changed the Bible and Why* (San Francisco: Harper, 2005), 178–186.

5 Quoted in Uta Ranke-Heinemann, *Eunuchs for the Kingdom of Heaven: Women, Sexuality and the Catholic Church* (New York: Viking Penguin Books, 1990), 127.
6 A thoughtful discussion on the ambivalence of Tertullian regarding women is set forth by Daniel L. Hoffman, *The Status of Women and Gnosticism in Irenaeus and Tertullian* (Queenstown, Ontario: Edwin Mellen Press, 1995), 145–182.
7 Ranke-Heinemann, *Eunuchs*, 179.
8 Heinrich Kramer and James Sprenger, *The Malleus Maleficarum* (New York: Dover, 1971). See pages 41–48 for descriptions of the supposed weaknesses of women.
9 John L. Allen Jr., *The Future Church: How Ten Trends are Revolutionizing the Catholic Church* (New York: Dover, 2009), 205.
10 See Cadence Woodland, "The End of the 'Mormon Moment'" (*New York Times*, Vol. 163, Tuesday, July 15, 2014), A21.
11 Ranke-Heinemann, *Eunuchs*, 177–182.
12 Sandra Lipsitz Bem, *The Lenses of Gender: Transforming the Debate on Sexual Equality* (New Haven, CT: Yale University Press, 1993), 6.
13 Quoted in Stephen J. Gould, *The Mismeasure of Man* (New York: W. W. Norton, 1981), 104.
14 Ibid., 103–104.
15 Nelson Sizer and H. S. Drayton, *Heads and Faces and How to Study Them: A Manual of Phrenology and Physiognomy for the People* (New York: Fowler & Wells, 1892), 23.
16 Francis Galton, *Hereditary Genius: An Inquiry into Its Laws and Consequences* (New York: D. Appleton and Company, 1900), 63.
17 T. S. Clouston, "Female Education from a Medical Point of View," *Popular Science Monthly* 17 (December 1883), 221.
18 Herbert Spencer, "The Psychology of the Sexes," *Popular Science Monthly* 4 (November 1873), 30–38.
19 Ely Van de Warker, "The Relations of Women to the Professions and Skilled Labor," *Popular Science Monthly* 6 (February 1875), 454–470.
20 Galton, *Hereditary Genius*, 196.
21 Sigmund Freud, "A Religious Experience," in *The Standard Edition of the Complete Psychological Works of Sigmund Freud*, Vol. 21, ed. and trans. James Strachey (London: Hogarth Press, 1961), 168–172.
22 Ernest Jones, "The Early Development of Female Sexuality," *Papers on Psycho-analysis* (Boston: Beacon Press, 1967), 438.
23 Sigmund Freud, "Future of an Illusion," in *The Standard Edition of the Complete Psychological Works of Sigmund Freud*, Vol. 21, ed. and trans. James Strachey (London: Hogarth Press, 1961), 3–56.
24 Grover Cleveland, "Would Woman Suffrage be Unwise?" *The Ladies Home Journal* 22 (October 1905), 7–8.
25 Grover Cleveland, "Woman's Mission and Woman's Clubs," *The Ladies Home Journal* 22 (May 1905), 3–4.
26 See, for example, Stephen Knowlton, "The Silence of Women in the Churches," *The Congregational Quarterly* 9 (October 1867), 329–334. A different opinion is offered by Charles W. Torrey, "Woman's Place in the Church," *The Congregational Quarterly* 9 (October 1867), 163–171.
27 Henrietta Irving Bolton, "Women in Science," *Popular Science Monthly* 53 (August 1898), 506–511.
28 Some of the early Biblical manuscripts include this story, others do not. The materials presented here were taken from the Authorized King James version of the Bible.
29 John Locke, *An Essay Concerning Human Understanding* (New York: Dover, 1959), 121.
30 Mary Wollstonecraft, *A Vindication of the Rights of Woman* (New York: Penguin, 2004).
31 John Stuart Mill, *The Subjection of Women* (Indianapolis, Cambridge: Hackett, 1988).

32 William Douglas Woody and Wayne Viney, *A History of Psychology: Emergence of Science and Applications*, 6th ed. (New York: Routledge, 2017), 147.
33 Todd D. Nelson, *Psychology of Prejudice*, 2nd ed. (Boston: Pearson, 2005).
34 Leta Stetter Hollingworth, "The Vocational Aptitudes of Women," in *Vocational Psychology: Its Problems and Methods*, ed. Harry Levi Hollingworth (New York: D. Appleton and Co., 1917), 224.
35 Karl Pearson, *The Chances of Death and Other Studies in Evolution* (New York: Edward Arnold, 1897), 376.
36 Ibid.
37 Helen Montague and Leta Stetter Hollingworh, "The Comparative Variability of the Sexes at Birth," *American Journal of Sociology* 20, No. 3 (November 1914), 335–370.
38 Harry Levi Hollingworth, *Leta Stetter Hollingworth: A Biography* (Lincoln, NE: University of Nebraska Press, 1943), 86.
39 Leta Stetter Hollingworth, "Functional Periodicity: An Experimental Study of the Mental and Motor Abilities of Women During Menstruation," *Contributions to Education* No. 69 (Teachers College, Columbia University, 1914).
40 Leta Stetter Hollingworth, *Vocational Aptitudes*, 227.
41 Rheta Childe Dorr, "Is Woman Biologically Barred from Success?" *The New York Times Magazine* 19 (September 1915), 75–76.
42 Claude M. Steele, "A Threat in the Air. How Stereotypes Shape Intellectual Ability and Performance," *American Psychologist* 52, No. 6 (June 1997), 613–629.
43 Gregory M. Walton and Steven J. Spencer, "Latent Ability: Grades and Test Scores Systematically Underestimate the Ability of Negatively Stereotyped Students," *Psychological Science* 20, No. 9 (September 2009), 1132–1139.
44 Francis Galton, *Inquiries into Human Faculty and its Development* (New York: E. P. Dutton, 1907), 36.
45 An examination of standard reference sources to popular literature in the late 19th and early 20th centuries such as *Poole's Index to Periodicals Literature* or *Readers Guide to Periodical Literature*, will reveal hundreds of references to women including opinions about suffrage, the status of women in many foreign countries, debates about old stereotypes, and the performance of women in various vocations. There was clearly an insatiable public appetite for information about women.
46 *Statistical Abstract of the United States* (Washington, D.C., U.S. Bureau of the Census, 1974), 238, 1028.
47 *Statistical Abstract of the United States* (Washington, D.C., U.S. Bureau of the Census, 2011), 1009–1010.
48 *Statistical Abstract of the United States* (Washington, D.C., U.S. Bureau of the Census, 1987), 137, Table 230.
49 Ibid., 137.
50 *Statistical Abstract of the United States*, 2011, 187.
51 Ibid.
52 Ibid., 190.
53 Reet Ann Howell and Max L. Howell, "The Games of the 2nd Olympiad," in *Historical Dictionary of the Modern Olympic Movement*, eds. John E. Findling and Kimberly D. Pelle (Westport, CT: Greenwood Press, 1996), 16.
54 Alice Domurat Dreger, *Hermaphrodites and the Medical Invention of Sex* (Boston, MA: Harvard University Press, 1998).
55 Melanie Blackless, Antony Charuvastra, Amanda Derryck, Anne Fausto-Sterling, Karl Lauzanne, and Ellen Lee, "How Sexually Dimorphic Are We? Review and Synthesis," *American Journal of Human Biology* 12 (2000), 151–166.
56 Ibid.
57 Ibid.

58 Faith Karimi and Dani Stewart, "Army Veteran not Legally Male or Female, Judge Rules," (*CNN*, June 12, 2016), http://www.cnn.com/2016/06/11/us/jamie-shupe-non-binary/ (Accessed August 24, 2016); Colleen Slevin and Thomas Peipert, "Navy Vet Pushes for Changes to Passport Gender Rule," (*Military.com*, July 21, 2016), http://www.military.com/daily-news/2016/07/21/navy-vet-pushes-changes-passport-gender-rule.html (Accessed August 24, 2016).
59 For example, in early 2014, Facebook added more than 50 gender options beyond "man" and "woman," see Brandon Griggs, "Facebook Goes beyond 'Male' and 'Female' with New Gender Options," http://www.cnn.com/2014/02/13/tech/social-media/facebook-gender-custom/ (Accessed June 18, 2016).
60 American Psychological Association, "APA Guidelines for Psychological Practice with Transgender and Gender Nonconforming People" (August 6, 2015), https://www.apa.org/practice/guidelines/transgender.pdf (Accessed August 24, 2016).
61 Singh, S. H. (April 29, 2014) "Transgender, Gay Indians Fight to Throw off Taboos, Stereotypes," http://www.cnn.com/2014/04/29/world/asia/india-transgender-gay-rights/ (Accessed June 20, 2014).
62 CNN, June 2, 2014, "Who Are Albania's 'Sworn Virgins'?" http://edition.cnn.com/video/data/2.0/video/world/2014/06/02/balkan-tradition-sworn-virgins.cnn.html (Accessed June 20, 2014).
63 Bob Drury and Tom Calvin, *The Heart of Everything That Is: The Untold Story of Red Cloud, An American Legend* (New York: Simon & Schuster, 2012).
64 Tony Horwitz, *Confederates in the Attic: Dispatches from the Unfinished Civil War* (New York: Vintage, 1998).
65 Katy Steinmetz, "Person of the Year, The Short List, No. 7: Caitlyn Jenner," http://time.com/time-person-of-the-year-2015-runner-up-caitlyn-jenner/ (Accessed August 24, 2016).
66 Ray Sanchez, "Feds' Transgender Guidance Provokes Fierce Backlash," *CNN*, May 14, 2016, http://www.cnn.com/2016/05/14/politics/transgender-bathrooms-backlash/index.html (Accessed August 24, 2016).
67 Ray Sanchez, "Feds' Transgender Guidance Provokes Fierce Backlash," paragraph 30.
68 Chris Isidor, "Target's $20 Million Answer to Transgender Bathroom Boycott," *CNN*, August 17, 2016, http://money.cnn.com/2016/08/17/news/companies/target-bathroom-transgender/index.html (Accessed August 24, 2016).
69 Michael Scherer, "Battle of the Bathroom," *Time* 187, No. 20 (2016), 35.

10

SEXUAL ORIENTATION

From Harmony to Discord to Diaspora

> *Both heterosexual and homosexual behavior are normal aspects of human sexuality.*[1]
>
> *If a man lies with a male as with a woman, both of them have committed an abomination; they shall be put to death; Their blood is upon them.*[2]

In recent decades there have been intense conflicts between science and selected faith communities over questions of sexual orientation. The questions are important because issues such as same-sex marriage and civil unions are closely tied to problems associated with employment discrimination, inheritance rights, and parenting privileges. The emotional intensity of the rhetoric illustrates what people on all sides of the issues refer to as "the culture wars." In this chapter, we review historical instances of intellectual warfare and accommodation as we review the rapidly evolving history of sexual orientation.

Sexual orientation refers broadly to the nature of enduring romantic, emotional, intellectual, and sexual attractions, attachments, and preferences. It has become increasingly clear that biological sexual identity as male or female does not predict the direction or locus of romantic or erotic appeal. Differential attachments and attractions are obvious even within those who identify as homosexual, heterosexual or bisexual, and there is growing recognition of greater diversity in human romantic attraction, including those who identify as asexual and do not feel sexual attraction for others.[3] There are mysteries about why we are attracted to one person and not another, but experts agree that aesthetic preferences and attractions surface spontaneously and naturally without any clear evidence of deliberative conscious choice.[4]

Sexual orientation is not necessarily tied to biological classifications as male or female; neither is gender identity. People assigned to be male at birth due to the appearance of their genitalia may sometimes identify as women, and people assigned female at birth may sometimes identify as men; as noted in the previous chapter, these are only some of the possible variations of human gender identity. Sexual orientation is separate from gender and refers to the nature of our attractions to others.

In the early 1900s, there was little difference among religious, legal, and scientific views of sexual orientation. People who were not heterosexual were simply regarded as deviant or even as pathological. From this early common ground, a series of scientific developments reshaped perspectives of same-sex behavior and relationships. Tensions between scientific and general cultural viewpoints came to a head in the late 1960s and early 1970s. The Stonewall Riots of 1969 and the growing gay-rights movement emerged as scientists challenged common conceptions of sexual orientation and mental illness.[5] Subsequently, in the 1990s there was an outpouring of legal activity including the national Defense of Marriage Act (DOMA) as well as statutory and constitutional changes in many states regarding access to marriage.[6] There was increasing discord between scientists and a large number of religious groups. Explosive changes gradually led to greater harmony of scientific and legal views but to diaspora about these questions in religious groups.

Prior to the proliferation of scientific studies on sexual orientation, religious groups remained largely unified in their views of people who are not heterosexual. Their unity was based on long-standing traditions, doctrines, and interpretations of scriptural passages. The earlier unity, however, has been challenged by the results of empirical studies on sexual orientation. Discord is evident in denominational politics and doctrines, in local churches, in religious colleges and universities and even in the Boy Scouts. The scientific and religious literature devoted to this question is monumental. This chapter explores these matters in detail and concludes with a discussion of the remarkable rate of change in public perceptions in recent years and the consequences of these ongoing changes for future conflicts and agreements between science and various faith traditions.

Religious and Legal Contexts

As noted, religious doctrine, tradition, and scripture shaped religious views of sexual orientation. The Old Testament includes claims such as Leviticus 18:22, which states, "Thou shalt not lie with mankind, as with womankind: it is abomination." Proscriptions against homosexuality are also encountered in the New Testament. Romans 1:27 speaks of "men leaving the natural use of the woman, burned in their lust one toward another." The Qur'an in Surah 7:81 speaks of the transgression of men feeling lust for other men instead of women. In the majority of Islamic groups, homosexuality in all forms continues to be strictly forbidden and severely punished.

Early legal constrictions on people who were not heterosexual were often based on religious views. In 1533, under Henry VIII, the English Parliament passed the Buggery Act, which criminalized anal and oral sex and defined these acts as capital crimes, functionally banning sexual contact between men.[7] This and similar laws defined acts of sodomy, often as "crimes against nature," and some laws, including those applied in British Colonies that would later be adopted in the United States, cited only Leviticus to justify the death penalty.[8] Such powerful religious and legal perspectives were dominant for centuries and undoubtedly obstructed early scientific and medical scholarship.

Early Medical Views

For long periods, there was harmony among various disciplinary areas regarding homosexuality. Anything outside of narrowly defined heterosexual attachments was pathologized in one way or another. Early scientific and medical investigations of gay men, lesbians, and people who were bisexual exploded in the 1800s. For example, Karl Heinrich Ulrichs and Karl Maria Kertbeny argued that gay men, lesbians, and people who were bisexual had congenital medical and psychological conditions.[9] Kertbeny coined the term *homosexual* in 1869,[10] replacing more negatively loaded descriptive labels such as *buggers* and *sodomites*. These developments shaped the culture along with emerging views that criminal prosecution should not be pursued for behaviors that are not under conscious voluntary control.[11] In this spirit, Ulrichs and Kertbeny argued for decriminalization of same-sex behaviors and relationships.[12] Many physicians, including Karl Friedrich Otto Westphal, lent their support to the arguments set forth by Ulrichs and Kertbeny.[13]

Several prominent medical scholars stepped into these discussions. The Italian physician Arrigo Tamassia used the term *inversion* to describe same-sex attraction. This term was widely accepted for several decades.[14] Jean Charcot and Valentin Magnan brought the notion of inversion into French, even as they confounded sexual orientation with gender identity.[15] Richard von Krafft-Ebbing and Havelock Ellis, described by some as sexologists, also blended questions of gender identity and sexual orientation, assuming that gay men were effeminate and that lesbians must possess what later observers called "mannishness."[16] Krafft-Ebbing viewed sexual orientation as a pathology acquired in one's lifetime, but Ellis argued that homosexuality was not a choice but a condition of birth, that it was not a medical condition or disease, and that homosexuals could make important contributions to society.[17] Despite the limitations of their views, particularly as seen through 21st century eyes, they made important contributions to the growing discussion of people who are sexually diverse. Individuals protesting anti-gay laws and attitudes were now able to introduce new medical perspectives that challenged older religious and legal perspectives.

Early Psychological Views

Although psychology as a science dates back only to the late 1800s, there has always been mystery associated with object attachments and aesthetic judgments. The Greeks had sexual fantasies about some of their Gods such as Aphrodite as well as erotic attachments to some of their statues – an attraction known as *agalmatophilia*.[18] The American psychologist Edward Bradford Titchener confessed he could hardly look at the color yellow without feeling excitement.[19] Aesthetic and even erotic appeal is attached to certain varieties of physical objects such as buildings, automobiles, and motorcycles along with more abstract attachments to specific ideas or fantasies. Specific regions of the body such as lips, eyes, hair, and legs have differential erotic appeal. How did religious groups respond to the wide diversity in human attachments?

Deeply aware of the profusion of object attachments, early church authorities struggled to control aesthetic expression via comprehensive ethical and legal structures designed to guide, constrain, reinforce, or punish the faithful. For example, men's attachments to women were denigrated and forbidden in celibate communities. Men who were tempted by the allure of women were encouraged to focus on the ugly internal workings of women's bodies, including their excrement, bile, saliva, blood, and guts. Such a focus, as noted by Arlo Karnen, could change the perception of a woman and presumably have curative value. Karnen refers to Jonathan Swift's poem "The Lady's Dressing Room."[20]

> Thus finishing his grand survey,
> Disgusted Strephon stole away
> Repeating his amorous Fits,
> Oh, Celia, Celia, Celia shits![21]

Most religious traditions have attempted to establish controls over aesthetic attachments and displays associated with dress modes, hair styles, use of cosmetics, wearing of jewelry, and general demeanor. Dress modes have been particularly significant as illustrated in Deuteronomy 22:5 "The woman shall not wear that which pertaineth to a man, neither shall a man put on a woman's garment: for all that do so are abomination unto the Lord thy God." The Qur'an in Surah 24, verse 31 advised believing women to cast down their looks, wear their head-coverings, and avoid displaying their ornaments in public. Controls have often run to the extremes as with castration as a "therapy" for those with weak wills who were unable to resist the temptations of the flesh or for women who struggle with lives that remain completely subjugated and controlled. Moreover, a major goal is for social controls to become internalized to the extent that the believer experiences restrictions, not as something imposed from without, but as a freely chosen conscious compliance. When believers voluntarily control their most intimate thoughts, expressions, and behaviors, it becomes easier for them to believe more strongly in the prohibitions and maintain stronger affinity to the group.[22]

A classic example of early psychological views of people who were not heterosexual is encountered in the work of Sigmund Freud, who hoped to explain human diversity in sexual orientation. His classic "Three Contributions to the Theory of Sex" is clearly typical of 19th century medical and psychological viewpoints.[23] Freud explicitly discusses gay men and lesbians, both of whom he calls "inverts." Unlike many of those who followed him, Freud did not commit to the belief that inversion must be hereditary or must be acquired. Additionally, he confounded sex and gender as he argued that bisexuality is the original human anatomical condition before transition to a "unisexual" condition.[24]

Freud's views have generated extensive discussion within psychology and related fields. As Jack Drescher noted, "Attempts to find 'the real Freud' are too often motivated by those who seek his agreement with their own point of view."[25] Freud's views on this complex topic are not tightly organized, and he presented at least four different explanations for diversity in sexual orientation; to complicate matters, in his discussions of sexual orientation he is often presenting other theoretical constructs in psychoanalysis. Additionally, Freud's explanations of sexual diversity were clearly products of late 19th and early 20th century Vienna.[26] For these reasons, his more global views are difficult to unpack.

A generalization of his work does suggest a "juvenilization" of gay men and lesbians.[27] Nevertheless, by 1930 Freud had affixed his name to a call for decriminalization of homosexuality in Germany and Austria. In a letter to an American mother about her son, Freud wrote that neither she nor her gay son should feel shame and that being gay is not a vice, something degrading, or an illness.[28] Freud did not regard homosexuality as a neurosis, but as a difficult-to-treat psychic disposition. Despite these statements, Freud at least once considered therapy to change a woman's sexual orientation from lesbian to heterosexual.[29] Despite the diversity of his views and the power of acceptance that he modeled, sometimes only in private letters, Freud saw people who were not heterosexual through the lenses of his time, as "the opposite of ... a normal person."[30] How did people who followed Freud in psychology and related fields evaluate people who were gay, lesbian, and bisexual?

Scientific Investigations into Sexual Orientation

Alfred Kinsey revolutionized the study of sexuality by seeking vast amounts of data about people's sexual fantasies and experiences, evidence drawn from thousands of interviews.[31] Kinsey demonstrated that sexual behavior varies extensively, even among men (i.e., as people with the same gender identity) in a single nation at one point in time. To fit his data, he eschewed categories of sexual orientation and constructed a six-point scale to describe the diversity of sexual attraction.[32] In ways that were particularly challenging for American society soon after World

War II, he found that many individuals who identified strongly as heterosexual had engaged in at least some same-sex sexual behavior and continued to have same-sex fantasies. Kinsey's revolutionary study helped challenge the notions that people who were gay, lesbian, or bisexual must be pathological and that such identities are categorical.

Kinsey's empirical approach was followed by the work of Evelyn Hooker, who in 1957 evaluated "The Adjustment of the Male Overt Homosexual."[33] After interviews and extensive psychological testing of men who identified as homosexual or heterosexual, she concluded that these groups did not differ significantly in psychological evaluations or clinical outcomes. She raised important questions about whether people of diverse sexual orientations were inherently pathological. Despite the work of Hooker and others, homosexuality was classified as a psychological disorder until 1973.

The work of Hooker, Kinsey, and others stood in stark contrast to other developments in psychology. In the early 1960s, a group of psychoanalysts claimed some degree of success in therapeutic procedures designed to convert clients from homosexuality to heterosexuality.[34] A raging controversy followed the claim, but the upshot was to lay the groundwork for "reparative therapy," or attempts to change a client's sexual orientation. The American Psychological Association now rejects reparative therapy as unscientific and dangerous.[35] Additionally, many psychologists continued to confound sexual orientation and gender and assumed that gay men must be more feminine and that lesbians must be more masculine.[36] We now recognize the distinction of sexual orientation and gender, but this confound persisted into the 1980s and beyond, despite evidence that sexual orientation is not associated with masculinity and femininity.[37]

The Emergence of Discord

Across the 20th century and into the present, psychology and psychiatry have played prominent roles in generating support for discrimination as well as later support for recognition and inclusion. Much of the foundation for mid-20th century scientific prejudice toward gay men, lesbians, and bisexuals comes from the *Diagnostic and Statistical Manual of Mental Disorders* (DSM), called by some the "psychiatric bible," the handbook of standardized definitions of psychological disorders that has recently emerged in its 5th edition.[38]

The 1952 first edition of the DSM included homosexuality as a "sociopathic personality disturbance" that required treatment.[39] Despite critics' questions about the scientific foundations of this claim, the DSM provided perceived "scientific support" for discrimination that remained prevalent in the larger culture. The DSM-II, which emerged in 1968, perpetuated these negative views, which did not change until the release of the DSM-III in 1973.

In the late 1960s, activists staged a series of protests at conventions of the American Psychological Association to challenge the authors of the DSM to remove homosexuality as a mental illness.[40] These protests came to a head in the early 1970s, with a series of high-profile presentations and debates about the status of homosexuality as a psychological disorder.

A persistent myth in psychology and related fields at this time was the notion that psychiatrists and psychologists could not possibly be gay, lesbian, or bisexual. Such a belief may seem absurd to 21st century readers but remained prominent well into the 1970s. There was a practical basis for such a belief; publicly identifying as gay or lesbian constituted a sufficient basis to be fired, ostracized, or removed from a graduate training program, government job, or academic position. Thus, few gay or lesbian psychologists or psychiatrists openly identified themselves.[41] The persistence of this false belief along with persistant discrimination was enough to merit a direct challenge.

An early opportunity arose in 1971, when Dr. Franklin E. Kameny, an astronomer who had been fired from his government job, physically grabbed a microphone and spoke directly to American Psychological Association convention attendees about psychology and gay rights.[42] This was inspirational for many in the "loose underground network of closeted gay psychiatrists" that called itself "the Gay-PA," but members of this group remained well aware of the potential repercussions and did not take any steps "that might expose us."[43] Subsequently, the 1972 American Psychological Association convention included an invited panel to discuss these issues, and on the panel was Dr. H. Anonymous.

Due to the legal, professional, religious, and scientific discrimination of the time, Dr. John Fryer, who had been terminated from a job and a psychological residency due to his sexual orientation, believed that if he spoke openly he would risk losing both his license and career, particularly because he did not have tenure in his academic appointment.[44] Therefore, when he joined a panel otherwise composed of "gays who were not psychiatrists and psychiatrists who were not gay," he hid his identity. This was a difficult task for a man 6'5" and approximately 300 pounds, but Fryer wore an oversized tuxedo and a Richard Nixon mask and used a voice-altering microphone. He introduced himself: "I am a homosexual. I am a psychiatrist. I am, like most of you in this room, a member of the American Psychiatric Association, and am proud of that membership."[45] His short but powerful statement moved several individuals and benefited the gay and lesbian community at large, particularly by galvanizing the push for changes to the DSM. Change, however, did not happen overnight. Many psychiatrists and psychologists remained staunchly opposed to these views, including an administrator who later fired Fryer from a job for being an openly gay man; the administrator had been in the front row for the speech of Dr. H. Anonymous but never knew that Fryer was under the mask.[46]

Extensive scientific and professional critique emerged of the DSM-III and its omission of sexual orientation, and some members called for a vote on the "APA's scientific process of reviewing the issue and [whether] to accept the expert consensus of their professional community" to remove homosexuality from the DSM.[47] The vote revealed that 58% of membership supported the decision, prompting those who called for the vote and then lost to argue ironically against the uses of votes to decide scientific questions.[48] The APA then released a strong statement against discrimination and in favor of civil rights legislation to protect gay rights.[49]

Although therapists strongly favored the decriminalization of homosexuality, even immediately after the changes to the DSM,[50] perceptions of people of diverse sexual orientations did not change overnight. Psychologists remained more likely to describe symptoms as more severe when presented from clients who were homosexual rather than heterosexual, not only immediately after the changes to the DSM but also 20 years later.[51] Institutional discrimination persisted; students who openly identified as sexual minorities continued to experience discrimination from faculty, administrators, and peers within their graduate programs.[52] Much psychological discussion then moved to questions of same-sex marriage and of gay men and lesbians as parents.

Cultural and Legal Conflicts

In the mid-20th century, scientific and religious perspectives continued to align in ways that devalued people who were not heterosexual, and the legal landscape in the United States reflected the assumptions that people who were sexually diverse were pathological and dangerous. In 1950, a U.S. Senate report, "Employment of Homosexuals and Other Sex Perverts in Government," raised concerns that people who were homosexual were pathological and therefore dangerous to U.S. military, intelligence, and other government operations, particularly in the fear-laden early days of the Cold War.[53] In 1953, President Dwight D. Eisenhower issued an executive order that prevented gay men and lesbians (along with people who had alcohol addictions and some psychological disorders) from working in government positions or for private contractors hired by the government.[54] A famous British casualty of similar regulations was Alan Turning, the pioneering British computer scientist who played critical roles in breaking German codes in World War II and who was arrested, fired, and disgraced for engaging in consensual sexual relations with another man.[55] In the United States, the assumption that people who engage in same-sex behavior must be pathological remained powerful in federal and state laws and in government actions through the mid-20th century and beyond.

Government intervention, or lack thereof, came to the forefront of the intersection of science and religion in response to the HIV/AIDS epidemic that most heavily struck the gay community in the United States.[56] It was initially called GRID (Gay-Related Immunodeficiency Syndrome) in congressional hearings, and the perception that it was a gay disease affected the political response and, in turn, funding and public support for the research that would eventually lead to treatments. Through the mid-1980s, the Secretary of Health and Human Services failed to increase research funding despite intense and repeated appeals from the Center for Disease Control.[57] Cleve Jones, the founder of the AIDS Memorial Quilt, recalls the struggles with grief, scientific uncertainty, political dismissal, and religious derision, all accompanied by bumper stickers that proclaimed, among other messages, "AIDS: It's Killing All the Right People."[58] Not until 1990 did Reagan deliver a speech in which he noted, "all kinds of people can get AIDS, even children."[59] The claim from some religious figures that AIDS is God's punishment on people who are gay continues to stigmatize people who struggle with the disease.[60]

Throughout this text, we have argued that religion is best understood in terms of historical and developmental perspectives and awareness. The same is true of scientific, philosophical, political, and legal systems of thought. The study of sexual orientation and sexual identities is a case study of development, movement, reversals, and of rapidly evolving epistemologies and ontologies. Comfortable and once stagnant cultural certitudes and agendas have been forced to yield to empirical evidence and to growing awareness of the alienating effects of old ideologies. Change was initiated by the extension of scientific methodologies into social and behavioral arenas and also by courageous political activism in those societies that are generally tolerant and open and that enfranchise doubt and curiosity.

The clash of scientific and conservative religious opinions about homosexuality is driven partly by the same epistemological issues that separated Galileo from official church doctrines in the 16th century. Galileo argued that "In discussions of physical problems we ought to begin not from the authority of scriptural passages, but from sense-experience and necessary demonstrations."[61] Arguments against homosexuality set forth by religious leaders are driven partly by references to scriptural passages, for example, from the Qur'an or the Bible, while scientific arguments have been driven by the results of empirical research. The weight of authority vs. empirical observation is playing out once again in divisive medical, legal, philosophical, psychological, religious, and cultural issues. To fail to appreciate fully the role of epistemological differences is to miss a major reason for the dispute.

Growing Diaspora

Scientific communities, including psychology, have people of diverse sexual orientations who have gradually gained inclusion and acceptance. Although scientific perspectives have recently aligned against ongoing prejudice and discrimination, many religious communities remain deeply divided even as others change rapidly. The changes have emerged through recent decades across the American religious landscape. For example, in 2003, the Episcopal Church challenged the international organization of Episcopal and Anglican Churches by ordaining Gene Robinson, an openly gay man, as bishop.[62] This and other actions supporting gay rights led several congregations to start their own organizations or to join Anglican groups that reject gay marriage and ordainment of gay leaders.[63] As congregations have divided, these intense disputes sometimes centered on theological questions and sometimes on practical questions such as land or building ownership.[64] Other denominations have faced similar issues.

The diversity of views has not come without backlash. In 2008, when Richard Cizik, Vice-President of Governmental Affairs for the National Association of Evangelicals (NAE), openly admitted his support for civil unions but not gay marriage, he faced such intense criticism that he resigned his position and left the NAE.[65] Matthew Vines' book, *God and the Gay Christian: The Biblical Case in Support of Same-Sex Relationships*, was aimed at Evangelical Christians. Immediately, R. Albert Mohler, Jr. of the Southern Baptist Theological Seminary at Louisville, Kentucky released a point-by-point critique and condemnation of his work in his book titled *God and the Gay Christian?: A Response to Matthew Vines*.[66]

Sadly, no conversation about religion and sexual orientation in the United States would be complete without discussion of the late Fred Phelps and the Westboro Baptist Church. Phelps represented an extreme minority of faith communities, but he commanded extensive media coverage and legislative pressure. After starting his career as a civil rights attorney, Phelps took a virulent stance against sexual orientation, arguing that "God hates" those who are not heterosexual.[67] He and his small congregation, composed largely of his extended family, gained national prominence as they protested the trial of those who were convicted of the brutal murder of Matthew Sheppard. The Westboro website and protest signs featured a photo of Sheppard's face surrounded by the flames of Hell. Westboro members later sought publicity by protesting churches, universities with anti-discrimination policies, and soldiers' funerals, claiming that soldiers' deaths are part of God's righteous punishment for the growing acceptance of gay men, lesbians, and bisexuals in the United States. Their aggressive language eventually led several states to enact legislation to limit Phelps's activities and to a free speech case that Phelps argued successfully in front of the U.S. Supreme Court.[68]

Although Phelps became increasingly controversial as public opinion in the United States moved toward acceptance of people with diverse sexual orientations, he unified disparate groups who came together to fight against his views. At the Sheppard trial in Cheyenne, a group called Angel Action shut down Phelps by silently surrounding him and blocking him from view of the crowd.[69] Other groups have taken similar actions. For example, the Patriot Guard coordinates counter-protests at soldiers' funerals; they protect family members of the fallen service personnel from Westboro members by waving large American flags and running loud motorcycles.[70] At a recent military funeral in Ohio, the Patriot Guard, a university group emulating Angel Action, and a diverse collection of religious leaders *all* joined together to protest Phelps.[71] Even when no formal groups can mobilize, Phelps inspires harmony in his opposition.[72] In 2003 when Phelps spoke at a university in Colorado, local ministers joined a panel to challenge Phelps; at the time all the ministers but one viewed homosexuality as wrong, but all spoke strongly against Phelps's claims of God's hatred.[73] Some observers have noted that Phelps may have inadvertently played the role of Bull Connor in the

Civil Rights movement, fighting for prejudice and discrimination so strongly as to motivate and unify the opposition.[74]

Changing perspectives on these questions have also reached across denominational lines into the intersection of theology, science, and psychological practice. For example, Jeffrey Paul recently investigated discussions of people who are sexual minorities in the peer-reviewed journal *Pastoral Psychology*. Since the 1950s, Paul found an historical "trend toward a more open and inclusive dialogue surrounding LGBT people."[75] In the 1950s, discussions of gay men emphasized deviance and pathology as well as the need for reparative therapy. By the 1990s, however, authors in *Pastoral Psychology* lament many congregations' persistent negative views. By the second decade of the new millennium, authors in *Pastoral Psychology* argue for inclusion of people of diverse sexual orientations, challenging ongoing homophobia in religious settings, and the inclusion of coming out stories as faith narratives. Paul argues that changes in this journal, while slower than psychology as a field, reflect growing religious inclusion of individuals who are gay, lesbian, and bisexual for religious as well as scientific reasons.[76]

A New Us

Much of the tension over the past 25 years of the struggle for gay rights has centered on marriage. We briefly review the recent history of progress and backlash related to gay marriage, and we address related issues such as employment discrimination, military service, and parenting.

Religious faith, at its best, results in a transition from the primacy of a "me" to the freedoms of an "us." Most people feel they live most fully, authentically, and joyfully when they can be in a sharing, intimate, reflective exchange with another. Marriage is one way we achieve such a feeling, but what is marriage and how are we to understand its multidimensional characteristics? This question has risen to the forefront of public consciousness in the United States following the 2015 Supreme Court ruling on gay marriage. In *Obergefell v. Hodges*, the court in a five to four decision declared that states must now recognize the right of same-sex couples to legal marriage.[77] Speaking for the majority Justice Kennedy said "No union is more profound than marriage, for it embodies the highest ideals of love, fidelity, devotion, sacrifice and family. In forming a marital union, two people become something greater than once they were."[78]

Just after the decision, Steve Blow spoke of those who opposed the Supreme Court ruling and their wish to maintain only traditional marriage. But then he raised questions about the meaning of traditional religious marriages. For example, there have been Biblical examples of polygamous marriages (2 Chronicles, 11:21), marriage as a prize for the winner of a contest (Joshua 15:16), marriage as a required consequence of sexual assault – the perpetrator *must* marry the victim and they may not divorce (Deuteronomy 22:28), and women to be married as spoils of war (Numbers 31:17).[79] In other faith traditions, as noted by Ayaan Hirsi Allie, there are marriages arranged by parents whose young girls have no choice in the matter, have no legal recourse, and have never met the man they must marry.[80] What is traditional marriage? These questions have shaped and confounded much of the scientific and religious dialogue.

Legal and religious questions about marriage have a long and contentious history. How should governments recognize and regulate intimate arrangements that are both religious and civil? For much of the history of the United States, regulation of marriage has been left to the states, and some states perpetuated discrimination against some forms of marriage, specifically based on the perceived or legally defined races of the parties involved. The term *miscegenation* referred to romantic, sexual, or marriage relations between white people and those who were not white,[81] and several states enforced anti-miscegenation laws.[82] Although often misconstrued as bans on inter-racial relationships, these laws defined and protected white identity and white advantage (including, depending on location, the abilities to vote, buy a home, send one's children to high-quality schools, and participate fully in society in many other ways) by narrowly defining who was white, namely people with two legally white parents.[83] There was even a national movement. In 1912, United States Representative Seaborn Roddenberry proposed a national constitutional amendment to defend marriage from the threat of miscegenation.[84]

Changes to anti-miscegenation laws remained slow and inconsistent for much of the 20th century until the U.S. Supreme Court addressed the issue. This legal dispute had religious foundations. The original 1959 trial court found the Lovings' marriage to be illegal (he was European American, she was African American) and based this decision on the belief that God wanted the races to remain separate.[85] The trial court's ruling was upheld by the Supreme Court of Appeals of Virginia. In 1967 the U.S. Supreme Court ruled that bans on miscegenation violated the equal protection clause of the 14th Amendment.[86]

Religious worldviews and texts were used extensively to support segregation and to fight interracial marriage, and these perpetuated earlier religious arguments not only against but *for* slavery.[87] In 1995, the largest Protestant Christian denomination in the United States publicly rejected the racism that drove its founding before the Civil War, and it apologized for its consistent support of slavery, segregation, and racism.[88] Across these events, questions related to the regulation of marriage have had a contentious religious and cultural history. Now we see these ideas applied to same-sex marriage.

Questions of marriage have been center stage in the recent so-called "culture wars" about sexual orientation. The growth of the movement for gay marriage has reflected the broader opinions about tolerance and sexual orientation, and the rapidly growing acceptance of same-sex relationships in general and of gay marriage in particular has paralleled a series of other developments related to parenting, military service, and adoption.

As recently as the early 1990s, questions of same-sex marriage remained below the horizon for many Americans. Questions related to people who were gay, lesbian, or bisexual revolved around issues of basic rights. In 1961 Illinois became the first state to eliminate its anti-sodomy law, and 20 more states did so through the 1970s, but states continued to regulate intimate contact between consenting adult volunteers. Not until 1999 did 50% of Americans believe that same-sex relations between consenting adults should be legal.[89] These views persisted until 2003, when the U.S. Supreme Court found anti-sodomy laws unconstitutional in *Lawrence v. Texas*.[90]

Other legal actions further demonstrate that concerns over basic rights remained dominant in the early 1990s. For example, in 1992, Oregon narrowly voted down Measure 9, which listed homosexuality alongside "pedophilia, sadism, and masochism as abnormal, wrong, unnatural, and perverse."[91] Also in 1992, Colorado voters passed Amendment 2, which emphasized the elimination of "special rights" for people who are gay, lesbian, and bisexual and eliminated the legal basis for any claim of discrimination based on sexual orientation.[92] In an atypical legal tactic, the governor of Colorado promptly sued his own state and pursued the case to the U.S. Supreme Court, which overturned Amendment 2.[93] Many other states took actions directly against gay marriage. Starting in the late 1990s and continuing through the first decade of the new millennium, 31 states amended their constitutions to limit same-sex marriage. Given that popular opinion would not swing to a consistent majority in favor of same-sex marriage until 2012, it is perhaps unsurprising that many states, including Colorado, passed laws *and* amended their constitutions to ban same-sex marriage.[94]

As states took these actions, the federal government also took steps against same-sex marriage, and these actions were popular with both major political parties. For example, in 1992, a speaker at the Republican National Convention noted that he stood with President George H. W. Bush "against the amoral idea that gay and lesbian couples should have the same standing in law as married men and women."[95] In 1996, President William J. Clinton signed the Defense of Marriage Act (DOMA), which banned same-sex marriage and strongly passed both houses of congress. As discussed previously, marriage had remained a state issue through much of the 20th century to enable discrimination based on race; ironically, at the close of the 20th century the federal government defined marriage, once again to enable discrimination.

DOMA defined marriage as being between one man and one woman, and many viewed it as a middle ground between acceptance of gay marriage and, at the other extreme, an amendment to the United States Constitution to ban gay marriage.[96] The Federal Marriage Amendment would eventually be proposed in 2004 by Marilyn Musgrave, who ran for U.S. congress from Weld County, Colorado and joined many others in emphasizing the issues of God, Guns, and Gays, two of which she endorsed.[97] Similarly, despite Clinton's promise to end the ban on military participation for gay men and lesbians, in 1994 he signed Don't Ask Don't Tell as a compromise between prior bans and those who supported the rights of gay military personnel to serve openly.[98] Don't Ask Don't Tell remained in place until 2010. Similar to the struggles for marriage rights regardless of race, the struggles for marriage equality for gay men and lesbians paralleled their pursuit of opportunity and equality in other areas.

Legal changes in favor of gay marriage began in some states even as bans continued to be passed in others. In 2000, Vermont became the first state to legalize civil unions, which were perceived as a middle ground between marriage bans and marriage. Civil unions incorporated many of the rights associated with marriage, but retained a separate status under the law.[99] Impressively, Vermont legalized these marriage-like relationships for gay men and lesbians when these relationships remained illegal in many states – before the Lawrence v. Texas case in 2003. In 2004, Massachusetts became the first state to legalize gay marriage. These decisions remained contentious; four years later, California passed Proposition 8, which banned gay marriage in the state. Additionally, the federal government continued to define marriage according to DOMA, and it provided federal funds to married couples in Massachusetts based on the federal definition of marriage rather than the Massachusetts definition of marriage, which included same-sex married couples. Massachusetts did not prevail against the federal government in court until 2010.[100] The Massachusetts case figured heavily when the U.S. Supreme Court finally overturned DOMA in a New York case.[101]

These changes occurred in parallel with ongoing changes in public opinion. The number of Americans who believe that consenting adult same-sex relationships should be legal and that gay marriage should be legal continued to grow through the new millennium, and, despite variations in religious and legal perspectives, other changes occurred that reflected public support for gay rights.[102] For example, during this time, laws changed in several states to provide legal protection from employment and housing discrimination.[103]

Same-sex couples and parents have faced vexing legal, psychological, cultural, and religious challenges. Statutes that prohibit parental rights and adoption rights to same-sex couples reflect the views encountered in a variety of faith communities. As we discussed previously, scientific views have changed since the early 1970s, and there are changing views across religious communities regarding gay parents. The strong consensus among researchers has emerged from decades of empirical data-based research demonstrating that the quality of parenting is not predicted by sexual orientation.[104] These findings are often challenged by conservative religious figures, many of whom fear that gay parents are unnatural or dangerous for children.[105]

Another front in these disputes has involved the Boy Scouts of America (BSA), which has consistently voiced concerns about gay men throughout its slowly changing perspectives on gay scouts and gay scoutmasters. The BSA defended its anti-gay stance all the way to the U.S. Supreme Court.[106] In 2000, BSA won their case; by defining the BSA as a private organization that promotes specific values, they retained the rights to discriminate in membership as a function of the

First Amendment. Over a decade later, after extensive backlash from gay rights groups, in 2013 the BSA opened membership to openly gay Scouts but not to openly gay adult Scoutmasters. Pressure continued, for example with BSA losing their charitable funding from sources such as Disney employees.[107] Robert Gates, former head of the CIA, assumed leadership of the beleaguered BSA, and he informed the membership in 2015 that their refusal to adapt could spell "the end of us as a national movement."[108] Immediately after the Supreme Court decided the gay marriage case, the Boy Scouts revised their position on gay scoutmasters. As an organization that relies on the support of a diverse array of sponsoring churches, the Boy Scouts walked a narrow line. On July 13, 2015, they revised their policy to allow gay Scoutmasters with local approval, but they emphasized local control for individual organizations; those who choose to deny gay Scoutmasters remained free to do so. Many criticized the decision for going only partway, and the Boy Scouts emphasized religious views in their response, stating that BSA "rejects any interference with or condemnation of the diverse beliefs of chartering organizations on matters of marriage, family and sexuality."[109] This particular middle ground lasted approximately two weeks; on July 27, 2015, the BSA announced that they had rescinded the ban at all levels of the BSA, not just Scoutmasters, but would continue to allow chartering organizations, many of which are religious institutions, to set their own standards, even if they continue to deny membership and participation to openly gay adults.[110] Among other religious backlash, the Church of Jesus Christ of the Latter Day Saints immediately announced that it would "re-evaluate" its relationship with BSA.[111] Other observers remained disappointed that the BSA did not completely eliminate discrimination based on sexual orientation.

Marriage continues to sit at the center of the conflicts about science, religion, and people of diverse sexual orientations. Perspectives on marriage have changed from the notion that gay marriage must be an "amoral idea" to a time when civil unions represented the middle ground to the recent United States Supreme Court decision that legalized same-sex marriage across the United States. Much like the long journey to *Loving v. Virginia*, the years leading to the legalization of gay marriage contained a complex mix of legislative actions and court orders to end discrimination based on sexual orientation.[112] The U.S. Supreme Court initially refused to hear the case, but as conflicting court decisions piled up across states and federal districts, the Supreme Court reconsidered its views. The plaintiffs prevailed in a divided court, and *Obergefell et al. v. Hodges et al.* has reached dramatically across the United States. The majority spoke very powerfully. Justice Kennedy wrote,

> It would misunderstand these men and women to say they disrespect the idea of marriage. Their plea is that they do respect it, respect it so deeply that they seek to find its fulfillment for themselves. Their hope is not to be condemned to live in loneliness, excluded from one of civilization's oldest

institutions. They ask for equal dignity in the eyes of the law. The Constitution grants them that right.[113]

This decision provides an opportunity to observe religion and science in both warfare and accommodation.

Warfare

Responses to the legalization of gay marriage have varied extensively, and some observers have employed the language of war, equating fighting the decision of the "imperialist court" with the American founders' Revolutionary War struggles against the British Monarchy.[114] Some figures at the extremes of the American religious landscape called for violence, including demanding the death penalty for anyone who is not heterosexual and for death by stoning for any minister who performs a same-sex wedding; other observers have described the ruling as a harbinger of the end of the world or of God's judgment.[115]

Other forms of backlash emerged as the court's ruling in favor of gay marriage appeared likely. In Michigan, the week before the U.S. Supreme Court issued the *Obergefell et al. v. Hodges et al.* decision, a state representative proposed legislation so that the state would only issue marriage licenses for weddings performed by religious officiants, and the explicit goal was to make same-sex marriages harder in Michigan.[116] Similarly, two weeks before the decision, Michigan enacted legislation that allowed private adoption agencies to discriminate against same-sex couples.[117] Other states have other forms of resistance to the legalization of gay marriage. For example, in Colorado, within a week of the decision, there were two proposed ballot initiatives, one of which would define all same-sex marriages in Colorado as civil unions rather than marriages and the other of which would allow businesses who reject gay marriage to hire a contractor to serve same-sex couples.[118]

Other resistant responses to the *Obergefell et al. v. Hodges et al.* were personal. For example, in some counties in Alabama, despite orders from the federal courts, county clerks refused to issue *any* marriage licenses rather than issue a license to two men or two women; the county clerk in Rowan County, Kentucky famously took a similar approach.[119] At time of writing, courts continue to untangle these legal questions.

Accommodation

In addition to responses that invoked the language and imagery of war and rejection, many religious figures responded positively to the change.[120] Well before the U.S. Supreme Court decision, when asked about gay priests in the Vatican, Pope Francis presented a perspective that differed significantly from his predecessors: "Who am I to judge?"[121] In the gay marriage ruling, some organizations saw the culmination of years of systematic effort, including Soulforce, a pro-gay Christian organization started by Mel White and others after White's ostracization at the hands of his former employers in the conservative Christian community.[122] Some individuals responded with accommodation to new options for legal marriage. Prior to the Supreme Court decision, the Health Director for the State of Ohio, Rick Hodges, followed state law and refused to list a man as a surviving spouse in a gay marriage. In this way, he was the most prominently named defendant in *Obergefell et al. v. Hodges et al.* One week after the Supreme Court decision that bears his name, he attended and performed a reading at a gay wedding. When asked, he replied that he did not perceive irony in being the defendant in this case and then participating in a gay wedding less than a week later; he had known one of the grooms for 25 years, and, as he told the reporter, "I love my friend."[123] Other political figures, even those who continued to oppose gay marriage, attended the same wedding and argued in favor of respecting the new law of the land.[124] In an editorial written just after the decision, David Brooks noted that some anti-gay marriage religious figures had responded with deeper commitment to continue the warfare against gay marriage and that others had accommodated to the new legal landscape. He recommended another accommodation approach for religious opponents: take the lead in a new area, such as building families or fighting economic and spiritual poverty.[125]

In the first year after *Obergefell et al. v. Hodges et al.* legalized same-sex marriage across the United States, accommodation continued, and approximately 123,000 same-sex couples got married.[126] The effects of this decision continue to ripple through American culture. Public acceptance of same-sex marriage and of people who identify as sexual minorities has remained high and continues to grow,[127] perhaps in part because the dire predictions of the culture warriors have not come true, despite nearly half a million married same-sex couples in the United States.

*****

This chapter and the previous two chapters have explored tensions and accommodations between science and religion with respect to topics such as the origins of males and females, social roles of men and women, and variations in sexual orientations and identities. These topics provide important insights into the relations between science and religion that are often neglected in standard historical sources. Ethics and norms associated with sexual behaviors were shaped and controlled for centuries by religious and political systems. Such systems functioned in the context of authority and abysmal ignorance of the molecular, chemical, neurological, and anatomical underpinnings of all matters associated with sex and gender. As a consequence there has been a long history of a tyrannical politics of exclusion and oppression that in many quarters persists into the 21st century. For centuries, the excluded had no champions in science, medicine, religion, or law.

Narrow identity politics are slowly giving way to more cosmopolitan perspectives. Many religious organizations have acquired a maturity that encourages critical self-reflection along with a quest for an increasingly inclusive and accommodating spirituality. It is a mistake to regard any system of thought, including religion, as forever static though movement can be agonizingly slow. Nevertheless, to the dismay of absolutists of every persuasion, horizons and their illuminations inevitably expand.

Notes

1. American Psychological Association, "Answers to Your Questions for a Better Understanding of Sexual Orientation and Homosexuality," https://apa.org/topics/lgbt/orientation.pdf (Accessed July 14, 2015).
2. Leviticus 20:13 (*The New Oxford Annotated Bible*).
3. Anthony F. Bogaert, "Asexuality: What it is and Why it Matters," *Journal of Sex Research* 52, No. 4 (2015), 364; Anthony F. Bogaert, *Understanding Asexuality* (Lanham, MD: Rowman & Littlefield, 2012).
4. American Psychological Association, "Sexual Orientation and Homosexuality," http://www.apa.org/topics/lgbt/orientation.aspx Posted 2015 (Accessed July 20, 2015).
5. Martin Duberman, *Stonewall* (New York: Plume, 1994).
6. The Defense of Marriage Act (DOMA) was a Federal Law passed in 1996 that restricted marriage to a legal union between one man and one woman. The law was found unconstitutional in 2010, as described subsequently.
7. See *Lawrence v. Texas*, 539 U.S. 558, 156 L Ed 2d 508, 123 S Ct 2472 (2003) at 519.
8. Lisa M. Lauria, "Sexual Misconduct in Plymouth Colony," *The Plymouth Colony Archive Project*, http://www.histarch.illinois.edu/plymouth/Lauria1.html Posted 1998 (Accessed June 15, 2015).
9. David M. Halperin, *How to Do the History of Homosexuality* (Chicago, IL: University of Chicago Press, 2009), 127.
10. Ibid.
11. Joseph F. Rychlak and Ronald J. Rychlak, "The Insanity Defense and the Question of Human Agency," *New Ideas in Psychology* 8 (1990).
12. Halperin, *How to Do*, 127.
13. Jeffrey Weeks, *Sex, Politics, and Society: The Regulations of Sexuality since 1800*, 3rd ed. (New York: Pearson Education, 2012), 129.
14. Halperin, *How to Do*, 127.
15. Vernon A. Rosario, II "Trans (Homo) Sexuality? Double Inversion, Psychiatric Confusion, and Hetero-Hegemony," in *Queer Studies: A Lesbian, Gay, Bisexual, and Transgender Anthology*, ed. Brett Beemyn and Michele Eliason (New York: New York University Press, 1996), 41.
16. Sherrie A. Inness and Michele E. Lloyd. "G.I. Joes in Barbie Land: Reconceptualizing Butch in 20th Century Lesbian Culture," in *Queer Studies: A Lesbian, Gay, Bisexual, and Transgender Anthology*, ed. Brett Beemyn and Michele Eliason (New York: New York University Press, 1996), 31 endnote 38 for "mannishness."
17. Paul A. Robinson, *The Modernization of Sex: Havelock Ellis, Alfred Kinsey, William Masters, and Virginia Johnson* (New York: Harper & Row, 1989).
18. Murray J. White, "The Statue Syndrome: Perversion? Fantasy? Anecdote?" *Journal of Sex Research* 14, No. 4 (1978), 246–249.
19. Edward Bradford Titchener, *A Textbook of Psychology* (New York: MacMillan, 1910), 269.

20 Arno Karlen, *Sexuality and Homosexuality: A New View* (New York: W.W. Norton, 1971), 49.
21 Jonathan Swift, "The Lady's Dressing Room," in *The Poetical Works of Jonathan Swift*, Vol. 1 (London: William Pickering, 1732), 251.
22 Carol Tavris and Elliot Aronson, *Mistakes Were Made but Not by Me: Why We Justify Fooling Beliefs, Bad Decisions, and Hurtful Acts* (New York: Harcourt, 2008).
23 Sigmund Freud, "Three Essays on Sexuality," in *The Standard Edition of the Complete Psychological Works of Sigmund Freud*, Vol. 7, ed. and trans. by James Strachey (London: Hogarth Press, 1953), 135–243.
24 Ibid., 141.
25 Jack Drescher, "I'm Your Handyman: A History of Reparative Therapies," *Journal of Homosexuality* 36, No. 1 (1998), 7.
26 Kenneth Lewes, *The Psychoanalytic Theory of Male Homosexuality* (New York: Simon and Schuster, 2008); Drescher, "I'm Your Handyman," 23.
27 Drescher, "I'm Your Handyman," 19.
28 Henry Abelove, "Freud, Male Homosexuality, and the Americans," in *The Lesbian and Gay Studies Reader*, ed. Henry Abelove, Michele Aina Barale, and David Halperin (New York: Routledge, 1993), 381–393; Sigmund Freud, "Anonymous (Letter to an American mother)," in *The Letters of Sigmund Freud*, ed. E. Freud (New York: Basic Books, 1960), 423–424 (original work published 1935).
29 Sigmund Freud, "The Psychogenesis of a Case of Homosexuality in a Woman," in *The Standard Edition of the Complete Works of Sigmund Freud*, Vol. 18, ed. and trans. by James Strachey (London: Hogarth Press, 1955), 221–232 (original work published 1920).
30 Freud, "Three Essays on Sexuality," 144.
31 Alfred Kinsey, Wardell B. Pomeroy, and Clyde E. Martin, *Sexual Behavior in the Human Male* (Bloomington, IN: Indiana University Press, 1948).
32 Ibid.
33 Evelyn Hooker, "The Adjustment of the Male Overt Homosexual," *Journal of Projective Techniques* 21, No. 1 (1957), 18–31.
34 See Karlen, *Sexuality and Homosexuality*, 572–606.
35 American Psychological Association, "APA Council of Representatives Passes Resolution on So-Called Reparative Therapy," http://psychology.ucdavis.edu/faculty_sites/rainbow/html/resolution97.html August 14, 1997 (Accessed July 21, 2015).
36 Clarence Arthur Tripp, *Homosexual Matrix* (New York: McGraw-Hill, 1975).
37 Michael D. Storms, "Theories of Homosexuality," *Journal of Personality and Social Psychology* 38, No. 5 (1980), 783–792. See also Louis J. Gooren and W. Byne, "Sexual Orientation in Men and Women," in *Hormones, Brain and Behavior*, 2nd ed., Vol. 5, ed. by D. W. Pfaff (New York: Elsevier, 2009), 2429–2448.
38 Herb Kutchins and Stewart A. Kirk, *Making Us Crazy: DSM: The Psychiatric Bible and the Creation of Mental Disorders* (New York: Free Press, 1997).
39 American Psychiatric Association, *Diagnostic and Statistical Manual of Mental Disorders* (Washington, DC: Author, 1952).
40 The DSM is produced by the American Psychiatric Association rather than the American Psychological Association, but the American Psychological Association convention remained the publicly accessible means to access practicing psychologists as well as the creators of the DSM.
41 David L. Scasta, "John E. Fryer, MD, and the Dr. H. Anonymous Episode," *Journal of Gay and Lesbian Psychotherapy* 6, No. 4 (2008), 73–84.
42 Dudley Clendinen, "John Fryer, 65, Psychiatrist Who Said He Was Gay in 1972, Dies." *New York Times*, http://www.nytimes.com/2003/03/05/obituaries/05FRYE.html March 5, 2003 (Accessed July 3, 2015). The Kameny Papers, *The Kameny Papers* (2015) http://www.kamenypapers.org/index.htm (Accessed July 20, 2015).

43 Scasta, "John E. Fryer," 79.
44 Ibid., 79–80.
45 Ibid., 80.
46 Ibid., 83.
47 Jack Drescher, "The Removal of Homosexuality from the DSM: Its Impact on Today's Marriage Equality Debate," *Journal of Gay and Lesbian Mental Health* 16, No. 2 (2012), 128.
48 Ibid.
49 J. J. Conger, "1974: Minutes of the Annual Meeting of the Council of Representatives," *American Psychologist* 30 (1975), 620–651.
50 Phyllis K. Robertson, "The Historical Effects of Depathologizing Homosexuality on the Practice of Counseling," *The Family Journal: Counseling and Therapy for Couples and Families* 12, No. 2 (2004), 163–169. On psychologists' support for decriminalization of homosexuality, see Nannette Gartell, Helena Kraemer, and H. Keith Brodie, "Psychiatrists' Attitudes Toward Female Homosexuality," *Journal of Nervous and Mental Disease* 159, No. 2 (1974), 141–144.
51 Gidi Rubinstein, "The Decision to Remove Homosexuality from the DSM: Twenty Years Later," *American Journal of Psychotheraphy* 49, No. 3 (1995), 416–427; Ellen M. Garfinkle and Stephen F. Morin, "Psychologists' Attitudes Toward Homosexual Psychotherapy Clients," *Journal of Social Issues* 34, No. 3 (1978), 101–112.
52 Neil W. Pilkinton and James M. Cantor, "Perceptions of Heterosexual Bias in Professional Psychology Programs: A Survey of Graduate Students," *Professional Psychology: Research and Practice* 27, No. 6 (1996), 604–612; see also Brad Walter Larsen, "Student Perceptions of Heterosexual Bias in Doctoral Level Psychology Programs," Unpublished master's thesis, 2007, Pacific University, http://commons.pacificu.edu/cgi/viewcontent.cgi?article=1139&context=spp (Accessed July 15, 2015).
53 U.S. Senate, 81st Congress, Committee on Expenditures in Executive Departments, "Employment of Homosexuals and Other Sex Perverts in Government," Washington, DC: Government Printing Office (1950).
54 Executive Order 10450 – Security Requirements for Government Employment, National Archives, http://www.archives.gov/federal-register/codification/executive-order/10450.html (Accessed July 20, 2015).
55 Andrew Hodges, *Alan Turing: The Enigma* (Princeton, NJ: Princeton University Press, 2012).
56 Randy Shilts, *And the Band Played On: Politics, People, and the AIDS Epidemic* (New York: St. Martin's Press, 1987).
57 William Cran and Renata Simone, *The Age of AIDS*, Frontline, http://www.pbs.org/wgbh/pages/frontline/aids/ May, 2006 (Accessed July 25, 2015).
58 Ibid. *The Beacon*, "Stories of a Gay Rights Activist Inspire," http://upbeacon.com/2012/01/25/stories-of-a-gay-rights-activist-inspire/ January 25, 2015 (Accessed July 25, 2015).
59 Cran and Simone, *The Age of AIDS*.
60 Cheryl K. Chumley, "Duck Dynasty's Phil Robertson says that AIDS, Syphilis God's Penalty for Gays," *Washington Times*, http://www.washingtontimes.com/news/2014/sep/11/duck-dynastys-phil-robertson-says-aids-syphilis-go/ September 11, 2014 (Accessed July 20, 2015).
61 Galileo Galilei, Letter to Madam Christina of Lorraine, Grand Duchess of Tuscany, 1615. Inters.org/Galilei-Madame-Christina-Lorraine (accessed July 3, 2015).
62 Jan Nunley, "New Hampshire Priest is First Openly Gay Man Elected Bishop," http://www.episcopalchurch.org/library/article/new-hampshire-priest-first-openly-gay-man-elected-bishop June 7, 2003 (Accessed July 15, 2015).
63 USA Today, "Conservatives Form Rival Group to Episcopal Church," http://usatoday30.usatoday.com/news/religion/2008-12-03-episcopal-split_N.htm December

4, 2008 (Accessed July 15, 2015); Church of Uganda, "Church of Uganda Declares Full Communion with Anglican Church in North America," http://anglicanchurch.net/?/main/page/9 June 25 Posted June 25, 2009 (Accessed November 14, 2016).
64 William Wan, "Episcopalians in Va. Divided over Decision Allowing Ordination of Gay Bishops," *Washington Post*, July 16, 2009, http://www.washingtonpost.com/wp-dyn/content/article/2009/07/15/AR2009071503697.html (Accessed July 15, 2015); Michael Gryboski, "Texas Diocese Wins Court Battle over Property Dispute with the Episcopal Church," *Christian Post*, March 3, 2015, http://www.christianpost.com/news/texas-diocese-wins-court-battle-over-property-dispute-with-the-episcopal-church-135047/ (Accessed July 15, 2015); The Episcopal Church, "Church Property Dispute," June 14, 2013 http://www.episcopalchurch.org/library/topics/church- property-dispute (Accessed July 15, 2015).
65 Sarah Pulliam, "Richard Cizik Resigns from The National Association of Evangelicals," *Christianity Today*, December 11, 2008, http://www.christianitytoday.com/ct/2008/decemberweb-only/150-42.0.html (Accessed July 15, 2015).
66 Matthew Vines, *God and the Gay Christian: The Biblical Case in Support of Same-Sex Relationships* (New York: Convergent Books, 2014). Also see R. Albert Mohler, Jr. (ed.), *God and the Gay Christian: A Response to Matthew Vines* (Louisville, KY: Southern Baptist Theological Seminary Press, 2014).
67 Louis Theroux (writer), *The most hated family in America*, BBC (2007).
68 *Snyder v. Phelps*, 562 U.S. 443; 131 S. Ct. 1207; 179 L. Ed. 2d 172 (2011).
69 Romaine Patterson, Angel Action, 2015, http://eatromaine.com/1/laramie-angels.html (Accessed July 20, 2015).
70 Patriot Guard Riders, "Welcome to the PGR," 2015, https://www.patriotguard.org/content.php?s=e0ebdd101162bc82fe85c8fc7bbf54dc (Accessed July 20, 2015).
71 Billie Murray, "Words that Wound, Bodies that Shield: Corporeal Responses to Westboro Baptist Church's Hate Speech," *First Amendment Studies* 50, No. 1 (2016), 33.
72 *Sun-Sentinel* Editorial. "Small Town Beats Westboro, Shows America at its Best," *Sun-Sentinel* December 1, 2010, http://articles.sun-sentinel.com/2010-12-01/news/fl-westboro-editorial-gs-20101201_1_westboro-baptist-church-missouri-town-fred-phelps (Accessed July 20, 2015).
73 Julio Ochoa, "Hate or Love? (Westboro Baptist Church of Topeka visits UNC," *Greeley Tribune* November 11, 2002, http://www.freerepublic.com/focus/news/767563/posts?page=78 (Accessed July 20, 2015).
74 Arnold H. Loewy, "Free Speech and the Anti-gay Shift," *Houston Chronicle*, December 29, 2011, http://www.chron.com/opinion/outlook/article/Free-speech-and-the-anti-gay-shift-2431590.php (Accessed June 20, 2015).
75 Jeffrey Paul, "The Varieties of Religious Responses to Homosexuality: A Content and Tonal Analysis of Articles in Pastoral Psychology from 1950 to 2015 Regarding Sexual Minorities," *Pastoral Psychology* 66, No. 1 (2017), 79.
76 Ibid.
77 *Obergefell v. Hodges*, decided June 26, 2015, slip opinion, http://www.supremecourt.gov/opinions/14pdf/14-556_3204.pdf (Accessed July 15, 2015).
78 *Obergefell v. Hodges* at 28.
79 Steve Blow, *Dallas Morning News*, "Blow: Beliefs about Marriage Evolve, even in the Bible." June 27, 2015, http://www.dallasnews.com/news/columnists/steve-blow/20150627-lesson-of-biblical-marriage-it-changes-and-for-the-better.ece (Accessed July 22, 2015).
80 Ayaan Hirsi Allie, *Infidel* (New York: Free Press, 2007), 170–199.
81 James W. Loewen, *Sundown Towns* (New York: The New Press, 2005), 28.
82 Loewen, *Sundown Towns*; James W. Lowen, *Lies My Teacher Told Me: Everything Your American History Textbook Got Wrong* (New York: The New Press, 2007).

83 Loewen, *Sundown Towns*; Isabella Wilkerson, *The Warmth of Other Suns: The Epic Story of America's Great Migration* (New York: Vintage, 2010).
84 Nicholas D. Kristof, "Marriage: Mix and Match," *New York Times*, March 3, 2004, http://www.nytimes.com/2004/03/03/opinion/marriage-mix-and-match.html (Accessed July 20, 2015).
85 *Loving v. Virginia*, 388 U.S. 1; 87 S. Ct. 1817; 18 L. Ed. 2d 1010 (1967).
86 Ibid.
87 See Theodore G. Bilbo, *Take Your Choice: Separation or Mongrelization* (Poplarville, MS: Dream House Publishing, 1947). Bilbo was former Governor of Mississippi, among other state and national offices. For Christian pro-slavery arguments, see Thornton Stringfellow, *Scriptural and Statistical Views in Favor of Slavery* (4th ed.) (Richmond, VA: J. W. Randolph, 1856). For additional reviews, see Stephen R. Haynes, *Noah's Curse: The Biblical Justification of Slavery in the United States* (Oxford: Oxford University Press, 2007); William Lee Miller, *Arguing about Slavery: John Quincy Adams and the Great Battle in the United States Congress* (New York: Vintage, 1998).
88 Southern Baptist Convention, "Resolution on Racial Reconciliation on the 150th Anniversary of the Southern Baptist Convention," 1995, http://www.sbc.net/resolutions/899/resolution-on-racial-reconciliation-on-the-150th-anniversary-of-the-southern-baptist-convention (Accessed July 20, 2015).
89 Gallup, "Gay and Lesbian Rights," 2015, http://www.gallup.com/poll/1651/gay-lesbian-rights.aspx (Accessed July 20, 2015).
90 Brent L. Pickett, *Historical Dictionary of Homosexuality* (Lanham, MD: Scarecrow Press, 2009); *Lawrence v. Texas*, 539 U.S. 558 (2003).
91 State of Oregon, Official 1992 General Voter's Pamphlet, http://www.glapn.org/6013AntiGayImages/Measure9BallotTitle.jpg (Accessed July 20, 2015).
92 Stephen Zamansky, "Colorado's Amendment 2 and Homosexuals' Right to Equal Protection of Law," *Boston College Law Review* 35 (1993), 221–258.
93 *Romer v. Evans*, 517 U.S. 620 (1996).
94 National Conference of State Legislatures, "Same-Sex Marriage Laws," June 26, 2015 http://www.ncsl.org/research/human-services/same-sex-marriage-laws.aspx (Accessed July 20, 2015); Gallup, "Gay and Lesbian Rights," (2015).
95 Patrick J. Buchanan, "1992 Republican National Convention Speech," http://buchanan.org/blog/1992-republican-national-convention-speech-148 (Accessed July 20, 2015), paragraph 34.
96 Some argued that legislation against gay marriage would defuse the push for a federal constitutional amendment to ban gay marriage.
97 U.S. Government Printing Office, H.R. 3396, Defense of Marriage Act, September 21, 1996, http://www.gpo.gov/fdsys/pkg/BILLS-104hr3396enr/pdf/BILLS-104hr3396enr.pdf (Accessed July 20, 2015); William J. Clinton, "Bill Clinton: It's Time to Overturn DOMA," *Washington Post*, March 7, 2013, https://www.washingtonpost.com/opinions/bill-clinton-its-time-to-overturn-doma/2013/03/07/fc184408-8747-11e2-98a3-b3db6b9ac586_story.html (Accessed July 20, 2015); U.S. Government Printing Office, Federal Marriage Amendment, May 13, 2004, http://www.gpo.gov/fdsys/pkg/CHRG-108hhrg93656/html/CHRG-108hhrg93656.htm (Accessed July 20, 2015); Stuart Steers, "The Gang of Four," *5280*, May 2005, http://www.5280.com/magazine/2005/05/gang-four?page=full (Accessed November 14, 2016); Karen Crummy, "The Republican Party Gets Ready," *The Denver Post*, August 29, 2008, http://www.denverpost.com/2008/08/29/the-republican-party-gets-ready/ (Accessed November 14, 2016).
98 *Washington Post*, "A History of 'Don't Ask, Don't Tell,'" November 30, 2010, http://www.washingtonpost.com/wp-srv/special/politics/dont-ask-dont-tell-timeline/ (Accessed July 20, 2015).
99 We ask readers to consider our long and dark history with "separate but equal" in the United States.

100 *Commonwealth of Massachusetts v. United States Department of Health and Human Services, et al.*, 698 F. Supp. 2d 234 (2010).
101 *United States v. Windsor*, 133 S. Ct. 2675; 186 L. Ed. 2d 808 (2013).
102 Gallup (2015).
103 Jennifer C. Pizer, Brad Sears, Christy Mallory and Nan D. Hunter, "LGBT Identity and the Law: Evidence of Persistent and Pervasive Workplace Discrimination against LGBT People: The Need for Federal Legislation Prohibiting Discrimination and Providing for Equal Employment Benefits," *Loyola of Los Angeles Law Review* 45 (2012), 715–779; Andrew Kravis, "Is the Inability to Marry a Marital Status? Levin V. Yeshiva University and the Intersection of Sexual Orientation and Marital Status in Housing Discrimination," *Columbia Journal of Gender and Law* 24 (2012), 1–24.
104 American Psychological Association, "APA on Children Raised by Gay and Lesbian Parents," June 11, 2012, http://www.apa.org/news/press/response/gay-parents.aspx (Accessed July 20, 2015).
105 Brittany Smith, "Family Expert on Studies: Same-Sex Parenting Does Affect Children," *Christian Post*, March 8, 2012, http://www.christianpost.com/news/family-expert-on-studies-same-sex-parenting-does-affect-children-71103/ (Accessed July 20, 2015). Importantly, the claims made by the expert described in this article do not have support from psychological science; see the previous note.
106 *Boy Scouts of America et al. v. Dale*, 530 U.S. 640 (2000).
107 Devon M. Sayers, "Disney to Pull Boy Scouts Funding by 2015 over Policy Banning Gay Leaders," *CNN*, March 2, 2015, http://www.cnn.com/2014/02/28/us/disney-pulls-boy-scouts-funding/ (Accessed July 20, 2015).
108 Sandhya Somashekhar, "Boy Scouts President Warns that Ban on Gay Leaders Threatens Organization," *Washington Post*, May 21, 2015, http://www.washingtonpost.com/politics/boy-scouts-president-warns-that-gay-ban-threatens-the-organization/2015/05/21/02ed19b0-fff1-11e4-8b6c-0dcce21e223d_story.html (Accessed July 20, 2015).
109 David Crary, "Boy Scouts Executive Committee OKs Ending Ban on Gay Leaders," *Associated Press*, July 14, 2015, http://www.denverpost.com/news/national/ci_28479144/boy-scouts-executive-committee-oks-ending-ban-on-gay-leaders (Accessed July 20, 2015).
110 Todd Leopold, "Boy Scouts Change Policy on Gay Leaders," *CNN*, July 27, 2015, http://www.cnn.com/2015/07/27/us/boy-scouts-gay-leaders-feat/ (Accessed July 28, 2015).
111 Church of Jesus Christ of the Latter Day Saints, Official Statement, "Church Re-evaluating Scouting Program: Concern Expressed over BSA Policy Change, Lack of Global Reach," July 27, 2015, http://www.mormonnewsroom.org/article/church-re-evaluating-scouting-program?cid=social_20150727_49844076&abid=625815481509806080&adbpl=tw&adbpr=10047382 (Accessed July 28, 2015).
112 For a concise synopsis of legislative and court decisions, see ProCon.Org "50 States with Legal Gay Marriage," June 26, 2015 *ProCon.org*, http://gaymarriage.procon.org/view.resource.php?resourceID=004857 (Accessed July 20, 2015).
113 *Obergefell et al. v. Hodges et al.* at 28.
114 Tom LoBianco, "GOP 2016 Hopefuls Seek Footing on Marriage Ruling," *CNN*, June 26, 2015, http://www.cnn.com/2015/06/26/politics/2016-candidates-gay-marriage-supreme-court/ (Accessed July 20, 2015).
115 Travis Gettys, "Pastors Call for Stonings and Warn of God's Wrathful Judgment after Marriage Equality Ruling," *Rawstory*, June 29, 2015, http://www.rawstory.com/2015/06/pastors-call-for-stonings-and-warn-of-gods-wrathful-judgment-after-marriage-equality-ruling/ (Accessed July 20, 2015); Czarina Ong, "Franklin Graham Issues New Comments on Christian Persecution, Same-sex Marriage," *Christianity Today*, July 2, 2015, http://www.christiantoday.com/article/franklin.graham.issues.new.comments.on.christian.persecution.same.sex.marriage/57794.htm (Accessed July 20, 2015).

116 Candace Williams, "Bills Would Require Clergy to Sign off on Marriages," *The Detroit News*, June 19, 2015, http://www.detroitnews.com/story/news/politics/michigan/2015/06/19/gay-marriage-legislation-religion-michian/29018125/ (Accessed July 20, 2015).
117 Reuters, "Michigan Governor Signs Bills Allowing Gay-couple Adoption Refusal," *Reuters*, June 11, 2015, http://www.reuters.com/article/2015/06/11/us-usa-michigan-adoption-idUSKBN0OR2LS20150611 (Accessed July 20, 2015).
118 Joey Bunch, "Two Ballot Proposals: Petitioners Seek Unions, not Marriage," *The Denver Post*, July, 4, 2015.
119 Campbell Robertson, "Most Alabama Judges Begin to Issue Licenses for Same-Sex Marriages," *The New York Times*, February 13, 2015, http://www.nytimes.com/2015/02/14/us/most-alabama-counties-are-granting-same-sex-marriage-licenses.html (Accessed November 14, 2016); Jason Hanna, Ed Payne and Catherine E. Shoichet, "Kim Davis Released, but Judge Bars her from Withholding Marriage Licenses," *CNN*, September 8, 2015, http://www.cnn.com/2015/09/08/politics/kim-davis-same-sex-marriage-kentucky/ (Accessed August 24, 2016).
120 Niraj Warikoo, "Religious Leaders' Reactions to Gay Marriage Mixed," *Detroit Free Press*, June 26, 2015, http://www.freep.com/story/news/2015/06/26/religious-same-sex-marriage-reaction/29328951/ (Accessed July 20, 2015).
121 Daniel Burke, "The Pope Said What?!?! More Stunners from Francis," January 19, 2015, http://www.cnn.com/2015/01/19/living/pope-said-what/ (Accessed July 20, 2015).
122 Soulforce. "Our Story," 2015, http://www.soulforce.org/#!our-story/cfvg (Accessed July 20, 2015); Mel White's story is told in his *Stranger at the Gate: To be Gay and Christian in America* (New York: Plume, 1995).
123 Associated Press, "Official Attends, Reads at Gay Wedding," *Dayton Daily News*, July 4, 2015, paragraph 7.
124 Ibid.
125 David Brooks, "The Next Culture War," *New York Times*, June 30, 2015, http://www.nytimes.com/2015/06/30/opinion/david-brooks-the-next-culture-war.html?_r=0 (Accessed July 20, 2015).
126 Gallup, "Same-Sex Marriages Up One Year After Supreme Court Verdict," June 22, 2016, http://www.gallup.com/poll/193055/sex-marriages-one-year-supreme-court-verdict.aspx?g_source=Social%20Issues&g_medium=newsfeed&g_campaign=tiles (Accessed August 26, 2016).
127 Gallup, "Satisfaction with Acceptance of Gays in U.S. at New High," January 18, 2016, http://www.gallup.com/poll/188657/satisfaction-acceptance-gays-new-high.aspx?g_source=position2&g_medium=related&g_campaign=tiles (Accessed August 26, 2016); Gallup, "Americans' Support for Gay Marriage Remains High, at 61%," May 19, 2016, http://www.gallup.com/poll/191645/americans-support-gay-marriage-remains-high.aspx?g_source=position1&g_medium=related&g_campaign=tiles (Accessed August 26, 2016).

11

RELIGION AND SOCIAL METRICS

All men are created equal[1]

It is in the most unqualified manner that I object to pretensions of natural equality[2]

The claim of Thomas Jefferson in the Declaration of Independence that all men are created equal is one of the most recognized and venerated ideas in American History. But the meaning of Jefferson's claim has never been completely clear. Obviously, this claim included only a few individuals, specifically wealthy, landowning, white men. Additionally, in Jefferson's day, individual differences, even among such highly privileged individuals, were often attributed to differences in will power. Thus, success was commonly viewed as a simple function of the "will to succeed." There was minimal appreciation for the idea that success may also be based on a more complicated formula that includes social and cultural contexts, individual aptitudes, and cognitive complexity or intelligence. Nevertheless, it is unlikely Jefferson meant to assert that all men are equal in mental or physical abilities. Rather, his famous claim refers to the political ideal of equality of opportunity and thus is intended to challenge pre-given social structures and differential starting points that promote and guarantee inequality.[3]

A century following the work of Thomas Jefferson, a fundamentally new way of thinking had gained momentum challenging earlier beliefs that achievements and destinies are based largely on will power. As noted in Chapter 9, empiricists such as Mary Wollstonecraft and John Stuart Mill had called attention to variations in circumstance that nurture inequality. They argued for universal education as an important corrective for this problem.

In addition to these questions about different educational opportunities, the 19th century witnessed a growing emphasis on advantages and constraints imposed by nature itself that pre-guarantee unequal starting points and different speeds of development based on inherent differences in individual aptitudes, abilities, and intelligence. The second epigraph at the beginning of this chapter is by Francis Galton, who challenged the idea of equality from one person to the next in bodily and mental attributes. In his book *Hereditary Genius*, Galton expressed "no patience with the hypothesis ... that babies are born pretty much alike" or that moral effort is the single reason for differences in achievement.[4] He declared with bold confidence that "There is no bodily or mental attribute ... which cannot be gripped and consolidated into an ogive with a smooth outline."[5] Thus, according to Galton, all bodily and mental events are quantifiable. Galton was also one of the first to challenge the idea of easy binary classifications into natural kinds. Instead, he promoted the idea that most things are distributed on a continuum from low to high. He acknowledged variations based on differences in environments and conditioning, but argued that heredity is the greater source of variation. Galton was also one of the leaders of the new discipline of social statistics.

Why are individual differences and their study important to the relations of science and religion? It is important because these fields represent an intrusion of "scientific evidence into problems over which theologians and moralists [had] long claimed jurisdiction."[6] Galton and earlier statisticians clearly demonstrated that physical and mental differences could be measured and plotted on various types of line graphs or charts that portrayed lawful distributions. Moral identities and behaviors would in time also be subjected to empirical quantitative studies.[7]

Galton was strongly influenced by the contributions of Belgian astronomer, mathematician, and statistician Lambert Adolphe Jacques Quetelet, who is properly regarded as the founder of social statistics. In his classic book *A Treatise on Man and the Development of his Faculties*, Quetelet opens with the claim that "Man is born, grows up, and dies, according to certain laws which have never been properly investigated either in whole or in the mode of their mutual reactions."[8] The failure to discern these laws, according to Quetelet, resulted from an exclusive focus on the individual. Such a focus hides generalities that surface when studies are conducted on specific behaviors in large groups. For example, Quetelet conducted extensive studies with very large sample sizes on moral issues such as propensity to commit crimes against persons and property. He examined criminal activity as a function of such variables as age, sex, literacy levels, seasons, and locations. His data revealed clear-cut lawful relations between likelihood of conviction for criminal activities and most of the variables he included in his studies such as age and sex of the offender, time of year, etc. He came to the conclusion that

> *everything that pertains to the human species considered as a whole, belongs to the order of physical facts:* the greater the number of individuals, the more does the influence of individual will disappear, leaving predominance to a series of general facts, dependent on causes by which society exists and is preserved.[9]

The moral implications of his extensive studies were troubling to Quetelet. Wherever he turned (e.g., mortality of infants, fecundity, physical characteristics, intellectual development, moral development) he uncovered lawful variations. Again, such variations are missed when the focus is exclusively on the individual. Individuals exist in extremely complicated interactive biological, physical, social, and cultural contexts, but specific causal effects of these contexts were easily overlooked prior to the advent of the science of statistics. Quetelet's data raised disquieting questions about the possible role of personal autonomy. Did moral responsibility lie exclusively within the individual, or does society itself bear some responsibility for the behavior and welfare of its constituents? The questions are highly pertinent to religion and to the many societies that face the consequences of failure to provide basic services, educational opportunities, and workable social and economic justice.

Interestingly, the older view that zeal and will power were the major causes of success had been embraced by no less a scientist than Charles Darwin. In 1870 Darwin forwarded a letter to his cousin Francis Galton, expressing his earlier doubts about inherited differences in intelligence. After reading Galton's book *Hereditary Genius*, Darwin noted "I have always maintained that, excepting fools, men did not differ much in intellect, only in zeal and hardwork."[10] But now, Darwin confessed that Galton's arguments had caused him to moderate his point of view, though he still believed in the importance of zeal and hard work. Galton's idea that intelligence is a highly variable natural characteristic and could be measured was "in the air" and shaped other scholars in the late 19th century.

The first intelligence test with some degree of predictive efficiency would surface in the work of Alfred Binet and Théodore Simon in 1905, a quarter of a century after Galton's claims.[11] It was becoming clear that there is not equality with respect to intellectual gifts, nor is there equality with respect to other mental attributes.

Religious Implications of Natural Variation

Natural inequalities are obvious and were recognized in the Bible in the "parable of the talents" as set forth in Matthew 25:14. A wealthy man planning to travel leaves five talents with one servant, two talents with a second servant, and only one talent with a third servant. According to the Bible, the talents are distributed to the men according to their respective abilities. The first two men invested their talents so that they grew in size. The third man simply saved his single talent so that its worth remained static. When the wealthy traveler returned he praised the first two men but was furious with the third man referring to him as wicked and slothful. There are many different interpretations of the parable. It is often interpreted to mean that humans should productively use the gifts available to them, but are those with fewer natural gifts as wise and accountable as those with greater gifts? Is risk taking itself a personality trait? There is no assurance that investments will grow; indeed, some economic conditions would greatly favor the person who simply saves and avoids the risk. The parable is not without troubling interpretive difficulties.

We may ask whether the discovery and measurement of natural variations in physical, emotional, motivational, moral, and intellectual attributes have yet to be fully understood or assimilated into larger religious worldviews. Early statisticians such as Quetelet and Galton opened up a new statistical methodology that revealed previously unrecognized laws of distribution with far reaching implications. On the practical side, Karl Pearson's classic book *The Chances of Death* uncovered remarkable laws associated with average life spans along with regularities in deviations from the average.[12] If predictions for a given individual were not yet possible, predictions were highly accurate for mortality in large groups suggesting the operation of natural laws at work and yet to be discovered. Subsequently, a great deal has been learned about genetic and environmental determinants of the life span for individuals.

It is clear there is natural variation associated with mortality and such variation has economic, scientific, political, theological, and ethical implications. Economic implications are obvious in the successes of the life insurance industry. Scientific implications are evident in increasing capacities to prolong life and to prolong quality of life and thus to manipulate mortality statistics. Political and religious implications are vast and play out most obviously in intense contemporary debates about issues such as "right to die" legislation. Discoveries of natural genetic and environmental laws of health and longevity also raise unavoidable theological questions about the role of the supernatural in life and death questions. Science has again invaded territory once dominated by theology.

The ethics of the human control of life, including extension and termination of life are in obvious transition. Few people reject the many scientific and technological interventions that prolong life and quality of life, but there are heated debates about the ethics of human control of death. Such debates are driven by many considerations including concerns in many faith communities that human intervention in the time and manner of death encroaches upon the prerogatives of deity.

The discovery of lawful variations in mental abilities has been even more perplexing than the discovery of lawful variations in mortality. For example, should moral accountability be considered as absolute, or is it a function of variations in intellectual capability and discernment? Judicial systems are increasingly troubled by the bewildering relations between mental variations and modern concepts of justice.[13] Should a person with a cognitive disability be accountable for a specific crime in the same way and to the same degree as a person who commits the same crime but is intellectually gifted? Is accountability absolute? Many faith traditions include beliefs in divine judgment of human actions and a system of rewards and punishments in an afterlife. How do traditional theological concepts of justice square with the discoveries of the complexities and the obvious natural variability in human mental abilities?

This chapter focuses on additional neglected dimensions of the relations between science and religion and science and theology. There had been clashes of opinion over the positions of the earth and sun in our immediate solar system, and there are continuing clashes between large segments of faith communities and biological scientists over human origins, but now new social and behavioral sciences such as psychology, sociology, and anthropology present a very different set of problems that challenge old assumptions and call for new and more nuanced interpretations of moral and theological issues. These sciences were sometimes viewed as presumptuous as they turned attention to naturalistic studies of religious beliefs and practices. Thus, there were new studies of such topics as the efficacy of prayer, conversion, religion and prejudice, religious experiences in relation to neurological events and processes, religion and violence, religion and a sense of well-being, and religion and sex. Science had invaded a new and previously sacrosanct arena with implicit and sometimes explicit "hands off" warning signs. Nevertheless, J. H. Leuba, an early psychologist of religion, argued that

> The subjective facts of religious life belong to psychology. It is the duty and the privilege of that science to extend its beneficial scepter over this realm also. The time is particularly favorable for such an annexation; the power that ruled during the past centuries has grown senile, its authority is denied; a painful anarchy prevails. Let psychology accept the succession that falls to it by right.[14]

Such claims resulted in understandable questions about the reach and presumed legitimacy of the audacious claims of the young science and the fit between scientific assumptions and methodologies and the deeper meanings of human religious experiences. Thoughtful critical treatment of psychology is nowhere better illustrated than in Holmes Rolston's scholarly book *Science and Religion: A Critical Survey*.[15] Rolston carefully explores classical psychoanalysis, behaviorism, and humanistic psychology along with a brief treatment of cognitive psychology. His work challenges the earlier claim of Leuba that "the subjective facts of religious life belong to psychology." Indeed, Rolston notes correctly that in the case of most behavioral psychologies, there is no inner life. Other psychological systems, according to Rolston, are equally inadequate in their attempts to explain human religious experiences. The reductionistic scientific frames in each case are insufficient for the profuse, robust, personal, and complex nature of the subject they hope to capture.

Rolston concludes that none of the psychological systems he explores "has enough historical rooting, evolutionary scope, cultural appreciation, or ontological insight. This does not fault what they can successfully abstract from life, but shows them to be incomplete explanations of what it means to live humanly in the world."[16] Science, however, never pretends to be complete. For that matter, it is doubtful there is any system of thought, be it psychological, philosophical, scientific, political, economic or religious, with sufficient "historical rooting, evolutionary scope, cultural appreciation or ontological insight" to address religious experience. There is nevertheless, as Rolston recognizes, much to be learned from partial perspectives for "what they can successfully abstract from life." In fact, the various systems of psychology, despite their metaphysical and methodological inadequacies and the overstated claims of Leuba, have contributed a great deal of useful knowledge about religious life and belief. Thus, in what is to follow, we explore the growth and extension of measurement techniques followed by selected examples of what scientific studies have contributed to our understanding of religion and the religious life. Prior to exploring the extension of scientific techniques into the study of religion, we will examine reasons for growing faith in innovative measurement techniques and their expansion into an increasing broad range of topical areas.

Growth of Measurement Techniques

In the 17th and 18th centuries there was an increasing capacity to measure and scale physical events, such as sound waves, light waves, and air pressure. The visible success of measurements of physical events helped set the stage for the belief that most things are numerable. The history of the measurement of something as seemingly abstract as air pressure is particularly suggestive of the reach of quantitative techniques. Aristotle believed that air was weightless. The earlier atomists, including Democritus believed there were two fundamental realities, atoms and the void. Atoms represent existence; the void is the absence of existence. The void presumably is unoccupied air space, a realm of non-being. The Eleatics, including Parmenides, argued logically that "being is" and "non-being is not." Thus, there were strong differences of opinion about whether there could be a void or a vacuum. Some believed there could be no such thing as a void or a vacuum because unoccupied air space could possibly be filled with something substantive but unseen and yet to be identified. The existence of a void raises interesting theological questions about the omnipresence of God. Would God occupy or be present in non-being?

The arguments of the philosophers about the existence or non-existence of a void were by no means trivial. The practical consequences were far reaching and nowhere better illustrated than in early attempts to explore the possible weight of air. In fact, the existence of a vacuum is central to early attempts to measure air pressure. Evangelista Torricelli (1608–47), who collaborated with Galileo, is credited with the development of early practical barometers as a means to measure atmospheric pressure. These early barometers demonstrated that air pressure at the base of a mountain is much higher than pressure at the top of the mountain. Aristotle was wrong; air does have weight. Measures of barometric pressure had enormous utility in the sciences along with practical applications as in weather forecasting. The upshot was unequivocal; air pressure exists in terms of a continuum from low to high as does temperature, pitch, light waves, and most other things.

Quantification and Prediction in the Social Sciences

The growing refinements and success of measurement in the physical sciences contributed to optimism about the possibility of measurement of human behaviors and mental processes such as memory, sensory acuity, and intelligence. If it seemed impossible to measure the weight of air, it seemed all the more impossible to measure something as apparently elusive as the speed of conduction of a nervous impulse. And yet, in 1849 German physicist and physiologist Hermann von Helmholtz (1821–94) successfully measured the speed of a nervous impulse as it crossed the length of the sciatic nerve of a frog. Commenting on the achievement, psychologist Edwin G. Boring suggested that Helmholtz had "brought the soul to time, as it were, measured what had been ineffable, actually captured the essential agent of mind in the toils of natural science."[17] Boring, speaking metaphorically, was suggesting the possibility of a science of psychology. If fundamental neural, mental, and behavioral processes could be measured and scaled then it might also be possible to conduct meaningful experimental studies in the social sciences. Following Helmholtz, the earliest psychological studies focused on the senses presumed to be the "windows to the mind."

Ernst von Weber (1795–1878) and Gustav Fechner (1801–87) were pioneers in psychophysics, one of the precursors of psychology. Psychophysics focused on the relationship between the properties of stimuli as measured by a physical scale and the psychological impressions of those stimuli. For example, auditory responses could be studied in relations to tones of measured frequencies on a physical scale. It was soon discovered that there are physical frequencies below and above the thresholds of human awareness. For example, humans normally cannot hear frequencies below 20 Hz or above 20,000 Hz. The limits of the senses were thus captured as well as capacities to discriminate differences between values within a sensory domain. For example, Ernst Heinrich Weber (1795–1878) was able to map cutaneous sensitivity by bringing a two-point compass into contact with body parts. Two points are often experienced as a single point if the points of the compass are too close together. How much spread is necessary for two points to be experienced as two points? This was known as a difference threshold. With such a simple technique, Weber was able to establish a great deal of knowledge about cutaneous sensitivity. For example ventral sensitivity (on the front of the body) is normally much more acute than dorsal sensitivity (on the back). This makes sense from an evolutionary standpoint as damage to the ventral parts of the body can often be more lethal than damage on the dorsal side.

The work of pioneers in the field of psychophysics resulted in practical knowledge along with the development of techniques that have been continuously refined and are now regularly employed in clinical work especially in the fields of vision and audition. Such studies demonstrated measurable connections between subjective experiences and physical variables and thus extended scientific inroads into hitherto inaccessible domains. Inspired by the promise of the field of psychophysics, Hermann Ebbinghaus (1850–1909) pioneered new techniques for the study of memory and forgetting. His work resulted in reliable demonstrations of the functions of memory along with demonstrable lawful generalizations about the course of forgetting. There was growing optimism that scientific methods could be expanded and extended to provide new ways to understand human experience and behavior.

Emerging psychological science and other new disciplines grew to a considerable extent out of the promise of new quantitative techniques. It would be only a matter of time before studies of religion would be included as a sub-disciplinary area within psychology and other new disciplines. Science, once subjected critically and appreciatively to religious scrutiny, would now subject religion to critical and appreciative scientific scrutiny with the hope that the results might be beneficial both to religion and science. Selected examples of insights provided by scientific studies are presented in the materials that follow.

Religion and Intolerance

A fundamental question centers on the possible role of religion in promoting ingroup cohesion and solidarity along with hostility toward outgroups.[18] Religion of course, is not alone in promoting ingroup solidarity. There is a sense of "we-ness" about any ingroup whether it be religious or not and a sense of "they-ness" about outgroups.[19] Religious groups are not exceptions to the general rule, but does religion itself exacerbate or sharpen ingroup–outgroup distinctions? Not necessarily, as noted by Sherif and Sherif, "every group regards some other groups as harmless, if not as friends and allies."[20] Hostilities between groups always have a history involving a multitude of causes including competition for resources, political differences, nationalism, perceived racial differences, and historical injustices. Hostilities between religious groups may include any or all of these causes, but there may also be theological perspectives that are not easily divorced from the problem of intergroup conflict. For example, scriptures that appear to be exclusivist often draw pointed and harsh demarcations between ingroups and outgroups. Jesus said "I am the way and the truth and the life. No one comes to the father except through me" (John 14:6). Acts 4:12 conveys the same idea that there is but one way to salvation. The Qur'an says "do not take the Jews and the Christians for friends" (Surah 5:51). Surah 9:29 says "Fight those who do not believe in Allah." As with all scriptures, the foregoing are subject to numerous interpretations and must be understood in complicated historical contexts that are often difficult to grasp. Many, however, take such scriptures literally and at apparent face value.

Exclusivist scriptures may not be the only way religion contributes to strong ingroup–outgroup distinctions. In a series of studies, Harvey Whitehouse and colleagues have explored varieties of rituals that "increase cohesion and tolerance *within groups* but [that] also intensify feelings of *hostility and intolerance towards outgroups*"[21] Highly aversive rituals employed in hazing and initiation procedures may produce pride of membership in an exclusive club or group along with a condescending attitude toward outsiders.[22] Whitehouse observes that the negative consequences of aversive rituals are less likely to be associated with milder rituals marked by blind repetition or routinization. He notes that such milder rituals create a sense of communal identity and "aid in the transmission of doctrinal orthodoxies." On the down side however, it seems possible that any blind repetitive ritualistic behavior may impede careful inquiry and innovation.[23] Whitehouse also cites a massive study of 644 rituals selected from a sample of 74 cultures demonstrating that frequency of rituals is negatively correlated with dysphoria.[24] This finding suggests that habitual practice of rituals may serve to reduce anxiety and general unease while affirming a sense of satisfaction, loyalty, and dedication to the norms of the group and a feeling of security in demonstrations that one is a loyal member in good standing. On the other hand, highly visible public rituals may remind outsiders of disconnections, barriers, or boundaries that distinguish between groups.

Such boundaries or demarcations are evident not only in public rituals but in dress, grooming modes, body language, observances, and avoidances that separate believers from others. For example, some deeply religious men refuse to sit next to an unknown woman on an airplane.[25] Such avoidances have caused troublesome tensions for travelers, including flight delays and other stressors. Additional research is needed to address the effects of such visible practices on outsiders. Another example is encountered in the possible cognitive and affective reactions to the athlete who makes the sign of the cross or who kneels with face to the ground following a successful performance. Onlookers may view such behaviors as humorous, puzzling, superstitious, trivial, petty, or admirable. Those who make highly visible public displays of their religious beliefs may be regarded positively as dedicated role models or negatively for a persistent in-your-face spirituality. The effects of purposefully visible public ritual displays on bonding with wider companies of human beings and on intergroup cooperation and harmony have yet to be investigated in sufficient detail. An extension of the effects of religion on in-group solidarity and out-group hostility is important because hostility often spills over into overt violence. The potential roles of religion in the promotion of such violence is a continuing source of disagreement among scholars.

Religion and Violence

Karen Armstrong, in her book *Fields of Blood: Religion and the History of Violence*, argues that it is not religion in itself that is the source of violence. She argues further that it is inaccurate "To claim that [religion] has a single, unchanging, and inherent violent essence."[26] Armstrong points out that so-called religious violence occurs in the context of real and/or perceived deprivations and injustices, geographic disputes, differing political and economic ideologies, and ethnic and racial differences. It is simplistic to single out religion as a singular cause of violence or to declare that religion has an essence that is inherently violent. Religion is many things, including the demonstrated non-violent religious beliefs and practices of leaders such as Martin Luther King Jr. and Mahatma Gandhi.

In contrast with Armstrong, Graeme Wood notes that "When a masked executioner says *Allahu akbar* while beheading an apostate, sometimes he's doing so for religious reasons."[27] This is all the more true if the executioner has been taught that the violent act will result in a highly desirable reward in an afterlife. The burning of women accused of witchcraft during the Inquisition appeared to be for religious reasons, even if there were also additional economic, gender, and cultural prejudices that drove these actions. Beliefs in demons and witches, whatever the origins of such beliefs, were supported by scriptures. Prescriptions for actions against such entities were also found in scriptures as in Exodus 22:18 which says "Thou shalt not suffer a witch to live." There are also scriptures that command the mass destruction of enemies, including innocent women and children.

Armstrong is correct in pointing to complexities in the origins of violence and she is also correct in denying that there is an inherent or essential violent nature associated with religion. She raises an interesting psychological question as to whether there is ever a single or pure motive for a given act. But even if there are no pure motives, there are dominant motives that may be of a religious nature. Thus, practically, it makes little difference whether one engages in violence exclusively for religious reasons. If religion plays a significant or dominant role in a complex of motives to engage in violence, then there is such a thing as religious violence just as there is religious charity or religious pacifism.

Another psychological question centers on whether there are motives, religious or otherwise, operating below the threshold of awareness. The philosopher Giles Deleuze, notes "We always start in the middle of things; thought has no beginning, just an outside to which it is connected."[28] If Deleuze is correct, the young executioner, under thoughtful philosophical interrogation, may be found to be profoundly ignorant of the reasons for his violent behavior. He may know very little about history, theology, or philosophy. He is radicalized by a complicated multidimensional belief system that may include religion, and he is simply caught in the exciting middle of things. But in contrast with Deleuze, it can be argued that the thought of the young executioner is connected to a narrow inside, and to an insulated and uncritical ideology. Critical thought, truly connected to a robust outside, is inevitably moderated by a plurality of perspectives including doubt and corrective self-criticism.

Concepts of God and God's commands and actions, as presented in sacred texts, are highly relevant to questions about religious violence. Ethical and moral behaviors are presumably modeled after, or even dictated by the commands and actions, attributed to God. "Godly behavior" is a common value in the religious life. But concepts of God, including the perceived nature of God, vary widely from one religion to the next and within various religious groups. God or Gods may be viewed as angry, peaceful, loving, vengeful, aloof, or deeply interested even in the finest unimaginable details of life. Gods may display benevolence or hate, favoritism for specific peoples or universal love for all peoples, and forgiveness and magnanimity. On the other hand, scriptures in some religious traditions tell of a God who inflicts horrific eternal punishments unequaled for their severity compared with anything encountered in the secular world.

What does it mean to live a "Godly life?" Practically, it appears that religion, as a strong factor within a larger belief system, is closely tied to concepts of God and may promote or even valorize violence or abandon it altogether as witnessed in the lives of numerous religious pacifists.

Another problem is that sacred scriptures, particularly when taken in naked literal meanings, are repeatedly used as justifications for violence. On the surface, there are in fact troublesome scriptures in many faith traditions as evidenced by intense apologetic efforts to soften or neutralize their meanings. The claim is made that if blinkered believers could only understand the context of such scriptures, they would quickly see that the scriptures do not at all mean what they clearly appear to mean. But emphasis on context is often used as a subterfuge, a term coming from the Latin *Subter* meaning below or underneath and *fugue* meaning flee. Subterfuge refers to deceptive strategies designed to conceal or hide. For example the painful and bald truths of slavery were covered, justified, and contextualized by the clam that it was the Fall of Man that "required the establishment of institutions of coercion, including slavery."[29]

Violence of a religious nature is also manifested in fantasies or ideas. Violence is normally understood in terms of overt acts that inflict harm, but there are also violent ideologies. Such ideology of a religious nature is manifested in thoughts and fantasies about hell and the nature of punishments inflicted on unbelievers, apostates, infidels, heretics, and reprobates. Dante's *Divine Comedy*, along with numerous sacred texts, provide evidence for virulent strains of violent religious ideology. "As a man thinketh in his heart, so is he" according to Proverbs 23:7. Such a statement, as well as the tragically numerous historical examples of religious violence, suggests that violent ideologies translate into violent behavior.

Religion and Prejudice

Most religious organizations embrace one of the many versions of the Golden Rule, they also engage in charitable outreach and preach the values of goodwill and universal "brotherhood." Such lofty ideals should be expected to translate into qualities such as tolerance, forbearance, magnanimity, altruism, benevolence, and generosity. Unfortunately, the translation does not always work and all too often suffers actual reversals when it comes to the treatment of specific outgroups. As Frederick Douglass observed, "I should regard being the slave of a religious master the greatest calamity that could befall me"; he noted that strong religious beliefs predicted owners' increased certainty that slavery was the will of God and increased willingness to abuse people who were also their property.[30] In the mid-twentieth century, in his classic book, *The Nature of Prejudice*, Gordon Allport outlined early evidence of prejudicial attitudes in various religious denominations.[31] C. Daniel Batson, in a study of religion and intolerance, summarized 44 findings "obtained across thirty-six different studies conducted between 1940 and 1975."[32] Batson found that "thirty-four of the forty-four findings reveal a positive relation between amount of intolerance and amount of interest in, involvement in, or adherence to religion."[33]

As early as 1954, Allport was troubled by the distressing results of early studies on religion and prejudice. The findings of the early studies seemed counterintuitive because, in Allport's words, they "belie the universalistic import of religious teaching."[34] Nevertheless, Allport came to the conclusion that "Two contrary sets of threads are woven into the fabric of all religion – the warp of brotherhood and the woof of bigotry."[35] Allport had collected extensive anecdotal evidence of clear-cut hostilities between various religious groups such as Catholics and Protestants and Jews and Christians. At the same time, he discerned high variability in prejudicial attitudes within Protestant and Catholic groups. For example, in one study, he found that Protestants and Catholics "who were considered most devout, more personally absorbed in their religion, were far less prejudiced than others."[36] Clearly, there was a need for a more nuanced examination of the relations between religion and prejudice. It was becoming apparent that there were very different motivations and reasons for affiliations, attachments, and memberships in religious organizations. For some church members, religion and spirituality were core values in themselves. For other members, religious affiliation was largely pragmatic or instrumental. For example, religious organizations were good places to establish social or business contacts with others, provide socialization skills for children, or provide comfort in times of distress. Allport suspected that "Belonging to a church because it is a safe powerful superior in-group is likely to be the mark of an authoritarian character and to be linked with prejudice."[37] The distinction between religion as an instrumental vs. a core value would inform a great deal of subsequent research.

In 1966 Allport published a classic study in pursuit of "sociocultural factors that predispose the churchgoer to prejudice."[38] He spoke of the vicious and shameful persecutions and inquisitions of the past that "occurred within religious contexts."[39] He also revisited the implications of religion as a core value vs. religion as an instrument to acquire personal benefits. Allport then reported on the results of pilot studies on religion as an *intrinsic* value vs. religion embraced for *extrinsic* purposes. In the intrinsic orientation a person would be likely to respond positively to a statement such as "My faith informs all aspects of my life." In the extrinsic orientation, a person would be more likely to respond positively to a statement such as "Church is a good place to make connections and meet friends." Preliminary results demonstrated that those with an intrinsic orientation were less prejudiced than those scoring high on the extrinsic orientation. The distinction between these two ways of being religious set off an outpouring of research on prejudice as a function of religious perspectives.

Study after study supported the findings that those who scored high on the intrinsic dimension were more tolerant and less prejudiced, particularly about members of other races, than those who scored high on the extrinsic dimension.[40] But there were numerous concerns about the advisability of basing conclusions regarding such an important topic on the basis of simple self-report responses to a questionnaire. Further, there were suspicions that the intrinsic–extrinsic distinction did not exhaust the ways of being religious. Accordingly, researchers introduced a third, more active way of being religious called "religion as quest."[41] Religion as quest enfranchises doubt, rejects dogmatic simplistic answers to life's perplexing questions, and embraces a general spirit of openness to change. Those who view the religious life as a quest are likely to be suspicious of certitude and easy answers. Indeed, they enjoy questions more than answers and deliberations more than pronouncements. They enjoy dealing with questions in the raw without having to embrace pre-digested solutions imposed beforehand by tradition and authority.

Studies conducted in the late 1980s and early 1990s examined the three orientations, but this time the emphasis was on non-proscribed intolerance – an intolerance not specifically forbidden by a church or scripture, such as intolerance for communists or atheists. Results of several studies revealed positive correlations between those in the intrinsic religious orientation and non-proscribed intolerance. The correlations were negative for those in the Quest orientation showing they were more tolerant than those in the intrinsic orientation. There was an absence of clear-cut patterns for those in the extrinsic orientation.[42] Though these results appear to contradict the results of earlier research on the extrinsic–intrinsic dimension, they actually supplement the earlier findings. Batson noted that the new results indicated that those in the intrinsic orientation are not really "free from enmity, contempt and bigotry [but instead they] are conforming to the 'right' tolerances and 'right' prejudices."[43]

Subsequent studies on religion and intolerance included actual behaviors in addition to self-reports on religious orientation. For example, researchers have examined willingness to lend assistance to students who self-identified as gay. It was found that those who scored above average on the intrinsic orientation were less likely to lend assistance to individuals who self-disclosed as gay than to lend assistance to individuals whose sexual orientation remained unknown.[44] Batson concluded that "in this experiment, intrinsic religion is at best associated with compassion that is circumscribed, not universal."[45] It has also been observed that those in the quest orientation are not free of selected kinds of intolerance. For example, it has been found that those who score high in the quest orientation are less likely to help those identified as fundamentalists compared to those who are not so identified. Apparently, those who regard themselves as tolerant have difficulty being tolerant with those they regard as intolerant.[46]

On a related theme, it has been argued that certain kinds of religious beliefs undermine the possibility of compromise. Walter Sinnott-Armstrong, in an article "How Religion Undermines Compromise" distinguishes between thin and thick compromises.[47] A thin compromise is illustrated in negotiations, for example, over the cost of an item. Each party gives in, resulting in middle ground that is not completely satisfactory to either party but is better than not doing business. A thick compromise is one in which a core value is involved.

To illustrate the distinction between thin and thick compromises, consider the following events. A new faith community representing conservative values was being built next to an existing older liberal church. One of the pastors of the older church suggested to leaders of the new group a way to share parking lots that would save both groups considerable money. One of the pastors of the liberal group was a woman who was openly lesbian. Leaders of the newly arrived conservative group believed it would be unacceptable to negotiate with a woman, especially a lesbian. They built a separate parking lot and a fence between the two worship facilities. Sinnott-Armstrong suggests that there are specific absolutistic and literalists doctrines that undermine abilities to compromise even when compromise would result in measurable benefits to all parties.

We return now to our basic question. What conclusions or permissible generalizations can be drawn regarding the relationship between religion and intolerance. There are any number of historical and contemporary examples of warfare between and within religious groups and between religious groups and secular interests and organizations. But there are often other political, economic, or territorial grievances or claims that complicate the picture. The larger question of interest centers on the effects of religion per se on intolerance and prejudice. As noted earlier there are exclusivist theological doctrines that undoubtedly contribute to intergroup conflict. The most generous conclusion that can be drawn from empirical studies on religion, intolerance, and prejudice is that there is strong evidence that religion often undermines tolerance and promotes prejudicial attitudes and behaviors. Nevertheless, there are ways of being religious that promote inclusive and tolerant behaviors and outlooks.

In a critique of research on religion and intolerance, John Perry and Nigel Biggar call attention to the dangers of treating religion as an explanatory category. Variation from one religious group to another is not the least of the problems confronting researchers. High variability on moral, political, and doctrinal issues is encountered within religious groups that are ostensibly homogeneous. Perry and Biggar also call attention to the importance of recognition that intolerance is not always bad, compromise is not always good, and war can be just. They go on to point out that prejudice is not peculiar to religious believers. The preceding materials focus on social-scientific studies of religious beliefs and practices. In fairness, such studies should also be directed at the beliefs and practices of scientists themselves. Further, atheists and people of various secular political persuasions have all too often defined and manifested the limits and extremes of intolerance and hatred. Discrimination against outgroups also results in part from ingroup favoritism as opposed to outright hostility toward outgroups.[48] Is it possible then, that regardless of the content of a belief system, simple preferences for one's own kind may have unintended negative consequences for outsiders?

Conversion Phenomena

Conversion from one belief system to another is a common occurrence and a central expectation or requirement in many faith communities. Conversion in religious contexts has traditionally been explained in terms of supernatural forces that beckon, directly influence, or even compel radical personality transformations. The Biblical story of the conversion of Paul in Acts 9 is a classic account of climacteric personality change prompted by the perceived action of a "light from heaven" and "voices" condemning Paul and directing him to a new life in the service of the Christian faith. The conversion of Aurelius Augustine is another example of a classic conversion experience. In a moment of crisis, Augustine heard the voice of a child commanding that he pick up a Bible and read it. Augustine's eyes fell on a scripture that provoked intense guilt and possible fear. This incident was a sudden and pivotal turning point in his transition to the religious life.

The conversion of Paul, according to the Biblical story, resulted from the direct action of God. Augustine's conversion was precipitated by "hearing a voice" presumably reflecting a powerful spiritual force. The claim has been made in Christian theology that "Only through God, can God be known."[49] A similar idea is set forth in the Qur'an in Surah 6:39 which says "whom Allah pleases He causes to err, and whom he pleases He puts on the right way." It also says in Surah 10:100, "It is not for a soul to believe except by Allah's permission."

The strength of the role of the supernatural in conversion phenomena has been a traditional source of disagreement among theologians. The aforementioned texts from the Qur'an indicate that human destiny, for better or worse, is under the absolute controlling influence of Allah though Surah 30:44 says "Whoever disbelieves, he shall be responsible for his disbelief." The same kind of tension between personal responsibility and divine control or coercion is encountered in Christian theology. Some theologians, such as John Calvin emphasize the absolute compelling foreknowledge of God including knowledge of the destiny of all souls.[50] Other theologians and religious leaders such as John Wesley have stressed the role of free will in the conversion process.[51] As noted in Chapter 3, it is deeply problematic to argue in support of the compatibility of the inviolate foreknowledge of God and the existence of human freedom of choice.

Naturalistic Approaches to Conversion

Scientists, employing the methodologies of science, must suspend judgment about the possible role of a God or of Gods in conversions. There are nevertheless, identifiable natural antecedents to conversion. Furthermore, it is clear that many radical personality conversions or changes are not of a religious nature. Dramatic shifts in beliefs and attitudes are regularly observed in political, economic, philosophical, scientific, and personal arenas.[52] There are multitudes of examples of sudden or gradual personality reversals whereby love turns to hate or vice versa. The philosopher Benedict Spinoza believed the human mind is subject to nature's laws and such laws are evident in all sorts of psychological matters. For example, he argued "if we develop hatred for a thing once loved, we hate with greater intensity than had we never loved it in the first place. Why? It is because the greater hatred is fueled by sorrow over the loss of love."[53]

The incidence of conversion phenomena in so many different arenas of life has stimulated research into natural antecedents and explanations of personality alterations. Naturalistic explanations of conversion, including religious conversions, may now be considered alongside supernatural explanations. Early psychologists such as William James, Ivan Pavlov, and Sigmund Freud were deeply interested in conversion phenomena and advanced descriptions and theories to enhance understanding of the experience and mechanics of radical personality changes.[54] Here again is a prime example of the encroachment of science into what was traditionally regarded as sacred territory, but extensive empirical studies have shed a great deal of light on the natural antecedents and experiences of those who have been converted from one system to another.

In 1900, Edwin Diller Starbuck, a pioneering psychologist interested in religion, published his classic work, *The Psychology of Religion, An Empirical Study of the Growth of Religious Consciousness*.[55] Starbuck conducted numerous empirical studies exploring conversion as a function of variables such as age, motivation, and emotional states that follow the conversion experience. Starbuck found consistent quantifiable patterns. One of his conclusions was that conversion "belongs almost exclusively to the years between 10 and 25. The number of instances outside that range appear few and scattered."[56] He goes on to note "The event comes earlier in general among the females than among the males, most frequently at 13 and 16. Among the males it occurs most often at 17 and immediately before and after that year."[57]

Starbuck found a range of emotions and motives present at the time of the conversion experience. The most dominant of the affective experiences included: fear of death and hell, conviction of sin, and a feeling of social pressure. Striving for a better life and seeking a moral ideal also played a role.[58] A range of positive emotions followed the conversion experience including: joy, bodily lightness, peace, happiness, relief, a sense of calm, but also a sense of responsibility. A relatively small number of the converted reported a sense of disappointment.[59]

Major evangelical religious leaders stress supernatural explanations of conversion, but do not deny the importance of social, physical, and psychological influences. John Wesley, for example, stressed the importance of beginning a sermon by preaching the law and this included the certainty of judgment and hell fire awaiting those who are unconverted. In his book, *Battle for the Mind: A Physiology of Conversion and Brainwashing*, William Sargant notes his own religious background in Methodism and cites Wesley's approach throughout his work, and Sargant describes common strategies for convincing large audiences and potential converts to break away from previous beliefs and behavior patterns and enter a "new life" that promises salvation.[60] An emotionally charged atmosphere including melodic and rhythmic music, testimonies from the faithful, heavy eye contact, love bombing, and dynamic, emotionally charged preaching are part of the equation. The induction of guilt and fear is followed by pointing to a path to salvation including fellowship in the elite company of believers, anticipation of a more fulfilling life in this world, and the promise of rich rewards in an afterlife. Those on the margins of society, dissatisfied with their lives or the direction of the world or at a difficult transition in life due to divorce, job loss, or bereavement are especially vulnerable.

Psychological studies of religious beliefs and practices have accelerated in modern times and are supported by scholarly journals such as the *Journal for the Scientific Study of Religion* and by Division 36 of the America Psychological Association.

*****

Scientific methodology has not been static and this would have come as no surprise to Francis Bacon who believed "the art of discovery may advance as discoveries advance."[61] Furthermore, as scientific methods have become more diverse and sophisticated, the reach of science has been extended. There was a time when Immanuel Kant could entertain doubts about whether chemistry was a science, though he believed chemistry might become a science.[62] Over time, the scientific canopy was extended to include increasing numbers of disciplines including all the biological sciences. The discoveries of lawful distributions of physical and behavioral characteristics added scientific legitimacy to disciplines such as anthropology, psychology, and sociology. These disciplines apply naturalistic methodologies to the study of a great range of experiential, behavioral, and social phenomena including those things we regard as religious.

Historically and in the present science has been, and is, subjected to religious scrutiny, but increasingly religion is now subjected to scientific scrutiny. Empirical studies have provided new ways to think about such topics as the efficacy of prayer, religion in relation to prejudice and violence, the positive and negative effects of ritual, and the natural antecedents of conversion. Religion is now observed with new eyes afforded by the methods of the sciences. Old certainties were challenged in the 16th century by the new astronomy and in the 19th century by evolution. The behavioral and social sciences also challenge older certainties but afford opportunities to understand the world at new and different levels of abstraction that broaden, challenge, and deepen spiritual sensitivities and understandings.

Notes

1 Decalaration of Independence, paragraph 2.
2 Francis Galton, *Hereditary Genius: An Inquiry into Its Laws and Consequences* (New York: D. Appleton & Company, 1900), 14.
3 It is most likely that Jefferson was challenging English belief in *Rex Lex* "The King is Law." The new American experiment in democracy rejected the rights of the King based on hereditary privilege. In this context, the notion that people are equal is revolutionary, particularly the claim that the King is not inherently better, either through noble (i.e., better) breeding or divine selection. Instead, the new nation would open leadership possibilities to all people. Jefferson obviously did not believe that all men are created equal. He owned people who were enslaved, voting privileges were restricted to white male property owners, and he undoubtedly understood that people are born with vastly different intellectual abilities, aptitudes, and physical characteristics.
4 Francis Galton, *Hereditary Genius*, 14.
5 Francis Galton, *Inquiries into Human Faculty and its Development* (New York: Dutton, 1883), 36.
6 Edward Burnett Tylor, "Quetelet on the Science of Man," *Popular Science Monthly* 1 (May 1872), 45–55.
7 Steven G. Hertz and Tobias Krettenauer, "Does Moral Identity Effectively Predict Moral Behavior?: A Meta-Analysis," *Review of General Psychology* 20, No. 2 (January, 2016), 129–140.
8 Lambert Adolphe Quetelet, *A Treatise on Man and the Development of his Faculties* (Gainsville, FL: Scholars' Facsimilies & Reprints, 1969), 5.
9 Ibid., 96.
10 Charles Darwin, Letter to Francis Galton December 23, 1870. In *More Letters of Charles Darwin* Vol. 2, ed. Francis Galton and A. C. Seward, Chapter 2, Letter 410, www.gutenberg.org/files/2740/2740-h/2740-h.htm (Accessed June 22, 2015).
11 Serge Nicholas, Aurélie Coubart, and Todd Lubart, "The Program of Individual Psychology (1895–1896) by Alfred Binet and Victor Henri," *L'Année Psychologique* 114, No. 1 (March, 2014), 5–60.
12 Karl Pearson, *The Chances of Death and Other Studies in Evolution* (New York: Edward Arnold, 1897).
13 For example, see Victor L. Streib, "Death Penalty for Children: The American Experience with Capital Punishment for Crimes Committed while under Age 18," *Oklahoma Law Review* 36, No. 3 (Summer, 1983), 613–641.
14 James Henry Leuba, "A Study in the Psychology of Religious Phenomena," *The American Journal of Psychology* 7, No. 3 (April, 1896), 312.
15 Holmes Rolston III, *Science and Religion: A Critical Survey* (New York: Random House, 1987), esp. Chapter 4.
16 Ibid., 193.
17 Edwin G. Boring, *A History of Experimental Psychology*, 2nd ed. (New York: Appleton-Century-Crofts, 1950), 42.
18 See Steve Clarke, Russell Powell, and Julian Savulescu (eds.), *Religion, Intolerance, and Conflict: A Scientific and Conceptual Investigation* (Oxford: Oxford University Press, 2013).

19 Muzafer Sherif and Carolyn Sherif, *Social Psychology* (New York: Harper & Row, 1969), 269.
20 Ibid., 227.
21 Harvey Whitehouse, "Religion, Cohesion, and Hostility," in *Religion, Intolerance, and Conflict: A Scientific and Conceptual Investigation*, eds. Steve Clarke, Russell Powell, and Julian Savulescu (Oxford: Oxford University Press, 2013), 36–47.
22 William Sargant, *Battle for the Mind: The Mechanics of Indoctrination, Brainwashing, and Thought Control* (New York: Pelican, 1957); Margaret T. Singer and Janja Lalich, *Cults in Our Midst: The Hidden Menace in Our Everyday Lives* (Hoboken, NJ: John Wiley and Sons, 1995); Michael D. Langone (ed.), *Recovery from Cults: Help for Victims of Psychological and Spiritual Abuse* (New York: Norton, 1993).
23 Whitehouse, "Religion, Cohesion, and Hostility," 42.
24 Ibid., 39.
25 Michael Paulson, "Refusing to Fly With a Woman in the Next Seat," *The New York Times* (Friday, April 10, 2015), 1, Vol. 164, No. 56.
26 Karen Armstrong, *Fields of Blood: Religion and the History of Violence* (New York: Alfred A. Knopf, 2014), 393.
27 Graeme Wood, "What ISIS Really Wants," *The Atlantic*, 315, No. 2 (March, 2015), 82.
28 Giles Deleuze, *Spinoza: Practical Philosophy* (San Francisco: City Lights Books, 1988), i.
29 Lester B. Scherer, *Slavery and the Churches in Early America, 1619–1819* (Grand Rapids, MI: William B. Eerdmans, 1975), 15; see also Stephen R. Haynes, *Noah's Curse: Biblical Justification of Slavery in the United States* (New York: Oxford University Press, 2002); Frederick Douglass, *Narrative of the Life of Frederick Douglass, An American Slave* (Boston, MA: The Anti-Slavery Office, 1845); Thorton Stringfellow, *Scriptural and Statistical Views of Slavery* (Richmond, VA: J. W. Randolph, 1856).
30 Douglass, *Narrative of the Life of Frederick Douglass*, 78.
31 Gordon Allport, *The Nature of Prejudice* (Garden City, NY: Doubleday Anchor Books, 1954), esp. Chapter 28.
32 C. Daniel Batson, "Individual Religion, Tolerance, and Universal Compassion," in *Religion, Intolerance and Conflict: A Scientific and Conceptual Investigation*, eds. Steve Clarke, Russell Powell, and Julian Savulescu (Oxford: Oxford University Press, 2013), 88–106.
33 Batson, *Individual Religion*, 90.
34 Allport, *The Nature of Prejudice*, 420.
35 Gordon W. Allport, "The Religious Context of Prejudice," *Journal for the Scientific Study of Religion* 5, No. 3 (Autumn, 1966), 447–457.
36 Allport, *The Nature of Prejudice*, 421.
37 Ibid., 422.
38 Allport, "Religious Context of Prejudice," 450.
39 Ibid., 447.
40 Batson, *Individual Religion*, 92.
41 Ibid., 95.
42 Ibid., 97.
43 Ibid., 98.
44 C. Daniel Batson, Randy B. Floyd, Julie M. Meyer, and Alana L. Winner, "And Who Is My Neighbor? Intrinsic Religion as a Source of Universal Compassion," *Journal for the Scientific Study of Religion* 38, No. 4 (December 1999), 445–457.
45 Batson, *Individual Religion*, 101.
46 Jerry Goldfried and Maureen Miner, "Quest Religion and the Problem of Limited Compassion," *Journal for the Scientific Study of Religion* 41, No. 4 (December, 2002), 685–695.
47 Walter Sinnott-Armstrong, "How Religion Undermines Compromise," in *Religion, Intolerance and Conflict*, eds. Steve Clarke, Russell Powell, and Julian Savulescu (Oxford: Oxford University Press, 2013), 221–235.

48 Anthony G. Greenwald and Thomas F. Pettigrew, "With Malice Toward None and Charity for Some: Ingroup Favoritism Enables Discrimination," *American Psychologist* 69, No. 7 (October 2014), 669–684.
49 See Hans Urs von Balthasar, *The Theology of Karl Barth* (San Francisco: Ignatius Press, 1992), 160.
50 John Calvin, "Institute of the Christian Religion," in *Classics of Protestantism*, ed. Vergilius Ferm (New York: Philosophical Library, 1959), 67–129.
51 John Wesley, "Free Grace," in *Classics of Protestantism*, ed. Vergilius Ferm (New York: Philosophical Library, 1959), 165–179.
52 For example of political conversions see Richard Crossman (ed.), *The God that Failed* (New York: Bantam Books, 1959).
53 As quoted in William Douglas Woody and Wayne Viney, *A History of Psychology: Emergence of Science and Applications*, 6th ed. (New York: Routledge, 2017), 159.
54 Pavlov's explanation of conversion can be found in William Sargant, *Battle for the Mind*. Freud's views are found in Sigmund Freud, "A Religious Experience," in *The Standard Edition of the Complete Psychological Works of Sigmund Freud*, Vol. 21, ed. and trans. James Strachey (London: Hogarth Press, 1961), 168–172. Williams James's views are set forth in his book *Varieties of Religious Experience* (New York: Routledge, 2002), esp. Lectures 9 and 10. See also William Douglas Woody, "Varieties of Religious Conversion,"*Streams of William James*, 5 (2003), 7–11.
55 Edwin Diller Starbuck, *The Psychology of Religion, An Empirical Study of the Growth of Religious Consciousness* (1900; repr., London: Dalton House, 2012).
56 Ibid., 28.
57 Ibid.
58 Ibid., 54, 63.
59 Ibid., 121.
60 Sargant, *Battle for the Mind*. See especially Chapter 5.
61 Francis Bacon, *The New Organon and Related Writings* (New York: Liberal Arts Press, 1960), 120.
62 See Eric Watkins and Marius Stan, "Kant's Philosophy of Science," *Stanford Encyclopedia of Philosophy*, plato.stanford.edu/entries/kant-science/ (Accessed May 23, 2015).

12

ABSOLUTISM

The Disease of Philosophical Thought

Nothing includes everything[1]

Nothing short of everything will really do[2]

This book has explored historical and contemporary relations between science and religion as well as some of the diverse treatments of the relations between these two important human endeavors. To say the least, relations have challenged and continue to bewilder scholars and the public at large. There is no one enduring generalization that captures or simplifies the history of the muddled interactions between scientific and religious worldviews. There are instances of accommodation, cooperation, partnership, mutual but tolerant suspicion, and specific instances of outright intellectual warfare as defined by the criteria set forth in our first chapter. The problem of characterizing the relations between science and religion is all the more difficult because of the absence of a consensus definition of religion. While science enjoys greater internal unities than religion, science nevertheless evolves resulting in widely different opinions about its ever changing nature and the expanding reach of its ever-improving methodologies.[3]

The previous chapters have covered a vast, though not exhaustive, range of historical and contemporary interactions between science and religion. How then, are we to arrive at a sensible and meaningful conclusion at this point in time? We stress the phrase "this point in time" because we agree with William James when he said "What really *exists* is not things made but things in the making."[4] James called for a nuanced developmental approach to all problems and repeatedly warned of the dangers inherent in the temptation to characterize things in terms of timeless absolutes. Our conclusions are informed by these two closely related ideas set forth by William James. That is, the relations between science and religion are best understood from a developmental or evolutionary perspective; and scholars including scientists, theologians, and historians, must work to avoid explanations that parade as finished, definitive, complete, or absolute.

Andrew Dickson White took a developmental approach when he suggested that there have been identifiable stages that characterize theological attacks on scientific discoveries.[5] A review of White's stages is informative, especially if such a review promotes thoughtful consideration about possible future directions. The first stage, according to White, is encountered in the argument that a given scientific discovery violates truths set forth in sacred scriptures. One example of this stage is illustrated in claims that the movement of the earth contradicts sacred scriptures such as I Chronicles 16:30, Psalms 93:1, and Psalms 96:10 that declare the earth to be immovable. This argument was used in the Galileo affair. A variation of the same argument has been employed more recently by religious conservatives and Biblical literalists who assess homosexuality in the context of ancient texts such as Leviticus 18:22 and Leviticus 20:13.

In White's analysis, the second stage is illustrated in the argument that a scientific discovery should be rejected because it violates a fundamental theological doctrine. This stage is illustrated in the theological doctrine that human origins are from a single primal pair such as Adam and Eve. Scientific discoveries in genomics however, point strongly to more diverse or complex beginnings. The rejection of a literal Adam and Eve raises deeply challenging questions about the doctrine of original sin as set forth in the second chapter of Genesis. Thus, scientific discoveries in genomics are pitted against a theological doctrine considered by some to be fundamental to the faith. As noted in Chapter 1, this proved to be one of the issues the Catholic Church had with Teilhard de Chardin who believed in multiple human origins.

The third stage is illustrated in attempts to reconcile once rejected scientific truths with sacred scriptures. Thus, the existence of dinosaurs was originally rejected in many faith traditions because such creatures are not referenced in sacred literature. Later with the advance of overwhelming scientific evidence, the existence of dinosaurs has been widely acknowledged. There are still disputes, however, about when they lived, the causes of their demise, and how to reconcile their existence with biblical stories, including whether dinosaurs co-existed with humans.

It is difficult to deny that there has been evolution if not stages in the relations of science and religion. Stage theories are popular, seductive, and often helpful in attempts to promote understanding of complex problems. Most stage theories however, are also beset with problems and should be approached with caution. One problem is that things do not always progress in terms of a linear sequential order. Stages are skipped or there are no clearly identifiable transitions. Another problem is that all stages are likely to be present at once in a given slice of time. "All of the above" is often the most appropriate answer to a given question. Still another problem is the temptation to valorize the most recently identified stage as the enlightened position that solves the deficiencies or oversights of earlier stages. Historians have often been vulnerable to this temptation as they celebrate the latest historical theory as the one true theory. For all the problems however, stage theories are useful and informative because they typically underscore the importance of evolution or development over time.

Stage theories encourage both prospective and retrospective thinking along with investigations of the forces that facilitate or inhibit change. There has been a fundamental shift in the relations between science and religion beginning with the dominance of religion as the older of the two orientations. Science is the youthful newcomer, and its gradual ascendance marks a new epoch in human history. Though some of the intellectual components necessary to the development of science are found in the works of scholars from ancient and medieval periods, science, as we know it today, has a relatively recent history. From the approximate time of Galileo, much of the world has witnessed a transition from religion as the dominant orientation to science as primary and dominant. It is difficult to argue that life in the 21st century, especially in developed nations, is not informed largely by science. The curriculum in any educational institution tells worlds about the centrality of science in modern life. Courses in mathematics, physics, chemistry, biology, the earth sciences, computer science, economics, psychology, sociology, anthropology, secular history, and political science are central to a proper education.

The centrality of science in modern life is also illustrated in any mindful monitoring of daily activities. Life in the 21st century is organized around, and almost unthinkable without, the products of science and its technological offshoots. We arise in the morning perhaps to the tunes coming from our cell phones, switch on the lights, and enjoy the ambient temperature regulated by so-called "intelligent" thermostats. We activate the television, microwave oven, and automatic dishwasher, and then we check the weather forecast augmented by satellite technology before getting into our automobiles also guided by satellite technology. We make a trip to the physician's office where we encounter a veritable world of images and tools afforded by science. We sit down in front of our computers or pick up our phones or tablets where we have near instant access to information sources larger by orders of magnitude than anything afforded by the greatest libraries in the world. We watch our favorite sport in high definition or enjoy a movie while moving close to the speed of sound as we travel over oceans and mountain ranges that were once formidable barriers. We hear an online lecture on the number and functions of neurons, synapses, and neurotransmitters in the human brain along with a description of some new sensory prosthetic that promises to change everything. The cognitive and pragmatic achievements we take for granted would be completely beyond the imaginative capacities of most of the peoples who lived prior to the scientific revolution.

It is clear; we have witnessed a transition out of a long period of history defined and dominated by tradition, authority, and revelation as central organizing features in matters of knowledge. Submission, obedience, surrender, and compliance, particularly to traditional authorities that were mysterious yet revered and feared, were celebrated as admirable virtues. We now live in a different world increasingly organized and dominated by the products that grew out of a new epistemology that prioritized the values of doubt, observation, reason, and experiment. But there is still something significant, pervasive, and deep that is missing. Few of us would want to return to a pre-scientific world; we would find such a world to be a miserable, dark, and ignorant habitation. Not only would we be immediately struck by major changes such as the lack of automobiles and the omnipresence of horses and other livestock, but we would also notice the small and innumerable differences in daily life in a world in which fire provides the only illumination, and we would likely dread a trip to the dentist. And yet, we are not entirely at home in a scientific age because we realize that, for all the benefits, there are dangers brought about by science that lurk below the surface of things and threaten our very existence.

Further, there are scholars who venture to suggest a larger "scientific viewpoint" on the significance, purpose, and meaning of individual life and of life in general and that the view is cold and stark. Bertrand Russell has characterized this picture as follows:

> That man is the product of causes which had no prevision of the end they were achieving; that his origin, his growth, his hopes and fears, his loves and beliefs, are but the outcome of accidental collocations of atoms; that no fire, no heroism, no intensity of thought and feeling can preserve an individual life beyond the grave; that all the labors of all the ages, all the devotion, all the inspiration, all the noonday brightness of human genius are destined to extinction in the vast death of the solar system, and that the whole temple of man's achievement must inevitably be buried beneath the debris of a universe in ruins – all these things, if not quite beyond dispute, are yet so nearly certain that no philosophy which rejects them can hope to stand.[6]

Carl Becker, in his book *The Heavenly City of the Eighteenth-Century Philosophers* suggests that we may "Edit and interpret the conclusions of modern science as tenderly as we like."[7] But an assessment somewhat comparable to that described by Russell is almost unavoidable in a world marked by a "blindly running flux of disintegrating energy."[8]

But does such a pessimistic "scientific view" run the risk of closing accounts with reality prematurely? William James insisted that *reality grows* just as our consciousness grows. He did not believe "human experience is the highest form of experience extant in the universe."[9] James did not believe that present worldviews are adequate to the future; he argued for openness to possible emergent realities, novelties, new worldviews, methodologies, and ways of existing that are completely beyond our present comprehension. He would not necessarily reject the pessimistic views outlined by Bertrand Russell and Carl Becker. Indeed, he might even view them as interesting scientistic parallels to the pessimistic end-of-the-world horrors encountered in some religious traditions. He would undoubtedly be equally captivated by the wildly imaginative and often more optimistic views set forth in modern futuristic science fiction works such as *The Day the Earth Stood Still* or *Guardians of the Galaxy*. James understood that our prospective reach is wild work. Perhaps we should enter such work more playfully or even joyfully and avoid the deadly serious tone encountered in the pessimism of scholars such as Russell and Becker as well as the cataclysmic end-of-the-world eschatologies encountered in some religious traditions. Above all else, James argued against narrow, pinched, and closed views of reality whether they be religious, political, historical, or scientific. He argued for a more open pluralistic philosophy that is moderate, disciplined, open to change, friendly to alternative perspectives, and deeply aware of our epistemic failures and limitations.

James spoke of a "something more" pluralistic philosophy as a kind of over-belief that amounts to a general philosophical orientation. This over-belief is captured in the epigraph that opens this chapter. James also acknowledged a monistic "nothing but" philosophy as an alternative over-belief captured by the second epigraph at the beginning of this chapter. A deeper grasp of these two orientations is relevant to discussions of the relations between science and religion because both orientations are commonly encountered in scientific as well as religious worldviews.

Nothing Short of Everything Will Really Do

This phrase from Aldous Huxley's book *Island* can be interpreted to mean that everything there is, in theory, can be grasped and that such a grasp is necessary to an adequate philosophy. Physicists speak of a "theory of everything" or of unifying the four forces of nature. A theory of everything is more manageable if everything reduces to one thing or one kind of thing. Monism is the belief that there is one and only one fundamental reality and that all things are intimately related to that one real thing. For example, according to monistic materialism all real things are composed of, or manifested in, matter. Without matter there is simply nothing. Thoughts or ideas are nothing more than complex materials (i.e., neurological and chemical) events.

Theoretical physicist Geoffrey West argues that the theory of everything is a theory that must die.[10] The meaning of the term *everything* eludes definition, and according to West, "smacks of arrogance and naïveté." Stephen Hawking has pointed out that a theory of everything is the grand dream of many physicists but is nevertheless a misnomer. Hawking notes that a theory of everything will fail to tell us "that Sinéad O'Conner will be at the top of the hit parade this week or that Madonna will be on the cover of *Cosmopolitan*."[11] It is highly doubtful that everything is so hard wired to every other thing that any history could be written in advance. Along these same lines, theoretical physicist Marcelo Gleiser suggests that grand unification schemes, or what he calls Überunification, must die.[12] The most we can hope for is more modest unifications within limited domains.

Nothing Includes Everything

The alternative perspective is manifested in the pluralistic belief that there are many different real things. Perhaps it is a multiverse rather than a universe. A pluralist can argue, for example, that an abstract formal principle such as the Pythagorean theorem exists as a formal truth, independent of any material manifestation, and that there are many such formal abstract truths. It is possible that these abstract truths do actually work only in a material context, but nevertheless have genuine ontological existence apart from their practical demonstrations in the material world.[13] It is reasonable to believe that a formal truth such as the Pythagorean theorem exists "out there" ontologically and prior to material entities including the existence of humans. James spoke of ontological pluralism; the belief that there are many real things including a real material world as well as other things encountered in ordinary experience such as real values, abstract truths, or time as a reality and not a mere human construction. This is the pluralistic "something more" faith that there is no one thing that includes everything. Pluralism also extends to epistemology as manifested in the belief, as explored in Chapter 2, that there are many legitimate methods in the quest for truth.

The exploration of the distinction between "nothing but" and "something more" attitudes moves us away from the mundane practice of religion per se and science per se and back to philosophy. Philosophy is the original discipline that seeks a way to rise above preoccupation with the on-going numbing routine and mindless immediacy of things including religious and scientific things. The heart and soul of philosophy involves consciousness of consciousness, thinking about thinking, and, for purposes of the present discussion, a demanding and challenging intellectual exercise that requires critical examinations of religion as well as science from the inside as well as the outside. Philosophers refer to this intellectual exercise as meta-level thinking or meta-cognition. The importance of such an exercise to education was illustrated by a university president confronted with a severe budget crisis and thus debating the possibility of eliminating an entire academic department as one possible solution to his problem. Someone suggested that enrollment in philosophy courses was lagging so that should be the department to be eliminated. The president said "A university without a philosophy department is not a university."[14] We agree, but is there any philosophical orientation that can provide ameliorative remedies for all the tensions, conflicts, and dilemmas associated with the relations of science and religion and with the historiographic differences we have encountered throughout this text? We believe the pluralistic, pragmatic, and radically empirical philosophy of William James provides a comprehensive grasp of the larger meanings of science and religion while recognizing workable accommodations and legitimate differences between the two. In what follows, we will try briefly to defend this position.

The Value of Pluralistic Perspectives

William James believed that pluralism, in contrast with monism, is more consistent with the flux of human experience and more likely to be open, moderate, and receptive to promising leads that fall outside the boundaries of orthodoxy. James argued that pluralism is less likely than monism to embrace absolutism, a philosophy that favors words such as *all, entire, total, finished, complete,* and *must*. Consistent with the Jamesian view, theologian John Haught argues that the desire to know "is most at home where there is an openness to a limitless horizon of being, and it begins to feel cramped whenever it hears phrases such as 'enough,' 'nothing but,' or 'all there is.'"[15] James's strong position against absolutism and radical singularity was based on his evolutionary belief that reality grows. Therefore, at this point in time, there is no final conclusion about anything because there are all sorts of connections even now in the making. For any problem, we may collect as much information as humanly possible assured that the future will inevitably bring new additions, challenges, surprises, deletions, adumbrations, and outright denials of earlier assured convictions. James's philosophy calls for a radical and deep sense of the limitations associated with our location in time along with a consequent epistemic humility. He found it sufficient to be content with a moderate and tentative inching forward as opposed to claims that we are already in possession of the grand conclusive sweep that brings everything together "in one vast instantaneous, co-implicated completeness."[16] This latter attitude provides the foundations for the species of absolutism undergirding the acts of terrorists.

Absolutism and Authority

Absolutism insists on conformity, ideological unity, and respect or even reverence for authority. Authoritarianism, as a personality trait, had its roots in low tolerance for compromise, doubt, and ambiguity. In a classic study, Adorno, Frenkel-Brunswik, Levinson, and Sanford found that, among other traits, authoritarians emphasize rigid views of right and wrong, fear of and submission to legitimate authorities, and authoritarian aggression toward those who challenge authority.[17] Psychologist Bob Altemeyer refined and further operationalized these ideas, all of which are prominent in people who embrace religious fundamentalism.[18] As we will see in the materials that follow, scientists may also be vulnerable to some of the characteristics of absolutism and authoritarianism.

Absolutism in Science

Science and religion have both been vulnerable to absolutistic thinking. Absolutism in science is encountered in claims that "only science can confer genuine (in contrast to apparent) knowledge about reality." Some observers claim that many of those who seek certainty from the inductive and probabilistic methods of science are actually seeking to replace fading religious certainty with non-existent scientific certainty. Such a claim is what Mikael Stenmark refers to as "epistemic scientism."[19] There is also a hint of absolutism when truth claims are made in the name of science that are unverifiable by the methodologies of science. Science has proven to be a powerful tool, but there are legitimate questions about this tool. Is the reach of science without limits and is scientific methodology adequate as a means of uncovering the truth in all imaginable arenas? Science itself grows with new methods, new perspectives that lead to new questions for research, and changing cultural worldviews. Can science answer the deepest most vexing questions the human mind can frame? If reality grows, is there any assurance that science, as we now know it, will be or even must be adequate to explain unexpected novelties? Is absolutistic certitude in keeping with the scientific spirit or is epistemic humility the more noble and appropriate trait? Could absolutism in science morph into totality and if so, what is to prevent the most egregious totalitarian actions by well-intentioned scientists?

Slife and Richardson, in a discussion of scientific naturalism and religion, make a helpful distinction between methodological naturalism and metaphysical naturalism.[20] The latter is more likely to result in explanatory monism because nature is all there really is; there is no possibility of any other order of reality.

Methodological naturalism, by contrast, allows for the practical use of all the observational tools of science, but stops short of saying that the natural world exhausts all the possibilities of reality or that the tools of science are completely adequate for all forms of inquiry. In short, methodological naturalism is inherently more open than metaphysical naturalism.

Presumably, the scientific attitude promotes tentative conclusions, openness to change, and probabilistic statements as opposed to absolute certainty. But some secular scholars have been, and are, as dogmatic and intolerant of diversity as any religious fundamentalist. Scientific and secular fundamentalism is encountered in uncompromising, narrow, and categorical treatments including scientific investigations of religion. The point is illustrated by the title of Christopher Hitchens' book *God Is Not Great: How Religion Poisons Everything*. The absolutistic all-inclusive "everything" is in stark contrast with the claim of William James that "nothing includes everything." One can admire the work of new atheists such as Christopher Hitchens, Richard Dawkins, and Sam Harris to expose abuses and absurdities associated with religion, but all too often the new atheists fall victim to the same authoritarian, absolutistic, steep, and evangelistic zealotry they find in the work of those with whom they disagree. Religion and science have a right to be understood in terms of their most noble and lofty achievements along with an obligation to also be understood in a critical perspective. The loss of the ability to criticize religion and science would amount to intellectual death, yet some organizations have called for international bans for some forms of criticism.[21] Religious and scientific absolutists, with their assured and comforting singularity of vision, attempt to characterize the whole of things they don't like in terms of the lowest possible denominators. Once again, words such as *everything* and *all* take center stage along with other warning signs such as "no trespassing" associated with intolerance for any kind of criticism of selected doctrines, books, or leaders.

Absolutism in Religion

Absolutism in religion surfaces repeatedly in claims that all truth is bottled up or contained in one relatively small sacred text or in one institution or in a single authority or representative of an institution. Claims of infallibility and inerrancy common in contemporary and religious history have led to the examples of certitude and abusive authority discussed in Chapter 2 and throughout this book. As with science, absolutism in religion slips easily into totality and totality into religious and political totalitarianism. Major tensions between science and religion have occurred historically and in the present by absolutistic religious attempts to bridle scientific ideas. Absolutism has been difficult to curb in those religions that denigrate the values of freedom of expression, doubt, and curiosity.

Absolutism in religion is also manifested in the work of evangelical believers who display an unquenchable appetite for uncompromising social unity including thoroughgoing uniformity of thought, speech, and action. Such religious absolutists feel an obligation to enforce unity via thought police, dress and grooming codes, a host of social and behavioral codes, and a mystical obsession with metaphysical oneness. The evangelical mission can brook no toleration for individuality or difference. For those with a more robust or full-bodied temperament, such a colorless, monotone, and monotonous world amounts to a death wish. For those outside the absolutist scheme, the message is clear, convert and conform or be ostracized, or, in more extreme applications, convert or die. The meaning of harmony in absolutism is tied up with mindless conformity whereas harmony from a pluralistic perspective refers to thoughtful agreement based on a measured quest for concord of genuinely independent parts. There can be no harmony in absolutism, because there can be no truly independent parts.

The Problem of Unity

In his *Notes on the State of Virginia*, Thomas Jefferson refers to the bed of Procrustes as he expresses concern that unity is too often achieved through coercion. He expressed doubts about any kind of natural unity and reminds his readers that the earth is "inhabited by a thousand millions of peoples [and that these] profess probably a thousand different systems of religion. That ours is but one of that thousand."[22] He laments the pervasive wish to force the other 999 to conform to the one "true way." He notes that, despite the abusive efforts of true believers, there has been no progress toward unification. In a discussion of the pathologies of freedom Matthew Stewart argues that "The eternal, implacable demand for unity of belief, Jefferson intimates, is worse than just impractical, it misconceives fundamentally the nature of human experience and the foundation of human community."[23]

In an early elaboration of the same ideas, William James launched a trenchant attack on Monistic philosophies. He understood that unifying efforts are relevant to many human interests including science and religion and their relations. But he argued that obsession with radical singularity is deeply problematic, partly because ordinary and reflective experience is of a bewildering profusion of different entities, sensations, concepts, principles, theories, contradictions, perplexities, and abstractions. He asked what oneness could possibly be or mean; is it of an ontological, epistemological, aesthetic, or axiological nature? If the answer is all of the above, how are such vastly different topical areas to be brought together? He doubted there could be any oneness anywhere that does not violate a welter of experiences elsewhere. Is oneness genuinely natural, or is it forced by conceptual prejudices? By what mystical magic could everything come down to one thing and then, what is that one thing? James was deeply suspicious of a "glut of oneness" that emerged from the mysticism he discerned in monistic philosophies, an over-emphasis on unity even in the face of contradictory evidence, a unity that he referred to as a "metaphysical monster."[24] We may also ask whether absolute oneness ever means anything other than intellectual death? For his part, James was interested not only in the theoretical problem of oneness, but also in the pragmatic implications of positing oneness or complete unity. We turn then briefly to the pragmatic problems of monistic absolutism.

Artificial Combinations

Expressions such as Marxist agriculture, Christian biology, Aryan physics, or Islamic chemistry are examples of artificial combinations. In each of these compound ideas, an over-belief forces a cherished worldview into a new combination. The boundaries of astronomy, for example, were too large to fit within privileged 16th century Biblically based Christian perspectives. Similarly, the reach of biology is far too extensive to be adequately understood by any of the favored theologies of the past. Their reach and content is insufficient for the vast subject matter of biology. What could Christian or Islamic biology possibly mean? Would Islamic chemistry lead to outcomes different to those of Christian chemistry? James understood that some things must stand alone and that forced or manufactured conjunctions undermine intellectual integrity.

The Wisdom of Moderation

James insisted that pluralism is not as extreme as monism. Belief in one all-embracing infallible truth is more likely to produce narrow loyalties along with evangelical zeal. In an absolutistic monistic religious or scientific system, a single point of contention can crack the entire foundation; therefore, any point of disagreement must be fought aggressively. The belief in a variety of vantage points is sure to be more open, more malleable, and more moderate compared to beliefs in the one true way. Fundamentalists, whether they are of religious, political, philosophical or scientific persuasions, are not known for their moderation.

Constraining Curiosity

Curiosity is constrained if one knows in advance that an investigation must yield data consistent with one overriding truth. The harnessing and limiting of curiosity stifles innovation and creativity. It may be no accident that literally hundreds of Nobel prizes have been awarded to scholars from countries that have a history of enfranchising curiosity and promoting liberal education as opposed to rote learning, routine memory work, training, and indoctrination.[25] Curiosity is constrained or dies outright when it is bridled, bounded, and channeled.

Distortion of Experience

One of James's major complaints against monistic absolutism is that it constrains and distorts experience. Although a beautiful, integrated, singular perspective may satisfy needs for aesthetic purity and simplicity, an absolutistic view fails to be adequate to the everyday tests of lived experience because experiences must be "cooked" to conform to the prescriptions of the monistic scheme. If we start with the view that all things *must be* connected, then we face the difficult challenge of connecting all things, even those that appear substantially different. For example, how does an obsolete grammatical rule in a dead language relate to the sound of a C-sharp note played on a piano in a basement bar in east London? These ideas and stimuli appear very different and serve different roles, but to monists the connections *must* exist, whether or not these connections can be observed. The word *all* simplifies cognition while the word *each* calls for a great deal of work and thought. James noted that when we employ the word *all* we can go on a "moral holiday." We know in advance the answers to our difficult questions without investigation of individual or exceptional cases with their ambiguities and complexities; these can be ignored or explained away as irrelevant exceptions.

James worried that *"we carve out* order by leaving the disorderly parts out."[26] The de-humanizing features of absolutistic schemes are illustrated by the character Javert in Victor Hugo's *Les Misérables*. Javert is an officer of the law known for his cold, rigid, absolutistic, obdurate, and uncompromising commitment to the letter of the law. He is robotic, without soul, grace, or feeling in his belief that there are no exceptions, concessions, mitigating circumstances, or complexities. It's all very simple. Such a philosophy is a death wish, and Javert dies by his own hand.

Freedom of Expression

Absolute oneness, wherever it is encountered, threatens freedom of expression and is threatened by free expression. Throughout this text, we have encountered examples of censorship, and suppression of thought, speech, and publications. These are the tools of paternalistic absolutists who restrict access to information, construct laws against blasphemy, or issue death threats against anybody who dares to think critically. George Packer has observed that "repression and violence against journalists is at record levels."[27] Indeed, according to one report, 66 journalists worldwide were murdered and 119 were abducted in 2014.[28] Violent attacks on freedom of expression and critical thinking in these opening years of the 21st century raises the larger question: "Why can't we all get along?" One reason is that absolutistic oneness is profoundly a-social in its insistence on unity, conformity, submission, and singularity of perspective. Pluralism, by contrast, is a more friendly social philosophy with emphasis on the values of multiple perspectives arising from numerous independent or quasi-independent sources. Compromise is a mark of weakness to the absolutist but a source of strength and new ideas to the pluralist.

Accommodation

The terms *accommodation* and *warfare* were purposefully employed throughout this book. Intellectual warfare, as defined in the first chapter, has been obvious in many of the previous chapters. We turn now to a treatment of accommodation. To accommodate is to adapt, assimilate, reconcile, or incorporate change. The goal is to seek harmonies where there have been conflicts, contradictions, or dissonance. Accommodation, where science and religion are concerned, appears superficially to have been a one-way street. Science has been the innovator as it has continually brought forth new facts and theories at an increasingly dizzying pace. Some of the new theories and facts have directly contradicted or challenged older religious intellectual constructions. As evidence accumulates, older religious traditions have been forced to change.

There is however, no disciplinary arena immune to needs for adaptation, accommodation, or even radical change. Science is often forced to construct a new picture of the origin and structure of some aspect of the world, to discard a theory once thought to be workable, and to adapt, sometimes quickly, to new methodologies. Legal codes and judicial systems once functional and taken to be inviolable, may with time become anachronistic, archaic, or even toxic. Lawmakers continually work to accommodate and adjust laws to new realities, changing physical and social structures, and changing belief systems and values. A speed limit in an earlier era with unpaved roads may be entirely inappropriate in a later period with modern paved roads and superior automobiles. A set of laws or a formal constitution may work for a period of time, but there will inevitably be a need for amendments, new interpretations, deletions, or additions. So called "originalism" where laws are concerned, in which observers attempt to discern the original intent of the writers who often lived in different times, places, and worldviews, may have a "feel good" quality, but there is a devastating price to be paid when eyes are reverted exclusively to the past. Religion, like science and legal systems, and all other systems of thought is also confronted with needs to adapt, accommodate, adjust, or incorporate new ways of seeing things or new ways of being in the world.

Historical perspectives can shape future accommodation. Recognition of past forces that led to substantial change can encourage open worldviews as well as scientific and religious humility. Scientists and religious leaders who have changed their views on race, sexual orientation, and gender identity can inspire future scholars to push the boundaries, even on topics once viewed as established or unassailable. We optimistically hope that historical perspectives such as the ones we have covered in this book will enfranchise curiosity about the future. To look to the future through the lenses of the past and the present will inspire scholars across fields to continue to accommodate and to shape our world.

The need to accommodate is not a weakness or a sign that a system is fatally flawed through and through. Indeed, it is the failure to accommodate that is a weakness if not pathological. Earlier beliefs, whether they were of a "scientific," political, economic, legal, or religious nature may be found to be wrong or unworkable. Though scientists may be stubborn, one of the virtues of science is that it is receptive to change. Most religious systems are conservative, but they do in fact gradually accommodate to changing circumstances. For this reason, it is a mistake to declare categorically that religion and science are inherently and irrevocably incompatible. Numerous religious groups, once guided exclusively by authority, tradition, and revelation, now valorize experience and reason as necessary epistemic guides. Such groups may have turned from a love of "unquestioned answers" to a new love for the exploration of "unanswered questions." Hillary Clinton said something to the effect that the earth is round, the sky is blue, and vaccination works. The vast majority of people of faith agree. A dramatic example of accommodation is encountered in the encyclical on climate change issued by Pope Francis in June of 2015. Numerous faith groups have been silent on the problem of climate change but the silence is giving way to deep concerns and to salutary actions including efforts to curb population growth. Science has led the way, but is now buttressed by increasingly strong support from a great range of faith communities.[29] This is not to downplay the large number of climate change deniers encountered in conservative religious and political organizations but to look to the future with curiosity, optimism, and hope.

*****

Relations between science and religion in history are not static, and it is a mistake to characterize them as such. Consciousness in all arenas inevitably expands with the evolution of languages, methodologies, technologies, cultural settings, and growing visions of the nature of reality. There are endemic differences between artistic, legal, religious, political, scientific, and technological endeavors. There are connections and disconnections among various disciplinary areas as well as common goals and goals that are unique to given disciplines. A certain degree of conflict or even intellectual warfare is inevitable but, as noted by Whitehead, "A clash of doctrines is not a disaster—it is an opportunity."[30] The opportunity is missed if informed dialogue is drowned out by absolutist pronouncements.

We believe the growth of process philosophy and theology holds out hope for meaningful cooperative work between science and religion. Process theory assumes that knowledge is best understood as ongoing, dynamic, and unending. This contrasts with older beliefs that revelation was a static absolute, once-for-all, timeless, frozen message. Andrew Dickson White believed in ongoing revelation and that revelation with religious implications may come from surprising sources including science. There can be no debate that science has inadvertently challenged retrograde views of religion and, overall, has had a profound influence on religious beliefs. With rare exceptions, faith communities joyfully use the products of science and technology, even including such products in their worship services. Religious views of the cosmos and of life have been dramatically altered by scientific discoveries. As noted in Chapter 1, Andrew Dickson White has been maligned by some historians for the errors he made in his classic *History of the Warfare Between Science and Theology in Christendom*. White should nevertheless be credited for his optimistic belief in a possible new stage in which faith, informed by, and compatible with scientific discoveries, leads to more comprehensive spiritualties that transcend local, nationalistic, and ethnocentric views. White suggested that a "new race of biblical scholars [points the way to] treasures of thought which have been inaccessible to theologians for two thousand years."[31] He was referring to research known as "higher criticism" which White viewed as a quasi-scientific endeavor. According to White, higher criticism of sacred texts casts doubt on theologies of tribal gods who are jealous and fitful over purely local concerns. The emerging new view is of a more universal value with a wide reach that includes all peoples. White speaks of moving beyond the theological concept of a "chosen people" and beyond an ethic based purely on authority to an ethic of doing right for the sake of right. Love based on obligatory duty to the command of a God is different from love that grasps the intrinsic worth of each human being. White believed in a revelation not of the "fall of human beings" but of the "ascent of human beings."[32]

We can add to White's vision by anticipating the growth of a faith consistent with science that embraces the value of doubt and to faith as a quest deeply sensitive to the many fundamentally new problems that did not exist when sacred texts were written. An example of such a problem is encountered in a world threatened by the prospect of 12 billion people by 2050. This is a problem that cries for new and relevant perspectives and programs to replace older brittle and fixed ideologies on the roles of women, birth control, and the protection of natural resources. There is a vast chasm between prescriptions for action informed by custom and tradition vs. prescriptions for action informed by modern innovations. Wisdom is understanding when we need the former and when we need the latter. Default settings driven by ideology that we must always begin with ancient texts will inevitably prove toxic in a changing world. But open, thoughtful, data-driven deliberations based on the best of scientific evidence serve as a basis for optimism. The philosophy of William James provides a guide for a more informed spirituality consistent with science and, as noted by John. J. McDermitt, will encourage "Confidence without arrogance, intelligibility without certitude, direction without totality."[33]

Notes

1 William James, *A Pluralistic Universe* (Lincoln, NE: University of Nebraska Press, 1996), 321.
2 Aldous Huxley, *Island* (New York: Harper-Perennial Modern Classics, 2009), 160.
3 See John Dupré, *The Disorder of Things: Metaphysical Foundations of the Disunity of Science* (Cambridge, MA: Harvard University Press, 1993) and Peter Galison and David J. Stump, *The Disunity of Science: Boundaries, Contexts, and Power* (Stanford, CT: Stanford University Press, 1996).
4 James, *A Pluralistic Universe*, 263
5 Andrew Dickson White, *A History of the Warfare of Science with Theology in Christendom*, Vol. 1 (Amherst, NY: Prometheus Books, 1993), 218.
6 These lines are extracted from Bertrand Russell's popular essay "The Free Man's Worship" first published in 1903, http://www.skeptic.ca/Bertrand_Russell_Collection.pdf (Accessed August 20, 2016).
7 Carl L. Becker, *The Heavenly City of the Eighteenth-Century Philosophers* (New Haven, CT: Yale University Press, 1970), 14.
8 Ibid., 15.
9 William James, *Pragmatism* (Cambridge, MA: Harvard University Press, 1975), 143–144.
10 Geoffrey West, "The Theory of Everything," in *This Idea Must Die*, ed. John Brockman (New York: Harper, 2015), 1–4.
11 Stephen Hawking, *Black Holes and Baby Universes and other Essays* (New York: Bantam Books, 1993), 134.
12 Marcello Gleiser, "Unification," in *This Idea Must Die*, ed. John Brockman (New York: Harper, 2015), 5–8.
13 *Ontology* is the study of what is real; "ontological status" refers to existence.
14 Personal communication to the senior author who at the time was a member of an accreditation site-visit team evaluating an American university. The president of the university was adamant, that so far as he was concerned, the philosophy department would be the last to go.

15 John F. Haught, *Is Nature Enough? Meaning and Truth in an Age of Science* (New York: Cambridge University Press, 2006), 41–42.
16 James, *A Pluralistic Universe*, 322.
17 Theodore W. Adorno, Else Frenkel-Brunswik, Daniel J. Levinson, and R. Nevitt Sanford, *The Authoritarian Personality* (New York: W. W. Norton, 1951).
18 Bob Altemeyer, *Right-Wing Authoritarianism* (Winnipeg: University of Manitoba Press, 1981). Altemeyer's formulation emphasized conventionalism, submission to authority, and authoritarian aggression; see also Wade C. Rowatt, Megan Johnson Shen, Jordan P. LaBouff, and Alfredo Gonzalez, "Religious Fundamentalism, Right-Wing Authoritarianism, and Prejudice: Insights From Meta-Analyses, Implicit Social Cognition, and Social Cognitive Neuroscience," in *Handbook of The Psychology of Religion and Spirituality*, 2nd ed., eds. Raymond F. Paloutz and Crystal L. Park (New York: Guilford Press, 2015).
19 Mikael Stenmark, "Science and the Limits of Knowledge," in *Clashes of Knowledge: Orthodoxies and Heterodoxies in Science and Religion*, eds. Peter Meusburger, Michael Welker, and Edgar Wunder (New York: Springer and Klaus Tschira Gemeinnützige GmbH, 2008), 113.
20 Brent D. Slife and Frank Richardson, "Naturalism, Psychology, and Religious Experience: An Introduction to the Special Section on Psychology and Transcendence," *Pastoral Psychology* 63 (2014): 319–322.
21 Elliot Friedland, "Saudi Arabia Calls on World to Ban Criticism of Religion," July 27, 2015, http://www.clarionproject.org/analysis/saudi-arabia-calls-world-ban-criticism-religion (Accessed August 3, 2015).
22 Thomas Jefferson, *Notes on the State of Virginia*. See Query 17. Avalon.law.yale.edu/18th_century/jeffvir.asp (Accessed June 25, 2015).
23 Matthew Stewart, *Nature's God: The Heretical Origins of the American Republic* (New York: W. W. Norton, 2014), 71.
24 James, *A Pluralistic Universe*, 46.
25 See List of Nobel Laureates by Country, https://en.wikipedia.org/wiki/List_of_Nobel_laureates_by_country (Accessed July 2, 2015).
26 James, *A Pluralistic Universe*, 9.
27 George Packer, "Mute Button," *The New Yorker* (April 13, 2015), 19–20.
28 David Stout, "66 Journalists Killed in 2014: Report," time.com/3635440/journalism-reporters-without-border-murder-kidnapping/ Posted December 16, 2014. (Accessed May 23, 2015.)
29 A list of faith based action groups can be found at www.interfaithpowerandlight.org/resources/religious-statements
30 Alfred North Whitehead, *Science and the Modern World* (New York: The Free Press, 1967), 186.
31 White, *A History*, Vol. 2, 395.
32 Ibid.
33 John J. McDermitt (ed.), *The Writings of William James* (New York: The Modern Library, 1968), xxvi.

BIBLIOGRAPHY

Abelove, Henry. "Freud, Male Homosexuality, and the Americans." In *The Lesbian and Gay Studies Reader*, eds. Henry Abelove, Michele Aina Barale, and David Halperin, 381–393. New York: Routledge, 1993 (original work published 1986).
Achenbach, Joel. "The Age of Disbelief." *National Geographic* 227, No. 3 (March 2015): 34–47.
Adorno, Theodore W., Else Frenkel-Brunswik, Daniel J. Levinson, and R. Nevitt Sanford. *The Authoritarian Personality*. New York: W. W. Norton, 1951.
The Advocate. "Focus on the Family Targeted by Protesters on Both Sides of Gay Issues Debate." *The Advocate*, April 25, 2005. http://www.advocate.com/news/2005/04/26/focus-family-targeted-protesters-both-sides-gay-issues-debate-15834 (Accessed July 15, 2015).
Al-Ghazālī. *The Incoherence of the Philosophers*. Trans. Michael E. Marmura. Provo, UT: Brigham Young University Press, 2000.
AlHajal, Khalil. "Doctors Not Liable for Death of Jehovah's Witness who Refused Blood Transfusion, Court Rules." http://www.mlive.com/news/detroit/index.ssf/2014/01/doctors_not_liable_for_death_o.html Posted January 10, 2014 (Accessed June 22, 2015).
Allen, John L. Jr. *The Future Church: How Ten Trends are Revolutionizing the Catholic Church*. New York: Dover, 2009.
Allie, Ayaan Hirsi. *Infidel*. New York: Free Press, 2007.
Allport, Gordon. *The Nature of Prejudice*. Garden City, NY: Doubleday Anchor Books, 1954.
Allport, Gordon. "The Religious Context of Prejudice." *Journal for the Scientific Study of Religion* 5, No. 3 (Autumn 1966): 447–457.
Altemeyer, Robert A. *Right-wing Authoritarianism*. Winnipeg: University of Manitoba Press, 1981.
American Psychiatric Association. *Diagnostic and Statistical Manual of Mental Disorders*. Washington, DC: Author, 1952.
American Psychiatric Association. "Answers to Your Questions for a Better Understanding of Sexual Orientation and Homosexuality." https://apa.org/topics/lgbt/orientation.pdf (Accessed July 14, 2015).

American Psychiatric Association. "APA Guidelines for Psychological Practice with Transgender and Gender Nonconforming People." August 6, 2015. https://www.apa.org/practice/guidelines/transgender.pdf (Accessed August 24, 2016).

American Psychiatric Association. "APA on Children Raised by Gay and Lesbian Parents." June 11, 2012. http://www.apa.org/news/press/response/gay-parents.aspx (Accessed July 20, 2015).

American Psychiatric Association. "Position on Ethics and Interrogations." http://www.apa.org/ethics/programs/position/ (Accessed July 20, 2015).

American Psychiatric Association. "Sexual Orientation and Homosexuality." http://www.apa.org/topics/lgbt/orientation.aspx2015 (Accessed July 20, 2015).

Armstrong, Karen. *Fields of Blood: Religion and the History of Violence*. New York: Alfred A. Knopf, 2014.

Associated Press. "Official Attends, Reads at Gay Wedding." *Dayton Daily News*, July 4, 2015 (Accessed July 20, 2015).

Attridge, Harold W. (ed.). *The Religion and Science Debate: Why Does It Continue?* New Haven, CT: Yale University Press, 2009.

Bacon, Francis. "Francis Bacon to his Brother," January 30, 1597. In *Francis Bacon: The Temper of a Man*, by Catherine Drinker Bowen. Boston: An Atlantic Monthly Press Book, 1963.

Bacon, Francis. *The New Organon and Related Writings*. New York: Liberal Arts Press, 1960.

Baird, Robert M. and Stuart E. Rosenbaum, (eds.). *Intelligent Design: Science or Religion? Critical Perspectives*. Amherst, NY: Prometheus Books, 2007.

Baker, Jean H. *Margaret Sanger: A Life of Passion*. New York: Hill and Wang, 2011.

Ball, Philip. *Curiosity: How Science Became Interested in Everything*. Chicago: University of Chicago Press, 2012.

Balthasar, Hans Urs, von. *The Theology of Karl Barth*. San Francisco: Ignatius Press, 1992.

Barstow, Anne Llewellyn. *Witchcraze: A New History of the European Witch Hunts*. San Francisco: HarperCollins, 1994.

Batson, C. Daniel. "Individual Religion, Tolerance, and Universal Compassion." In *Religion, Intolerance and Conflict: A Scientific and Conceptual Investigation*, eds. Steve Clarke, Russell Powell, and Julian Savulescu, 88–106. Oxford: Oxford University Press, 2013.

Batson, C. Daniel, Randy B. Floyd, Julie M. Meyer, and Alana L. Winner. "And Who is My Neighbor? Intrinsic Religion as a Source of Universal Compassion." *Journal for the Scientific Study of Religion* 38, No. 4 (December 1999): 445–457.

Baumeister, Roy F. and Kathleen D. Vohs (eds.). *Encyclopedia of Social Psychology*. New York: Oxford University Press, 2000.

Baumgartner, Frederic J. *Longing for the End: A History of Millenialism in Western Civilization*. New York: Palgrave, 1999.

BBC News. "Ovulation Moment Caught on Camera." Posted June 11, 2008. http://news.bbc.co.uk/1/hi/health/7447942.stm (Accessed November 14, 2016).

The Beacon. "Stories of a Gay Rights Activist Inspire." http://upbeacon.com/2012/01/25/stories-of-a-gay-rights-activist-inspire/ January 25, 2015 (Accessed July 25, 2015).

Becker, Carl. *The Heavenly City of the Eighteenth-Century Philosophers*. Hew Haven, CT: Yale University Press, 1970.

Behe, Michael J. *Darwin's Black Box: The Biochemical Challenge to Evolution*. New York: Simon & Schuster, 1996.

Beins, Barney. "Skeptical but not Cynical: The Importance of Critical Thinking" (Invited Lecture, annual meeting of the Rocky Mountain Psychological Association, Salt Lake City, UT, April 2014).

Bellarmine, Robert. Letter on Galileo's Theories, April 12, 1615. http://sourcebooks.ford ham.edu/mod/1615bellarmine-letter.asp (Accessed November 14, 2016).
Bem, Sandra Lipsitz. *The Lenses of Gender: Transforming the Debate on Sexual Equality*. New Haven, CT: Yale University Press, 1993.
Berenda, Carlton W. *World Visions and the Image of Man*. New York: Vintage, 1965.
Berger, Peter and Anton Zijderveld. *In Praise of Doubt: How to Have Convictions Without Becoming a Fanatic*. New York: HarperCollins, 2009.
Berkman, Michael and Eric Plutzer. *Evolution, Creationism, and the Battle to Control America's Classrooms*. Cambridge: Cambridge University Press, 2010.
Bilbo, Theodore G. *Take Your Choice: Separation or Mongrelization*. Poplarville, MS: Dream House Publishing, 1947.
Blackless, Melanie, Anthony Charuvastra, Amanda Derryck, Anne Fausto-Sterling, Karl Lauzanne, and Ellen Lee. "How Sexually Dimorphic Are We? Review and Synthesis. *American Journal of Human Biology* 12(2000): 151–166.
Blackwell, Richard J. *Behind the Scenes of the Galileo Trial*. Notre Dame, IN: University of Notre Dame Press, 2000.
Blow, Steve. *Dallas Morning News*. "Blow: Beliefs about Marriage Evolve, even in the Bible." June 27, 2015. http://www.dallasnews.com/news/columnists/steve-blow/20150627-lesson-of-biblical-marriage-it-changes-and-for-the-better.ece (Accessed July 22, 2015).
Bogaert, Anthony F. *Understanding Asexuality*. Lanham, MD: Rowman & Littlefield, 2012.
Bogaert, Anthony F. "Asexuality: What it is and Why it Matters." *Journal of Sex Research* 52, No. 4 (2015): 362–379.
Bolton, Henrietta Irving. "Women in Science." *Popular Science Monthly* 53 (August, 1898): 506–511.
Boone, Kathleen C. *The Bible Tells Them So*. Albany, NY: State University of New York Press, 1989.
Borchart, Donald M. (ed.). *Encyclopedia of Philosophy*. Detroit: Thompson/Gale, 2006.
Boring, Edwin G. *A History of Experimental Psychology*, 2nd ed. New York: Appleton-Century-Crofts, 1950.
Bowen, Catherine Drinker. *Francis Bacon: The Temper of a Man*. Boston: Atlantic Monthly Press, 1963.
Box, Ian. "Bacon's Moral Philosophy." In *The Cambridge Companion to Bacon*, ed. Markku Peltonen, 260–282. New York: Cambridge University Press, 1966.
Boy Scouts of America et al. v. Dale, 530 U.S. 640(2000).
Bratten, Ellen B. and Wayne Viney. "Some Late Nineteenth-Century Perspectives on Sex and Emotional Expression." *Psychological Reports* 86 (April, 2000): 575–585.
Bridgman, Percy W. *Reflections of a Physicist*. New York: Philosophical Library, 1955.
Brooke, John Hedley. *Science and Religion: Some Historical Perspectives*. New York: Cambridge University Press, 1991.
Brooks, David. "The Next Culture War." *New York Times*, June 30, 2015. http://www.nytimes.com/2015/06/30/opinion/david-brooks-the-next-culture-war.html?_r=0 (Accessed July 20, 2015).
Broun, Haygood and Margaret Leech. *Anthony Comstock: Roundsman for the Lord*. New York: Albert & Charles Boni, 1927.
Brown, Simon. "Creationism Crusade." *Church and State* 64 (February, 2012).
Browning, Robert. "A Woman's Last Word." In *Robert Browning's Poetry*, eds. James F. Loucks and Andrew M. Stauffer, 147. New York: W. W. Norton & Company, 2007.

Brush, Stephen. "Should the History of Science by Rated X?" *Science* 183, No. 4130 (March, 1974): 1164–1172.
Brush, Stephen G. "The Prayer Test." *American Scientist* 62, No. 5 (September–October, 1974): 561–563.
Buchanan, Patrick J. "1992 Republican National Convention Speech." http://buchanan.org/blog/1992-republican-national-convention-speech-148 (Accessed July 20, 2015), paragraph 34.
Buffon, Comte de. *Selections from Natural History General and Particular.* Vol. 1. New York: Arno, 1977.
Bullough, Vern L. "Science and Religion in Historical Perspective." In *Science and Religion: Are They Compatible?* ed. Paul Kurtz, 129–138. Amherst, NY: Prometheus Books, 2003.
Bunch, Joey. "Two Ballot Proposals: Petitioners Seek Unions, Not Marriage." *The Denver Post,* July 4, 2015.
Burke, Daniel. "The Pope Said What?!? More Stunners from Francis." January 19, 2015. http://www.cnn.com/2015/01/19/living/pope-said-what/ (Accessed July 20, 2015).
Butler, Samuel. *Erewhom Revisited.* New York: E. P. Dutton, 1920.
Butterfield, Herbert. *The Whig Interpretation of History.* New York: Norton, 1931.
Caiazza, John. "The Evolution Versus Religion Controversy: How Two Mystiques Devolved into Politics." *Modern Age* 47, No. 2 (Spring 2005): 104–120.
Calvin, John. "Institute of the Christian Religion." *Classics of Protestantism,* ed. Vergilius Ferm, 67–129. New York: Philosophical Library, 1959.
Capra, Fritjof. "The Role of Physics in the Current Change of Paradigms." In *The World View of Contemporary Physics,* ed. Richard F. Kitchener, 144–155. Albany, NY: State University of New York Press, 1988.
Caputo, John D. *Philosophy and Theology.* Nashville, TN: Abingdon Press, 2006.
Carlson, Allan. *Godly Seed: American Evangelicals Confront Birth Control, 1873–1973.* New Brunswick, NJ: Transaction, 2012.
Carroll, William E. "Galileo Galilei and the Myth of Orthodoxy." In *Heterodoxy in Early Modern Science and Religion,* eds. John Brooke and Ian Maclean, 115–144. New York: Oxford University Press, 2005.
Chadee, Derek (ed.). *Theories in Social Psychology.* Malden MA: Wiley-Blackwell, 2011.
Chopra, Deepak and Leonard Mlodinow. *War of the Worldviews: Science vs. Spirituality.* New York: Harmony Books, 2011.
Chumley, Cheryl K. "Duck Dynasty's Phil Robertson says that AIDS, Syphilis God's Penalty for Gays." *Washington Times.* http://www.washingtontimes.com/news/2014/sep/11/duck-dynastys-phil-robertson-says-aids-syphilis-go/ September 11, 2014 (Accessed July 20, 2015).
Church of Jesus Christ of the Latter Day Saints, Official Statement. "Church Re-evaluating Scouting Program: Concern Expressed over BSA Policy Change, Lack of Global Reach" July 27, 2015. http://www.mormonnewsroom.org/article/church-re-evaluating-scouting-program?cid=social_20150727_49844076&adbid=625815481509806080&adbpl=tw&adbpr=10047382 (Accessed July 28, 2015).
Church of Uganda. "Church of Uganda Declares Full Communion with Anglican Church in North America." http://anglicanchurch.net/?/main/page/9 June 25 Posted June 25, 2009. (Accessed November 14, 2016).
Clark, Ronald W. *Einstein: The Life and Times.* New York: World Publishing Company, 1971.
Clarke, Steve, Russell Powell, and Julian Savulisecu. *Religion, Intolerance, and Conflict: A Scientific and Conceptual Investigation.* Oxford: Oxford University Press, 2013.

Clendinen, Dudley. "John Fryer, 65, Psychiatrist Who Said He Was Gay in 1972, Dies." *New York Times*. http://www.nytimes.com/2003/03/05/obituaries/05FRYE.html March 5, 2003 (Accessed July 3, 2015).

Cleveland, Grover. "Would Woman Suffrage be Unwise?" *The Ladies Home Journal* 22 (October 1905): 7–8.

Cleveland, Grover. "Woman's Mission and Woman's Clubs." *The Ladies Home Journal* 22, (May 1905): 3–4.

Clinton, William J. "Bill Clinton: It's Time to Overturn DOMA." *Washington Post*. March 7, 2013. https://www.washingtonpost.com/opinions/bill-clinton-its-time-to-overturn-doma/2013/03/07/fc184408-8747-11e2-98a3-b3db6b9ac586_story.html (Accessed July 20, 2015).

Clouston, T. S. "Female Education from a Medical Point of View." *Popular Science Monthly* 24 (December 1883): 214–228, 319–334.

CNN. June, 2014, "Who are Albania's 'Sworn Virgins'?"http://edition.cnn.com/video/data/2.0/video/world/2014/06/02/balkan-tradition-sworn-virgins.cnn.html (Accessed June 20, 2014).

Cohen, I. Bernard. "Isaac Newton." In *Lives in Science: A Scientific American Book*, ed. Dennis Flanagan, 21–30. New York: Simon and Schuster, 1957.

Cohen, Richard. *"There is no Why Here."* Editorial, in *The New York Times*, Tuesday, September, 30, 2014. A23.

Commonwealth of Massachusetts v. United States Department of Health and Human Services, et al., 698 F. Supp. 2d 234(2010).

Conger, J. J. "Proceedings of the American Psychological Association, Incorporated, for the Year 1974: Minutes of the Annual Meeting of the Council of Representatives." *American Psychologist* 30 (1975): 620–651.

Cottingham, John, Robert Stoothoff, and Dugald Murdoch, (eds.). *The Philosophical Writings of Descartes*, 2 vols. Cambridge: Cambridge University Press, 1984–1985.

Coyne, Jerry A. *Faith vs. Fact: Why Science and Religion are Incompatible*. New York: Viking, 2015.

Cran, William and Simone Renata. "The Age of AIDS." *Frontline*, http://www.pbs.org/wgbh/pages/frontline/aids/ May, 2006 (Accessed July 25, 2015).

Crary, David. "Boy Scouts Executive Committee OKs Ending Ban on Gay Leaders." *Associated Press*, July 14, 2015. http://www.denverpost.com/news/national/ci_28479144/boy-scouts-executive-committee-oks-ending-ban-on-gay-leaders (Accessed July 20, 2015).

Cresswell, James. "Can Religion and Psychology Get Along?: Toward a Pragmatic Cultural Psychology of Religion That Includes Meaning and Experience." *Journal of Theoretical & Philosphical Psychology* 34, No. 2 (May 2014): 133–145.

Cronon, William. "Two Cheers for the Whig Interpretation of History." *Perspectives on History: The News Magazine of the American Historical Association* 50, No. 6 (September 2012).

Crosby, Donald A. *Novelty*. New York: Lexington Books, 2005.

Crosby, Donald A. *Faith and Reason: Their Roles in Religion and Secular Life*. Albany, NY: State University of New York Press, 2011.

Crossman, Richard (ed.). *The God that Failed*. New York: Bantam Books, 1959.

Crummy, Karen. "The Republican Party Gets Ready." *The Denver Post*, August 29, 2008. http://www.denverpost.com/2008/08/29/the-republican-party-gets-ready/ (Accessed November 14, 2016).

Cummings, Elizabeth. "Education as an Aid to the Health of Women." *Popular Science Monthly* 17 (1880): 823–827.
Cuneo, Michael W. *American Exorcism: Expelling Demons in the Land of Plenty.* New York: Broadway Books, 2001.
Danielson, Dennis R. "That Copernicanism Demoted Humans from the Center of the Cosmos." In *Galileo Goes to Jail and Other Myths about Science and Religion*, ed. Ronald L. Numbers, 50–58. Cambridge, MA: Harvard University Press, 2009.
Darwin, Charles. Letter to Francis Galton, December 23, 1870. In *More Letters of Charles Darwin*, Vol. 2, eds. Francis Darwin and A. C. Seward, Ch. 2, Letter 410. www.gutenberg.org/files/2740/2740-h/2740-h.htm Posted December 1, 2008 (Accessed June 22, 2015).
Darwin, Charles. *Journal of Researches Into the Natural History and Geology of the Countries Visited During the Voyage of the H. M. S. Beagle Around the World Under the Command of Capt. Fitzroy, R. N.* New York: D. Appleton, 1897.
Darwin, Charles. *On the Origin of Species.* London: The Folio Society, 2006.
Daston, Lorraine and Elizabeth Lunbeck. "Introduction." In *Histories of Scientific Observation*, eds. Lorraine Daston and Elizabeth Lunbeck, 1–9. Chicago: University of Chicago Press, 2005.
Dawkins, Richard. *The God Delusion.* New York: Houghton Mifflin, 2006.
Dawkins, Richard. *The Greatest Show on Earth.* New York: The Free Press, 2009.
Deleuze, Giles. *Spinoza: Practical Philosophy.* San Francisco, CA: City Lights Books, 1988.
De Rosa, Peter. *Vicars of Christ: The Dark Side of the Papacy.* New York: Crown, 1988.
Descartes, René. "René Descartes to Marin Mersenne, April, 1634." In *Descartes' Philosophical Letters*, ed. Anthony Kenny, 25–27. Oxford: Clarendon Press, 1970.
Descartes, René. "Treatise on Man." In *Philosophical Writings of Descartes* Vol. 1, eds. John Cottingham, Robert Stoothoff, and Dugald Murdoch, 99–108. Cambridge: Cambridge University Press, 1985.
Desmond, Adrian and James Moore. *Darwin: The Life of a Tormented Evolutionist.* New York: W. W. Norton, 1991.
Dewolf, David K., John G. West, Casey Luskin, and Jonathan Witt. *Trapsing into Evolution, Intelligent Design and the Kitzmiller v. Dover Decision.* Seattle, WA: The Discovery Institute, 2006.
Dierenfield, Bruce J. *The Battle Over School Prayer: How Engel v. Vitale Changed America.* Lawrence, KS: University of Kansas Press, 2007.
Dorr, Rheta Childe. "Is Woman Biologically Barred from Success?" *The New York Times Magazine* 19 (September 1915): 75–76.
Douglas, Frederick. *Narrative of the Life of Frederick Douglas, An American Slave.* Boston, MA: The Anti-Slavery Office, 1845.
Dowe, Phil. *Galileo, Darwin, and Hawking.* Grand Rapids, MI: William B. Eerdmans, 2005.
Draper, John W. *History of the Conflict Between Religion and Science.* London: Kegan Paul, Trench Thrübner, 1874.
Dreger, Alice Domurat. *Hermaphrodites and the Medical Invention of Sex.* Cambridge, MA: Harvard University Press, 1998.
Drescher, Jack. "I'm Your Handyman: A History of Reparative Therapies." *Journal of Homosexuality* 36 No. 1 (1998): 19–42.
Drescher, Jack. "The Removal of Homosexuality from the DSM: Its Impact on Today's Marriage Equality Debate." *Journal of Gay and Lesbian Mental Health* 16 No. 2 (2012): 124–135.

Drury, Bob and Tom Calvin. *The Heart of Everything that Is: The Untold Story of Red Cloud, An American Legend.* New York: Simon & Schuster, 2012.
Duberman, Martin. *Stonewall.* New York: Plume, 1994.
Dupré, John. *The Disorder of Things: Metaphysical Foundations of the Disunity of Science.* Cambridge, MA: Harvard University Press, 1993.
Durant, Will and Ariel Durant. *The Story of Civilization: Part VII The Age of Reason Begins.* New York: Simon & Schuster, 1961.
Earle, Alice Morse. *Curious Punishments of Bygone Days.* Detroit, MI: Singing Tree Press, 1968.
Eco, Umberto. *The Name of the Rose.* New York: Harcourt, Brace, & Co., 1980.
Edmundson, Mark. "Body and Soul." *Hedgehog Review: Critical Reflections on Contemporary Culture* 17, No. 2 (Summer, 2015).
Egner, Robert and Lester E. Denonn (eds.). *The Basic Writings of Bertrand Russell.* New York: Routledge, 2009.
Ehrman, Bart D. *Misquoting Jesus: The Story Behind Who Changed the Bible and Why.* San Francisco: Harper, 2005.
Eig, Jonathan. *The Birth of the Pill: How Four Crusaders Reinvented Sex and Launched a Revolution.* New York: W. E. Norton & Company, 2012.
Eiseley, Loren C. "Charles Darwin." In *Lives in Science: A Scientific American Book*, ed. Dennis Flanagan, 195–214. New York: Simon & Schuster, 1957.
Ekman, Paul and Erika L. Rosenberg (eds.). *What the Face Reveals: Basic and Applied Studies of Spontaneous Expression.* New York: Oxford University Press, 2005.
Emerson, Ralph Waldo. "Self Reliance." In *The Works of Ralph Waldo Emerson in One Volume*, assembled by Editorial Staff, 97–114. Roslyn, NY: Black's Readers Service (no date).
The Episcopal Church. "Church Property Dispute." June 14, 2013. http://www.episcopalchurch.org/library/topics/church-property-dispute (Accessed July 15, 2015).
Epstein, Cynthia F. "Great Divides: The Cultural, Cognitive and Social Bases of the Global Subordination of Women." *American Sociological Review* 72, No. 1 (February, 2007): 1–22.
Euteneur, Thomas. *Exorcism and the Church Militant.* San Francisco, CA: Ignatius Press, 2010.
Evans, Richard I. *B. F. Skinner: The Man and His Ideas.* New York: E. P. Dutton and Co. Inc., 1968.
Executive Order 10450 – Security Requirements for Government Employment, National Archives. http://www.archives.gov/federal-register/codification/executive-order/10450.html (Accessed July 20, 2015).
Fantoli, Annibale. *Galileo: For Copernicanism and the Church*, 2nd ed. Notre Dame, IN: University of Notre Dame Press, 1996.
Fantoli, Annibale. *The Case of Galileo: A Closed Question?* Notre Dame, IN: University of Notre Dame Press, 2012.
Ferngren, Gary B. (ed.). *The History of Science and Religion in the Western Tradition: An Encyclopedia.* New York: Garland, 2000.
Ferngren, Gary B. (ed.). *Science and Religion: A Historical Introduction.* Baltimore, MD: The Johns Hopkins University Press, 2002.
Feynmann, Richard P. "The Value of Science." In *Frontiers of Science*, ed. Lee A. Dubridge, 260–267. New York: Basic Books, 1958.
Finocchiaro, Maurice A. *Retrying Galileo: 1633–1992.* Berkeley, CA: University of California Press, 2005.

Finocchiaro, Maurice A. "That Galileo was Imprisoned and Tortured for Advocating Copernicanism." In *Galileo Goes to Jail and Other Myths about Science and Religion*, ed. Ronald L. Numbers, 68–78. Cambridge, MA: Harvard University Press, 2009.

Fischer, Sara. "Cheney Has No Regrets: I Would Do It Again in a Minute." http://www.cnn.com/2014/12/14/politics/dick-cheney-torture-report-meet-the-press/ (Accessed May 20, 2015).

Flanagan, Dennis. (ed.). *Lives in Science*. New York: Simon & Schuster, 1957.

Forrest, Barbara. "Intelligent Design: Creationism's Trojan Horse, A Conversation with Barbara Forrest." In *Intelligent Design: Science or Religion? Critical Perspectives*, eds. Robert M. Baird and Stuart E. Rosenbaum, 87–102. Amherst, NY: Prometheus Books, 2007.

Frame, Donald M. (ed.). *The Complete Essays of Montaigne* (2 Vols.). Garden City, NY: Anchor & Doubleday, 1960.

Frank, John. "Bob Beauprez's IUD Remark in Debate Generates Controversy." *Denver Post* (October 1, 2014).

Frankenberry, Nancy K. *The Faith of Scientists in Their Own Words*. Princeton, NJ: Princeton University Press, 2008.

Freud, Sigmund. "Three Essays on Sexuality." In *The Standard Edition of the Complete Psychological Works of Sigmund Freud*, Vol. 7, ed. and trans. James Strachey, 135–243. London: The Hogarth Press, 1953.

Freud, Sigmund. "The Psychogenesis of a Case of Homosexuality in a Woman." In *The Standard Edition of the Complete Psychological Works of Sigmund Freud*, Vol. 18, ed. and trans. James Strachey, 221–232. London: Hogarth Press, 1955.

Freud, Sigmund. "Leonardo Da Vinci and a Memory of His Childhood." In *The Standard Edition of the Complete Psychological Works of Sigmund Freud*, Volume 11, ed. and trans. James Strachey, 59–137. London: The Hogarth Press, 1957.

Freud, Sigmund. "Anonymous (Letter to an American mother)." In *The Letters of Sigmund Freud*, ed. E. Freud, 423–424, New York, NY: Basic Books, 1960.

Freud, Sigmund. "Civilization and Its Discontents." In *The Standard Edition of the Complete Psychological Works of Sigmund Freud*, Vol. 9, ed. and trans. James Strachey, 55–145. London: Hogarth Press, 1961.

Freud, Sigmund. "Future of an Illusion." In *The Standard Edition of the Complete Psychological Works of Sigmund Freud*, Vol. 21, ed. and trans. James Strachey, 3–56. London: Hogarth Press, 1961.

Freud, Sigmund. "A Religious Experience." In *The Standard Edition of the Complete Psychological Works of Sigmund Freud*, Vol. 21, ed. and trans. James Strachey, 168–172. London: Hogarth Press, 1961.

Friedland, Elliot. "Saudi Arabia Calls on World to Ban Criticism of Religion." July 27, 2015. http://www.clarionproject.org/analysis/saudi-arabia-calls-world-ban-criticism-religion (Accessed August 3, 2015).

Froese, Paul and Christopher Bader. *America's Four Gods: What We Say about God and What That Says about Us*. New York: Oxford University Press, 2010.

Furcht, Leo and William Hoffman. *The Stem Cell Dilemma*. New York: Arcade Publishing, 2008.

Galchen, Rivka. "Weather Underground: The arrival of Man-Made Earthquakes." *The New Yorker* (April 13, 2015): 34–40.

Galileo, Galelei. "Letter to the Grand Duchess Christina of Tuscany, 1615." www.fordam.edu/halsall/mod/Galileo-tuscany.asp (Accessed May 19, 2015).

Galileo, Galelei. "Letter to Madam Christina of Lorraine, Grand Duchess of Tuscany, 1615." http://inters.org/Galilei-Madame-Christina-Lorraine (Accessed July 3, 2015).
Galileo, Galelei. From the Dedication in *Dialogues Concerning Two New Sciences*. http://ebooks.adelaide.edu.au/g/Galileo/dialogues/complete.html (Accessed July 12, 2015).
Galison, Peter and David J. Stump. *The Disunity of Science: Boundaries, Contexts, and Power*. Stanford, CA: Stanford University Press, 1996.
Gallup. "Gay and Lesbian Rights." 2015. http://www.gallup.com/poll/1651/gay-lesbian-rights.aspx (Accessed July 20, 2015).
Gallup. "Satisfaction with Acceptance of Gays in U.S. at New High." January 18, 2016. http://www.gallup.com/poll/188657/satisfaction-acceptance-gays-new-high.aspx?g_source=position2&g_medium=related&g_campaign=tiles (Accessed August, 26, 2016).
Gallup. "Americans' Support for Gay Marriage Remains High, at 61%." May 19, 2016. http://www.gallup.com/poll/191645/americans-support-gay-marriage-remains-high.aspx?g_source=position1&g_medium=related&g_campaign=tiles (Accessed August 26, 2016).
Gallup. "Same-Sex Marriages Up One Year After Supreme Court Verdict." June 22, 2016. http://www.gallup.com/poll/193055/sex-marriages-one-year-supreme-court-verdict.aspx?g_source=Social%20Issues&g_medium=newsfeed&g_campaign=tiles (Accessed August 26, 2016).
Galton, Francis. *Hereditary Genius: An Inquiry into Its Laws and Consequences*. New York: D. Appleton and Company, 1900.
Galton, Francis. *Inquiries into Human Faculty and its Development*, 2nd ed. New York: E. P. Dutton, 1907.
Garfinkle, Ellen M. and Stephen F. Morin. "Psychologists' Attitudes toward Homosexual Psychotherapy Clients." *Journal of Social Issues* 34 No. 3 (1978): 101–112.
Gartell, Nannette, Helena Kraemer, and Brodie, H. Keith. "Psychiatrists' Attitudes toward Female Homosexuality." *Journal of Nervous and Mental Disease* 159 No. 2 (1974): 141–144.
Gasking, Elizabeth B. *Investigations into Generation 1651–1828*. Baltimore, MD: Johns Hopkins University Press, 1967.
Gettys, Travis. "Pastors Call for Stonings and Warn of God's Wrathful Judgment after Marriage Equality Ruling." *Rawstory*, June 29, 2015. http://www.rawstory.com/2015/06/pastors-call-for-stonings-and-warn-of-gods-wrathful-judgment-after-marriage-equality-ruling/ (Accessed July 20, 2015).
Gleiser, Marcello. "Unification." In *This Idea Must Die*, ed. John Brockman, 5–8. New York: Harper, 2015.
Goldfried, Jerry and Maureen Miner. "Quest Religion and the Problem of Limited Compassion." *Journal for the Scientific Study of Religion* 41, No. 4 (December 2002): 685–695.
Gomes, Peter J. *The Good Book: Reading the Bible with Mind and Heart*. New York: Harper Collins, 1996.
Gooren, Louis J. and W. Byne "Sexual Orientation in Men and Women." In *Hormones, Brain and Behavior*, 2nd ed., Vol. 5, ed. D. W. Pfaff, 2429–2448. New York: Elsevier, 2009.
Gould, Stephen Jay. *The Mismeasure of Man*. New York: W. W. Norton, 1981.
Gould, Stephen Jay. *Rocks of Ages: Science and Religion in the Fullness of Life*. New York: Ballantine, 1999.
Granhag, Pär Anders, Aldert Vrij, and Christian A. Meissner. "Information Gathering in Law Enforcement and Intelligence Settings: Advancing Theory and Practice." *Applied Cognitive Psychology* 28 No. 6 (November/December 2014): 815–816.

Green, Samuel. "The Different Arabic Versions of the Qur'an." http://www.answering-islam.org/Green/seven.htm (Accessed May 11, 2015).

Greenwald, Anthony G. and Thomas Pettigrew. "With Malice Toward None and Charity for Some: In-group Favoritism Enables Discrimination." *American Psychologist* 69, No. 7 (October 2014): 669–684.

Grendler, Paul F. "Printing and Censorship." In *The Cambridge History of Renaissance Philosophy*, ed. Charles B. Schmitt, 25–53. New York: Cambridge University Press, 1988.

Gribbin, John. *History of Western Science*. London: The Folio Society, 2006.

Griggs, Brandon. "Facebook Goes beyond 'Male' and 'Female' with New Gender Options." http://www.cnn.com/2014/02/13/tech/social-media/facebook-gender-custom/ (Accessed June 18, 2016).

Gryboski, Michael. "Texas Diocese Wins Court Battle Over Property Dispute with the Episcopal Church." *Christian Post*, March 3, 2015. http://www.christianpost.com/news/texas-diocese-wins-court-battle-over-property-dispute-with-the-episcopal-church-135047/ (Accessed July 15, 2015).

Haack, Susan. *Defending Science Within Reason*. Amherst, New York: Prometheus, 2003.

Haidt, Jonathan. *The Righteous Mind: Why Good People are Divided by Politics and Religion*. New York: Pantheon, 2012.

Halperin, David M. *How to Do the History of Homosexuality*. Chicago: University of Chicago Press, 2009.

Hameed, Salman. "Bracing for Islamic Creationism." *Science* 322, No. 5908 (December 2008): 1637–1638.

Hameed, Salman. "An Old Earth for All Muslims: But How does Evolution Fit In?" *Earth* 56, No. 10 (October 2011): 79.

Hanna, Jason, Ed Payne, and Catherine E. Shoichet. "Kim Davis Released, but Judge Bars her from Withholding Marriage Licenses." *CNN*, September 8, 2015. http://www.cnn.com/2015/09/08/politics/kim-davis-same-sex-marriage-kentucky/ (Accessed August 24, 2016).

Harmon, Amy. "A Teacher on the Front Line as Faith and Science Clash." *New York Times*, August 24, 2008.

Harris, Sam. *The End of Faith: Religion, Terror, and the Future of Reason*. New York: W. W. Norton, 2004.

Harrison, Peter. "Curiosity, Forbidden Knowledge, and the Reformation of Natural Philosophy in Early Modern England." *ISIS* 92, No. 2, 2001.

Haught, John F. *Is Nature Enough? Meaning and Truth in an Age of Science*. New York: Cambridge University Press, 2006.

Haught, John F. *Science and Faith: A New Introduction*. New York: Paulist Press, 2012.

Hawking, Stephen. *Black Holes and Baby Universes and Other Essays*. New York: Bantam Books, 1993.

Hawking, Stephen (ed.). "Albert Einstein." In *On the Shoulders of Giants: The Great Works of Physics and Astronomy*. ed. Stephen Hawking, 1161–1167. Philadelphia: PA: Running Press, 2002.

Haynes, Stephen R. *Noah's Curse: The Biblical Justification of Slavery in the United States*. Oxford: Oxford University Press, 2007.

Hecht, Jennifer Michael. *Doubt: A History*. New York: HarperCollins, 2003.

Heilbron, John L. *Galileo*. New York: Oxford University Press, 2010.

Henle, Mary, Julian Jaynes, and J. J. Sullivan (eds.). *Historical Conceptions of Psychology*. New York: Springer, 1973.

Henry, John. "Causality." In *The History of Science and Religion in the Western Tradition: An Encyclopedia*, ed. Gary B. Ferngren, 31–37. New York: Garland Publishing, 2000.

Hertz, Steven G. and Tobias Krettenauer. "Does Moral Identity Effectively Predict Moral Behavior?: A Meta-Analysis." *Review of General Psychology* 20 No. 2 (January 2016): 129–140.

Hilgard, Ernest R. and Gordon H. Bower. *Theories of Learning*, 3rd ed. New York: Appleton-Century-Crofts, 1966.

Hitchens, Christopher. *God Is Not Great: How Religion Poisons Everything*. New York: Hachette Book Group, Inc., 2007.

Hodges, Andrew. *Alan Turing: The Enigma* (centenary edition). Princeton, NJ: Princeton University Press, 2012.

Hoffer, Eric. *The True Believer*. New York: Mentor, 1951.

Hoffman, Daniel L. *The Status of Women and Gnosticism in Irenaeus and Tertullian*. Queenstown: Edwin Mellen, 1995.

Hollingworth, Harry Levi. *Leta Stetter Hollingworth: A Biography*. Lincoln, NE: University of Nebraska Press, 1943.

Hollingworth, Leta Stetter. "Functional Periodicity: An Experimental Study of the Mental and Motor Abilities of Women During Menstruation." *Contributions to Education*, No. 69, Teachers College, Columbia University, 1914.

Hollingworth, Leta Stetter. "The Vocational Aptitudes of Women." In *Vocational Psychology: Its Problems and Methods*, ed. Harry Levi Hollingworth, 222–244. New York: D. Appleton and Co., 1917.

Hood, Ralph W. W. (ed.). *Handbook of Religious Experience*. Birmingham, AL: Religious Education Press, 1995.

Hooker, Evelyn. "The Adjustment of the Male Overt Homosexual." *Journal of Projective Techniques* 21, No. 1 (1957): 18–31.

Howell, Reet Ann and Max L. Howell. "The Games of the 2nd Olympiad." In *Historical Dictionary of the Modern Olympic Movement*, eds. John E. Findling and Kimberly D. Pelle, 12–17. Westport, CT: Greenwood Press, 1996.

Horwitz, Tony. *Confederates in the Attic: Dispatches from the Unfinished Civil War*. New York: Vintage, 1998.

Hull, Clark. *Principles of Behavior*. New York: D. Appleton-Century, 1943.

Humes, Edward. *Monkey Girl: Evolution, Education, Religion, and the Battle for America's Soul*. New York: Harper Collins, 2007.

Huxley, Aldous. *Island*. New York: Harper Perennial Modern Classics, 2009.

Inness, Sherrie A. and Michele E. Lloyd. "G.I. Joes in Barbie Land: Reconceptualizing Butch in 20th Century Lesbian Culture." In *Queer Studies: A Lesbian, Gay, Bisexual, and Transgender Anthology*, eds. Brett Beemyn and Michele Eliason, 9–34. New York: New York University Press, 1996.

Isidor, Chris. "Target's $20 Million Answer to Transgender Bathroom Boycott." *CNN*, August 17, 2016. http://money.cnn.com/2016/08/17/news/companies/target-bathroom-transgender/index.html (Accessed August 24, 2016).

James, Henry (ed.). *The Letters of William James*, 2 Vols. Boston, MA: The Atlantic Monthly Press, 1920.

James, William. "Letter to Shadworth H. Hodgson, 1885." In *Letters of William James*, Vol. 1, ed. Henry James, 243–247. Boston, MA: The Atlantic Monthly Press, 1920.

James, William. "Letter to Mrs. Henry Whitman, 1899." In *The Letters of William James*, Vol. 2, ed. Henry James, 88–90. Boston, MA: The Atlantic Monthly Press, 1920.

James, William. *The Meaning of Truth*. Cambridge, MA: Harvard University Press, 1975.
James, William. *Pragmatism*. Cambridge, MA: Harvard University Press, 1975.
James, William. *The Will to Believe*. Cambridge, MA: Harvard University Press, 1979.
James, William. *A Pluralistic Universe*. Lincoln, NE: University of Nebraska Press, 1996.
James, William. *Some Problems of Philosophy*. Lincoln, NE: University of Nebraska Press, 1996.
James, William. *The Varieties of Religious Experience*. New York: Routledge, 2002.
Jaynes, Julian. "The Problem of Animate Motion in the Seventeenth Century." In *Historical Conceptions of Psychology*, eds. Mary Henle, Julian Jaynes, and J. J. Sullivan. New York: Springer, 1973.
Jefferson, Thomas. *Notes on the State of Virginia*. http://avalon.law.yale.edu/18th_century/jeffvir.asp (Accessed June 25, 2015).
Jones, Ernest. *The Life and Work of Sigmund Freud*, Vol. 3. New York: Basic Books, 1957.
Jones, Ernest. "The Early Development of Female Sexuality." *Papers on Psychoanalysis*, 438–451. Boston, MA: Beacon Press, 1967.
Jurinski, James John. *Religion on Trial: A Handbook with Cases, Laws, and Documents*. Santa Barbara, CA: ABC Clio, 2004.
Kane, Robert. *A Contemporary Introduction to Free Will*. New York: Oxford University Press, 2005.
Karimi, Faith and Stewart, Dani. "Army Veteran not Legally Male or Female, Judge Rules." *CNN* (June 12, 2016), http://www.cnn.com/2016/06/11/us/jamie-shupe-non-binary/ (Accessed August 24, 2016).
Karlen, Arno. *Sexuality and Homosexuality: A New View*. New York: W.W. Norton, 1971.
Kaufmann, Stuart A. *The Origin of Order: Self-Organization and Selection in Evolution*. New York: Oxford University Press, 1993.
Kellaway, Jean. *The History of Torture and Execution: From Early Civilization Through Medieval Times and the Present*. Ludlow: Talamus Publishing, 2000.
Kennerly, June. "Paleontologists Brought to Tears, Laughter by Creationist Museum." http://phys.org/news/2009-06-paleontologists-brought-laughter-creation-museum.html Posted June 30, 2009. (Accessed January 8, 2012.)
Kinsey, Alfred, Wardell B. Pomeroy, and Clyde E. Martin *Sexual Behavior in the Human Male*. Bloomington, IN: Indiana University Press, 1948.
Kirk, Geoffrey Stephen and John Earle Raven. *The Presocratic Philosophers: A Critical History with a Selection of Texts*. Cambridge: Cambridge University Press, 1962.
Kirsch, Irving. "Demonology and the Rise of Science: An Example of the Misperception of Historical Data." *Journal of the History of the Behavioral Sciences* 14, No. 2 (April 1978): 149–157.
Kitzmiller v. Dover, Tennessee (Middle District) 707(2005).
Knowlton, Stephen. "The Silence of Women in the Churches." *The Congregational Quarterly* 9 (October 1867): 329–334.
Köhler, Wolfgang. *Gestalt Psychology*. New York: Liveright, 1970.
Kramer, Heinrich and James Sprenger. *Malleus Maleficarum*. New York: Dover, 1971.
Kramer, Stanley. (Dir.). *Inherit the Wind*. DVD with Spencer Tracy, Frederic March and Gene Kelly. Hollywood, CA: MGM Home Entertainment, Inc. 2001.
Kravis, Andrew. "Is the Inability to Marry a Marital Status? Levin V. Yeshiva University and the Intersection of Sexual Orientation and Marital Status in Housing Discrimination." *Columbia Journal of Gender and Law* 24 (2012): 1–24.

Kristof, Nicholas D. "Marriage: Mix and Match." *New York Times*, March 3, 2004. http://www.nytimes.com/2004/03/03/opinion/marriage-mix-and-match.html (Accessed July 20, 2015).

Krueger, Joachim I. "Attribution Theory." In *Encyclopedia of Social Psychology*, Vol. 1, eds. Roy F. Baumeister and Kathleen D. Vohs, 320–325. New York: Oxford University Press, 2000.

Kuhse, Helga and Peter Singer. "Individuals, Humans and Persons: The Issue of Moral Status." In *Embryo Experimentation: Ethical, Legal and Social Issues*, eds. Peter Singer, Helga Kuhse, Stephen Buckle, Karen Dawson, and Pascal Kasimba, 65–76. Cambridge: Cambridge University Press, 1993.

Kurtz, Paul (ed.). *Science and Religion: Are They Compatible?* Amherst, NY: Prometheus Books, 2003.

Kutchins, H. and S. A. Kirk. *Making Us Crazy: DSM: The Psychiatric Bible and the Creation of Mental Disorders*. New York: Free Press, 1997.

La Mettrie, Julien Offray de. *Man a Machine*. La Salle, IL: Open Court, 1912.

Langone, Michael D. *Recovery from Cults: Help for Victims of Psychological and Spiritual Abuse*. New York: Norton, 1993.

Larsen, Brad Walter. "Student Perceptions of Heterosexual Bias in Doctoral Level Psychology Programs." Unpublished master's thesis, Pacific University, 2007. http://commons.pacificu.edu/cgi/viewcontent.cgi?article=1139&context=spp (Accessed July 15, 2015).

Larson, Edward J. *Summer for the Gods: The Scopes Trial and America's Continuing Debate over Science and Religion*. Cambridge, MA: Harvard University Press, 1997.

Larson, Edward J. *The Creation–Evolution Debate*. Athens, GA: University of Georgia Press, 2008.

Lauria, Lisa M. "Sexual Misconduct in Plymouth Colony." *The Plymouth Colony Archive Project*, 1998. http://www.histarch.illinois.edu/plymouth/Lauria1.html (Accessed June 15, 2015).

Laycock, Joseph P. "Why are Exorcisms as Popular as Ever." Posted December 28, 2015. https://newrepublic.com/article/126607/exorcisms-popular-ever (Accessed January 1, 2016).

Lebo, Lauri. *The Devil in Dover*. New York: New Press, 2008.

Leibniz, Gottfried Wilhelm von. *Essays on the Goodness of God, the Freedom of Man, and the Origin of Evil*, eds. Austin M. Farrer and trans. E. M. Huggard. New York: Cosimo Classics, 2010.

Leopold, Todd. "Boy Scouts Change Policy on Gay Leaders." *CNN*, July 27, 2015. http://www.cnn.com/2015/07/27/us/boy-scouts-gay-leaders-feat/ (Accessed July 28, 2015).

Leuba, James Henry. "A Study in the Psychology of Religious Phenomena." *The American Journal of Psychology* 7, No. 3 (April 1896): 309–385.

Lewes, Kenneth. *The Psychoanalytic Theory of Male Homosexuality*. New York: Simon and Schuster, 2008.

Lincoln, Abraham. "Letter to H. W. Herndon, 1856." In *The Lincoln Encyclopedia The Spoken and Written Words of A. Lincoln Arranged for Ready Reference*, ed. Arthur H. Shaw, 149. New York: The Macmillan Co., 1950.

Lindberg, David. "Natural Adversaries?" *Christian History* 21, No. 4 (November 2002): 44–46.

Lindberg, David. "Galileo, the Church, and the Cosmos." In *When Science and Christianity Meet*, eds. David C. Lindberg and Ronald L. Numbers, 33–60. Chicago: University of Chicago Press, 2003.

Lindberg, David C. and Ronald L. Numbers (eds.). *When Science and Christianity Meet.* Chicago: University of Chicago Press, 2003.
LoBianco, Tom. "GOP 2016 Hopefuls Seek Footing on Marriage Ruling." *CNN*, June 26, 2015. http://www.cnn.com/2015/06/26/politics/2016-candidates-gay-marriage-supreme-court/ (Accessed July 20, 2015).
Locke, John. *An Essay Concerning Human Understanding.* New York: Dover, 1959.
Loewen, James W. *Sundown Towns*, New York: The New Press, 2005.
Loewen, James W. *Lies my Teacher Told Me: Everything your American History Textbook Got Wrong* (revised and updated version). New York: The New Press, 2007.
Loewy, Arnold H. "Free Speech and the Anti-Gay Shift." *Houston Chronicle*, December 29, 2011. http://www.chron.com/opinion/outlook/article/Free-speech-and-the-anti-gay-shift-2431590.php (Accessed June 20, 2015).
Lofholm, Nancy. "Couple Gets 20 Years Probation." *The Denver Post*, November 9, 2001.
Loucks, James F. and Andrew M. Stauffer (eds.). *Robert Browning's Poetry*. New York: W. W. Norton, 2007.
Loving v. Virginia, 388 U.S. 1; 87 S. Ct. 1817; 18 L. Ed. 2d 1010(1967).
MacKenna, Stephen (trans.). *The Enneads*, London: Faber and Faber, 1956.
Magill, Frank N. (ed.). *World Philosophy*, Vol. 2. Englewood Cliffs, NJ: Salem Press, 1982.
Maienschein, Jane. *Embryos Under the Microscope: The Diverging Meanings of Life.* Cambridge, MA: Harvard University Press, 2014.
Malle, Bertram F. "Attribution Theories: How People make Sense of Behavior." In *Theories of Social Psychology*, ed. Derek Chadee, 72–95. Malden, MA: Wiley-Blackwell, 2011.
Marius, Richard. *Martin Luther: The Christian Between God and Death.* Cambridge, MA: Harvard University Press, 1999.
Marsh, Margaret and Wanda Ronner. *The Fertility Doctor: John Rock and the Reproductive Revolution.* Baltimore, MD: Johns Hopkins University Press, 2008.
Martin, Malachi. *Hostage to the Devil: The Possession and Exorcism of Five Living Americans.* New York: Readers Digest, 1976.
McDermitt, John J. (ed.) *The Writings of William James.* New York: The Modern Library, 1968.
McGrath, Alister. *Dawkins' God: Genes, Memes, and the Meaning of Life.* Malden, MA: Blackwell, 2005.
McHenry, Lawrence C. Jr. *Garrison's History of Neurology.* Springfield, IL: Charles C. Thomas, 1969.
McLaughlin, Loretta. *The Pill, John Rock, and the Church.* Boston, MA: Little Brown, 1982.
McLaughlin, Mary Martin. "Survivors and Surrogates: Children and Parents from the Ninth to the Thirteenth Centuries." In *The History of Childhood*, ed. Lloyd DeMause, 101–181. New York: The Psychohistory Press, 1974.
McNeill, William H. *Plagues and Peoples.* New York: History Book Club, 1976.
Medawar, Peter B. *The Limits of Science.* New York: Harper & Row, 1984.
Meli, Domenico Bertoloni. "Early Modern Experimentation on Live Animals." *Journal of the History of Biology* 46, No. 2 (Summer 2013): 199–226.
Meusburger, Michael Welker and Edgar Wunder (eds.). *Clashes of Knowledge: Orthodoxies and Heterodoxies in Science and Religion.* New York: Springer and Klaus Tschira Gemeinnützige GmbH, 2008.
Mill, John Stuart. *The Subjection of Women.* Indianapolis, Cambridge: Hackett, 1988.
Miller, Kenneth R. "An Idea that Provoked, but Didn't Deliver." In *Intelligent Design: Science or Religion? Critical Perspectives*, eds. Robert M. Baird and Stuart E. Rosenbaum, 45–47. Amherst, NY: Prometheus, 2007.

Miller, Kenneth R. "Expert Statement at the Dover, Pennsylvania Trial." In *Intelligent Design: Science or Religion? Critical Perspectives*, eds. Robert M. Baird and Stuart E. Rosenbaum, 23–44. Amherst, NY: Prometheus, 2007.

Miller, William Lee. *Arguing about Slavery: John Quincy Adams and the Great Battle in the United States Congress.* New York: Vintage, 1998.

Milton, John. *Paradise Lost.* Franklin Center, PA: Franklin Library, 1979.

Mohler, R.Albert Jr. (ed.). *God and the Gay Christian?: A Response to Matthew Vines.* Louisville, KY: Southern Baptist Theological Seminary Press, 2014.

Montague, Helen and Leta Stetter Hollingworth. "The Comparative Variability of the Sexes at Birth." *American Journal of Sociology* 20, No. 3 (November 1914): 335–370.

Montaigne, Michel de. "Apology for Raimond Sebond." In *The Complete Essays of Montaigne,* Vol. 2, trans. Donald M. Frame, 112–308. Garden City, NY: Doubleday, 1960.

Mora, George (ed.). *Witches, Devils, and Doctors in the Renaissance.* Binghamton, NY: Center for Medieval & Renaissance Studies, State University of New York, 1991.

Murphy, Cullen. *God's Jury: The Inquisition and the Making of the Modern World.* New York: Houghton Mifflin Harcourt, 2012.

Murray, Billie. "Words that Wound, Bodies that Shield: Corporeal Responses to Westboro Baptist Church's Hate Speech." *First Amendment Studies* 50, No. 1 (2016): 32–47.

Myers, Paul Zachary. "The Creation 'Museum.'" http://scienceblogs.com/pharyngula/2009/08/10/the-creation-museum-1/ Posted August 10, 2009. (Accessed November 14, 2016.)

National Conference of State Legislatures. "Same-Sex Marriage Laws." June 26, 2015. http://www.ncsl.org/research/human-services/same-sex-marriage-laws.aspx (Accessed July 20, 2015).

Nelson, Todd D. *Psychology of Prejudice,* 2nd ed. Boston, MA: Pearson, 2005.

Newport, Frank. "Four in 10 Americans Believe in Strict Creationism." In *The Gallup Poll: Public Opinion, 2010,* 445–446. New York: Rowman & Littlefield, 2011.

Nicholas, Serge, Aurélie Coubart, and Todd Lubart. "The Program of Individual Psychology (1895–1896) by Alfred Binet and Victor Henri." *L'Année psychologie* 114, No. 1 (March 2014): 5–60.

Nietzsche, Friedrich. *The Genealogy of Morals.* New York: Anchor, 1956.

Numbers, Ronald L. *The Creationists: The Evolution of Scientific Creationism.* New York: Alfred A. Knopf, 1992.

Numbers, Ronald L. (ed.). *Galileo Goes to Jail and Other Myths About Science and Religion.* Cambridge, MA: Harvard University Press, 2009.

Nunley, Jan. "New Hampshire Priest is First Openly Gay Man Elected Bishop." http://www.episcopalchurch.org/library/article/new-hampshire-priest-first-openly-gay-man-elected-bishop June 7, 2003 (Accessed July 15, 2015).

Nye, Robert D. *The Legacy of B. F. Skinner: Concepts and Perspectives, Controversies and Misunderstandings.* Pacific Grove, CA: Brooks/Cole, 1992.

Obergefell v. Hodges, decided June 26, 2015, slip opinion, http://www.supremecourt.gov/opinions/14pdf/14-556_3204.pdf (Accessed July 15, 2015).

Ochoa, Julio. "Hate or Love? (Westboro Baptist Church of Topeka Visits UNC)." *Greeley Tribune,* November 11, 2002. http://www.freerepublic.com/focus/news/767563/posts?page=78 (Accessed July 20, 2015).

Ong, Czarina. "Franklin Graham Issues New Comments on Christian Persecution, Same-sex Marriage." *Christian Today,* July 2, 2015. http://www.christiantoday.com/ article/

franklin.graham.issues.new.comments.on.christian.persecution.same.sex.marriage/57794. htm (Accessed July 20, 2015).

Osborne, Kenan B. and Ki Wook Min. *Science and Religion: Fifty Years After Vatican II*. Eugene, OR: Wipf & Stock Publishers, 2014.

Owen, Richard. "Katrina – Controversial Prelate Now a Bishop." *The Times* (London) February 2, 2009.

Packer, George. "Mute Button." *The New Yorker*, April 13, 2015.

Pagels, Elaine H. *The Origin of Satan*. New York: Random House, 1995.

Paine, Thomas. "The Age of Reason." In *Common Sense and Other Writings*, Introduction and notes by Joyce Appleby, 255–320. New York: Barnes & Noble Classics, 2005.

Pastoral Psychology, paragraphs 1 and 2, http://link.springer.com/journal/11089 (Accessed July 15, 2015).

Patriot Guard Riders. "Welcome to the PGR." http://www.patriotguard.org/content.php?s=eOebdd101162be82fe85c8fc7bbf54dc (Accessed July 20, 2015).

Patterson, Romaine. "Angel Action." 2015http://eatromaine.com/1/laramie-angels.html (Accessed July 20, 2015).

Paul, Jeffrey. "The Varieties of Religious Responses to Homosexuality: A Content and Tonal Analysis of Articles in Pastoral Psychology from 1950 to 2015 Regarding Sexual Minorities." *Pastoral Psychology* 66, No. 1 (2017): 79.

Paulson, Michael. "Refusing to Fly with a Woman in the Next Seat." *The New York Times* (Friday, April 10, 2015), 1 Vol. 164, No. 56.

Peach, Bernard. "Leviathan." In *World Philosophy, Essays-Reviews of 225 Major Works*, Vol. 2, ed. Frank N. Magill, 839–846. Englewood Cliffs, NJ: Salem Press, 1982.

Pearson, Karl. *The Chances of Death and Other Studies in Evolution*. New York: Edward Arnold, 1897.

Peck, Tom and Jerome Taylor. "Scientist Imam Threatened over Darwinist Views." *The Independent* (London), News, March 5, 2011, 16.

Peltonen, Markku (ed.). *The Cambridge Companion to Bacon*. New York: Cambridge University Press, 1996.

Pickett, Brent L. *Historical Dictionary of Homosexuality*, Lanham, MD: Scarecrow Press, 2009.

Pilkinton, Neil W. and James M. Cantor. "Perceptions of Heterosexual Bias in Professional Psychology Programs: A Survey of Graduate Students." *Professional Psychology: Research and Practice* 27 No. 6 (1996): 604–612.

Pinto-Correia, Clara. *The Ovary of Eve: Egg and Sperm and Preformation*. Chicago: University of Chicago Press, 1997.

Pisa, Nick. "Pope's Exorcist Squads Will Wage War on Satan." http://www.dailymail.co.uk/news/article-504969/Popes-exorcist-squads-wage-war-Satan.html Updated December 2007. (Accessed August 20, 2010).

Pizer, Jennifer C., Brad Sears, Christy Mallory, and Hunter, Nan D. "LGBT Identity and the Law: Evidence of Persistent and Pervasive Workplace Discrimination against LGBT People: The Need for Federal Legislation Prohibiting Discrimination and Providing for Equal Employment Benefits." *Loyola of Los Angeles Law Review* 45 (2012): 715–779.

Plotinus. *The Enneads*, Vol. 5, London: Faber and Faber, 1956.

Principe, Lawrence. *Science and Religion*. DVD-ROM. Chantilly, VA: The Teaching Company, 2006.

ProCon.Org "50 States with Legal Gay Marriage." June 26, 2015. *ProCon.org*http://gaymarriage.procon.org/view.resource.php?resourceID=004857 (Accessed July 20, 2015).

Prothero, Stephen. *God is Not One: The Eight Rival Religions that Run the World – and Why Their Differences Matter*. New York: HarperCollins, 2010.
Pulliam, Sarah. "Richard Cizik Resigns from the National Association of Evangelicals." *Christianity Today*, December 11, 2008. http://www.christianitytoday.com/ct/2008/decemberweb-only/150-42.0.html (Accessed July 15, 2015).
Quetelet, Lambert Adolphe. *Treatise on Man and the Development of his Faculties*. Gainsville, FL: Scholars Facsimiles & Reprints, 1969.
Ranke-Heinemann, Uta. *Eunuchs for the Kingdom of Heaven: Women, Sexuality and the Catholic Church*. New York: Penguin, 1990.
Rauch, Jonathan. *Kindly Inquisitors*. Chicago: University of Chicago Press, 1994.
Reilly, Robert R. *The Closing of the Muslim Mind*. Wilmington, DE: Robert R. Reilly, 2010.
Reuters. "Michigan Governor Signs Bills Allowing Gay-couple Adoption Refusal." *Reuters*, June 11, 2015. http://www.reuters.com/article/2015/06/11/us-usa-michigan-adoption-idUSKBN0OR2LS20150611 (Accessed July 20, 2015).
Robertson, Campbell. "Most Alabama Judges Begin to Issue Licenses for Same-Sex Marriages." *The New York Times*, February 13, 2015. http://www.nytimes.com/2015/02/14/us/most-alabama-counties-are-granting-same-sex-marriage-licenses.html (Accessed November 14, 2016).
Robertson, Pat. "Pat Robertson on Haiti Earthquake by Pact with Devil." http://www.huliq.com/3257/90436/pat-robertson-haiti-earthquake-caused-pact-devil Posted January 14, 2010 (Accessed December 2, 2010).
Robertson, Phyllis K. "The Historical Effects of Depathologizing Homosexuality on the Practice of Counseling." *The Family Journal: Counseling and Therapy for Couples and Families* 12 No. 2 (2004): 163–169.
Robinson, Paul A. *The Modernization of Sex: Havelock Ellis, Alfred Kinsey, William Masters, and Virginia Johnson*. New York: Harper & Row, 1989.
Rogers, Eric M. *Physics for the Inquiring Mind: The Methods, Nature, and Philosophy of Physical Science*. Princeton, NJ: Princeton University Press, 1960.
Rolston III, Holmes. *Science and Religion: A Critical Survey*. New York: Random House, 1987.
Romer v. Evans, 517 U.S. 620 (1996).
Rosario II, Vernon A., "Trans (Homo) Sexuality? Double Inversion, Psychiatric Confusion, and Hetero-hegemony." In *Queer Studies: A Lesbian, Gay, Bisexual, and Transgender Anthology*, eds. Brett Beemyn and Michele Eliason, 35–51. New York: New York University Press, 1996.
Rosenfield, Leonora Cohen. *From Beast Machine to Man Machine: Animal Soul in French Letters from Descartes to LaMettrie*. New York: Octagon, 1968.
Rosenstein, Diana and Harriet Oster. "Differential Facial Responses to Four Basic Tastes in Newborns." In *What the Face Reveals: Basic and Applied Studies of Spontaneous Expression*, eds. Paul Ekman and Erika L. Rosenberg, 302–319. New York: Oxford University Press, 2005.
Rowatt, Wade C., Megan Johnson Shen, Jordan P. LaBouff, and Alfred Gonzalez. "Religious Fundamentalism, Right-wing Authoritarianism, and Prejudice: Insights from Meta-analyses, Implicit Social Cognition, and Social Cognitive Neuroscience." In *Handbook of The Psychology of Religion and Spirituality*, 2nd ed., eds. Raymond F. Paloutz and Crystal L. Park. New York: Guilford Press, 2015.
Rowland, Wade. *Galileo's Mistake: A New Look at the Epic Confrontation Between Galileo and the Church*. New York: Arcade, 2001.

Rubinstein, Gidi. "The Decision to Remove Homosexuality from the DSM: Twenty Years Later." *American Journal of Psychotherapy* 49, No. 3 (1995): 416–427.

Rubenstein, Richard E. *Aristotle's Children: How Christians, Muslims, and Jews Rediscovered Ancient Wisdom and Illuminated the Dark Ages*. New York: Harcourt, 2003.

Rubinsky, Yuri and Ian Wiseman. *A History of the End of the World*. New York: Quill, 1982.

Ruse, Michael. "Introduction." *Religion and Science* by Bertrand Russell, v–xxiii. New York: Oxford University Press, 1997.

Russell, Bertrand. *Religion and Science*. New York: Oxford University Press, 1997.

Russell, Bertrand. "A Free Man's Worship." In *The Basic Writings of Bertrand Russell*, eds. Robert Egner and Lester E. Denonn. New York: Routledge, 2009.

Russell, Jeffrey Burton. *Inventing the Flat Earth: Columbus and Modern Historians*. New York: Praeger, 1991.

Rutherford, Donald. *Leibniz and the Rational Order of Nature*. New York: Cambridge University Press, 1995.

Rychlak, Joseph F. and Ronald J. Rychlak. "The Insanity Defense and the Question of Human Agency." *New Ideas in Psychology* 8 (1990): 3–24.

Sacks, Jonathan. *The Great Partnership: Science and Religion and the Search for Meaning*. New York: Schocken, 2011.

Sagan, Carl. *The Demon Haunted World: Science as a Candle in the Dark*. New York: Ballantine Books, 1996.

Salmon, Jacqueline L. "Most Americans Believe in a Higher Power, Poll Finds." *The Washington Post*, June 24, 2008.

Sanchez, Ray. "Feds' Transgender Guidance Provokes Fierce Backlash." *CNN*, May 14, 2016. http://www.cnn.com/2016/05/14/politics/transgender-bathrooms-backlash/index.html (Accessed August 24, 2016).

Sanger, Margaret. *Motherhood in Bondage*. Columbus, OH: Ohio State University Press, 2000.

Santillana, Giorgio, de. *The Crime of Galileo*. Chicago, IL: University of Chicago Press, 1955.

Sargant, William. *Battle for the Mind: The Mechanics of Indoctrination, Brainwashing and Thought Control*. Baltimore, MD: Penguin, 1961.

Sayers, Devon M. "Disney to Pull Boy Scouts Funding by 2015 over Policy Banning Gay Leaders." *CNN*, March 2, 2015. http://www.cnn.com/2014/02/28/us/disney-pulls-boy-scouts-funding/ (Accessed July 20, 2015).

Scasta, David L. "John E. Fryer, MD, and the Dr. H. Anonymous Episode." *Journal of Gay and Lesbian Psychotherapy* 6, No. 4 (2008): 73–84.

Scherer, Lester B. *Slavery and the Churches in Early America, 1619–1819*. Grand Rapids, MI: William B. Eerdmans, 1975.

Scherer, Michael. "Battle of the Bathroom." *Time* 187, No. 20 (2016): 30–37.

Schmitt, Charles B. (ed.). *The Cambridge History of Renaissance Philosophy*. New York: Cambridge University Press, 1988.

Seidel, George E. Jr. and R. Peter Elsden. *Embryo Transfer in Dairy Cattle*. Milwaukee, WI: Hoard & Sons, 1997.

Shakespeare, William. *Measure for Measure: An Old-Spelling and Old-Meaning Edition*, ed. Ernst Leisi. New York: Hafner, 1964.

Shaw, Arthur H. (ed.). *The Lincoln Encyclopedia The Spoken and Written Words of A. Lincoln Arranged for Ready Reference*. New York: The Macmillan Co., 1950.

Sherif, Muzafer and Carolyn Sherif. *Social Psychology*. New York: Harper & Row, 1969.

Shilts, Randy. *And the Band Played On: Politics, People, and the AIDS Epidemic*. New York: St. Martin's Press, 1987.

Shorto, Russell. *Descartes' Bones: A Skeletal History of the Conflict Between Faith and Reason*. New York: Doubleday, 2008.
Singer, Margaret T. and Janja Lalich. *Cults in Our Midst: The Hidden Menace in Our Everyday Lives*. Hoboken, NJ: John Wiley & Sons, 1995.
Singer, Peter, Helga Kuhse, Stephen Buckle, Karen Dawson, and Pascal Kasimba (eds.). *Embryo Experimentation: Ethical, Legal, and Social Issues*. Cambridge: Cambridge University Press, 1993.
Singh, S. H. "Transgender, Gay Indians Fight to Throw off Taboos, Stereotypes." April 29, 2014. http://www.cnn.com/2014/04/29/world/asia/india-transgender-gay-rights/ (Accessed June 20, 2014).
Sinnott-Armstrong, Walter. "How Religion Undermines Compromise." In *Religion, Intolerance, and Conflict: A Scientific and Conceptual Investigation*, eds. Steve Clark, Russell Powell, and Julian Savulesco, 221–235. Oxford: Oxford University Press, 2013.
Sizer, Nelson and H. S. Drayton. *Heads and Faces and How to Study Them: A Manual of Phrenology and Physiognomy for the People*. New York: Fowler & Wells, 1892.
Slevin, Colleen and Thomas Peipert. "Navy Vet Pushes for Changes to Passport Gender Rule." *Military.com*, July 21, 2016. http://www.military.com/daily-news/2016/07/21/navy-vet-pushes-changes-passport-gender-rule.html (Accessed August 24, 2016).
Slife, Brent and J. Reber. "Is There a Pervasive Implicit Bias Against Theism in Psychology?" *Journal of Theoretical & Philosphical Psychology* 29 (2009): 63–79.
Slife, Brent D. and Frank C. Richardson. "Naturalism, Psychology, and Religious Experience: An Introduction to the Special Section on Psychology and Transcendence." *Pastoral Psychology* 63 (2014): 319–322.
Smith, Brittany. "Family Expert on Studies: Same-Sex Parenting Does Affect Children." *Christian Post*, March 8, 2012. http://www.christianpost.com/news/family-expert-on-studies-same-sex-parenting-does-affect-children-71103/ (Accessed July 20, 2015).
Snyder v. Phelps, 562 U.S. 443; 131 S. Ct. 1207; 179 L. Ed. 2d 172(2011).
Sobel, Dava. *A More Perfect Heaven: How Copernicus Revolutionized the Cosmos*. New York: Walker, 2011.
Somashekhar, Sandhya. "Boy Scouts President Warns that Ban on Gay Leaders Threatens Organization." *Washington Post*, May 21, 2015. http://www.washingtonpost.com/politics/boy-scouts-president-warns-that-gay-ban-threatens-the-organization/2015/05/21/02ed19b0-fff1-11e4-8b6c-0dcce21e223d_story.html (Accessed July 20, 2015).
Sotirin, Patty. "Becoming-woman." In *Giles Deleuze: Key Concepts*, ed. Charles J. Stivale, 98–109. Ithaca, NY: McGill Queen's University Press, 2005.
Soulforce. "Our Story." 2015. http://www.soulforce.org/our-story (Accessed July 20, 2015).
Southern Baptist Convention. "Resolution on Racial Reconciliation on the 150th Anniversary of the Southern Baptist Convention." 1995. http://www.sbc.net/resolutions/899/resolution-on-racial-reconciliation-on-the-150th-anniversary-of-the-southern-baptist-convention (Accessed July 20, 2015).
Spencer, Herbert. "The Psychology of the Sexes." *Popular Science Monthly*, 4 (November, 1873): 30–38.
Spilka, Bernard, and Daniel N. McIntosh. "Attribution Theory and Religious Experience." In *Handbook of Religious Experience*, ed. Ralph W. Hood, Jr., 421–445. Birmingham, AL: Religious Education Press, 1995.
Spilka, Bernard, Phillip Shaver, and Lee A. Kirkpatrick. "A General Attribution Theory for the Psychology of Religion." *Journal for the Scientific Study of Religion* 24, No. 1 (March, 1985): 1–20.

Spilka, Bernard and Kevin L. Ladd. *The Psychology of Prayer: A Scientific Approach*. New York: Guilford, 2013.
Stanley, Tiffany. "Praying for Bad Things to Happen to Bad People." *The Salt Lake Tribune*, July 1 (2009).
Starbuck, Edwin Diller. *The Psychology of Religion: An Empirical Study of the Growth of Religious Consciousness*. London: Dalton House 2012 (Reprint of 1900 edition).
Stark, Rodney. *For the Glory of God*. Princeton, NJ: Princeton University Press, 2003.
State of Oregon. Official 1992 General Voter's Pamphlet. http://www.glapn.org/6013Anti-GayImages/Measure9BallotTitle.jpg (Accessed July 20, 2015).
Statistical Abstract of the United States. Washington D.C., U.S. Bureau of the Census, 1974.
Statistical Abstract of the United States. Washington D.C., U.S. Bureau of the Census, 1987.
Statistical Abstract of the United States. Washington D.C., U.S. Bureau of the Census, 2011.
Steele, Claude M. "A Threat in the Air. How Stereotypes Shape Intellectual Ability and Performance." *American Psychologist* 52, No. 6 (June 1997): 613–629.
Steers, Stuart. "The Gang of Four." *5280*, May 2005. http://www.5280.com/magazine/2005/05/gang-four?page=full (Accessed November 14, 2016).
Steinmetz, Katy. "Person of the Year, The Short List, No. 7: Caitlyn Jenner." 2015. http://time.com/time-person-of-the-year-2015-runner-up-caitlyn-jenner/ (Accessed August 24, 2016).
Stenger, Victor J. *God: The Failed Hypothesis*. New York: Prometheus Books, 2008.
Stenmark, Mikael. "Science and the Limits of Knowledge." In *Clashes of Knowledge: Orthodoxies and Heterodoxies in Science and Religion*, eds. Peter Meusburger, Michael Welker, and Edgar Wunder, 111–120. New York: Springer and Klaus Tschira Gemeinnützige GmbH, 2008.
Stewart, Matthew. *Nature's God: The Heretical Origins of the American Republic*. New York: W. W. Norton, 2014.
Stoddard, Ed. "Poll Finds more American Believe in Devil than Darwin." http://uk.reuters.com/article/iduKN2922875820071129 Posted November 29, 2007. (Accessed June 25, 2015).
Storms, Michael D. "Theories of Homosexuality." *Journal of Personality and Social Psychology* 38, No. 5 (1980): 783–792.
Stout, David. "66 Journalists Killed in 2014: Report." http://time.com/3635440/journalism-reporters-without-border-murder-kidnapping/ Posted December 16, 2014. (Accessed May 23, 2015).
Streeter, Michael. *Witchcraft: A Secret History*. Hauppauge, NY: Quarto, 2002.
Streib, Victor L. "Death Penalty for Children: The American Experience with Capital Punishment for Crimes Committed While Under the Age of Eighteen." *Oklahoma Law Review* 36, No. 3 (Summer 1983): 613–641.
Stringfellow, Thornton. *Scriptural and Statistical Views in Favor of Slavery*, 4th ed. Richmond, VA: J. W. Randolph, 1856.
Sun-Sentinel Editorial. "Small Town Beats Westboro, Shows America at Its Best." *Sun-Sentinel*, December 1, 2010. http://articles.sun-sentinel.com/2010-12-01/news/fl-westboro-editorial-gs-20101201_1_westboro-baptist-church-missouri-town-fred-phelps (Accessed July 20, 2015).
Swammerdam, Jan. *The Book of Nature*. Trans. T. Flloyd. London: C. G. Seyffert, 1758.
Taves, Ann. *Religious Experience Reconsidered: A Building Block Approach to the Study of Religion and Other Special Things*. Princeton, NJ: Princeton University Press, 2009.
Tavris, Carol. *The Mismeasure of Woman: Why Women Are Not The Better Sex, The Inferior Sex, or the Opposite Sex*. New York: Simon & Schuster, 1992.

Tavris, Carol and Eliot Aronson. *Mistakes Were Made but Not by Me: Why We Justify Fooling Beliefs, Bad Decisions, and Hurtful Acts*. New York: Harcourt, 2008.
Taylor, Richard. "Determinism." In *The Encyclopedia of Philosophy*, Vol. 2, ed. Paul Edwards, 359–373. New York: Macmillan, 1967.
Tennessee Sixty-Fourth General Assembly. An Act Prohibiting the Teaching of Evolution Theory in all the Universities, Normals, and all other Public Schools of Tennessee, which are Supported in Whole or in Part by the Public School Funds of the State, and to Provide Penalties for the Violations Thereof, *Public Acts of the State of Tennessee* Chapter No. 27, (March 13, 1925) HB185. http://law2.umkc.edu/faculty/projects/ftrials/scopes/tennstat.htm (Accessed January 6, 2012).
Tennessee, Public Act, Chapter 237, No 48. An Act to Repeal Section 498–1922, Tenessee Code Annotated, Prohibiting the Teaching of Evolution, 1967.
Teo, Thomas. "Critical Psychology: A Geography of Intellectual Engagement and Resistance." *American Psychologist* 70, No. 3 (April 2015): 243–254.
Theroux, Louis (writer). *The Most Hated Family in America*, BBC (2007).
Thompson, Keith. "Introduction." In *The Religion and Science Debate: Why Does it Continue?*, ed. Harold W. Attridge, 1–14. New Haven, CT: Yale University Press, 2009.
Tiffany, Stanley. "Praying for Bad Things to Happen to Bad People." *The Salt Lake Tribune*, July 1, 2009.
Titchener, Edward Bradford. *A Textbook of Psychology*. New York: MacMillan, 1910.
Tooler, Michael. "Causation: Metaphysical Issues." In *Encyclopedia of Philosophy*, 2nd ed., Vol. 2, ed. Donald M. Borchart, 95–103. Detroit: Thompson/Gale, 2006.
Torrey, Charles W. "Woman's Place in the Church." *The Congregational Quarterly* 9 (1867): 163–171.
Tripp, C. A. *Homosexual Matrix*. New York: McGraw-Hill, 1975.
Twain, Mark. "The War Prayer." In *The Complete Essays of Mark Twain*, ed. Charles Neider, 679–682. Garden City, NY: Doubleday, 1963.
Tylor, Edward Burnett. "Quetelet on the Science of Man." *Popular Science Monthly* 1 (May, 1872).
United States v. Windsor, 133 S. Ct. 2675; 186 L. Ed. 2d 808(2013).
U.S. Senate, 81st Congress, Committee on Expenditures in Executive Departments. "Employment of Homosexuals and Other Sex Perverts in Government." Washington, DC: Government Printing Office, 1950.
U.S. Government Printing Office, H.R. 3396, Defense of Marriage Act. http://www.gpo.gov/fdsys/pkg/BILLS-104hr3396enr/pdf/BILLS-104hr3396enr.pdf (Accessed July 20, 2015).
U.S. Government Printing Office, Federal Marriage Amendment, May 13, 2004. http://www.gpo.gov/fdsys/pkg/CHRG-108hhrg93656/html/CHRG-108hhrg93656.htm (Accessed July 20, 2015).
USA Today. "Conservatives Form Rival Group to Episcopal Church." December 4, 2008. http://usatoday30.usatoday.com/news/religion/2008-12-03-episcopal-split_N.htm (Accessed July 15, 2015).
Vail, Tom. *Grand Canyon: A Different View*. Green Forest, AZ: Master Books, 2006.
Van de Warker, Ely. "The Relations of Women to the Professions and Skilled Labor." *Popular Science Monthly* 6 (February 1875): 454–470.
Vickers, Brian. "Bacon and Rhetoric." In *The Cambridge Companion to Bacon*, ed. Markku Peltonen, 222–227. New York: Cambridge University Press, 1996.
Vines, Matthew. *God and the Gay Christian: The Biblical Case in Support of Same-Sex Relationships*. New York: Convergent Books, 2014.

Viney, Donald Wayne. *A Philosopher Looks at the Bible*. Pittsburg, KS: Friends of Timmons Chapel, 1992.
Viney, Donald Wayne. "Teilhard: Le philosophe malgré l' église." In *Recovering Teilhard's Fire*, ed. Kathleen Duffy, 69–88. Philadelphia: St. Joseph's University Press, 2010.
Viney, Donald Wayne (ed. and trans.). *Translation of Works of Jules Lequyer*. Queenston, Ontario: The Edwin Mellen Press, 1998.
Viney, Donald Wayne. "The Nightmare of Necessity: Jules Lequyer's Dialogue of the Predestinate and the Reprobate." *The Journal for the Association of the Interdisciplinary Study of the Arts* 5, No. 1 (1999): 19–32.
Viney, Wayne and William Douglas Woody. "Psychogeny: A Neglected Dimension of the Mind-Brain Problem." *The Teaching of Psychology* 22, No. 3 (October 1995): 173–177.
Viney, Wayne and Elizabeth Parker. "Necessity as a Nightmare or as a Pathway to Freedom: Freud's Dilemma, a Human Dilemma." *Psychoanalytic Psychology* 33 (2016): 299–311.
Vohs, Katherine D. and Jonathan W. Schooler. "The Value of Believing in Free Will: Encouraging a Belief in Determinism Increases Cheating." *Psychological Science* 19, No. 1 (January 2008): 49–54.
Voltaire, François-Marie Arouet. *Candide*. Trans. Robert M. Adams. New York: Norton, 1991.
Walton, Gregory M. and Steven J. Spencer. "Latent Ability: Grades and Test Scores Systematically Underestimate the Ability of Negatively Stereotyped Students." *Psychological Science* 20, No. 9 (September 2009): 1132–1139.
Wan, William. "Episcopalians in Va. Divided Over Decision Allowing Ordination of Gay Bishops." *Washington Post*, July 16, 2009. http://www.washingtonpost.com/wp-dyn/content/article/2009/07/15/AR2009071503697.html (Accessed July 15, 2015).
Warikoo, Niraj. "Religious Leaders' Reactions to Gay Marriage Mixed." *Detroit Free Press*, June 26, 2015. http://www.freep.com/story/news/2015/06/26/religious-same-sex-marriage-reaction/29328951/ (Accessed July 20, 2015).
Washington Post. "A History of 'Don't Ask, Don't Tell.'" November 30, 2010. http://www.washingtonpost.com/wp-srv/special/politics/dont-ask-dont-tell-timeline/ (Accessed July 20, 2015).
Watkins, Eric and Marius Stan. "Kant's Philos Sci." In *Stanford Encyclopedia of Philosophy*. Revision posted July 18, 2014. http://plato.stanford.edu/entries/kant-science/ (Accessed May 23, 2015).
Watts, Fraser and Kevin Dutton (eds.). *Why the Science and Religion Dialogue Matters: Voices from the International Society for Science and Religion*. Philadelphia, PA: Templeton Foundation Press, 2006.
Webb, George E. *The Evolution Controversy in America*. Lexington, KY: University of Kentucky Press, 1994.
Weeks, Jeffrey. *Sex, Politics, and Society: The Regulations of Sexuality Since 1800*, 3rd ed. New York: Pearson Education, 2012.
Wennberg, Robert N. *Faith at the Edge: A Book for Doubters*. Grand Rapids, MI: William B. Eerdmans, 2009.
Wertheimer, Michael. "Gestalt Theory, Holistic Psychologies, and Max Wertheimer." In *Personale Psychologie: Beitraege zur Geschichte, Theorie und Therapie*, ed. Günther Bittner, 32–49. Göttingen: C. J. Hogrefe, 1983.
Wertheimer, Michael. *A Brief History of Psychology*, 5th ed. New York: Psychology Press, 2011.
Wesley, John. "Free Grace." In *Classics of Protestantism*, ed. Vergilius Ferm, 165–179, New York: Philosophical Library, 1959.

Wesleyan Quadrilateral, Wikipedia entry. http://en.wikipedia.org/wikiWesleyan_Quarilateral. (Accessed May 11, 2015).
West, Geoffrey. "The Theory of Everything." In *This Idea Must Die*, ed. John Brockman, 1–4. New York: Harper, 2015.
Westminster Assembly. *The Westminster Confession of Faith*. Charleston, SC: Forgotten Books, 2007.
Weyer, Johann. "De Praestigiis Daemonum." In *Witches, Devils, and Doctors in the Renaissance*, ed. George Mora, 1–584. Binghamton, NY: State University of New York at Binghamton, 1991.
White, Andrew Dickson. *A History of the Warfare of Science with Theology in Christendom*. Amherst, NY: Prometheus Books, 1993.
White, Mel. *Stranger at the Gate: To be Gay and Christian in America*. New York: Plume, 1995.
White, Murray J. "The Statue Syndrome: Perversion? Fantasy? Anecdote?" *Journal of Sex Research* 14, No. 4 (1978): 246–249.
Whitehead, Alfred North. *Science and the Modern World*. New York: The Free Press, 1967.
Whitehouse, Harvey. "Religion, Cohesion, and Hostility." In *Religion, Intolerance, and Conflict: A Scientific and Conceptual Investigation*, eds. Steve Clarke, Russell Powell, and Julian Savulescu, 36–47. Oxford: Oxford University Press, 2013.
Wilkerson, Isabella. *The Warmth of Other Suns: The Epic Story of America's Great Migration*. New York: Vintage, 2010.
Williams, Candace. "Bills Would Require Clergy to Sign Off on Marriages." *The Detroit News*, June 19, 2015. http://www.detroitnews.com/story/news/politics/michigan/2015/06/19/gay-marriage-legislation-religion-michian/29018125/ (Accessed July 20, 2015).
Wilson, David B. "The Historiography of Science and Religion." In *Science and Religion: A Historical Introduction*, ed. Gary B. Ferngren, 13–29. Baltimore, MD: Johns Hopkins University Press, 2002.
Wolfe, Harry Kirke. Distinguished Lecture, American Psychological Association presented at the April, 2014 meeting of the Rocky Mountain Psychological Association, Salt Lake City, UT.
Wollstonecraft, Mary. *A Vindication of the Rights of Women*. New York: Penguin, 2004.
Wood, Graeme. "What ISIS Really Wants." *The Atlantic* 315, No. 2 (March 2015): 78–94.
Woodland, Cadence. "The End of the 'Mormon Moment'." *New York Times* 163, July 15, 2014.
Woody, William Douglas. "Varieties of Religious Conversion." *Streams of William James* 5 (2003): 7–11.
Woody, William Douglas. "The Use of 'Cult' in the Teaching of Psychology." *Psychology of Religion and Spirituality* 1, No. 4 (2009): 218–232.
Woody, William Douglas and Wayne Viney. *A History of Psychology: The Emergence of Science and Applications*, 6th ed. New York: Routledge, 2017.
Wootton, David. *Galileo: Watcher of the Skies*. New Haven, CT: Yale University Press, 2010.
Wray, Herbert. "The Science of Interrogation: Rapport, Not Torture." www.huffingtonpost.com/wray-herbert/the-science-of-interrogat_b_6309296.html (Accessed March 20, 2015).
Zamansky, Stephen. "Colorado's Amendment 2 and Homosexuals' Right to Equal Protection of Law." *Boston College Law Review* 35 (1993): 221–258.
Zorn, Eric. "Dateline Gettysburg: The Tribune Regrets the (Minor) Errors." *Chicago Tribune*, November 17, 2013. http://articles.chicagotribune.com/2013-11-17/news/ct-get tysburg-lincoln-anniversary-zorn-1117-zorn-20131117_1_abraham-lincoln-book-shop -four-score-gettysburg-address (Accessed November 14, 2016).

INDEX

abortion 54; evolving attitudes 135; and Comstock Law 143; and intellectual warfare 146–7, 169
absolutism 217–31; in science 224–5; in religion 225
accommodation 173, 188, 228–30
Adam 25, 68, 136–7, 153, 156, 218
agalmatophilia 176
Albertus Magnus (Albert the Great) 154
Al-Ghazali 49
Allah 39; as cause of error 50, 55, 211; as cause of death and all things 53, 69, 211; creative acts of 68
Allen, J. 154
Allie, A. H. 184
Allport, G. 208
American Civil Liberties Union 97
American Psychiatric Association 179
American Psychological Association 178–9
Angel Action 182
angels 23, 44, 71, 76; popular belief in 63; as causal forces 63–5, 69; fallen 64; created by Allah 68; relation to humans 68; Spinoza and denial of 76; *see also* Iblis, Jinn, Satan
animal spirits 84–7
animate motion 83–4, 86; *see also* motion
Anonymous, H. 179
Aquinas, T. 9, 37, 132, 156; on faith and reason 36; on instantiation of the soul 89; on masturbation 134; and essentialism 154

Aristotle 81, 89, 118; classification of causes 51–2; on animal generation 132, 139; weight of air 202
Armstrong, K. 5, 205–6
attribution theory 44, 59
Augustine, A. 14, 36, 68, 132; conversion of 211
authority 31; in science 32–3; in religion 33–5
Authoritarian control 32–3

Bacon, F. 5, 41; value of curiosity 25–6; role of doubt 29–30; disdain for tradition and authority 36, 113; superiority of observation and experience 38, 128; common errors or idols 113
Bader, C. 96
Baer, K. E. von 136
Barberini , M. 121, 123–4
Batson, C. D. 208
Becker, C. 220
Behe, M. J. 100, 106; *see also* intelligent design
Bellarmine, R. 120–3
Benedict XIV, Pope 64, 129
Berenda, C. 17
Bible 10, 37, 68, 97, 99, 102–3, 107, 181, 211; trust in 17; higher criticism and interpretation 27, 34; inerrancy 34, 102; effect of printing press 40; and imprecatory prayer 48; on the forces of

evil 64–5; geocentrism 114, 120, 124; and natural inequalities 199
Biggar, N. 210
birth control 135, 142–8; *see also* Comstock, Sanger
bisexual 173–85
Boring, E. G. 86, 203
Boy Scouts of America 174, 186–7
Broca, P. 156–7, 161
Brooke, J. H. 15
Brooks, D. 189
Bryan, W. J. 97, 104
Buggery Act 175
Bush, George H. W. 185
Butler Act 97–8

Caiazza, J. 9
Calvin, J. 116, 211
Capra, F. 140
Cashire, A. D. J. 168
Catholic 28, 35, 40, 48, 75, 88, 108, 115, 135, 144, 145, 151, 154, 208, 218; birth control 146–7; exorcism 64–5; Index of Prohibited Books 74, 112, 116; protection of church doctrines 7, 9, 116, 120, 124, 147
Causality 44–77, 99; God as cause 49–51; demons and causality 63–7, 69–73; prayer and causality 45–9; naturalism and causality 51–2
Charcot, J. 175
Chopra, D. 2
Christianity 3, 9, 10, 40, 70, 100, 104
Church of Jesus Christ of Latter Day Saints 187; *see also* Mormon Church
Cizik, R. 182
Clement of Alexandria 153
Cleveland, G. 158, 161
Clinton, H. 229
Clinton, W. J. 185
compulsions 6, 7, 59; *see also* ritual
Comstock, A. 143–4, 146
conversion 211–13
Copernicus, N. 107; and heliocentrism 115–16, 120; suppression of his work 116, 120–1, 123, 128
Coyne, J. 1
creationism 5, 97; and perception of warfare 95; teaching of in the United States 95; balanced treatment 99; "creation science" 99; and intelligent design 99, 100–1, 104–6; and teleology 105–6

Creationist Museum 103
critical psychology 40
Crosby, D. A. 13, 140
curiosity 24–6; and science, 26; and religion, 26–8

Daniel v. Waters 99
Danielson, D. 17
Darrow, C. 97, 104
Darwin, C. 6, 36, 96; doubts purposive explanations 105–6; moral sensitivities 108–9; technical points in his theory 148; 161, 199
Dawkins, R. 13, 96, 224
Defense of Marriage Act (DOMA) 174
Deleuze, G. 132, 206
Democritus 202
demons 63–77; reasons for belief in 64–7
Descartes, R. suppression of his book *The World* 7–8; procedural rules 29–30; thinking and existence 41; mechanistic theory of movement 75–6, 83–8; 117, 128, 139
determinism 54–9, 138
devils: persistence of belief in 63–7; presumed work of 68–71; demise of belief in 73–6, 143, 153–4
Diagnostic and Statistical Manual (DSM) 178–80
Donnez, J. 136
Don't Ask Don't Tell 185–6
doubt 28–9; and science 29–30; and religion 30
Draper, J. W. 1, 13–14, 18, 95
Dutton, K. 3

Ebbinghaus, H. 204
Eco, U. 27
efficient cause 51
Einstein, A. 54–5, 127
Eisenhower, D. D. 180
Ellis, H. 175
Emerson, R. W. 127
epigenesis 135, 138–9
Episcopal Church 181
epistemology 13, 24; fear of knowledge 25; and Montaigne 75; 32, 37, 41, 75, 101, 220, 222; *see also* authority, curiosity, doubt, experience, and critical psychology
Epperson v. Arkansas 98–9
essentialism 152, 158, 165, 168; in relation to gender and sex 151–69; theological

views 152–6; "scientific" and secular views 156–60; challenged 158, 160–6, 165, 168; *see also* gender, sex
Euteneuer, T. 64, 77
Eve 25, 156, 218
evolution 5, Teilhard and 8–9; 11–12, 28, 95–109; U. S. belief in 95–6; and Islam 96–7; and warfare thesis 97–109, 114, 148, 169
exorcism 64–5
experience 37–8; in science 38–9; in religion 39–40

Fechner, G. 203
Feynman, R. P. 6
final cause 51; *see also* teleology and purpose
Finocchiaro, M. A. 15
foreknowledge 50, 59, 138, 211; *see also* predestination
Forest, B. 12
formal cause 51–2
Francis, Pope 188, 229
Frankenberry, N. K. 2
free will 54–9, 211
Freud, S. 73, 212; and determinism 54, 59; on human happiness 65–6; views on women 157–8; on sexual orientation 177
Fryer, J. 179

Galileo 8, 9; conflict with the Catholic Church 15–19, 112–29; 26; Inquisition trial of 122–6; 147, 148, 181, 203, 218, 219
Gallup Poll 96, 114, 147
Galton, F. 162; efficacy of prayer 48–9; on women 157; measurement 164–5, 198–200
Galvani, L. 86–7
Garabedian, D. 57–8
gay rights movement 174–90; early medical views, 175; early psychological views, 176–7; *see also* homosexual and homosexuality
gender 28; and souls 89, 92; origins of 92; and microcosmic gametes 136; bias 152–8; challenges to gender inequalities 159–69; and sexual orientation 173–189; *see also* sex, transgender, lesbian, gay rights, bi-sexual
God: presumed attributes of 10, 50, 54–5, 68, 70, 76, 182, 207; as cause of all things 49–50; relation to evil 70–2; foreknowledge of 55–9, 137–8, 211; human knowledge of 36–7, 39, 211; presumed human influence on 47; presumed purposes of 53, 66, 106; word of 128
Gregory IX, Pope 122
Gross, P. R. 101

Haack, S. 5
Harris, S. 13, 225
Harrison, P. 25
Hasan, Usama 96
Haught, J. F. 15, 223
heliocentrism 102, prohibition of works on 16; early emotional reaction to 17–18; heresy of belief in 115–16; problems of proving 118–19; and Galileo 121–4, 126
Helmholtz, H. von 86, 203
historiography 4; complexity thesis 15–19; 126–8
Hitchens, C. 13, 224
Hobbes, T. 75
homosexual 173–82, 185
homosexuality 109, 135, 148; and sacred literature 174–5, 181; pathologized 175, 178–9, 182, 185; decriminalized 177, 180 *see also* Buggery Act, inversion, sodomites
Humanae Vitae 146–7

Iblis 68; *see also* angels, Satan, jinn
idealism 80–1
immutability 30, 47, 55
Index of Prohibited Books 112, 116
Innocent IV, Pope 122
Innocent VIII, 69
Inquisition 69, 71; use of torture 16–17, 72, 75; Galileo's trial 8, 120–5, 128–9; mistakes of 129; 154, 206, 208
instantiation 89–92
intelligent design 99–101, 106
intersex 167
inversion 175, 177
Islam 3, 10, 34–5, 49, 55, 64–5, 96, 166, 174, 226

James, W. 6, 38, 68 ; on prayer 48; on free will and determinism 54–5; on individualism 127; on process and pluralism 220–4; 217
Jaynes, J. 83–4

Jefferson, T. 197, 225–6
Jesus 30, 34, 39, 47, 158–9, 204
jinn 68; *see also* angels
John Paul II, Pope 64
Johnson V. 144
Jones, J. E. 100–1
Judaism 3

Kauffman, S. A. 139
Kelly, K. 155
Kepler, J. 74, 107
Kinsey, A. C. 144, 177–8
Kitzmiller, V. Dover 100, 106
klinefelter syndrome 167
knowledge 23–41, ; God's 50, 55, 105; absence of and shaky foundations of 65, 76; effects of microscope and telescope 119; limits of 119, 230; and the "word of God" 128; and science 13, 102
Köhler, W. 140
Kraft-Ebbing, R. von 175
Kramer, H. 69–72, 81, 154

LaMettrie, J. O. 87
Larson, E. J. 3–4, 104
Le Bon, G. 156–7, 161
Lebo, L. 101
Leibniz, G. W. 137, 139
Lequyer, J. 56
Leuba, J. H. 201
LGBT (Lesbian, Gay, Bisexual, Transgender) 183
Locke, J. 117, 150–60
Loving v. Virginia 187
Luther, M. 36–7, 39, 116, 127

Maienschein, J. 133, 140
Malleus Maleficarum 69, 73, 81, 154
Masters, W. 144
masturbation 134–5, 148
material cause 51
materialism 80–1, 221
Maxwell, J. C. 83
McCormick, K. 145
Middle Ages 10, 25, 82, 135
Mill, J. S. 127, 159–60, 165, 197
Miller, K. 12, 106
Min, K. W. 3
miscegenation 184
mitochondrial DNA 141
Mlodinow, L. 2–3
monism 221–2
Montague, H. 162–3, 165

Montaigne, M. 28–9, 75–6, 113
Mormon Church 137, 151, 155; *see also* Church of Jesus Christ of Latter Day Saints
motion 82–4, 86–8, 117, 125, 136, 138, 141; *see also* animate motion
Murphy, C. 17

natural variation: religion implications 199–202
neurology 75–6, 82, 87–8
Newton, I. 6–7, 59, 74, 127
Numbers, R. 5

Obergefell v. Hodges 183, 187–9
olympic games: and women 166
omnipotence 55
omniscience 55
Osborne, K. B. 3
ovists 135–6

Paine, T. 31
Parmenides 202
Paul IV, Pope 112
Paul VI, Pope 112
Pearson, K. 161–6, 200
Phelps, F. 182
Pincus, G. 145–6
Pinto-Correia C. 133–4, 138
Pius XII, Pope 64
plague 53, 106
Plotinus 80–1
pluralism 222–3
Pope: see Benedict, Gregory IX, Francis, Innocent IV, Innocent VIII, Paul IV, Paul VI
prayer: efficacy of 47–9, 53, 64–5, 201, 213
predestination 55–7; *see also* foreknowledge
preformationism 137–9
press: and warfare 11–12
pricking 74
Principe, L. 2
Protestant 28, 34–5, 39–40, 64, 75, 108, 112, 146, 184
psychogeny 89, 91

Quetelet, L. A. J. 165, 198–200
Qur'an 55, 64–5; 107, 181, 204 doubt and curiosity 25, 32; authority of 34–5; foreknowledge of Allah 52–3, 211; creation of Adam 68; age of the earth 96; teleology and Allah's absolute knowledge 105; men and women 53, 176; homosexual behavior 174

Ranke-Heinemann, U. 75, 154–5
Rauch, J. 24
reason 35–6; in science 36; in religion 36–7
religion: variation in 5–7, 210–11; and intolerance 204–5; violence 205–7; and prejudice 207–11; as quest 209; and compromise 210–11; developmental approach 218–21
ritual 6, 64–5, 205, 213; *see also* compulsions
Robertson, P. 69, 102
Rock, J. 145–7
Rogers, E. 68
Rolston, H. 201–2
Russell, B. 1, 14, 220
Russell, J. B. 114

Sacks, J. 2
Sanger, M. 127, 142–5
Satan 68, 77, 152
scientism 13, 41, 224
Scopes, J. 8, 97–8, 100, 104
sex 131–48; defined 131; sexual orientation 174–90; early medical views of homosexuality 176; early psychological views of homosexuality; scientific investigations 177, 180; cultural and legal conflicts 180–1; growing diaspora 181–90; warfare 188; accommodation 188–9
Sheppard, M. 182
Sinnott-Armstrong, W. 210
Skinner, B. F. 6, 54
Slife, B. 224
sodomites 175
soul 44, 55, 93, 145, 203, 211; as cause of locomotion 44, 74, 81–2; Descartes on 75, 83–7; in relation to body 80, 81; instantiation 89–91; problem of gendered souls 92; *see also* psyche
sperm 91, 131–8, 146
spermists 135–6
Spilka, B. 251
Spinoza, B. 76, 212
Sprenger, J. 69–72, 81, 154
Starbuck, W. D. 212
Stark, R. 1, 9, 10
Stenger, V. 49
Stensen, N. or (Nicolaus of Steno) 85
stonewall riots 174

Swammerdam, J. 85–6
Swift, J. 176

Teilhard, de Chardin Pierre 8, 9, 218
teleology 51–2, 105–6, 139; extrinsic 52, 139; intrinsic 52, 130 *see also* final cause, and purpose
Tertullian 153
Thales 82
Thomson, K. 1
Thorndike, E. L. 163–4
Torricelli, E. 202
torture 4, 16–17, 72–3, 75, 122, 124
Turing, A, 180
Tyndall, A. 180

unisexual 176
unity 225–8
Urban VIII, Pope 121

Vail, Y. 102
Viney, D. W. 8, 34, 68, 76
Viney, W. 160
Voltaire, F. M. A. 16, 76

warfare 1–19; intellectual warfare defined 3–4; arguments against the warfare thesis 5–12; conflict over evolution 95–104; and birth control 144–8; gender and sex issues 169, 188–9; warfare between science and religion 210, 217, 230
Watts, F. 3
Wertheimer, M. 139–40
Wesley, J. 56, 127, 211, 213
Westboro Baptist Church 182
Weyer, J. 73–5
whig history 11, 15
White, A. D. 1, 5, 12, 13–14, 16, 18, 95, 144, 218, 230–1
Whitehead, A. N. 10, 230
Whitehouse, H. 205
Whytt, R. 86
Wilson, D. B. 11, 15
Wilson, E. O. 92
witches 45, 70–5 206
Wollstonecraft, M. 159–60, 165–6, 197
Wood, G. 206
Woody, W. D. 160
Wootton, D. 116, 118, 125

Yousafzai, Malala 166